Victorian Alchemy

Victorian Alchemy

Science, magic and ancient Egypt

Eleanor Dobson

First published in 2022 by
UCL Press
University College London
Gower Street
London WC1E 6BT

Available to download free: www.uclpress.co.uk

Text © Author, 2022
Images © Contributors and copyright holders named in captions, 2022

The authors have asserted their rights under the Copyright, Designs and Patents Act 1988 to be identified as the authors of this work.

A CIP catalogue record for this book is available from The British Library

Any third-party material in this book is not covered by the book's Creative Commons licence. Details of the copyright ownership and permitted use of third-party material is given in the image (or extract) credit lines. If you would like to reuse any third-party material not covered by the book's Creative Commons licence, you will need to obtain permission directly from the copyright owner.

This book is published under a Creative Commons Attribution-Non-Commercial 4.0 International licence (CC BY-NC 4.0), https://creativecommons.org/licenses/by-nc/4.0/. This licence allows you to share and adapt the work for non-commercial use providing attribution is made to the author and publisher (but not in any way that suggests that they endorse you or your use of the work) and any changes are indicated.

Attribution should include the following information:

Dobson, E. 2022. *Victorian Alchemy: Science, magic and ancient Egypt*. London: UCL Press. https://doi.org/10.14324/111.9781787358485

Further details about Creative Commons licences are available at http://creativecommons.org/licenses/

ISBN: 978-1-78735-850-8 (Hbk.)
ISBN: 978-1-78735-849-2 (Pbk.)
ISBN: 978-1-78735-848-5 (PDF)
ISBN: 978-1-78735-851-5 (epub)
ISBN: 978-1-78735-852-2 (mobi)
DOI: https://doi.org/10.14324/9781787358485

For Anne Ardis, Rosie Armstrong, Mary Brennan, Patrick Dehm, Niels Kelsted, Sara Krishna, Ingrid Larroque, Michaela Phillips, Richard Presland and Sue Wright

Contents

List of figures	viii
Acknowledgements	xii
Introduction: enchanted pasts	1
1 Ghostly images: magic, illusion and technology	20
2 Worlds lost and found: journeys through time and space	77
3 Weird physics: visible light, invisible forces and the electromagnetic spectrum	120
4 Occult psychology: dream, trance and telepathy	177
Conclusion: afterlives	231
Bibliography	244
Index	258

List of figures

0.1   Paul Hardy, 'Into the mouthpiece of the machine I spoke, asking "Do you hear me?"', in Ernest Richard Suffling, *The Story Hunter: or tales of the weird and wild* (London: Jarrold & Sons, 1896), p. i. Author's own.   2

0.2   Émile Bayard, '*Isis écrivant ses mystères*', in P. Christian, *Histoire de la magie: Du Monde surnaturel et de la fatalité à travers les temps et les peuples* (Paris: Furne, Jouvet et Cie [1876]), p. viii. Source: Hathi Trust. Public Domain; Google digitised.   6

0.3   [Louis] Poyet, 'Heron's Marvellous Altar', in Albert A. Hopkins, *Magic: stage illusions and scientific diversions, including trick photography* (London: Sampson Low, Marston and Co., 1897), p. 236. Author's own.   8

1.1   'Exterior view of the Egyptian Hall: c.1900'. © Museum of London.   24

1.2   Evans, 'The Sphinx', in Professor Hoffmann, *Modern Magic: a practical treatise on the art of conjuring*, 9th edn (London: George Routledge and Sons, 1894), p. iv. Source: Library of Congress, Rare Book and Special Collections Division, Professor Hoffmann and Harry Houdini Collection, GV1547.L6 1894.   26

1.3   H. R. Millar, 'A faint, beautiful voice began to speak', *Strand Magazine* 29 (173) (May 1905): 592; and H. R. Millar, 'The children cast down their eyes – and so did everyone', *Strand Magazine* 31 (184) (April 1906): 471. Source: Internet Archive.   33

1.4   Edward Whymper, illustrated capital, in H. Rider Haggard, *Cleopatra* (London: Longmans, Green, and Co., 1889), p. 101. Author's own.   38

1.5   R. Caton Woodville, 'I saw the world as it had been before man was', in H. Rider Haggard, *Cleopatra* (London: Longmans, Green, and Co., 1889), facing p. 58. Author's own.   49

1.6   M. Greiffenhagen, 'She looked; she saw the awful shapes', in H. Rider Haggard, *Cleopatra* (London: Longmans, Green, and Co., 1889), facing p. 323. Author's own.   50

1.7   James Deering and Abby Deering Howe, c.1880s, taken in Egypt, seemingly by Heymann and Co. Courtesy of Vizcaya Museum and Gardens Archives, Miami, Florida.   55

1.8   'Photograph of "Spirits"', in Albert A. Hopkins, *Magic: stage illusions and scientific diversions, including trick photography* (London: Sampson Low, Marston and Co., 1897), p. 436. Author's own.   57

1.9   'Painting by N. Sichel', in Albert A. Hopkins, *Magic: stage illusions and scientific diversions, including trick photography* (London: Sampson Low, Marston and Co., 1897), p. 437. Author's own.   58

2.1   'Claude Ptolémée dans l'observatoire d'Alexandrie' and 'Mort de la philosophe Hypatie, à Alexandrie', in Louis Figuier, *Vies des Savants illustres: Depuis l'antiquité jusqu'au dix-neuvième siècle*, 3rd edn (Paris: Librairie Hachette et Cie, 1877), facing p. 406 and facing p. 458. Author's own.   85

2.2   'La grande comète vue des Pyramides d'Égypte, le 23 octobre 1882. (D'après le croquis d'un officier de l'armée anglaise.)', in 'La grande comète de 1882', *La Nature* 10 (2) (1882): 409. Source: Cnum – Conservatoire numérique des Arts et Métiers.   86

2.3   [Louis] Poyet, 'Prêtres de l'ancienne Egypte observant les astres dans la grande Pyramide', in F. de Ballore, 'La grande Pyramide: Instrument des passages', *La Nature* 19 (1) (1891): 292. Source: Cnum – Conservatoire numérique des Arts et Métiers.   88

2.4   P. Gray, 'The Martians built the sphinx', in Garrett P. Serviss, 'Marvellous Discoveries', *New York Evening Journal*, 3 February 1898. Courtesy of Greg Weeks.   91

2.5   Fred T. Jane, 'Have you married him, female?', in Fred T. Jane, *To Venus in Five Seconds: an account of the strange disappearance of Thomas Plummer, pillmaker* (London: A. D. Innes, 1897), facing p. 111. Source: Internet Archive.   96

2.6   H. G. Wells, *The Time Machine* (London: William Heinemann, 1895). Courtesy of the Rare Book & Manuscript Library, University of Illinois at Urbana-Champaign.   103

2.7   H. R. Millar, 'The opening of the arch was small,
but Cyril saw that he could get through it', in E. Nesbit,
The Story of the Amulet (New York: E. P. Dutton, [1907]),
p. 78. Source: Internet Archive.   110

3.1   'Première expérience publique d'eclairage par l'électricité
sur la place de la Concorde faite par Deleuil et Léon
Foucault (en décembre 1844)', in Louis Figuier, *Les Nouvelles
Conquêtes de la Science*, vol. 1: *L'Électricité* (Paris: Librairie
Illustrée, 1884), p. 9. Author's own.   129

3.2   'Electric Lighting of the British Museum', *Illustrated
London News*, 8 February 1890, p. 164. Courtesy of the
Cadbury Research Library: Special Collections,
University of Birmingham, f AP 4.I5.   132

3.3   W. H. Gardiner, photograph depicting the interior
of the Western Electric Company's Egyptian temple
exhibit at the World's Columbian Exposition, 1893.
Chicago History Museum, ICHi-061755.   134

3.4   T. H. McAllister, Lantern slide 'View 082: Egypt –
Shepherd's [*sic*] Hotel, the Hall, Cairo' [n. d.], lantern
slide 3.25 in × 4 in, Brooklyn Museum, New York.   137

3.5   Henry Le Keux, *The Seventh Plague of Egypt*, after
John Martin, c.1828, engraving, 7.3 cm × 10.5 cm, Victoria
and Albert Museum, London, http://collections.vam.ac.uk/
item/O692702/the-seventh-plague-of-egypt-print-le-keux-
henry/ (accessed 7 April 2022) © Victoria and Albert
Museum, London.   143

3.6   Joseph Mallord William Turner, *The Fifth Plague of Egypt*,
1808, etching and mezzotint, 20.6 cm × 29.2 cm, The
Metropolitan Museum of Art, New York, https://www.
metmuseum.org/art/collection/search/382982 (accessed
7 April 2022).   144

3.7   Gilbert, 'Conférence de M. Tesla devant la Société de
physique et la Société internationale des électriciens,
le 20 février 1892', in E. Hospitalier, 'Expériences de
M. Tesla sur les courants alternatifs de grande fréquence',
La Nature 20 (1) (1892): 209. Source: Cnum –
Conservatoire numérique des Arts et Métiers.   152

3.8   Alec Ball, 'Queen Cleopatra lifted her hands and stood thus
for a while', in H. Rider Haggard, 'Smith and the Pharaohs',
Strand Magazine 45 (265) (1913): 2. Source:
Visual Haggard.   157

3.9   'Main de momie égyptienne (Photographie)' and
       'Main de momie égyptienne (Radiographie négative)',
       in Albert Londe, 'Les rayons Röntgen et les momies',
       La Nature 25.2 (1897), 105. Source: Cnum – Conservatoire
       numérique des Arts et Métiers.   160

3.10   H. R. Millar, 'The word was spoken, and the two great arches
       grew', in E. Nesbit, *The Story of the Amulet* (New York:
       E. P. Dutton, [1907]), p. 342. Source: Internet Archive.   166

4.1   'Pauline Frederick – Potiphar's Wife', Bain News Service,
       c.1913. Source: Library of Congress, Prints & Photographs
       Division, LC-DIG-ggbain-12499.   179

4.2   Maurice Greiffenhagen, 'And they whispered each to
       each', in H. Rider Haggard and Andrew Lang, *The World's
       Desire* (London: Longmans, Green and Co., 1894),
       new edn, facing p. 192. Author's own.   200

4.3   Cheiro, *The Hand of Fate; or, A Study of Destiny* (New York:
       F. Tennyson Neely, 1898), cover design by T. Di Felice.
       Source: Internet Archive.   202

4.4   Edward Tennyson Reed, 'Horrible result of using the
       "Egyptian fur-tiliser"', *Punch* 98 (2536) (15 February
       1890): 81. Author's own.   203

4.5   Aleister Crowley c.1909. Courtesy of Ordo Templi
       Orientis Archives.   209

4.6   Theda Bara in a promotional photograph for
       Cleopatra (1917). Source: The Cleveland Press
       Collection. Special Collections, Michael Schwartz
       Library, Cleveland State University.   215

4.7   David Allen & Sons, 'The Progress of Hypnotism',
       c.1890–1910?. Source: John Johnson Collection,
       Bodleian Library, University of Oxford, Entertainments
       folder 11 (13).   223

Acknowledgements

This book has been nearly a decade in the making and has benefited from the guidance of a great number of friends and colleagues, many of whom will likely have forgotten – or perhaps were never truly aware of – the extent of their contribution to my thinking. It is my pleasure to record my gratitude to them here.

I am, first and foremost, indebted to Jim Mussell, who read and critiqued this work in its earliest stages, always responding with characteristic patience and positivity. My thanks extend to Rex Ferguson, Deborah Longworth and Martin Willis for their own suggestions and guidance at a crucial moment in the project's development. That Jennie Challinor knows the project better than anyone (through no fault of her own!) is testament to her generosity and endurance.

This work has also been shaped by conversations with Gemma Banks, Howard Carlton, Ross Conway, Melissa Dickson, Careena Fenton, Rosalind Fursland, David Gange, Matt Hayler, Oliver Herford, John Holmes, Rebecca Mitchell, Daniel Moore, Jimmy Packham, Richard Parkinson, Fariha Shaikh, Will Tattersdill and Nathan Waddell; I am so thankful for their expertise and encouragement. I am equally grateful to the delegates and attendees of the 'Do Ancient Egyptians Dream of Electric Sheep?' conference, held at the University of Birmingham in 2021. I owe a special debt to them, Megan Lewis and Leire Olabarria, for stimulating exchanges over several days that really illuminated the twentieth- and twenty-first-centuries legacies of the Victorian material at the heart of this project.

My thanks extend to William Breeze at Ordo Templi Orientis, Richard Dabb at the Museum of London, Julie Anne Lambert at the Bodleian Libraries, Elizabeth Piwkowski at Cleveland State University, Ana D. Rodriguez at the Rare Book and Manuscript Library of the University of Illinois at Urbana-Champaign, Karen Urbec at Vizcaya Museum and Gardens, and Greg Weeks, for their aid in finding and reproducing sources pertinent to this study. An early version of

Chapter 3 appeared as 'Gods and Ghost-Light: Ancient Egypt, Electricity, and X-Rays' in *Victorian Literature and Culture* in 2017 (volume 45 issue 1), and I am indebted to the anonymous reviewers for their recommendations for improvements, as well as the editors and publishers for their permission to reprint material here.

As ever, I am grateful to my family, Georgia, Mike and Cleo Dobson, in each of whom I find twin enthusiasms for the sciences and the arts. It is certainly thanks to them that this book was written. Vital encouragement from Param Bains, Jade Buttery, Joshua Chamberlain, Theresa Clement, Gaynor Martin, Bernard Pressdee, Jason Schaub and Darren Tambourini kept me going. Frank, in particular, put in a good shift wearing out Wilbur.

Finally, much credit is due to my former teachers, who had such a formative impact on me at a time when my lab coat doubled up as an artist's smock. This book is dedicated to them.

Introduction: enchanted pasts

> Setting my apparatus in order, I commenced work by unrolling the head of the mummy … I worked away upon my subject, and having at length uncovered the whole head, I made a small hole through the apex of the cranium with a brad-awl. This done, I inserted, into the space once occupied by the brain, the ends of the wires connected with a certain electric instrument … I am a thought-reader, and my hope was that, if my query were understood by the soul (or brain-ether) of the mummy, I could, by the exercise of my peculiar function of reading thought, obtain a reply … I put the question 'Do you hear me?'
>
> Nothing at first transpired; but, on repeating the question several times, my brain became aware of the power of thought working in the dead skull, and this thought-voice gradually became coherent, until I could actually detect the vibration of certain words being formed.[1]

Thus, the fictional 'Doctor Nosidy, scientist, mesmerist, thought-reader, and electrician', begins his experiments into communicating with the 'brain-ether' of the ancient Egyptian dead.[2]

'The Strange Discovery of Doctor Nosidy' is the first of several short stories that make up a collection of tales entitled *The Story Hunter: or tales of the weird and wild* (1896) by the British stained-glass artist and writer Ernest Richard Suffling (1855–1911). That *The Story Hunter*'s front cover features an image of Doctor Nosidy as he attempts to communicate with the mummy laid out before him, which appears again as a frontispiece (figure 0.1), suggests that either Suffling or his publisher were aware that the ancient Egyptian aspect of 'The Strange Discovery of Doctor Nosidy' would have particular appeal to *fin-de-siècle* readers interested in fiction

Figure 0.1 Paul Hardy, 'Into the mouthpiece of the machine I spoke, asking "Do you hear me?"', in Ernest Richard Suffling, *The Story Hunter: or tales of the weird and wild* (London: Jarrold & Sons, 1896), p. i. Author's own.

of the *weird and wild* variety. The 'weird' can be understood as a category that emerges at the point of intersection between science fiction and the Gothic: a mode that takes contemporaneous science as a starting point 'to produce narratives of strange horror' and which, towards the end of the nineteenth century, was increasingly informed by 'occult and spiritualist ideas'.[3] The illustration by Paul Hardy (1862–1942) encapsulates both aspects of the weird. The Gothic and occult are suggested by the unravelled Egyptian mummy lying before the scientist, while the depiction of Nosidy himself reinforces an allusion to contemporaneous science encoded in the eponymous doctor's surname: 'Nosidy' reversed spells 'Ydison', a clear allusion to the American inventor and 'electrician' Thomas Edison (1847–1931). Hardy's visual depiction of Nosidy appears to have been based on Edison, too; the man of science is pictured in formal attire, surrounded by and using his inventions, as Edison himself was regularly photographed or illustrated. Nosidy even resembles Edison, though it is something of an unflattering portrait, with an exaggeratedly austere profile and a more advanced receding hairline; in fact, these overstated features indicate something of a textual and illustrative caricature. An illuminated lamp that occupies the space between Nosidy's head and the face of the ancient Egyptian as depicted on his sarcophagus not only associates the scientist with light (albeit gas rather than electric), reinforcing the connection with Edison, but serves as a metaphor for enlightenment, as well as symbolising the attempted channel of communication – at once scientific and occult – that Nosidy attempts to open up between these ancient and modern, dead and living, men.

I open *Victorian Alchemy: science, magic and ancient Egypt* with a spotlight on 'The Strange Discovery of Doctor Nosidy' and its reception as it unites several of the themes central to this study. Suffling weaves a tale that involves communication with the ancient Egyptian dead, Nosidy putting modern electric apparatus and his own telepathic abilities to an arcane purpose. The tales that make up *The Story Hunter* are united by a frame narrative in which Suffling's narratorial voice (identified only as 'Mr. S—' and therefore implied to be Suffling himself)[4] assures his readers that the tales he relates are true, and that he has accessed them by hypnotising both willing and unwilling storytellers. Indeed, the frame narrative suggests that the stories should be read in tandem rather than separately, the tales united by a framework that relies upon the hypnotic abilities of the narratorial voice. Other stories flesh out Suffling's conception of the 'brain-ether' as introduced in the collection's first tale. 'A Visitor from Mars', for instance, reveals that after the deaths of 'learned men' their 'etherealized bodies' migrate to the red planet, a decidedly

INTRODUCTION 3

theosophical concept (known as 'metempsychosis') outlined by the matriarch of the Theosophical Society, Helena Blavatsky (1831–91) in *Isis Unveiled* (1877).[5] When visible, these spirit forms appear with 'luminous eyes', 'shadowy fingers' that emit 'a rush of little sparks', and ethereal brain-matter than looks 'like revolving smoke, curling this way and that, and taking fantastic forms'.[6] The spirit form in 'A Visitor from Mars', while not an ancient Egyptian, is an alchemist, a devotee of a practice suspended between notions of science and magic, and that has long been held (whether erroneously or not) as originating – theoretically and etymologically – in ancient Egypt.[7]

Suffling's collection is somewhat unusual in that it unites ancient Egypt, electricity, interplanetary travel, parapsychology, alchemy and magic, all in the space of around 200 pages. These themes themselves were by no means unusual in fiction of the late nineteenth century, yet to find them together in one collection of narratives is something of a rarity, making the volume a pertinent launchpad for this project, which is as interested in the little-known popular fiction of the long nineteenth century as it is in the texts that have received plentiful scholarly attention. Suffling's text, like many of those at the heart of this book, is as responsive to contemporaneous science as it is to esotericism, and while 'The Strange Discovery of Doctor Nosidy' establishes a rather one-sided dialogue between ancient and modern worlds, its pursuit of establishing meaningful communication between the two is central to *Victorian Alchemy*.

In the nineteenth century, to quote Dominic Montserrat, ancient Egypt was considered 'the beginning of everything'.[8] The tradition of heralding Egypt as the origin point of human civilisation stretches back to the ancient Greeks who, as Alison Butler points out, held 'Egypt as the source of all learning'; the ancient Greek historian Diodorus Siculus, for instance, praised Egyptian knowledge of medicine and astrology.[9] While, as David Gange records, 'claims of ancient Greek writers to have received their wisdom from Egypt' were 'unfashionable' early in Victoria's reign; by the latter half of the nineteenth century they 'were suddenly treated with great credulity'.[10] In the Scottish writer Charles Mackay's (1814–89) occult novel *The Twin Soul; or, The Strange Experiences of Mr. Rameses* (1887), to provide one example of such a view as expressed in fiction, the titular Rameses asserts that it was from ancient Egypt that 'the Greeks borrowed everything they knew'; more so, '[c]ompared with the Phœnicians and Egyptians, the Greeks were only babes and sucklings'.[11]

While Victorian Christianity is commonly understood to have been a faith in crisis, shaken by geological discoveries and the impact of theories by the likes of Charles Darwin (1809–82), Christianity remained the dominant system of belief across the nineteenth century, and the Bible a powerful driving force in early Egyptology.[12] Egypt's priests and necromancers, according to the Bible, had powers that could rival God's own miracles; meanwhile, discoveries such as that of the Westcar Papyrus in the early 1820s helped to reinforce the notion of ancient Egyptian sorcery as unparalleled.[13] Such beliefs sat fairly comfortably with emerging alternative faiths. The latter half of the nineteenth century was particularly significant for the growth of esoteric movements such as spiritualism and theosophy, along with a more generalised 'surge in popular interest in all things esoteric, mystical, and magical', now termed the 'occult' or 'magical revival'.[14] Over the course of a decade, the London Lodge of the Theosophical Society was founded in 1878, the Society for Psychical Research was established in 1882 (the same year in which Britain invaded Egypt), and 1888 saw the formation of the Hermetic Order of the Golden Dawn, the first occult society to create a rigorous programme of practical magical education.[15] That Freemasonry had long drawn upon ancient Egyptian iconography played a significant role in the widespread interest in ancient Egypt across the occult revival, as did increasing public interest in Egyptology. The magical revival was largely devoted to the rediscovery of the occult wisdom of the ancients (often conceiving this in relation to contemporaneous science) – and while the theosophists also looked to India and the Golden Dawn to Celtic traditions, ancient Egypt was vital to the beliefs of both groups at key points in their history. 'Egypt ... frequently traverse[d] gaps between' belief systems and occult groups, from spiritualism to theosophy, in a sense bringing together a 'variety of magical or occult practitioners' in the late nineteenth and early twentieth centuries.[16]

Ancient Egypt was touted as a point of origin for ritual magic and occult power central to such alternative faiths. In Jean-Baptiste Pitois's (1811–77) *Histoire de la magie* (1870), published under the pseudonym Paul Christian, the frontispiece (figure 0.2) by illustrator Émile Bayard (1837–91) depicts the goddess Isis *'écrivant ses mystères'* ('writing her mysteries'). Sitting atop a sphinx (whose lack of nose indicates that it is the Great Sphinx of Giza), Isis pays no mind to the viper writhing at her feet; in various ancient sources she has the ability to create snakes and to cure their venomous bites, boasting great healing powers. A temple and three pyramids in the background call to mind the acolytes devoted

Figure 0.2 Émile Bayard, 'Isis écrivant ses mystères', in P. Christian, *Histoire de la magie: Du Monde surnaturel et de la fatalité à travers les temps et les peuples* (Paris: Furne, Jouvet et Cie [1876]), p. viii. Source: Hathi Trust. Public Domain; Google digitised.

to her. Behind her, on a ruined column (the image, somewhat unusually, blending ruined and intact Egyptian architecture), perches an ibis, symbolic of the god Thoth, the inventor of writing, who would go on to be combined with the Greek god Hermes as Hermes Trismegistus, the fabled discoverer of alchemy. The presence of the ibis aligns Isis and

Thoth, both deities being masters of magic. While these details underline Isis's occult powers, she is also surrounded by scientific instruments: an astrolabe, telescope and compass. Isis may well be a goddess of magic, but she is also a scientist. Tellingly, when the American chemist and historian George Sarton (1884–1956) established a history of science journal in 1913 he named it *Isis*.[17]

Indeed, a deferral to ancient Egypt as the birthplace of scientific knowledge in texts of the latter half of the nineteenth century is so prevalent as to become a cliché. This includes knowledge of technologies that could produce seemingly mystical illusory effects. In *Magic: stage illusions and scientific diversions, including trick photography* (1897), for instance, the American magician and historian of magic Henry Ridgely Evans (1861–1949) opens the introduction: 'Far back into the shadowy past, before the building of the pyramids, magic was a reputed art in Egypt, for Egypt was the "cradle of magic".'[18] A substantial volume boasting more than 400 illustrations, *Magic* credits ancient Egypt (albeit after it had been conquered by the Greeks) with knowledge of steam power, providing a description and illustration (figure 0.3) of an altar at a temple of Minerva constructed so as to be understood by the priesthood but to bamboozle the uninitiated masses.[19] The illustration of the device by Louis Poyet (1846–1913), whose precise scientific engravings filled popular science journals such as *La Nature* and *Scientific American*, underscores the technological basis for the altar's seemingly magical effects. Just as Egyptians were talented magicians and illusionists, they were also understood to be skilled engineers. The pyramids were lauded as miraculous feats of construction on a par with modern railways, created using jewel-edged tools that anticipated nineteenth-century diamond-tipped drills.[20] Along with ancient Egypt's reputation for phenomenal mathematical and astronomical knowledge, imparted to the ancient Greeks, such speculations as to and celebrations of Egypt's supposed technological abilities cemented its reputation as a major scientific power.

Ancient Egypt's status as an advanced civilisation was understood in both scientific and magical terms, the ancient Egyptians themselves not having made any distinction between these classifications. Recent scholarship has, intriguingly, also established these categories' nebulousness in Victorian culture, providing a useful framework within which to examine nineteenth-century engagements with Egypt. One might refer to 'mesmerism, spiritualism, modern Theosophy and psychical research as "alternative sciences"', as the historian of science Richard Noakes does, in order to recognise the perceived 'scientific potential that these controversial subjects had for so many nineteenth-century individuals'.[21]

Figure 0.3 [Louis] Poyet, 'Heron's Marvellous Altar', in Albert A. Hopkins, *Magic: stage illusions and scientific diversions, including trick photography* (London: Sampson Low, Marston and Co., 1897), p. 236. Author's own.

Indeed, Olav Hammer's useful definition of 'scientism' applies here, which demarcates an esotericism that is:

> position[ed] … in relation to the manifestations of any academic scientific discipline, including, but not limited to, the use of technical devices, scientific terminology, mathematical calculations, theories, references and stylistic features—without, however, the use of methods generally approved within the scientific community.[22]

This certainly chimes with nineteenth-century esoteric cultures, particularly theosophy and spiritualism, though organisations such as the Society for Psychical Research attempted to investigate the supernatural with scientific rigour. Noakes warns against binary ways of thinking when it comes to approaching 'mesmerism, spiritualism and psychical research', avoiding enforcing artificial 'distinctions between natural and supernatural, material and spiritual, manifest and occult'.[23] Julie Chajes's recent claims that in the late nineteenth century 'the boundaries of "legitimate" science were more contested than they are today', support such a stance; she observes, in particular, that esotericists such as 'Blavatsky contributed to spreading the ideas of leading scientists'.[24] Scholars such as Alex Owen and Mark S. Morrisson have, in Owen's words, demonstrated that 'Victorian science itself was sometimes less divorced from occultism than its practitioners might care to admit'.[25] Developments in fields as diverse as telegraphy, radioactivity and psychology were theorised by eminent scholars to be connected to occult phenomena.

Equally useful is Karl Bell's understanding of the 'magical imagination' in the mid-nineteenth century: Bell laments that '[h]istorians of modern popular magical beliefs and historians of magical entertainments tend to pursue their research in parallel' despite 'the frequent symbiotic links between them'.[26] He insists that contemporaneous public fascination for both illusory magic – based on optical science and technological devices – and phenomena held to be genuinely supernatural should encourage us to 'challenge simplistic tripartite divides between magic, religion, and science'.[27] The full range of these activities can be understood to have appealed to the socially widespread 'magical imagination'.

Indeed, the aforementioned critical works invite us to recognise – and dismantle – binary divisions that have proved particularly impactful in the study of how ancient Egypt has been understood by the modern world. Erik Hornung's influential division of ancient Egypt in the Western cultural consciousness between objective, scholarly Egyptology and spiritual 'Egyptosophy' – 'the study of an imaginary Egypt viewed as the profound source of all esoteric lore' – is an oft-used starting point for an analysis of the ways in which ancient Egypt is and has recently been perceived.[28] Certainly, this separation seems appropriate in the twenty-first century, where scientific Egyptology and mystical Egyptosophy are kept, for the most part, distinct. Recent scholarship on the two has shown, however, that in the late nineteenth and early twentieth centuries any divide between academic Egyptology and its esoteric cousin was far less precise; this current project, too, is more interested in the ambiguous points where boundaries collapse than where they are maintained.[29] Equally, this culture complicates Edward Said's understanding of Orientalism in the nineteenth century, whereby the Orient was generally aligned with magic, mysticism and superstition, in contrast to Occidental science and rationality. While Said's broader thesis holds true (certainly in the case of modern Egypt, which was often painted as degenerate in order to justify imperialistic ideologies), ancient Egypt often resists a cultural positioning as 'inferior',[30] even when it otherwise conforms to Orientalist stereotypes or is made to serve imperialist ends. Neither fully oriental nor occidental, ancient Egypt occupies something of a unique space, its wisdom straddling categories of the magical and the scientific.

For the purposes of this book, it is useful to bring together both Noakes's understanding of 'alternative sciences' and Bell's 'magical imagination' to conceive of these fascinating grey areas between (or across) Hornung's and Said's binaries as 'alchemical'. While some nineteenth-and early twentieth-century texts that feature ancient Egypt draw explicitly upon an alchemical tradition that stretches back to ancient practices and are particularly interested in the medieval alchemical tradition, alchemy is useful more widely as a metaphor to capture the cultural space where science and magic not only coexist but are often thought indistinguishable. In ancient Egypt itself, science and magic were inseparable, and the general belief that alchemy had originated in Egypt, and that the practice had even inherited its name from the country's ancient name 'Kemet', has only encouraged the enduring association between ancient Egypt and magical and scientific sophistication.[31] Nonetheless, even while alchemy is more useful as a broad metaphor for the purposes of this study, alchemy proper looms large in myriad texts in the period, and lurks perceptibly in the background of others. Alchemy was, as historians have shown, of increasing interest in the latter half of the nineteenth century both to those with esoteric interests and in terms of cultural perceptions of scientific advancement and innovation.

Susan Hroncek, for instance, has noted the disparities between certain nineteenth-century scientists' and historians' acknowledgement of modern chemistry as historically rooted in ancient Egyptian 'alchemy, and Eastern mysticism', and others' downplaying or rejection of this outright.[32] Across the sources she consults, various writers position the Egyptians in relation to the Greeks, arguing for the superiority of one over the other. The trend that emerges as the century progresses, however, is one whereby 'histories of chemistry seem to become more accepting of Middle Eastern and occult influences'.[33] Hroncek observes 'the public image of chemistry as a pseudo-magical study' and 'the occult revival's fascination with ancient Egyptians' ability to seamlessly blend the magical with the scientific', demonstrating how, particularly towards the *fin de siècle*, chemists, historians of chemistry and popularisers of science contributed to 'the erosion of boundaries between science and the occult, and East and West'; this resulted, ultimately, in 'an increasingly narrowing gap … between science and the occult' 'explicitly link[ed] with the Middle East'.[34] This corresponds with Martin Willis's understanding of late nineteenth-century science's 'return to secrecy' 'outside the usual apparatus of culture and society', therefore aligning its various emerging disciplines with 'magical and alchemical traditions'.[35]

As Lawrence M. Principe observes, the late nineteenth century saw an alchemical revival with the rise of Victorian occultism, but that in this context alchemy was largely 'reinterpreted … as a spiritual practice, involving the self-transformation of the practitioner and only incidentally or not at all the transformation of laboratory substances'.[36] Nevertheless, the pattern that Hroncek recognises in histories, and that which Willis reads in the sciences more broadly, shows the re-emergence of alchemy as a useful means of understanding nineteenth-century science. There are intriguing parallels in fiction, too, which show authors keen to interrogate alchemy's ancient origins and its reimagining in modern contexts. The number of nineteenth- and early twentieth-century fictions that credit the ancient Egyptians with alchemical knowledge is striking. The peculiar events of Fred T. Jane's (1865–1916) novel *The Incubated Girl* (1896) are set in motion by the antagonist's chemical creation of a child following instructions given on an Egyptian papyrus. This alchemical document, 'being Egyptian', 'had a good deal of mysticism wrapped around it', though its scientific basis is underlined by its 'chemical formulæ'.[37] The protagonist of Henry Ridgely Evans's novel *The House of the Sphinx* (1907) is employed by a patron (who, tellingly 'look[s] like a mummy just emerged from a sarcophagus') to act as an assistant conducting alchemical research in a laboratory replete with 'the multifarious apparatus of the working chemist, ancient and modern'.[38] Most of the latter novel's seemingly supernatural events – which orbit its powerful

Egyptian antagonist, Ramidan – are shown by its close to be illusory, but *The House of the Sphinx* nonetheless relies upon an understanding of Ramidan's potent mental powers (understood in overlapping occult and medical terms) as entirely genuine.

Mummy stories were particularly quick to pay homage to the advanced wisdom of ancient Egypt, and are especially interested in alchemy's promises of extended life.[39] George Griffith's 'The Lost Elixir' (1903) concerns an ancient Egyptian who retrieves the mummified body of his wife in order to counteract the effects of 'the Elixir of Long Drawn Days', said to be composed of the tears of the goddess Isis and, contained within a hollowed-out emerald, is clearly meant to evoke the fabled philosopher's stone.[40] He kisses his deceased wife's lips, still wet with the antidote, in order to be able to die with her. Another mummy tale, and likely the inspiration for 'The Lost Elixir', Arthur Conan Doyle's (1859–1930) short story 'The Ring of Thoth' (1890), features an ancient Egyptian, Sosra, who has lived for centuries as a result of injecting himself with an alchemical elixir of life. To Sosra, despite his 'train[ing] in all those mystic arts' referred to in the Bible and his experiments taking place in the Temple of Thoth, the secret behind his extreme longevity is 'simply a chemical discovery', which modern Western civilisation has yet to duplicate.[41] The text is saturated with references to modern apparatus in an ancient setting including 'test-tubes', distillers and injecting devices, which facilitate the experiments conducted in temples-turned-laboratories.[42] In creating this hybrid space characterised by its simultaneous antiquity and modernity, Doyle responds and contributes to an ongoing association between the latest scientific breakthroughs and alchemy as the fabled pinnacle of scientific refinement.

Decades before 'The Ring of Thoth', other authors including Edgar Allan Poe (1809–49) and Grant Allen (1848–99) had already published humorous fiction suggesting that ancient Egyptian achievements in science, medicine and engineering matched or surpassed their Victorian equivalents. In Poe's tale, 'Some Words with a Mummy' (1845), the reanimated Allamistakeo reveals that his ancient civilisation had superior microscopes, and equivalents of the railway and steam engine.[43] In Edward Bulwer-Lytton's (1803–73) *The Coming Race* (1871), an advanced subterranean civilisation with ancient Egyptian elements has technologies akin to the steam engine and telegraph, while in Grant Allen's 'My New Year's Eve Among the Mummies' (1878), first published under the *nom de plume* J. Arbuthnot Wilson, the protagonist stumbles upon a group of mummified Egyptians who enjoy the benefits of watches and chloroform. When lit with a Lucifer match, 'brilliant gas-lamps' illuminate the interior of their pyramid tomb, '[g]aslight', at this time, according to Wolfgang Schivelbusch, 'reign[ing] supreme as a symbol of human and intellectual progress'.[44] The late nineteenth-century present does not symbolise progress or innovation in the American physician Thomas C. Minor's (1846–1912) *Athothis: a satire on modern medicine* (1887), either, as is also the case in Mackay's *The Twin Soul* (published the same year), with its proposition that 'all the inventions and discoveries of … modern civilization … are but accidental and imperfect re-discoveries of what was once familiar' in ancient Egypt.[45] Although ancient Egyptian civilisation is long gone, its scientific achievements continue to match – in some cases to literally outshine – those of the modern Western world.

It is on such fictions – that demonstrate how ancient Egypt was drawn upon in relation to overlapping understandings of science and magic – that this book focuses, analysing predominantly nineteenth- and early twentieth-century anglophone culture. While the earliest material I consider predates the beginning of Victoria's reign, the majority of the works addressed in this study accumulate around the end of the nineteenth century, spilling over into the twentieth. According to Gange, '[b]y the mid-1890s many more works of fiction set in ancient Egypt were being produced each year than had been written in the whole of the first half of the century put together' and, as such, the *fin de siècle* is of particular interest within this project's wider temporal remit.[46]

I argue for the significance of ancient Egypt in the long nineteenth century, especially in *fin-de-siècle* popular culture, scrutinising its manifestation in a variety of literary genres, as well as in theatre, art, and more serious scholarly investigations into diverse scientific (and pseudo-scientific) subjects, ranging from electricity and X-rays to trance and clairvoyance. Science and magic were categories in flux, coming together in metropolitan centres, in lecture halls, museums, theatres, and private rooms used for occult rituals, where ancient Egypt was often drawn upon to evoke a sense of genuine magic, or unparalleled scientific advancement. Major cities, such as London, Paris, New York and, in Egypt itself, Cairo, saw the creation of immersive ancient Egyptian spaces where magic seemed real and science alchemical in its mystical sophistication. As such, my readings of these texts are also informed by and particularly sensitive to metropolitan contexts.

The texts considered in this study are most often prose fictions. This is due to these sources' consideration of fantastical, supernatural and scientific subject matter which, while not exclusive to novels and short stories, largely suggest themselves as the bread and butter of popular prose writing, from the Gothic to science fiction, adventure tales to historical fantasy, theosophical fiction to children's literature. As generic categories were then, more than now, hazier as these genres emerged, it is best to understand the disparate texts considered in this book as belonging to the more generalised category of 'speculative fiction'. The material that this book takes as its primary subject matter traverses divides between intended audience (including class, gender and age) and publication format (from books to periodicals). Separated from modernity by thousands of years, ancient Egypt evidently emerged as newly relevant to the present through its association with the origins of modern science and magic in an enormous variety of fora.

A note on authorship is pertinent here. Most of the writers whose works are of interest to this study are men, many of whom – Bram Stoker (1847–1912), H. Rider Haggard (1856–1925), H. G. Wells (1866–1946), Algernon Blackwood (1869–1951) and Sax Rohmer (1883–1959) – are well known as authors whose names are bywords for the Gothic, imperial fantasy, science fiction and the weird. The women who contributed to ancient Egypt's legacy in speculative fiction include the literary juggernaut Marie Corelli (1855–1924), though her aptitude as a writer was much derided at the time and, despite record-breaking sales, she still receives far less critical attention than any of her aforementioned contemporaries.[47] I thus endeavour to shed light on women's contributions, even when there is little in the historical record to illuminate who these women were. Literary criticism may well recognise the contributions of E. Nesbit (1858–1924) and the pioneer of the reanimated mummy tale Jane Webb (1807–58), but *Victorian Alchemy* also spotlights lesser-known shorter writings by women including the American writers Florence Carpenter Dieudonné (1850–1927), Charlotte Bryson Taylor (1880–1936) and Lucy Cleveland (1850–?), and the Welsh author Marie Hutcheson (1854–1914). Anonymous or pseudonymous publication was widespread in the nineteenth century, complicating the provenance of some pertinent texts, and several women considered in this study published under names that concealed their feminine identities. Of these women, Edith Nesbit published using her first initial, as did Charlotte Bryson Taylor.[48] Webb's groundbreaking mummy novel was published anonymously, Henrietta Dorothy Everett's novel *Iras; A Mystery* (1896) was published under the masculine *nom de plume* Theo Douglas, while Marie Hutcheson retained her initials in her eccentric alias, Mallard Herbertson. While some of the men I consider in this study embraced pseudonymous or anonymous publication, none (as far as I can determine) saw fit to adopt a feminine moniker.

Even trickier is concretely ascertaining the ethnic and racial identities of authors under pressure to conform in white-majority contexts.

As Scott Trafton has shown, even among the 'unorthodox thinkers' of spiritualism and Theosophy, racism proliferated'; 'spiritualism … was a community marked by whiteness'.[49] Thus, when we turn to the American occultist and author Thomas Jasper Betiero's (1864–1917) *Nedoure, Priestess of the Magi: an historical romance of white and black magic* (1916) in this book's final chapter, we engage with a text by a mixed-race writer who claimed Spanish ancestry and to have been born in Egypt in order to evade the racial prejudices that would have inevitably impacted on his career. Other authors addressed in this study but about whom little is known may well have found themselves in a similar situation. Beyond anglophone literature, I am indebted to the work of scholars who have shone light on texts published in other languages. Projit Bihari Mukharji, for instance, in his analysis of the Bengali author Dinendra Kumar Roy's (1869–1943) translation and adaptation of the Australian writer Guy Boothby's (1867–1905) novel *Pharos the Egyptian* (1898; 1899), is key in illuminating some of the shared tropes between the focal texts of this study and South Asian literature. Roy's *Pishach purohit* ('The Zombie Priest') appeared in 1910, and chimes in intriguing ways with the material I cover (far more so than Boothby's original), underscoring the potential for 'alchemical' cultural understandings of ancient Egypt on a far broader cultural and geographical scale than one study alone can tackle. It does, however, suggest exciting possibilities for such work in future.

Victorian Alchemy is organised thematically, each chapter centring on a particular area of intersection between science and magic. The first chapter studies the way in which Spiritualist séances, stage magic and the visual technologies behind photography and early cinematography interacted with ancient Egypt. This section identifies a trend in fiction that describes the ancient Egyptian magical and occult in terms that situate it somewhere between stage conjuring and genuine spiritual occurrence, and pays particular attention to the role of London's Egyptian Hall in blurring these boundaries. Haggard's Egyptian-themed texts are discussed – particularly his *Cleopatra* (1889) – along with various supernatural romances including Everett's *Iras* (1896), Corelli's *Ziska* (1897), Nesbit's *The Story of the Amulet* (1906), Taylor's *In the Dwellings of the Wilderness* (1904), the fiction and non-fiction of magician Henry Ridgely Evans, and short stories by Blackwood, Charles Webster Leadbeater (1854–1934) and Marie Hutcheson. Drawing parallels between the gloom of the photographer's darkroom, the shadowy séance, and the dim Egyptian temple, darkness in these contexts comes to represent an appropriate setting for the magical as much as it does technological innovation, in which both real or illusory spirits might be summoned, and where coloured lights signal the arrival of the genuine supernatural, the gaudy theatrical, or something altogether more ambiguous.

While the aforementioned imaging technologies allowed unprecedented access to ancient Egypt, authors speculated as to other ways in which the chasm between antiquity and modernity might be broached. The second chapter charts three such routes, encouraged by contemporary scientific and esoteric interests. The first is contact with a remote civilisation related to ancient Egypt, either subterranean as in Haggard's *She* (1886–7), and Baroness Orczy's (1865–1947) *By the Gods Beloved* (1905), or somewhere little explored, as in Jules Verne's (1828–1905) *Le Sphinx des glaces* (1897), which ends with the discovery of Egyptian hieroglyphs in Antarctica, responsive to contemporaneous archaeological enquiry. The second is a similar conceit by which, instead of being located on earth, the offshoot of ancient Egyptian civilisation is extraterrestrial, reflecting contemporaneous astronomical interests, as in Fred T. Jane's *To Venus in Five Seconds* (1897), or in which alien civilisations are responsible for constructing the Egyptian monuments, as in Garrett P. Serviss's (1851–1929) *Edison's Conquest of Mars* (1898). Finally, time travel makes possible the bridging of a temporal rather than or in addition to a geographical divide, as in Nesbit's *The Story of the Amulet*, Wells's *The Time Machine* (1895), and William Henry Warner's (fl. 1919–34) *The Bridge of Time* (1919). This chapter ultimately unearths fantasies of exploration spurred on by scientific advancements on the one hand, and imaginative speculation by scientists, spiritualists and occultists alike, on the other, that ancient Egyptian civilisation somehow lived on, elsewhere. I draw this chapter to a close with a gesture to the marriage of scientific and esoteric ideas in the French astronomer Camille Flammarion's (1842–1925) *La Fin du monde* (1894), lingering on the symbol of the sphinx as representing scientific and esoteric knowledge across this chapter's focal texts.

The third chapter investigates the collision between developments in physics – specifically understandings of the electromagnetic spectrum – alongside references to ancient Egypt. It examines the prevalent use of electrical lighting in nineteenth-century exhibitions of ancient Egyptian artefacts, the common trope of electrical reanimation of mummies in literature, and connections between ancient Egyptian monuments and unusual electrical phenomena that bring these disparate themes together in the cultural consciousness. The chapter goes on to discuss scientific developments in radiation and X-rays, suggesting that their use in mummy examination had a significant impact on literature. In turn, this implies that the most radical and innovative breakthroughs were being ascribed to this ancient civilisation in a way that aligned science with magic and the figure of the scientist with the figure of the god. I make connections between the scientist-*cum*-showman Nikola Tesla (1856–1943), the anatomist Grafton Elliot Smith (1871–1937), the physicist and chemist Marie Curie (1867–1934), and characters in Haggard's *Ayesha: the return of She* (1905), his 'Smith and the Pharaohs' (1912–13), and Stoker's *The Jewel of Seven Stars* (1903; 1912). Haggard and Stoker, I show, build on a literary inheritance that saw physics put to use in awakening ancient Egypt, transferring these powers onto the ancient Egyptians themselves.

The fourth and final chapter discusses connections between ancient Egypt and a variety of psychological topics related to the occult. Trance, telepathy and powers of prophecy are examined in contexts that emphasise the ancient Egyptian as a way of lending legitimacy to potentially magical mind powers. This chapter focuses on the symbol of the eye – itself deeply important to ancient Egyptian culture – as the site of uncanny abilities, and the effects of these powers on bodies that are reduced to automata. Ancient Egypt's erotic and seductive power is also highlighted as particularly significant, exemplified in feminine bodies, which themselves become hypnotic weapons, from late nineteenth-century literary representations through to early twentieth-century actresses at the advent of cinema. Nightmares of Egypt reside just below the surface of the conscious mind and threaten to cause psychological disturbances. With reference to texts including Richard Marsh's (1857–1915) *The Beetle* (1897), Griffith's *The Mummy and Miss Nitocris*, Betiero's *Nedoure* and psychological practitioners as eminent as Sigmund Freud (1856–1939), I consider unusual mind powers in the context of contemporaneous scientific conceptions of evolution and degeneration, which categorise these ancient concepts as distinctly modern phenomena.

At the end of *Victorian Alchemy*, in a brief conclusion, I look forward to the legacies of this material in the 100 years that followed. After the opening decades of the twentieth century, these tropes, ideas and theories did not simply dissipate. While as Richard Noakes rightly claims, 'the heyday of "physics and psychics"' was well and truly over by the late 1930s, in theory driving a wedge between the concepts of the scientific and the magical that had previously seemed so close, this entwinement nevertheless persisted in fictional media (and, to a lesser extent, non-fiction), and is very much essential to reimaginings of ancient Egypt to this day.[50] I chart the afterlives of the kinds of stories scrutinised in each of the chapters, from the fringe theories of Erich von Däniken (1935–) to Hollywood blockbusters including *Stargate* (1994). Subsequently, I turn to modern narratives that are not only interested in ancient Egypt, science and magic, but are also set in the nineteenth- or early twentieth-century past, lingering especially on the fantasy adventure movie *Les Aventures extraordinaires d'Adèle Blanc-Sec* (2010). An echo of the nineteenth-century 'magical imagination' is evident in the supernatural elements of these texts, as are the thrilling occult possibilities of scientific discovery. In these examples we can read refashionings of earlier literary material, and a continuation of an appetite among consumers not just for narratives that revel in speculating as to the knowledge of the ancients but also for encounters with ancient Egypt via the Victorian and Edwardian world – a time and place on which we now look back as itself enchanted.

Notes

1. Suffling 1896, 20, 21, 23.
2. Suffling 1896, 20.
3. Alder 2020, 2, 17.
4. Suffling 1896, 62.
5. Suffling 1896, 91; Chajes 2019, 4, 50–1.
6. Suffling 1896, 93.
7. Haage 2006, 16–7, 22.
8. Montserrat 2000, 154.
9. Butler 2011, 87.
10. Gange 2006, 1091.
11. Mackay 1887 I, 31.
12. For the relationship between Christianity and Egyptology, 1822–1922, see Gange 2013.
13. Mangan 2007, 1–6; Muhlestein 2004, 139; Luckhurst *The Mummy's Curse* 2012, 213. Part of the document describes a magician, Dedi, who can behead and then revive animals, a power achieved through devotion to the gods.
14. Chajes 2019, 2.
15. Butler 2011, 2.
16. Dobson 'The Sphinx at the Séance' 2018, 85.
17. Sarton 1953, 232–42. Sarton established the journal *Osiris* in 1936 as a venue for the lengthier papers that had been submitted for consideration in *Isis*.
18. Evans 1897, 1.
19. Hopkins 1897, 234–5.
20. Gange 2013, 156.
21. Noakes 2019, 8.
22. Hammer 2004, 206.
23. Noakes 2019, 9.
24. Chajes 2019, 16.
25. Owen 2004, 6.
26. Bell 2012, 12.
27. Bell 2009, 27–8.
28. Hornung 2002, 3.
29. See, for instance Dobson 2021, 186–220.
30. Said 2014, 62.
31. Colla 2007, 21; Elliott 2012, 1; Nye 1994, 4.
32. Hroncek 2017, 214.
33. Hroncek 2017, 219.
34. Hroncek 2017, 215, 219, 220.

35. Willis 2006, 9. As Willis notes, while '[i]n the first three decades of the century, science was still closely allied, at least in the public imagination, with magic, alchemy, and the occult ... the scientific successes of the midcentury – especially in the applied sciences and technology – rid the image of that association'. As the century progressed, however, science's 'relationship with the public became as equivocal as it had been at the beginning of the century. The scientific community's perceived secrecy appeared to parallel the opacity of alchemical work that was science's inheritance in the early nineteenth century'; Willis 2006, 10.
36. Principe 2011, 307.
37. Jane 1896, 22.
38. Evans 1907, 61.
39. Brantlinger 2011, 81.
40. Griffith 1903, 161.
41. Doyle 1890, 55.
42. Doyle 1890, 55, 58.
43. Poe 1845, 369–70.
44. Wilson 1878, 101; Schivelbusch 1995, 152.
45. Mackay 1887 I, 32.
46. Gange 2006, 1102n75.
47. Donawerth 1997, xvii.
48. Fitzsimons. Fitzsimons records that '[s]everal critics expressed astonishment' upon finding out that Nesbit was a woman, and that 'H.G. Wells ... had been so convinced that she was a he that he insisted on calling her Ernest'.
49. Trafton 2004, 28, 32.
50. Noakes 2019, 328.

1

Ghostly images: magic, illusion and technology

> Any sufficiently advanced technology is indistinguishable from magic.[1]

Throughout the nineteenth century and beyond, city centres saw the side-by-side existence of all varieties of spectacle for the purposes of entertainment, scientific or spiritual demonstration. This chapter explores the crossover between ancient Egypt, magic and illusion, with tropes and conventions exchanged between a variety of discourses that thrived, especially in metropolitan spaces: stage magic, spiritualist demonstrations, photography and projection technologies leading up to and including early moving pictures. There is a high degree of reciprocity between them, and in turn these media influenced fiction that deals with themes of the supernatural or the illusory in ancient Egyptian contexts. Technologies of magic and illusion were constantly being updated or employed so as to produce new effects, and these developments contributed to the broader association between ancient Egypt and modernity. As Antonia Lant has established, '[t]he alliance between optically novel and illusory forms of representation and ideas about Egypt … is detectable at least since the French Revolution and persists throughout the nineteenth century'; there is 'an imaginative association pulling together the ancient culture and modern spectacular invention' evident 'across lantern shows, panoramas, dioramas, photographs … and on into the emerging sphere of cinema itself'.[2] Expanding Lant's understanding of these technologies' enduring association with antiquity, this chapter posits the indelibility of the association between ancient Egypt and magic (both illusory and occult power) as vital to Egypt's continued relevance as visual subject matter to be rendered on stage sets, in photographs and projected as ethereal light.

First, this chapter investigates the significance of London's Egyptian Hall, a popular entertainment venue, in aligning ancient Egypt with cutting-edge optical effects and magical technologies, leading to a closer examination of the exchanges between the spiritualist séance and stage-magic performances (both of which were performed at the Egyptian Hall across its history) in media of the age. Whether stage conjuring or purportedly genuine occult ritual, the apparitions and mysterious lights, sounds and sensations associated with these performances found their counterparts in written descriptions of ancient Egyptian magic. When we look to representations of genuine ancient Egyptian magic in fiction, and to instances of Egyptian-themed optical illusion and spectacular trickery, we see authors – notably E. Nesbit and the magician Henry Ridgely Evans, in fiction and non-fiction – playfully blur the lines between these categories. Nesbit and Evans, in their interest in the Egyptian Hall respond to a particularly potent popular reference point in the visual culture of nineteenth- and early twentieth-century magic, infusing this venue famous for its performers' optical trickery with a keen sense of genuine supernatural power.

The chapter moves on to discuss optical technologies that were supposedly used to capture spirit materialisations – namely, photography – and the technologies of entertainment which created and projected luminous images. These include the magic lantern and early moving picture cameras, the Egyptian Hall being the second venue in Britain (by a matter of days) to show projected moving pictures. Such technologies may well have appealed to rapt audiences through their innovations, yet, as we shall see, they also facilitated imaginative access to antiquity on a hitherto unrealisable scale; photography, in particular, promised to facilitate personal creative engagements with ancient Egypt in which one could assume an ancient Egyptian identity in the guise of a mummy or a sphinx, while other photographs apparently captured glimpses of genuine Egyptian spirits. In. H. Rider Haggard's historical novel *Cleopatra* (1889) the rites of Isis appear half séance, half magic-lantern display, while other texts that depict Egyptian magic also turn to the spectacle of the panorama or phantasmagoria (magic-lantern shows featuring dynamic effects) to aid readers in visualising Egyptian magic. Notably, such metaphors and similes were exploited by stage magicians and occultists alike, magician Henry Ridgely Evans and occultist Charles Webster Leadbeater among those turning to the same language of visual theatrics, juxtaposing modern and ancient in their fictional descriptions of primeval landscapes, supernatural powers, and their psychological effects in relation to up-to-date optical techniques.

The final sections of the chapter turn to dissolve techniques, used in magic-lantern displays but also integral to an understanding of the depiction of supernatural materialisations and transformations in early film. In Marie Corelli's *Ziska*, the novel's climax deep within a pyramid sees the ancient Egyptian woman metamorphose from woman to translucent spirit, while the short moving pictures of filmmakers with links to the Egyptian Hall also use ancient Egypt as an immediate visual marker for magic. Artefacts and individuals hailing from Egypt are, in these works, impossible to pin down, shifting, vanishing and re-emerging in depictions of supernatural powers effected entirely by new technological possibilities. As this chapter draws to a close, we find ourselves back at the Egyptian Hall, underscoring its centrality to the visual culture of magic, its importance in histories of spectacular and technological innovation, and the windows to the ancient world that such venues, their performers and apparatus conjured up.

Before turning to the Egyptian Hall, it is useful to ascertain a sense of the range of magical activities whose practitioners emphasised their associations with ancient Egypt. Karl Bell's understanding of the magical imagination is useful here, which he specifies 'not only embod[ies] specific magical practices such as witchcraft and astrology, but also encompass[es] a fantastical mentality informed by supernatural beliefs, folkloric tropes, and popular superstitions'.[3] Bell's examples from the latter half of the nineteenth century are particularly intriguing for their intertwinement with Egyptian imagery; these '[l]ater Victorian expressions of "magical" mentalities' include 'spiritualism, the stage shows of Jean Eugene Robert-Houdin or John Maskelyne, "Pepper's Ghost", [and] the occult activities of the Order of the Golden Dawn'.[4] Bell ultimately contends that 'the magical imagination testifies to the previously underestimated extent of genuine belief in the fantastical in the nineteenth century'.[5] Belief across these settings varied enormously, of course. Spiritualist séances were held to manifest genuine supernormal phenomena by some, though others approached these occasions with more scepticism; others still chastised mediums for what they held to be outright charlatanerie. Stage-magic shows often involved the magician's assertion that what audiences witnessed was real; and while many (if not most) audience members believed that what they observed was exclusively illusory, they nonetheless indulged in the pretence of the magician's claims to the contrary (a mentality that has been termed the 'ironic imagination' by Michael Saler).[6] The Golden Dawn, meanwhile, a secret society devoted to occult practices, sincerely pursued the paranormal at the *fin de siècle*. What I seek to add to Bell's work on this variety of contexts that invited and facilitated the magical imagination is ancient

Egyptian iconography's usefulness as a kind of shorthand for magic, not just in settings reliant upon an atmosphere of occult gravitas as in the Golden Dawn's rituals, but equally in settings where cutting-edge technological innovations were being showcased and in which the magical atmosphere necessitated the suspension of disbelief. In each case, Egypt aided in establishing an air of authenticity. The Egyptian Hall's role in encouraging this, as a site where past and present met in nineteenth- and early twentieth-century culture, was crucial.

The Egyptian Hall

If ancient Egypt was customarily held as the source of ritual magic, then it was equally considered the place where illusory stage magic originated. As with histories of occult power, common to many nineteenth-century books on illusion is the claim – usually in the introduction – that its roots were in antiquity, most often in Egypt itself. *The Boy's Own Conjuring Book: being a complete handbook of parlour magic* (1859), for instance, relates that 'sleight of hand … and various miraculous deceptions, were the means by which the priests of Egypt, Greece, and Rome, used to subjugate mankind'.[7] That the ancient Egyptians who honed these illusory skills belonged to the priesthood is a fairly common assumption, their craft purportedly employed for the purposes of tricking laypeople into believing that the gods were performing miraculous feats or granting the priests supernatural powers. Magic is cast in such volumes not as a potent force, but as deceptive trickery involving *legerdemain*, misdirection and optical technologies. For residents of London across the nineteenth century, the Egyptian Hall reinforced the close association between ancient Egypt and illusion outlined in such publications.

The Egyptian Hall (figure 1.1) in Piccadilly was England's first major public building with a neo-Egyptian façade, its distinctive frontage inspired by the temple of Hathor at Dendera.[8] Built in 1812, the Egyptian Hall was an ethnographical and natural history museum until 1819, subsequently housing art exhibitions, panoramas, spiritualist performances and, eventually, anti-spiritualist demonstrations, illusion and moving picture shows, before its demolition to make way for flats and offices in 1905. Its distinctive Egyptianised aesthetic imparted something of antiquity's glamour onto what took place within, as was the case with other London venues that drew upon ancient Egypt in their décor. Ancient Egyptian iconography suffused the city's meeting spaces used by the Freemasons, who had promoted their connection with ancient Egypt

Figure 1.1 'Exterior view of the Egyptian Hall: c.1900'. © Museum of London.

since the latter half of the eighteenth century.[9] In the nineteenth century's closing decades, newer occult orders such as the Hermetic Order of the Golden Dawn would also meet in Egyptianised settings.[10]

The Egyptian Hall's Orientalised style (not authentically ancient Egyptian, but a fantastical interpretation loosely informed by archaeological sources) was sometimes mirrored in the acts and exhibitions it housed. Early in its history, in 1821, it was the venue for the Italian circus-strongman-turned-explorer Giovanni Battista Belzoni's (1778–1823) exhibition of the tomb of Seti I, an immersive recreation of Egyptian spaces, replete with mummified remains that Belzoni had transported from Egypt. Subsequently, the Hall was home to many exhibitions without an overt Egyptian connection. It was after the mid-point of the nineteenth century that the Hall became strongly associated with both spiritualist performances and stage magic, and when a relationship between the Hall's exterior and what took place within began to be re-established. An illusion by the name of Stodare's Sphinx, for example, first performed by the British magician Joseph Stoddart (1831–66) in 1865, drew upon ancient Egypt's mysterious aura. The trick involved the use of angled mirrored glass to make the head of the magician's accomplice, enclosed within a box and topped with a kind of *nemes* headdress (symbolic of royalty), appear dismembered. The 'Sphinx' would open its eyes, answer questions posed by Stodare (Stoddart's stage persona), and recite poetry, after which Stodare would close the box. Stodare would next reveal that his ability to 'revivify ... the ashes of an ancient Egyptian, who lived and died some centuries ago' only lasted for 15 minutes before the Egyptian must return to dust; he would then open the box to reveal a pile of ash.[11] Charles Dickens (1812–70) saw the illusion and praised it for being 'so extraordinarily well done'.[12] The trick was evidently impressive enough to have been deemed fit for the eyes of Queen Victoria and her children that same year; of the illusions performed by Stodare, the Sphinx was one of two to receive an encore from the royal family.[13] Stodare's illusion was so celebrated that a diagram of the trick appears as the first image in several guides to magic of the latter half of the nineteenth century (figure 1.2), notably being reprinted over the course of at least 16 editions of Louis Hoffmann's (1839–1919) *Modern Magic: a practical treatise on the art of conjuring*, which first appeared in 1876, stretching to editions appearing as late as the 1910s.[14]

The American magician Henry Ridgely Evans painted a vivid picture both of Stodare's Sphinx and the Egyptian Hall in his magical history, *The Old and the New Magic* (1906), published the year after the Egyptian Hall's demolition:

> What is the meaning of this Egyptian Temple, transplanted from the banks of the Nile to prosaic London? The smoke and grime have attacked it and played sad havoc with its sandstone walls, painted with many hieroglyphics. The fog envelops it with a spectral embrace ... The temple ... is guarded by two up-to-date, flesh-and-blood Sphinxes in swallow-tail coats and opera hats ... See the long line of worshippers waiting to obtain admission to the Mysteries. Has the cult of Isis and Osiris been revived?[15]

In this passage, Evans evidently enjoys stage magic's tongue-in-cheek claims to be genuine, the theatricality of its venues, and indeed the suspension of disbelief, imagining what transpires within the Hall to be real. The Egyptian Hall was by no means a convincing Egyptian temple – at least to early twentieth-century onlookers in the final years of the Hall's existence; its hieroglyphs were nonsense signs (major breakthroughs in decipherment were made a decade after the Hall was constructed) and the statues of Isis and Osiris were executed in a style that was far from Egyptianate. Nevertheless, Evans revels in imagining the Egyptian Hall as an authentic temple for the best part of a page, before going on to

Figure 1.2 Evans, 'The Sphinx', in Professor Hoffmann, *Modern Magic: a practical treatise on the art of conjuring*, 9th edn (London: George Routledge and Sons, 1894), p. iv. Source: Library of Congress, Rare Book and Special Collections Division, Professor Hoffmann and Harry Houdini Collection, GV1547.L6 1894.

explain the illusion behind Stodare's Sphinx. More than 40 years after Stodare's illusion was performed, and even once the Egyptian Hall itself had ceased to stand, this famed optical trick is most dramatically imagined – in Evans's work at least – after an evocation of the enchanting atmosphere of the Egyptian Hall.

While many illusionists brought Egyptian elements into their performances – the scientist Gertrude Bacon (1874–1949) records in an article on the Hall's history that 'the Fakir of Ooloo, Hermann [*sic*], and Dr. Lynn, well-known conjurers of their day, strove to introduce Egyptian Magic into the London temple of Isis and Osiris'[16] – even illusions without their own obvious Egyptian connections were marketed using the imagery of ancient Egypt. One of the most influential illusions in the nineteenth century (still in use today) was the British scientist and inventor John Henry Pepper's (1821–1900) 'Pepper's Ghost'. The trick is based on reflections in angled glass, a translucent image appearing and disappearing as a light source brightens and dims. Pepper's Ghost began as an optical illusion used for scientific demonstrations, before finding its way into theatrical and magical performances.

Pepper first exhibited his Pepper's Ghost at the Royal Polytechnic Institution, then under his own management, before taking the illusion to the Egyptian Hall. The programme for Pepper's show from 1872 employs ancient Egyptian imagery in keeping with this new setting; it features a face wearing a *nemes* headdress and hands emerging from a cloud of dark smoke that pours forth from a lit amphora.[17] With a background sporting the pyramids of Giza, the programme draws upon ancient Egypt's reputation for the mystical, situating Pepper's performance within two magical traditions: one that claims to be able to produce 'true' supernatural magic, and the other that promises to delight – or to deceive – with illusion or *legerdemain*. Emblazoned with a ribbon declaring the title of Pepper's performance as 'The new and the wonderful!', the programme makes explicit the tension between novelty and 'newness' in the programme's text, and antiquity and 'oldness' in its visual imagery. Inside the programme, the running order begins with a lecture 'On some of the Realities of Science', underneath which are listed Pepper's academic credentials to bolster his credibility as a man of science: 'Fellow of the Chemical Society; Associate of the Institution of Civil Engineers; Hon. Diploma in Physics and Chemistry of the Lords of the Committee of Council on Education; late Professor of Chemistry and Honorary Director of the Royal Polytechnic Institution.' After readings from famous dramatic and poetic works by another performer, an interval and a musical interlude, 'Professor Pepper's Ghost' illusion featured as part of a 'historical and dramatic sketch' promising 'Scenic and Spectral Effects'. Such details demonstrate that even while the cover of the programme entices with imagery of ancient Egypt – the birthplace of magic(s) – this is not at the expense of underlining that the illusion, and the individual performing it, are, first and foremost, aligned with science.

From 1873, the British magicians John Nevil Maskelyne (1839–1917) and George Alfred Cooke (1825–1905) performed shows at the Egyptian Hall that exposed the mechanisms behind faked spiritualist phenomena, breaking down the boundaries between illusory and supernatural categories of magic.[18] As Catherine Wynne elegantly puts it, in Maskelyne and Cooke's shows, '[s]cience and séance converged on the late Victorian stage'.[19] The kinds of activity that Maskelyne and Cooke attempted to replicate and explain were the most sensational wonders of the séance, summarised by author and prominent member of the Society for Psychical Research, Frank Podmore (1856–1910):

> Inexplicable sounds; the alteration of the weight of bodies; the movement of chairs, tables and other heavy objects, and the playing of musical instruments without contact or connection of any kind; the levitation of human beings; the appearance of strange luminous substances; the appearance of hands apparently not attached to any body; writing not produced by human agency; the appearance of a materialised spirit-form.[20]

Like Pepper's before them, the programmes for Maskelyne and Cooke's debunking performances, which ran from 1873 to 1904, often emphasised the ancient Egyptian architectural style of the Hall – imagery of gods, goddesses, flaming torches and coiled serpents – rather than the kinds of illusion that they actually produced in their shows.[21] This, along with the Hall's architecture, lent an exotic tone to the proceedings.[22] The pylon-shaped architrave at the building's entrance, reproduced on some programmes, evokes an Egyptian temple, and so passing over this threshold, in reality or in the turning of the programme's page, appeals directly to the magical imagination.

While geographically confined to a fairly affluent area of London, the Egyptian Hall's cultural impact was such that ripples of its influence could be felt across the Atlantic Ocean. The American magician Harry Kellar (1849–1922), who had previously worked with the infamous Davenport brothers fraudulently producing spiritualist phenomena (which they had performed at the Egyptian Hall), was so inspired by this venue that he gave the name to his own theatre, housed in a Masonic Temple on Philadelphia's Chestnut Street.[23] Kellar's Egyptian Hall was only active from 1884 to 1885 before he left Philadelphia. Upon his return, he found that his Hall had burned down, prompting him to open a second Egyptian Hall on the same street in 1891.

Posters of Kellar represent him alongside recognisable ancient Egyptian symbols and scenery. One depiction of his 'Levitation of Princess Karnac' illusion in the early 1900s (inspired by a levitation trick he saw performed by Maskelyne at the Egyptian Hall), features the pyramids in the background, while Kellar himself stands at the top of the steps approaching a pylon-shaped temple and flanked by twin sphinxes.[24] An assistant in exotic costume floats in the air in a reclining position before him. Another version of the poster shows him with a far more detailed background featuring seated colossi evocative of those of the Great Temple of Ramses II at Abu Simbel or perhaps the Colossi of Memnon, handily relocated to a position adjacent to the Sphinx so as to form a composite image of Egypt at its most monumental.[25]

Kellar was one of the most successful magicians of the late nineteenth and early twentieth centuries, and the Egyptian Hall's iconography, by which he was so influenced, was in turn inherited by his successors and emulators. The 'Levitation of Princess Karnac' illusion was passed down by Kellar to Howard Thurston (1869–1936) and duplicated by Charles Joseph Carter (1874–1936), both of whom drew upon ancient Egypt's glamour in advertisements for their own shows. Carter advertised his levitation trick in the early 1900s using a design based heavily on one of Kellar's.[26] A poster of Thurston from around 1914, meanwhile, shows an ancient Egyptian-inspired stage set featuring technicolour columns and a gilded cabinet into which a boy and girl (in ancient Egyptian-themed costume) – along with a donkey – enter and vanish.[27] Atop the cabinet is a winged solar disc, giving the structure the appearance of a miniature temple. The apparatus was, likely, a large-scale version of Stodare's Sphinx.[28]

Another Egyptian Hall appeared in 1895 when a small theatre of this name was built in Ohio by the American politician and magician William W. Durbin (1866–1937). The theatre would go on to become a magic museum and was the site of the first ever convention devoted to magic in 1926. In the years after the demolition of London's Egyptian Hall in 1905, then, its influence still resonated with some of the most celebrated magicians of the early twentieth century; it survived, too, in various other Egyptian Halls that sought something of the original's cultural success. Intriguingly, it is in the aftermath of London's Egyptian Hall's demolition that we see authors specifically drawing upon this venue when describing genuine Egyptian magic in their texts, once it, like ancient Egyptian civilisation before it, had become consigned to the past. Literary allusions attest to its ever-presence in the Edwardian magical imagination, however. The effect is a curious blending of real magic and trickery, which mirrors the Egyptianised programmes advertising the shows of Pepper, and Maskelyne and Cooke.

For example, when the children in E. Nesbit's *The Story of the Amulet* (1906) – first serialised in *The Strand Magazine* as *The Amulet: a story for children* between 1905 and 1906 – seek entertainment towards the novel's end, they set off for 'the Egyptian Hall, England's Home of Mystery', for '[a]ll children, as well as a good many grown-ups, love conjuring'.[29] But when they arrive in Piccadilly they cannot see the 'big pillars outside'; the Egyptian Hall, demolished in 1905, temporally eludes the time-travelling children, and after a policeman informs them of the whereabouts of Maskelyne and Cooke's new premises – St George's Hall in Langham Place – they finally enjoy 'the most wonderful magic appearances and disappearances, which they could hardly believe – even with all their knowledge of a larger magic – was not really magic after all'.[30]

While Nesbit's Edwardian protagonists are not granted an encounter with the Egyptian Hall itself, they do witness a performance by the magician David Devant (1868–1941), a member of Maskelyne and Cooke's company, at which an ancient Egyptian priest, Rekh-marā, materialises. Devant witnesses the sudden appearance of the Egyptian priest amidst his audience and smoothly incorporates this into his own show:

> Though the eyes of the audience were fixed on Mr David Devant, Mr. David Devant's eyes were fixed on the audience … So he saw quite plainly the sudden appearance, from nowhere, of the Egyptian Priest.
>
> 'A jolly good trick,' he said to himself, 'and worked under my own eyes, in my own hall. I'll find out how that's done.' He had never seen a trick that he could not do himself if he tried.
>
> By this time a good many eyes in the audience had turned on the clean-shaven, curiously-dressed figure of the Egyptian Priest.
>
> 'Ladies and gentlemen,' said Mr Devant, rising to the occasion, 'this is a trick I have never before performed. The empty seat, third from the end, second row, gallery—you will now find occupied by an Ancient Egyptian, warranted genuine.'
>
> He little knew how true his words were.[31]

While the Egyptian Hall is gone, the Egyptianised trappings of stage magic persisted, and so Rekh-marā, 'curiously dressed', is not out of place in the modern magic venue: in fact, his costume marks him out as stage-magical. The moment is redolent of Henrietta Dorothy Everett's novel *Iras, A Mystery* (1896), published under the pseudonym Theo Douglas, in which the narrator is invited to attend an event where a fortune teller is to provide the entertainment and, before the proceedings begin, finds his 'attention ... arrested by a totally unexpected figure': 'a man in the sacerdotal costume of ancient Egypt'.[32] With no clear explanation as to the man's identity, the narrator's friend suggests that he might be 'some satellite' of the fortune teller, and so the narrator – a sceptic – expects to 'discover him ... in conjunction with the rest of the *diablerie*'.[33] Ancient Egyptian costume is misleading in both Nesbit's and Everett's texts, falsely indicating stage magic rather than the genuine occult power accessible to both of these ancient Egyptian priests. In Nesbit's novel, although Devant does not realise it, this is the first 'jolly good trick' he sees that he cannot replicate himself.

Egyptian magic in *The Story of the Amulet* as a whole is, after all, rit-ualistic and supernaturally powerful, rather than mundane productions of spectacular illusory effects. Rekh-marā threatens, 'I can make a waxen image of you, and I can say words which, as the wax image melts before the fire, will make you dwindle away and at last perish miserably'.[34] Dedicated to E. A. Wallis Budge (1857–1934), then Keeper of the Department of Egyptian and Assyrian Antiquities at the British Museum, Nesbit's novel integrates much that was considered Egyptologically accu-rate at the time she was writing, and Nesbit's detail about the employ-ment of wax in magic echoes details from Budge's book *Egyptian Magic* (first published in 1890, but which appeared in several later formats). Budge notes 'that the use of wax figures played a prominent part in cer-tain of the daily services which were performed in the temple of the god Amen-Ra at Thebes' and 'that these services were performed at a time when the Egyptians were renowned among the nations of the civilized world for their learning and wisdom'.[35] The parallels indicate that the detail of Egyptian magic involving wax figures certainly came from Budge, and that Nesbit's anchoring of the magic that Rekh-marā claims to be able to enact in historical fact attests to its authenticity.

The sinister threat of the Egyptian priest's claim is undercut, how-ever, by his awe at one of the children, Cyril, being able to 'make *fire* itself' through the use of a modern matchstick, a moment illustrated in the seri-alised version of the text that depicts Rekh-marā shrinking back into the shadows, away from this symbol of modernity.[36] Nevertheless, the text does not disprove the veracity nor indeed the potency of genuine Egyptian magic, even when faced with the stagier gimmicks of the children's supposedly magical productions. Indeed, when the children perform other acts of magic to dazzle the ancient Egyptians, they are simply employing the titular Egyptian amulet (as anyone with the 'word of power' could) to travel through time and space, making it seem as if objects are instantaneously appearing (using the amulet rather like an enchanted trapdoor). Through this method they produce 'a magic flower in a pot',[37] presumably a tongue-in-cheek reference to stage magicians' production of bouquets of flowers as if out of thin air (usually with the apparatus concealed up their sleeve). Intriguingly, the manifestation of flowers – including plants replete with pots – was also popular in spiritualist séances; in 1890 the medium Elizabeth d'Espérance (1855–1919) materialised a potted lily, seven feet in height, and with a piece of mummy bandage impaled by its stem, confirming – so d'Espérance claimed – that the plant had come to the séance directly from Egypt.[38]

There is certainly irony in that the children's production of fire from a match is considered to be the result of genuine supernatural power, while the creation of an archway to their own time via the amulet is held to be nothing more than a 'conjuring trick', specifically one produced by '[s]ome sort of magic-lantern' by a woman that they meet in the future.[39] Indeed, there is comedy in the frequent misunderstandings as to what type of magic is being witnessed by the novel's various audiences. When the Queen of Babylon wishes that the Babylonian artefacts in the British Museum 'would come out … slowly, so that those dogs and slaves can see the working of the great Queen's magic', the smashing of the glass display cases and the artefacts 'floating steadily through the door' is not effected through her magic at all (she does not display any magical abilities of her own throughout the text), but the work of the wish-granting sand fairy, the Psammead. When a journalist assumes the Queen to be 'Mrs. Besant' and the sight he witnesses to be the result of 'theosophy' – a reference to the British theosophist Annie Besant (1847–1933) – the range of magical possibilities is broadened further still, expanding to the powers claimed to have been developed by key players in the occult revival.[40]

Other representations of Egyptian magic in the novel suggest séance-like activities, as when the children 'prepare the mystic circle and consult the Amulet'.[41] Such moments are categorised by 'a silence and a darkness' out of which emerges 'a light and a voice'.[42] The children ask questions of the voice – implied to be that of the goddess Isis – and the voice answers, granting, at the novel's conclusion, a spiritual union between a modern

Egyptologist and the ancient Egyptian priest in something akin to a wedding ceremony, as they join hands underneath an arch illuminated by celestial radiance. Nesbit's repeated simile of magical conjoining – 'as one quick-silver bead is drawn to another quick-silver bead'[43] – underlines this union's alchemical associations, and so alchemy too is subsumed into the novel's broader magical melting pot. Séance-like images of the magical use of the amulet bookend the first and final instalment of the narrative as it first appeared in *The Strand Magazine* (figure 1.3). This version of the text visually represents the darkness in which the amulet operates, the amulet itself casting a spectral glow onto the faces of the participants who are positioned around it in a circle. In the first image, the children and the Psammead are the participants witness to its magic, while in the second, at the story's conclusion, they are joined by both the ancient Egyptian Rekh-marā and the modern Egyptologist.[44] Ancient Egyptian presences in séances were not uncommon; often, Egyptian spirits were said to have manifested, and several mediums reported having Egyptian spirit 'controls' who would help them to open a line of communication with individuals on the other side. Genuine artefacts – and modern forgeries – appeared from out of the gloom and some participants brought ancient Egyptian items with them to the séance, at times to test the abilities of the medium.[45] The caption accompanying the first image – 'A faint, beautiful voice began to speak' – reinforces the aural as well as visual phenomena that characterise this séance-like experience.

Figure 1.3 H. R. Millar, 'A faint, beautiful voice began to speak', *Strand Magazine* 29 (173) (May 1905): 592; and H. R. Millar, 'The children cast down their eyes – and so did everyone', *Strand Magazine* 31 (184) (April 1906): 471. Source: Internet Archive.

The Story of the Amulet thus presents a varied array of magical activity interpreted as occupying an enormous range of what Bell terms 'magical thinking', from optical illusion and stage magic to the spiritualist séance, from theosophy to alchemy. While the Egyptian Hall is aligned in Nesbit's novel with the first of these categories, Egyptian Hall magicians are also confronted by real ancient Egyptian power that is – to their eyes and to the eyes of audience – merely a magic trick yet to be comprehended.

Published in the same year as the novel version of Nesbit's text, the British author and explorer George Griffith's *The Mummy and Miss Nitocris: a phantasy of the fourth dimension* (1906) similarly features an ancient Egyptian with genuine occult powers, which onlookers compare to Egyptian Hall performances. In this moment, a crowd reacts to the novel's antagonist, Phadrig, hypnotising the novel's heroine, Nitocris:

> It might have been expected that the miracle, or at least the extraor-dinary defiance of physical law ... would have produced something like consternation among the bulk of the spectators ... but they only saw something wonderful ... Nothing would have persuaded them that it was not the result of such skill as produced the marvels of the Egyptian Hall.[46]

This passage in Griffith's text underscores the Egyptian Hall's reputation for spectacular visual effects, but it also reads alongside Nesbit's novel in interesting ways. Phadrig, who was an ancient Egyptian in a former life, uses a genuine occult force in order to coerce Nitocris and, as with the materialisation of Rekh-marā out of thin air in Nesbit's novel, that this is assumed to be nothing more than an impressive magic trick reveals the indistinguishability of real ancient Egyptian magic and the modern routines that sought to produce similar effects on stage. That Phadrig's audience includes sceptical professors who 'each wore the scalps of many spiritualistic mediums' (one – Nitocris's father – being a member of the 'Psychical Research Society') means that Phadrig is subject to scrutiny that ultimately seeks to determine whether he has genuine occult power or is 'merely a conjurer'.[47] That Phadrig describes the other effects that he can produce in relation to spiritualism and theosophy further recontextu-alises his powers in relation to the modern world, but also suggests these belief systems as the direct inheritors of genuine ancient occult forces.[48] Even after the Egyptian Hall was gone, its legacy was evidently still felt in literature depicting ancient Egyptian magic. The Egyptian Hall, in *The Story of the Amulet* and *The Mummy and Miss Nitocris*, is the nearest thing in the crowds' experience to the real magical abilities that they witness, and is thus emblematic of the meeting point between illusion and genuine enchantment, modern technologies and ancient iconographies.

The séance and stage magic

The séance and stage magic were, in some respects, very similar performances, particularly when stage magic set out to emulate and explain the ways in which certain common séance phenomena could be produced. Peter Lamont claims that nineteenth-century audiences differentiated between the two practices simply by relying on what the conjuror claimed to be able to achieve: direct contact with spirits of the deceased or else illusions and tricks often designed to replicate such acts.[49] This was certainly the case in the 'anti-Spiritualist' performances by the likes of Maskelyne and Cooke, as well as in the shows of other magicians who explicitly set out to undermine spiritualist mediums' claims to authenticity. Spiritualists, meanwhile, retorted that magicians were conjuring these effects with real supernatural power without realising or admitting to it.[50] Ultimately, while stage magicians' and spiritualist mediums' claims varied, as did audiences' responses to what they witnessed, both kinds of conjuring shared much of the same imagery.

As Michael Saler notes, although stage magic was perceived as something unknowably ancient, it also simultaneously came to express modernity through its fashionability, the audience's hunger for novelty and new technological developments that facilitated innovative tricks; Karl Bell similarly observes that stage magic 'promot[ed] bourgeois conceptions of a technological modernity'.[51] Of the many features that stage magic and spiritualist séances had in common, 'innovation and novelty' were key to the success of both.[52] Audiences were eager to see something that they had not experienced before. Nevertheless, the novel was often disguised in such terms as to evoke antiquity: the Ouija board, one method by which the spirits could apparently be contacted, produced at the *fin de siècle* (first marketed as a game, and subsequently acquiring greater occult credibility), had another name in this period: the 'Egyptian luck board'.[53] While the Ouija board was 'new', the suggestion of its origin in Egypt provided it some kind of mystical authenticity.

Often depicted in literature as a curious mingling of the spiritualist séance and the stage-magic performance, demonstrations of ancient Egyptian occultism relate back to contemporaneous notions of illusion, with traces of novel tricks and phenomena essential to securing the reputation of the medium or stage magician. Intriguingly, the blending of these types of magical performance means that the 'genuineness' of the phenomena remains hazy for original readers and those encountering the texts now; is the Egyptian magic presented in these narratives real or merely an optical effect? Is this an occult achievement or a scientific one? In most cases, it appears to be both, occupying an alchemical middle ground.

Myriad texts that feature ancient Egyptian magic blend the supernatural with the theatrical in this way. H. Rider Haggard provides a compelling case study, his own texts having made a particular impact upon the world of stage magic and other kinds of illusory performance.[54] In his novel *Cleopatra* (1889), the protagonist Harmachis communes with the goddess Isis, who appears before him as a 'dark cloud upon the altar' that 'grew white ... shone, and seemed at length to take the shrouded shape of a woman'.[55] Surrounded by 'bright eyes', 'strange whispers' and 'vapours [that] burst and melted', the descriptions of what Harmachis sees might equally apply to a séance in a fashionable London drawing room or, as David Huckvale suggests, a Masonic initiation ceremony.[56] The ancient Egyptian spiritual rite and the cosmopolitan Victorian experience of the supernatural ritual are rendered virtually indistinguishable, particularly through the depiction of the goddess Isis as a 'shrouded ... woman', suggestive of the manifestation of draped spirit forms in the séance room, or the veiled medium herself.[57] Haggard had attended séances in his youth and, although he claimed to have ridiculed these experiences at the time, these events may well have impacted upon the representation of occult practices in his fiction.[58] Later, when Isis appears again, she takes the form of 'the horned moon, gleaming faintly in the darkness, and betwixt the golden horns rested a small dark cloud, in and out of which the fiery serpent climbed'.[59] With Isis's entrance and exit heralded by the music of invisible sistra and her voice emerging from within the smoky cloud, Haggard might be seen to allude to the common séance phenomena of disembodied voices and music (the sistra suggestive of the tambourine, used by many spiritualists), and strange light effects in the darkness.

Harmachis, like the psychic medium, can summon the forms of spirits, requesting that 'the curtains' be 'drawn and the chamber' 'a little darkened', 'as though the twilight were at hand' in order to perform his illusion.[60] He summons 'the shape of royal Caesar' wearing 'a vestment bloody from a hundred wounds', who materialises first as 'a cloud' before taking the shape of a man 'vaguely mapped upon the twilight, and [which] seemed now to grow and now to melt away'.[61] Harmachis makes the image dematerialise after a mere instant, admitting that it was nothing more than a 'shadow', an illusory image projected from his own imagination.[62] This admission complicates the scene, which here transitions into a kind of anti-spiritualist demonstration. The effects may be convincing, and they may still demonstrate Harmachis's occult powers, but the conjuror confesses that they are not what they seem.

In keeping with his claim to be an illusionist rather than a medium, Harmachis performs with an ebony wand tipped with ivory, a playful wink to the black and white magic wand that was, by this point, common stage-magic apparatus. This variety of wand was allegedly first used by the French magician Jean Eugène Robert-Houdin (1805–71) in the early 1800s.[63] Such a detail would have likely been too glaringly anachronistic to appear in the novel's rather sombre narrative illustrations by the artists R. Caton Woodville (1856–1927) and Maurice Greiffenhagen (1862–1931), though it does feature in one of the illuminated capitals (figure 1.4) designed by explorer and illustrator Edward Whymper (1840–1911).[64] In this image the wand rests atop a scroll inscribed with hieroglyphs. Small stars surrounding and seemingly resting atop the wand suggest a genuine magical power at odds with the depiction of the wand itself. To Haggard's credit, the ancient Egyptians did use magic wands in their rituals (the earliest surviving examples date from around 2800 BCE) and, while his use of a black and white magic wand is anachronistic, he does take care to describe this relatively modern magical prop as constructed from suitably exotic materials.[65] Ancient Egyptian wands were, after all, usually made from hippopotamus ivory.[66] Even Whymper's capital, with its rather curvaceous shape for the capital t it represents,[67] is suggestive of the curvature of genuine ancient Egyptian examples rather than the thin straightness of the modern baton, the ram and serpent that make up the ends of this shape evocative of the protective mythical creatures and deities inscribed onto their ivory surfaces. As a result, Haggard – along with one of his illustrators, perhaps in on the 'joke' – maintains a degree of historical accuracy, while injecting an element of nineteenth-century stage-magical convention, closely aligning the two.

The history of ancient Egyptian magic had a significant impact on modern magical performances. Both modern stage magic and occult ceremonies inherited a greater sense of legitimacy through their links to ancient Egyptian ritual and illusory conventions, interplay evident not just in Haggard's novel, but across broader cultural contexts. As Catherine Wynne points out, 'Victorian [stage] magicians liked to invoke Pharaonic practices', 'the period's excavation of Egyptian tombs add[ing] an occult frisson and contemporaneity to their rituals'.[68] While Haggard grants his ancient Egyptian conjuror a modern nineteenth-century magician's wand, magic wands based on ancient Egyptian iconography were

Figure 1.4 Edward Whymper, illustrated capital, in H. Rider Haggard, *Cleopatra* (London: Longmans, Green, and Co., 1889), p. 101. Author's own.

used by nineteenth-century occult groups, including the Golden Dawn, lending their ceremonies a kind of iconographical weight. Haggard's frame narrative in *Cleopatra* is one of modern archaeology; opening his novel is an account of how the narrative that follows – a purportedly genuine ancient Egyptian text – had been unearthed and translated. Its revelations of magical rites and demonstrations of illusion in antiquity (which, though the trappings of nineteenth-century stage magic transpire to be surprisingly familiar to Haggard's readers), establish, from the narrative's opening pages, a collision between the modern moment and Egyptian antiquity.

Séance phenomena – tempered with the conventions of anti-spiritualist demonstration as theatre – also feature in Everett's aforementioned novel, *Iras*. Early in the narrative, Ralph Lavenham, a man sceptical about all things paranormal, attends a London *soirée* where private consultations with a psychic are the evening's entertainment. The room in which the sessions take place is described as 'arranged in semi-darkness', illuminated only by 'a single lamp with a deep red shade' and 'the embers of a dying fire left in the grate'.[69] While no psychic phenomena occur in this environment other than some cryptic (but prescient) warnings from the medium, Lavenham sees a man in ancient Egyptian attire elsewhere in the house. Although he assumes the man to be the psychic's accomplice, the medium discloses that the ancient Egyptian is in fact a spirit that only she and Lavenham are able to see as a result of their clairvoyant powers. The man, Savak, is an ancient Egyptian priest, who reappears multiple times to steal amulets from Lavenham's ancient Egyptian love interest, Iras, at one point materialising simply as 'a slender hand'.[70] The hand, which has 'no appearance of detachment … seemed to reach over from behind [Iras] as if the figure to which it belonged were concealed by the back of the sofa, and the arm passed through it'.[71] This description conjures up the kinds of techniques used by some of the most famous mediums of the age who claimed to be able to produce the hands of spirits, including the Italian spiritualist medium Eusapia Palladino (1854–1918).[72] These phantom appendages were often seen to be detached, when in many cases they seem to have been the hands of the performer, or else a prosthetic that was manipulated to give the appearance of suspension in mid-air. The very idea of furniture with false backs, or which had been otherwise been modified, also suggests the 'spirit cabinet' – famously introduced to spiritualist demonstrations by the Davenport brothers, and subsequently used by mediums as (in)famous as Florence Cook (c.1856–1904) – or indeed the duplicate apparatus of anti-spiritualist magicians exposing such phenomena.[73] The Davenports' cabinet featured a hole cut out of the door for the purposes of supplying air to the mediums inside; conveniently, it also offered an orifice through which hands – claimed to be those of the spirits – could emerge. That Savak's real magic is conceived of as appearing like the fraudulent manifestations of modern mediums casts him as an antagonist. Despite the fact that it is Savak's occult abilities that allow him to foil Lavenham and Iras's plans to live as a married couple in the modern world, his powers' appearance as trickery paints him as one of the deceptive priests who appear at the beginnings of histories of illusory magic; for Savak, like his forerunners, magic is put to nefarious ends: to beguile and to overpower.

This is in direct contrast to Iras, who is presented as a genuine psychic medium, and whose abilities are coded as more passive – therefore more feminine – and put to ends exclusively in pursuit of romantic love and in avoiding Savak's sinister designs. Iras awakens after having been put into a trance by Savak lasting thousands of years, and this, along with her prophetic dreams about the loss of the amulets on her necklace, indicate that her occult power is connected (unlike Savak's) to states of unconsciousness. She also reveals to Lavenham that during her life in ancient Egypt she had seen his image 'in the divining-cup, and in the smoke above the altar'.[74] Conjuring images of her lover thousands of years before they meet, Iras has access to genuine future truths, just as the psychic medium at the soirée offers words that predict later events. While Savak's magic is understood in terms of fraudulent spiritualist illusion, Iras's is only ever described in terms that suggest a higher power, and ritual magic whose veracity is never in doubt.

To take one final example, Algernon Blackwood's short story 'The Nemesis of Fire' (1908) also adopts the conventions of the séance to depict ancient Egyptian supernatural forces. A member of the Golden Dawn, Blackwood was well acquainted with contemporary ritual magic, especially that which had its roots in ancient Egyptian lore. He was also a theosophist and, as a result, was dedicated to the study of esoteric wisdom passed down from ancient Egypt and India.[75] Outside of these quasi-religious organisations, he nurtured a keen interest in the supernatural. He was a member of the Ghost Club and although he was not a member of the Society for Psychical Research, he often participated in their investigations into haunted houses.[76] As David Punter and Glennis Byron point out, Blackwood was 'one of the few writers of Gothic fiction actually to have believed in the supernatural', and his experiences in these groups that bridged scientific and occult interests had a distinct impact upon his writing.[77] His work is laced with traces of authentic mysticism and the modes of scientific inquiry put to use in investigating occultists' claims, echoing the aims and beliefs of the diverse circles in which Blackwood moved.

In 'The Nemesis of Fire', Blackwood describes the materialisation of a fire elemental, which was originally conjured by ancient Egyptian necromancers to protect a mummy. At midnight, the elemental is summoned in a darkened room lit only by red lamps, and provided with an offering of a bowl of blood. Sat at a round table and taking each other's hands, the participants experience a plethora of typical séance phenomena, beginning with the subtle sensations of the skin being touched with 'a silken run'.[78] Scraps of silk and other light or diaphanous fabrics were often used by mediums to suggest ectoplasm, supposedly a visible spiritual energy that first appeared in the 1880s, while the feeling of being touched (usually on the face or hands) was another common occurrence for sitters.[79] One of the characters present, Colonel Wragge, is then possessed by the elemental, his expression changing to one that is 'dark, and in some unexplained way, terrible' and speaking with a 'changed voice, deep and musical', at once 'half his own and half another's'.[80] Here, Blackwood draws upon contemporaneous concepts of the supernatural rather than those of ancient Egyptian culture; the ancient Egyptians did not believe in spirit possession, and yet this trope is found in several late Victorian and Edwardian texts with ancient Egyptian supernatural themes.[81] In the case of Blackwood's text, ancient and contemporaneous occultism are brought together, creating a hybrid account of the supernatural in which the ancient world returns via the conventions of modern spiritualist enquiry.

After the Colonel's possession, 'a pale and spectral light' within which can be seen 'shapes of fire' begins to materialise from the shadows.[82] In the passage that follows, the shapes move and interact with the possessed participant:

> They grew bright, faded, and then grew bright again with an effect almost of pulsation. They passed swiftly to and fro through the air, rising and falling, and particularly in the immediate neighbourhood of the Colonel, often gathering about his head and shoulders, and even appearing to settle upon him like giant insects of flame. They were accompanied, moreover, by a faint sound of hissing.[83]

The passage reads almost as a catalogue of some of the more impressive séance phenomena of the time. Glowing lights resembling will-o'-the-wisps were part of the repertoires of some of the most notorious psychic mediums, and were sometimes captured in séance photographs. One of the most famous images of a séance, taken by the German psychical researcher Albert von Schrenck-Notzing (1862–1929), seemingly depicts the French spiritualist medium Eva Carrière (1886–1943) with a luminous apparition like a streak of electricity emerging from between her hands. Although the effect was almost certainly the result of a coincidental fault on the film or else the product of subsequent manipulation, photographs showing manifestations of light remained popular because of the compelling nature of the images. Blackwood's use of lights and also inexplicable sounds – in this case hissing – conforms to accounts of some of the most notorious psychic mediums as investigated and reported on by eminent scientists of the Society for Psychical Research.[84] Thus, in his nod to the fraudulent use of fabric to simulate ectoplasm, along with lights and sounds of a more convincing nature, Blackwood combines elements of the séance that hint at fraudulence as much as they gesture to something more genuine.

There are also elements of the theatrical in Blackwood's text that allude to stage magic, further complicating the representation of the scene. The shape that emerges from the shadows does so 'as though slowly revealed by the rising of a curtain', aligning the materialising elemental with the dramatic conventions of the theatre.[85] Although curtains were used to drape cabinets in séances, these were meant to shield the medium from view, rather than to be raised dramatically in this manner. Popular visual spectacle and optical technologies are referred to later when the narrator experiences a vision. When he touches the face of the mummy, 'time fled backwards like a thing of naught, showing in haunted panorama the most wonderful dream of the whole world'.[86] The spiritual experience and popular entertainment collide in Blackwood's narrator's evocation of the panorama, blending fashionable metropolitan visual spectacle with profound supernatural encounter.

The likening of such a psychic experience to a panorama – which Markman Ellis describes as 'among the most astonishing and popular of visual spectacles from the early 1790s through most of the next century'[87] – further calls into question what is a genuine apparition and what a theatrical visual effect. With its origins in the late eighteenth century, the panorama was an optical technology emblematic of modernity through the various innovations that enhanced the illusion across the nineteenth century. The panorama offered a 360-degree view, essentially being an enormous painting suspended on the inside of a circular room. Dioramas – 'extensions of the panorama' that 'added movement to the image' – 'unfolded like a story-board in time'.[88] Of course, Egypt was a popular subject for such entertainments; the Egyptian Hall showcased 'a moving panorama of the Nile in July 1849'.[89] *The Grand Moving Panorama of the Nile* was 'conceived and created by Egyptologist Joseph Bonomi (1796–1872) as a means of introducing people to the scenes and wonders of Egypt, both ancient and modern'. S. J. Wolfe has uncovered that either this same panorama, or a duplicate, was shown in New York before touring America, its afterlife extending into the second half of the nineteenth century.[90] Gentle lighting combined with the translucency of the panorama itself gave this particular entertainment an ethereal quality, and its final scene – a fading view of the Great Sphinx of Giza as the lights were dimmed – concluded the spectacle with a dreamlike experience as if travelling back in time from Egypt's present to its ancient past.

Indeed, decades before Blackwood, otherworldly visions of Egypt were described in relation to the panorama in popular literature. Among them is Grant Allen's burlesque 'My New Year's Eve Among the Mummies' (1878), published under the pseudonym J. Arbuthnot Wilson. When Allen's protagonist 'enters a pyramid only to find ancient Egyptian mummies restored to life, he describes the sight as a 'strange living panorama'.[91] Later, when he commits to be mummified himself so as to spend eternity with the princess Hatasou, he is anaesthetised, and relates that 'the whole panorama faded finally from my view'.[92] Allen's story, intended as a comic relation of an adventure that his narrator claims to be true, but is, more likely, a vision brought about by malarial fever, uses the panorama as a means to describe a visually exciting experience, altogether immersive and dreamlike. Blackwood's narrator's relation of 'time fl[ying] backwards like a thing of naught, showing in haunted panorama the most wonderful dream of the whole world' reads in a similar way, only with a differing tone to suggest a genuine – rather than dreamed – psychological journey brought about by the ancient Egyptian occult. The narrator's experience in Blackwood's text reads very much like *The Grand Moving Panorama of the Nile*, with its journey back through time to conclude on an image of the distant past. While Blackwood would not have encountered this particular panorama, such technologies evidently made an impression on him, and are evoked again in relation to supernatural Egyptian experiences in his later short story 'Sand' (1912), this time set in Egypt itself. His protagonist experiences 'something swift and light and airy' flashing '[b]ehind the solid mass of the Desert's immobility … Bizarre pictures interpreted it to him, like rapid snap-shots of a huge flying panorama'.[93]

The indistinctness of the line between magic and illusion in ancient Egyptian contexts is striking across these accounts. Haggard, Everett and Blackwood seem unable to resist the allure of describing genuine supernatural events in the language of the theatre, with costumes, curtains and specialist props being central to their depictions of the occult. Almost anticipating Hollywood portrayals of ancient Egypt, each more opulent than the last, the rich symbolism, fire, smoke, blood and celestial music of these accounts create a proto-cinematic effect. These writers focus on the multisensory, but particularly on the visual, relating what is seen and what is unseen in terms that describe ancient Egyptian magic in relation to the séance, the anti-spiritualist demonstration, the magic show, and – in Blackwood's case – the panorama. Magic is thus cast as occupying a hazy middle ground between truth and trickery, genuine manifestation and the products of optics and bespoke equipment. It is to imaging technologies that we now turn in even greater detail, specifically to such apparatus that promised glimpses of the dead.

Phantasmagoria

Across the nineteenth century, images of disembodied spirits were produced via ever-changing technologies. Magic lanterns, photographs and, at the end of the century, early moving pictures manifested images of ancient Egypt in various ways and for different purposes, often for entertainments with an emphasis on the magical or supernatural. In turn, the ways in which ancient Egypt was represented by these technologies impacted upon literature; methods of projection, including the magic lantern, are often discernible beneath the text's surface. Dissolve effects frequently used to depict ghosts in magic-lantern displays, particularly in phantasmagorical shows that relied on more elaborate effects – often involving multiple magic lanterns put to use at once, or the projection of images onto moving surfaces, such as smoke – and, later, film are evoked in literary portrayals of ancient Egyptian characters fading in and out of the material world. We can trace the imagery of such technologies in Haggard and Blackwood, but beyond these authors to fiction including that of the magician Henry Ridgley Evans and the theosophist Charles Webster Leadbeater, too, evidencing how such technologies were employed by those who, respectively, saw Egypt as the origin of optical illusion passing as magic and of genuine supernatural power.

The magic lantern has a history that stretches back to the seventeenth century, though it was not until the eighteenth century that the technology became widely used. That this history was fairly well known did not stop sources such as the children's penny periodical *Young England* from recording in 1880 that:

> Some suppose that the ancient Egyptians … were the first to use lenses in such a way as to produce effects similar to those now shown with the lantern. No doubt the clever magi, or priests, used to impose upon the poor superstitious people with some kind of mysterious exhibition of shadowy figures.[94]

The author attributes knowledge of sophisticated illusory effects to the ancient Egyptians, conjuring an image of performance magic facilitated by optical technologies before, ultimately, asserting that '[t]he real inventor' of the magic lantern was, in fact, the German polymath Athanasius Kircher (1602–80). A reference to similar technologies in ancient Egyptian also exists in the introduction to Henry Ridgley Evans's novel, *The House of the Sphinx* (1907); '[w]ith the aid of polished convex mirrors of metal' the ancient Egyptian priests 'were able to cast image upon the smoke rising from burning incense, and thus often deceived their votaries into the belief that they beheld visions of the gods'.[95] Egypt is, once again, imagined as the origin of all things, in this case optical technologies, credited, if not with the invention of the magic lantern itself, then with its precursors.

Ever since the magic lantern's (true) origins, hand-painted slides had been used to project Gothic subject matter, which likely suggested itself as particularly appropriate imagery given the hazy and luminous effects that the lantern produced, most effective in darkened spaces. These morbid displays evolved into the more complex phantasmagoria from the final decades of the eighteenth century onwards. Painted slides in phantasmagorical displays occasionally depicted ancient Egyptian mummies. Barbara Maria Stafford, for instance, draws attention to the use of the mummy in the phantasmagorical shows of the Belgian magician and physicist Étienne-Gaspard Robertson (1763–1837) in the late eighteenth and early nineteenth centuries. In these performances, 'by illuminating a single slide with several candles, Robertson could multiply one figure into many to produce a host of frightening creatures, which he advertised as the "Dance of the Witches" and the "Ballet of the Mummies"'.[96] Some narratives 'evoked the context of Egyptian archaeology', one featuring a bejewelled skeleton discovered by a would-be tomb robber.[97] Robertson would also move the projectors closer to and further away from projection surfaces, causing the images to shrink or grow. As Marina Warner notes, Robertson's most successful shows were performed in an abandoned Parisian convent, decorated with hieroglyphs, which he claimed appeared 'to announce the entrance to the mysteries of Isis'.[98] Lant observes that in London in 1801, the magician Paul de Philipsthal's (d.1829) phantasmagoria was housed in the same venue as a show entitled 'Aegyptiana', a series of Egyptian scenes; that the poster for phantasmagoria expressly warned that patrons should not mistakenly attend the 'Aegyptiana' suggests 'imaginary and physical alliances' between the phantasmagoria and Egyptian subject matter in the minds of viewing publics.[99] In America, meanwhile, audiences were thrilled by phantasmagoria produced from 1803 onwards; one performer by the name of William Bates showcased a 'particularly intriguing image' in 1804 of 'An Egyptian Pigmy Idol, which instantaneously changes to a Human Skull'.[100] Egyptian subject matter was, therefore, evident in phantasmagorical shows on both sides of the Atlantic from early in the nineteenth century.

Subsequently, the Victorian era saw an explosion in the use of the magic lantern in illusory contexts; its 'popularity … as a visual storytelling device peaked in the middle to late nineteenth century', with venues such as the Royal Polytechnic Institute hosting 'displays that often involved up to six lanterns, and pioneered technology such as dissolving views that foreshadowed the cinematograph's moving images'.[101] The magic lantern and early cinema were, as Simone Natale outlines, part of a web of technologies that produced superimposed images that included spirit photography and stage-magic devices.[102] While the magic lantern itself did not originate in the nineteenth century, it was refined and put to innovative purposes across this era, beginning with the phantasmagoria and culminating, in several historians' accounts, in the special effects that we witness in some of the earliest moving pictures.[103]

Photographic lantern slides became available from the mid-nineteenth century onwards, a development that meant hand-painted and photographic slides could be used in combination to produce new and exciting results, theatrically accompanied by music and sound effects.[104] Fantasy and reality collided at venues such as the Royal Polytechnic, where the traditional subject matter of magic-lantern shows depicting 'popular fairy stories, cautionary tales, old jokes, ghostly apparitions, [were] all mixed up with recent reports of explorers' exploits and the latest news', giving the undertakings an exotic and sometimes archaeologically inflected twist, and suggesting the presence of the fantastic in the real world.[105] The influence of such visual collages is suggested in Algernon Blackwood's short story 'A Descent into Egypt' (1914). Blackwood's narrator recounts the tale of the loss of his friend, who is drawn to the mysteries of Egypt and is ultimately consumed by them. The narrator is one of three men who all feel Egypt's pull, and describes the effects that they experience as they come to be possessed by the spirit of Egypt:

VICTORIAN ALCHEMY

> In rapid series, like lantern-slides upon a screen, the ancient symbols flashed one after ... and were gone ... The successive signatures seemed almost superimposed as in a composite photograph, each appearing and vanished before recognition was even possible, while I interpreted the inner alchemy by means of outer tokens familiar to my senses.[106]

In 'A Descent into Egypt' the 'ancient symbols' of the past are visualised as 'flash[ing]', on the faces of the men, as if illuminated and projected onto these receptive forms by a magic lantern. The narrator is aware that something alchemical is taking place in their psyches, and that this is manifesting externally in their physical appearances, which reveal something Sphinx or Horus-like. As in earlier examples, this occult experience is meant to be real, although the language of optical illusion means that these ancient archaeological horrors are conceived of in relation to modern visualisation technologies. The use of simile reveals how Blackwood's narrator's grasp of the situation is shaky: he turns to the magic lantern and to the photograph as a means to express his experience and ultimately to comprehend it, but modernity is no match for the Egyptian supernatural. Blackwood's narrator is evidently lucky to survive this experience.

The introduction of fantastical and ghostly imagery into archaeological settings via projection technologies can be read in earlier texts too, notably in Haggard's *Cleopatra*. Indeed, magic-lantern technology may well have been on Haggard's mind at the time: a photographic portrait of Haggard from around the mid-1880s was made into magic-lantern slides by York & Son as part of a series entitled 'Celebrities From Life', likely around the time that *Cleopatra* was published.[107] When Haggard's protagonist, Harmachis, is first shown visions of the past by a priest of Isis, the pictures seem very similar to those produced by magic-lantern slides. Harmachis's account of the experience, in which 'the end of the chamber became luminous, and in that white light [he] beheld picture after picture' emphasises the way in which the images are shown in quick succession and against a flat surface suitable for projection.[108] Passages describing the individual images are separated by observations revealing the way in which each image gives way to the next: 'the picture passed and another rose up in its place.'[109] Here, Haggard de-emphasises the supernatural and makes the whole spiritual experience seem a surprisingly pragmatic affair. Nevertheless, it is significant that lantern slides were by no means devoid of atmosphere; their use in Masonic initiation ceremonies suggests that they maintained something of their mystical aura (Haggard was a Freemason), and here too Harmachis is initiated into the mysteries of Isis.[110]

The scenes themselves have several features in common with contemporaneous slides showing images of Egypt. Harmachis mentions one in which he could see 'the ancient Nile rolling through deserts to the sea'.[111] Nile scenes were a common subject of hand-painted slides of Egyptian subjects, and photographic slides too once the technology became available. The accompanying illustration only serves to further the parallel between this scene and the projected image created by optical technologies (figure 1.5). The stream of light towards the image implies that the picture is being projected from behind the figures of Harmachis and the priest. The area of the scene taken up by the vision is also represented as existing within a defined rectangle, while the smoking lamp in the foreground perhaps alludes to the practice of projecting onto smoke, which was used to create a more ghostly effect, or else acted as a visual reminder of the light source required for such apparatus. The image representing the appearance of the ghosts later in the novel (figure 1.6) also conforms to conventions of image projection. Again, the magic lantern appears to be referenced, both in the situation of a light source behind Cleopatra and Harmachis and, of course, in the subject matter of phantoms, which almost seem to materialise on a flat plane as if they were Pepper's Ghosts.

The imagery of the phantasmagoria is further apparent in *Cleopatra* in the spirit of the dead pharaoh, Menkau-ra, which appears in the form of a 'mighty bat', 'white in colour', with 'bony wings' and 'fiery eyes'.[112] Bats, like phantoms, were popular in phantasmagorical displays, which tended to favour the established imagery of Gothic horror. The pale colouring of Haggard's bat, and its 'fiery eyes' in particular, denote it as a being of light. A set of nineteenth-century magic-lantern slides in the Richard Balzer Collection creates the illusion of an animated bat flapping its wings, and Haggard's bat's repetitive movements – not just in flight but 'rocking itself to and fro' – suggest the simple but effective visuals that sets of mechanical magic-lantern slides could create.[113] Witnessed in conjunction with the beautiful woman and the hideous corpse, and appearing and disappearing with supernatural speed, the bat reveals Haggard's reliance on the tropes and practices of the phantasmagoria when creating his ancient Egyptian horrors.[114] Indeed, the bat's final appearance in the novel heralds the arrival of the crowd of spirits, as if one set of slides were giving way to another as part of a phantasmagorial display.

Beyond Haggard's historical novel, the impact of magic-lantern technology on narratives of Egypt is palpable in a range of other genres,

Figure 1.5 R. Caton Woodville, 'I saw the world as it had been before man was', in H. Rider Haggard, *Cleopatra* (London: Longmans, Green, and Co., 1889), facing p. 58. Author's own.

from children's fiction to theosophical publications. The British politician James Henry Yoxall's (1857–1925) children's adventure novel *The Lonely Pyramid* (1892) has, at its opening, a scene like an eccentrically coloured magic-lantern slide: 'Yonder … are fair low rounded hills; at their feet a

Figure 1.6 M. Greiffenhagen, 'She looked; she saw the awful shapes', in H. Rider Haggard, *Cleopatra* (London: Longmans, Green, and Co., 1889), facing p. 323. Author's own.

patch of emerald sward and feathery palms, a gleam of silver water; and amidst it all a loft, lonely Pyramid, of purple hue!'[115] As John Plunkett observes, '[m]ore than any other genre, children's books drew on optical recreations like the ... magic lantern', modest versions of this technology having become, by the late nineteenth century, available for domestic use and, as such, had entered the middle-class home to be enjoyed as a family activity.[116] Intriguingly, for an illustrated book, however, these magic-lantern-esque views are not pictured, but left to the child reader's imagination. A divide emerges between the rather more straightforward narrative illustrations and the more mystical optical effects conjured up in the mind's eye and not permitted to appear materially on the page. Nonetheless, Yoxall's textual depictions of these effects are evidently crafted to capture the young imagination and to suggest the spectacular. A reviewer for the *Spectator*'s literary supplement admired its 'vividness and picturesqueness', praising Yoxall's 'descriptions of pyramid interiors and desert scenery'.[117]

Our hero, Roy Lefeber, is in Egypt for the purposes of studying optics, specifically 'the laws that govern the production of mirage', and the descriptions of the Egyptian desert certainly linger on its unusual optical effects in spectacular terms:

> The lovely landscape wavered, shifted, changed like the transformation scene at a theatre. A shaft of fuller light smote it like a sword; it shuddered, it shredded into filaments, it wavered ... it rose, it rolled apart, it melted into rainbow-tinted haze, it disappeared.[118]

Yoxall's listing and use of alliteration – 'lovely landscape', 'it shuddered, it shredded', 'it rose, it rolled' – provides a sense of rhythm to the descriptions of the constantly changing image, suggesting an almost trance-like captivation on Roy's part. The theatrical simile further underlines the fascination commanded by these dramatic light effects. The child fears that the scene he witnesses is nothing more than a mirage – described in technological terms as 'the magic-lantern of the desert' – and indeed, when it disappears from view 'like a silken, flashing curtain split and rolled asunder' it is with the theatricality of seemingly instantaneous appearances and disappearances concealed and then revealed by curtains, common in stage magic.[119] Once the protagonists arrive at the purple pyramid, Roy witnesses 'a white and ghostly figure, gliding with silent foot', and while this transpires not to be a revenant as they first suppose, is does mark the beginning of a litany of imagery that associates the pyramid with phantasmagorical horrors, from a statue of a crocodile so lifelike as to be presumed by the protagonist to be real – 'the spirit of ancient Egypt ... set to guard the mysteries of Isis' – to the mummy of the female pharaoh Hatshepsut fixed in position, crouching before the goddess's altar.[120] As in Haggard's text, the horrors of the Egyptian mysteries are best expressed in modern terms.[121]

Charles Leadbeater, a leading member of the Theosophical Society, also used the magic lantern to capture the phenomenology of the Egyptian occult. 'The Forsaken Temple', included in his collection of short narratives, *The Perfume of Egypt and Other Weird Stories* (1911), is one of several 'true' 'stories', among which are 'personal experiences of [Leadbeater's] own'.[122] While he claims that 'it may be difficult for one who has made no study of the subject to believe them, those who are familiar with the literature of the occult', he assures, 'will readily be able to parallel most of these experiences'.[123] The tale begins with the relation of how the narrator was working as a music teacher for two young brothers and that, after their lessons were finished, as 'these two boys were good physical mediums', they would participate in séances.[124] One evening, after the boys have left, the narrator wakes in the night to see one of the brothers in his bedroom, seemingly in a trance. The narrator then experiences 'a change ... in [his] surroundings': 'I found that we were in the centre of some vast, gloomy temple, such as those of ancient Egypt.'[125] In this post-séance state, the narrator experiences a split consciousness, in which he is both looking at the boy, while he also '[sees]the wonderful paintings on the walls pass before [him] like the dissolving views of a magic lantern'.[126] That he describes what he witnesses as an 'exhibition' furthers the simile comparing astral scenes of ancient Egypt to a modern visual display.

Henry Ridgely Evans, also referred to the phantasmagoria to describe his protagonist's visual encounter with Egypt, in his *The House of the Sphinx*:

> When night, with its blue-black canopy, studded with brilliant stars, has fallen upon the world of the Orient, these ancient ruins seem to breathe forth mystery ... The silvery moon, sacred disk of Isis, floods the faces of the colossi, images of the gods, and intensifies their grotesque shadows. In this solemn hour of slumber and silence a weird phantasmagoria presents itself to our entranced vision. We behold the ruins restored, as if by magic; pylon and pillar, obelisk and avenue of sphinxes, are all intact, as of old.[127]

The moon provides the light needed to effect a near-magical transformation of the scene (the moon is not a light source, of course, but functions essentially as an enormous mirror, reflecting the light of the sun), and Evans invokes Isis to imbue this light with an occult association. As in his enchanting description of the Egyptian Hall, however, Evans knows that there is no genuine magic taking place, however, though it certainly appears '*as if*' this is the case, and his presentation of this passage, just as his description of the Egyptian Hall, in the present tense, belies an effort to immerse his readership in lush descriptions that feel immediate. We (Evans uses the plural to include us along with his protagonist-narrator) are 'entranced' by the 'weird phantasmagoria' (the soft sibilance of Evans's description maintains this dreamy quality), beguiled by something that looks magical but which is, in fact, just a convincing optical effect. With the breaking dawn – like the theatrical rising of the house lights – the scene reverts back to the mundane (and the narrative reverts to the past tense).

Intriguingly, what these disparate texts have in common is the visualisation of ancient Egypt as it was – its temples in a state of perfection rather than in ruin, its mysteries still to be revealed – via the imagery of modern technologies. Moreover, all of these texts' protagonists experience visions involving Egypt (whether occult or the result of optical illusion) specifically as akin to the visual effects of the magic lantern. On the one hand, this infuses the texts with references to the kinds of technology with which these authors' readers would undoubtedly have been familiar, magic lanterns being widely used in the late nineteenth and early twentieth centuries in all manner of settings, from education to entertainment. This is not to say that this technology had lost its chilling potential – the antagonist of Sax Rohmer's (1883–1959) supernatural horror novel, *Brood of the Witch-Queen* (1918), to take an even later example, has magical powers whose effects are experienced as a 'horrible phantasmagoria'.[128] On the other hand, it re-enchants the lantern, suggesting this device as a magical tool in both senses of the word, both in terms of illusion and supernatural experience. In all three of the texts that we have considered in detail in this section, the magic lantern is the closest thing in their protagonists' – or their writers' – experience to an actual encounter with Egypt as it existed in antiquity. As we shall see, just as the magic lantern opened up opportunities to engage with fantastical views of Egypt, photographic technologies also promised meaningful visual engagements with ancient Egyptian culture, in personal snapshots, posed portraits, and in images purportedly infiltrated by spirits.

Photography

In her short story 'The Paraschites' (1889), the now little-known author Marie Hutcheson (publishing under the pseudonym Mallard Herbertson) imagines a supernatural encounter with ancient Egyptian art. The tale's protagonist, a modern man, is brought face-to-face with an ancient Egyptian embalmer. Before this meeting between representatives of the modern and ancient worlds, however, Hutcheson sets the scene for the paranormal; using light to ascertain a better glimpse of the paintings within an Egyptian tomb, the protagonist unwittingly produces supernatural results:

> The series of mummies represented in tombs … was the object of my present visit, and as I reached the spot I lighted the magnesium wire to examine them by a better light. The effect was startling. The figures seemed to wake up and step forward as the bright light fell on them … One after another the light fell on them with the same curious effect.[129]

Magnesium, which had been sold in wire form from the 1860s for the purposes of providing an intense flash of light to aid in the capture of photographic images, appears to awaken the painted figures depicted.

Hutcheson imbues the photographer's accoutrements with magical power, suggesting their ability to literally reanimate the past.

Photography had an enormous impact on engagements with and understanding of ancient and modern Egypt. The first documented photograph of an Egyptian scene was taken on 7 November 1839, '[w]ithin ten months of the official announcement of the invention of photography'.[130] Before mass travel, photographs from Egypt were as close to the country as most Europeans could get, depicting both modern views and Egypt's ancient sites. By the latter half of the nineteenth century, Thomas Cook & Son had transformed affordable travel, and a visit to Egypt itself became possible for thousands with the time and money to spare. As Donald Malcolm Reid notes, it was in the 1890s with the development of Kodak cameras that people could first photograph foreign landscapes for themselves, rather than buying postcards.[131]

As the pastime of photography increased in popularity, more individuals became well-versed in image manipulation and, as these techniques became more widely understood, the demand for novelty photographs increased. These were available at holiday destinations including Cairo, where tourists could have their picture taken while they posed in apertures cut out of 'cardboard sphinx molds and mummy cases' (figure 1.7).[132] The earliest examples of these photographs as taken in Egypt date from the late nineteenth century, though the trend was still popular in the following decades; as one journalist records in 1908, 'American and English faces peer out from' the 'hole … where the inscrutable face of the sphinx should be'.[133] Most surviving Cairene examples appear to have been produced by A. Strommeyer and J. Heymann (spellings of both names vary), recorded by Baedecker's 1885 guide to Egypt as being the proprietors of a 'well-equipped studio'.[134] Similar services were offered in Cairo at the studio of an Armenian photographer named Gabriel Lékégian.[135] That one could also acquire personalised mummy portraits in Paris and New York speaks to the fact that demand extended beyond Egyptian-based tourist contexts, and that metropolitan centres were the technological hubs where trick photography became a readily accessible commodity. Such novelties were apparently especially popular in Paris in the closing years of the nineteenth century; another anonymous writer documenting the subject reports that:

> in Paris, where the rage for the bizarre and the weird is highly developed, some whimsical mind has conceived the idea of having a real Egyptian mummy photographed with the head of a live person in place of its own.[136]

Figure 1.7 James Deering and Abby Deering Howe, c.1880s, taken in Egypt, seemingly by Heymann and Co. Courtesy of Vizcaya Museum and Gardens Archives, Miami, Florida.

The most famous individual to have had their portrait taken in this style is the Austrian Archduke Franz Ferdinand (1863–1914), whose assassination would lead to the onset of the First World War. Franz Ferdinand is captured in a photograph from 1896, with his face emerging from a hole within a prop sarcophagus. On the photograph is written this hybrid individual's name: 'Amenhotepp XXIII'. With the death of his father, Karl Ludwig (1833–96), earlier that year, Franz Ferdinand became the heir presumptive to the Austro-Hungarian throne. The caption thus acknowledges his royal lineage, while bridging the gap between the ancient pharaohs and modern royalty in the number of Amenhoteps imagined to have ruled between the last Amenhotep of ancient Egypt (Amenhotep IV, more famously known as Akhenaten) and Franz Ferdinand, recast as the 23rd pharaoh of this name. These light-hearted photographs function as a kind of opposite to the panoramas and dioramas at their peak of popularity earlier in the century. Rather than losing oneself in an immersive, spectacular recreation of foreign lands, including amidst ancient Egyptian ruins, 'sitters' for these photographs themselves assumed ancient Egyptian identities. These are not photos of modern Egypt that a tourist might capture with their own Kodak, but images that reimagine the individual in a fantastical antiquated context, imbuing sarcophagi and sphinx statues with life.

The latter half of the nineteenth century also saw the emergence and the popularisation of the spirit photograph. Although they were often linked to the kinds of sensational occurrences that characterised late Victorian séances, spirit photographs were frequently produced without the help of a medium or participant claiming to have access to supernatural powers. A spirit photograph usually showed a living sitter, and in the space around them one or more 'spirits', often hazier, translucent faces or figures. An example is reproduced in Albert A. Hopkins's *Magic: stage illusions and scientific diversions including trick photography* (1897), in a section derived from Walter E. Woodbury's *Photographic Amusements: including a description of a number of novel effects obtainable with the camera* (1896), indicating that the spirit photograph might be understood as an entertaining optical diversion for the amateur photographer, or an illusory magical production. Woodbury provides an image of a so-called 'spirit photograph' (figure 1.8), in which can be seen a smartly dressed gentleman in fine detail, and at least two mistier faces, the features of a third, far less distinct face suggested in the space above the man's top hat. Woodbury reveals this image to be fraudulent – not capturing spirits along with the living sitter at all – by providing the source for the face of the spirit on the right of the composite picture

Figure 1.8 'Photograph of "Spirits"', in Albert A. Hopkins, *Magic: stage illusions and scientific diversions, including trick photography* (London: Sampson Low, Marston and Co., 1897), p. 436. Author's own.

(figure 1.9). He relates, 'Mr. W. M. Murray, a prominent member of the Society of Amateur Photographers of New York, called our attention to the similarity between one of the "spirit" images and a portrait painting by Sichel'.[137]

The reference is to the German artist Nathaniel Sichel (1843–1907), whose subjects were often beautiful Oriental women. One of Sichel's paintings of ancient Egypt – *Joseph Before the Pharaoh* – won the Prix de Rome in 1864, while a later painting, *Almée* (1886), saw him tackle

Figure 1.9 'Painting by N. Sichel', in Albert A. Hopkins, *Magic: stage illusions and scientific diversions, including trick photography* (London: Sampson Low, Marston and Co., 1897), p. 437. Author's own.

another Egyptian subject, depicting a woman playing an ancient Egyptian harp (or else a modern instrument modelled on ancient examples). That Sichel also produced other images of ancient Egyptian women is clear from reproductions of such works. I have encountered several of these where I have been unable to trace the original. A painting entitled *An Egyptian Princess* featuring a woman wearing the vulture crown donned by female royalty exists, for instance, as a full-page engraving in an issue of *The Illustrated London News* from 1888.[138]

The painting identified by Murray as featuring in the spirit photograph is yet another Egyptian image. A decorative piece produced by the German porcelain manufacturers Hutschenreuther from around 1900 is the closest I have come in finding a visualisation of the original painting, and this clearly shows the woman from the spirit photograph in flowing gold and white drapery, clasping a sistrum.[139] The title of this ornamental work is *Cleopatra*, suggesting the ancient Egyptian queen as the spirit supposedly materialising in Woodbury's example of the spirit photograph. That Sichel's original painting was of Cleopatra is indicated, too, in a spirit portrait produced by the American spiritualist mediums Elizabeth (1859–1920) and Mary Bangs (1862–1917), together known as the 'Bangs sisters'. The Bangs sisters began to produce spirit portraits in 1894, claiming them to be images of the spirits that the dead themselves manifested (they maintained that these images materialised in a medium unknown to artists on Earth, though visually many of their pictures resemble chalk pastels). The similarities between their portrait of ancient Egypt's final pharaoh and Hutschenreuther's decorative porcelain copy reveals that the Bangs sisters' image, too, is derived from Cleopatra as imagined by Sichel.

Progress in photographic technologies directly enabled such images to be produced: evidently, the spirit photographer and the Bangs sisters had access to Sichel's painting, almost certainly not the original, but rather a reproduction appearing in a mass medium, making this imagery cheap and accessible. The Bangs sisters' version of Cleopatra wears a different coloured robe to the Cleopatra in the Hutschenreuther ornament, sporting, in the spiritualist image, drapery in Virgin Mary-esque blue. This being the major difference between the two images underlines that the Bangs sisters – and perhaps even Hutschenreuther – had a greyscale engraving from which to work, leaving room for some artistic licence. The risk run by spirit photographers and spiritualist mediums was that, in using images published in the mass press in their own purportedly genuine images of the ancient dead, the very modernity of the photographic technologies that made reproductions of the original available to an audience of thousands would lead to their exposure as frauds.

The most famous narrative involving a spirit photograph with an ancient Egyptian element seems to combine the imagery of tourist photographs that saw living faces emerging from within sarcophagi, with the spirit photograph that promised to make the dead visible. An artefact known as the 'Unlucky Mummy' (not human remains as the name suggests, but rather a wooden mummy board) acquired by the British

Museum in 1889, was supposedly cursed and responsible for the deaths of the handful of people who arranged for it to be brought into the country.[140] In the early years of the twentieth century, rumours abounded that an ancient Egyptian priestess had made contact at séances attended by the artefact's modern 'owner', that fire that could be seen flashing from its painted eyes, and that it had been donated to the Museum as the result of a warning from theosophical *doyenne* Helena Blavatsky that evil forces were at work.[141] Most significant for our purposes were stories that the mummy-board had been photographed, the photographer dying shortly afterwards, and the picture developing with a vengeful human face superimposed over the painted likeness of the unknown woman.[142] If this particular image ever existed, and was not merely another supernatural element to a snowballing tale, it is now lost. Nonetheless, the narrative underlines how photography, which was often lauded as a revolutionary scientific tool representative of modern advances in technology, was also imagined as a means of visualising the ancient Egyptian supernatural at the *fin de siècle*: photography could produce amusing illusions but it could also, according to some, capture something truly paranormal.

The influence of the spectral images made possible by photographic technologies can be read in Marie Corelli's *Ziska* (1897), a novel set amidst Cairo's fashionable hotels. Corelli, who received letters from fans interested in liminal subjects ranging from theosophy to psychical research, repeatedly alluded to Egypt as a setting for or the origins of the supernatural in her works.[143] Although she never visited the country, she had earlier expressed a sense of bitterness that Haggard was able to do so in a letter to her publisher, George Bentley (1828–98). She lamented that after Haggard's literary successes (presumably his recently published *She*) 'he [had] gone comfortably off to Egypt on the proceeds, which I wish I could do!'[144] Her envy – and sense of her own mystical connection to Egypt – leads her, in *Ziska*, to lampoon the 'Cook's Tourist'.[145] A perceptive reviewer in *The Sketch* jests that 'a "Cook's Tour" is evidently not good enough for Miss Corelli, the development of her narrative suggesting that nothing short of a Maskelyne and Cooke's tour can satisfy her longings after the mysterious and magical'.[146] Indeed the reviewer furthers this parallel between the supernatural elements of Corelli's tale and 'conjuring tricks—located … in Egypt itself instead of the Egyptian Hall'.[147]

Corelli's desire to visit Egypt manifests itself in the level of real detail she includes when referring to the hotels.[148] In *Ziska*, she dedicates a passage to describing the facilities available for the amateur photographer at the Mena House:

> That ubiquitous nuisance, the 'amateur photographer,' can there have his 'dark room' for the development of his more or less imperfect 'plates'; ... With a ... 'dark room,' what more can the aspiring soul of the modern tourist desire?[149]

This scathing passage is curious for several reasons, not least for the remarkable response to Corelli's critique that took the form of a poem first appearing in *The Journal of the Amateur Photographic Society of Madras* before it was reprinted in *The Photographic Times*. Describing Corelli as 'deal[ing ...] | With mouldy kings, or mummies cold, | Princesses,— anything that's old | Or somewhat mystical' rather than more mundane '[v]isibles', the amateur photographer laments Corelli's derision, which they encounter as they hold '*Ziska* open in my hand, | And chapter thirteen roughly scanned'.[150] The poet speculates as to the impetus behind Corelli's jibe, suggesting that perhaps she has had an unfortunate experience of being photographed in an unflattering manner – specifically imagining a scenario in which Corelli might be photographed smoking, blaming the appearance of a cigarette on an '"imperfect" plate' – or indeed failed '[t]o take a photograph' herself.[151] Most interesting is the opposition that the poet establishes between 'mystical' entities and '[v]isibles', the former being of more interest to the supernaturally inclined Corelli, and the latter the domain of the more grounded photographers. Speculating that a photograph of Corelli ascending 'Gizeh's awful pyramid' might reveal her to be '[a] biped plain to all' – that she herself was nondescript, mundane 'visible' rather than the otherworldly, draped image of herself that she cultivated in the publicity photographs – the poet circumvents recognising the flourishing trade in photographs of the once-invisible spirits ('anything that's old | Or somewhat mystical') that Corelli herself takes as her subject matter.[152]

This poetic rebuttal is clearly in jest, picking up on a supposedly throwaway remark on a subject of minor interest to the novel, its characters and plot. Yet, despite the fact that Corelli does not return to the dark room later in the novel, it is of broader thematic significance. Instead of simply acting as a sarcastic attack on the concerns of contemporary socialites (which the novel, as a whole, certainly is), it also highlights the spectral image as one of the text's key themes. Corelli's reference to the imperfection of the photographic plates is striking. While this may seem a simple criticism of the amateur photographer at first glance, imperfections on photographic plates often produced unusual effects that were thought to be visual representations of supernatural phenomena invisible to the naked eye and yet somehow captured by the photographic process. Flawed photographic plates were also used by the Society for Psychical Research and other paranormal investigators to test those who claimed to be able to photograph such anomalies.[153] As a result, Corelli makes reference to the technology behind the imagery of occultism and psychic investigation, reinforcing her emphasis on modernity and real liminal science. Corelli was aware of the extent to which photographic images could be altered through her own personal experience. Notoriously secretive about her age, Corelli had a number of her publicity photographs doctored to make her appear younger, slimmer and altogether more ethereal, something that Jill Galvan has connected to the production of fake spirit photographs through their similar image manipulation techniques.[154]

While the novel does not include spirit photographs, it does feature paintings that capture and reveal the supernatural in a similar way. The French artist, Armande Gervase, himself the reincarnation of an ancient Egyptian warrior, Araxes, paints the portrait of the mysterious and eponymous Ziska who, unknown to him, is the ghost of the lover he murdered in his past life. While Gervase is able to produce a good likeness of Ziska while she sits for him, when he returns to the painting he is disturbed to discover it inexplicably changed. Corelli appears to borrow many of the portrait's details from Oscar Wilde's (1854–1900) *The Picture of Dorian Gray* (1890; 1891), a text which also draws upon the conventions of spiritualist image-making and the language of psychical research.[155] Like Wilde's supernatural painting, the image reveals the evil nature of an otherwise captivatingly beautiful individual, is kept covered, and simultaneously evokes repulsion and fascination. Gervase claims that the picture 'isn't the Princess' and that he 'can only get the reflection of a face which is not hers'.[156] Later, the picture is defined as having 'no real resemblance ... to the radiant and glowing loveliness of the Princess Ziska, yet, at the same time, there was sufficient dim likeness to make an imaginative person think it might be possible for her to assume that appearance in death'.[157] It is at once 'like the Princess Ziska, and yet totally unlike', comprising both 'a dead face and a living one'.[158] While initially, the painting is said to resemble Ziska's face 'in torture', 'agony' and 'death', later her expression is described as 'half-watchful, half-mocking', the picture appearing 'almost sentient'.[159] The juxtaposition of the living and the dead in the same image is, of course, the very foundation of the spirit photograph.

Ziska herself is described in such a way as to make her seem visually similar to spirits as depicted in spirit photographs, or indeed spirits as they manifested in séances. The way she moves is repeatedly described as being akin to floating – she is 'like an aërial vision'.[160] She appears to be 'all fire and vapour and eyes in the middle', her features are often darkened by 'a curious shadow' and, while her skin is ethereally white, within it is a colour 'dark and suggestive of death'.[161] Her clothing is also evocative of grave cerements in which phantoms in spirit photographs commonly appear. Most of her clothes are diaphanous, gauzy and white, simultaneously suggesting the bridal gown, the shroud and mummy wrappings. In the latter half of the novel, she is depicted as being 'veiled entirely in misty folds of white', 'her exquisite form scarcely concealed by the misty white of her draperies', also suggesting the delicate fabrics used by fraudulent mediums to simulate ectoplasm.[162]

Yet, it is at the novel's climax when the full extent of Corelli's engagement with contemporary imaging technologies becomes apparent. Exhibiting her ghostly powers, Ziska's body changes until it becomes 'thin and skeleton-like, while still retaining the transparent outline of its beauty'.[163] Corelli had already imagined a similar transformation from corpse to skeleton in her novel *Wormwood* (1890), although in this earlier work this metamorphosis is hallucinatory rather than supernatural, brought on by the consumption of absinthe. Notably, *Wormwood*'s narrator describes his vision as a 'magic lantern of strange pictures', directly invoking the kind of technologies that Corelli's Ziska calls to mind.[164] The changes to Ziska's body evoke the kinds of transformations visualised by magic lanterns; fade effects could be created to transition one slide to the next, giving the impression of transfiguration.[165] Douglas's *Iras* draws upon similar optical techniques, where sinister shadows often appear and disappear from walls illuminated by 'a flood of moonlight'.[166] Iras herself, like the fading out of a single magic-lantern slide, becomes physically insubstantial, eventually invisible to everyone except Lavenham. Instead, he sees her as 'growing more ethereal under the advancing Shadow'.[167] Thus, like Ziska, Iras too undergoes this transformation, from the physically solid ancient Egyptian, to a dwindling ghost, to a mummy. As she does, all evidence of her existence in the modern world fades, including her signature on her wedding certificate, which by the time Lavenham examines it is 'barely legible', 'gradually disappearing' and likely to have completely vanished in 'a few more months'.[168]

The opposite transformation takes place in the American writer Charlotte Bryson Taylor's (1880–1936) *In the Dwellings of the Wilderness* (1904), when one of the protagonists finds himself trapped in a tomb with a mummy:

his gaze fell on the mummy. This time he stared at it ... The light was dim, his head swimming. What he saw, watching in a fascination of interest, was a slow, indefinable change in the thing, which took place under his eyes, yet whose stages he could not follow. He saw the dead face turn slowly towards him – so slowly that, try as he might, he could not see it move – saw the sunken cheeks grow rounded, covered no longer with shrivelled parchment, but with velvety brown skin; saw full crimson lips which hid the twin rows of perfect teeth; saw the shrunken arms firm and gracious; the billowy curves and soft hollows of breast and throat, the sudden brilliancy of unknown jewels.[169]

As in *Ziska*, the darkness of the tomb space suggests itself as the perfect setting for Gothic projections. The 'slow, indefinable change' 'whose stages [the protagonist] could not follow' is a slow, dissolving effect, the reverse of the transformation undertaken by Iras.

The precursor to these ancient Egyptian bodies, shifting between various states, appears to be the moment of transformation of H. Rider Haggard's Ayesha in *She* who, while not of ancient Egyptian heritage herself, is described in terms that code her as Egyptian. Haggard's narrator's first glimpse of Ayesha evokes the imagery of the phantasmagoria – indeed, his thoughts upon seeing her entirely swathed form are of 'a corpse in its grave-clothes', a 'ghost-like apparition' and of a 'swathed mummy-like form'.[170] At the novel's climactic moment, after Ayesha emerges from the pillar of fire, she transforms and dies, 'her face ... growing old before my eyes', her body 'shrivelling up' until she resembles 'a badly-preserved Egyptian mummy'.[171] The impact of Haggard's novel on later texts that depicted the visuals of Egyptian magic, on stage-magic performances and in early film is itself noteworthy.[172] And, as we shall see, the effects produced by magicians, magic-lantern technologies and those as described in the novels discussed in this section themselves fed into the ways in which ancient Egyptian presences were imagined in early moving pictures. In looking now to the early history of film, we come full circle, returning to the Egyptian Hall.

Moving pictures

In December 1895, using their projection device, the 'Cinématographe', the Lumière brothers showed 10 short films in Paris.[173] Within a matter of weeks, this equipment had reached London; on 20 February 1896, the

Cinématographe's moving pictures were shown at the Royal Polytechnic Institution by the French magician Félicien Trewey (1848–1920). By coincidence, that very day, the British inventor Robert W. Paul (1869–1943) showed his 'Theatrograph', another moving picture projector, at Finsbury Park College. Daniel Devant (the magician who was to be confronted by an Egyptian priest in Nesbit's *The Story of the Amulet*) promptly purchased a Theatrograph for the Egyptian Hall, establishing the Hall's status as one of London's major moving picture venues, and the second cinema in Britain. The Egyptian Hall showed its first short films – often incorporated into magic acts – in the spring of 1896.[174]

We have already noted the impact of the illusory performances of the Egyptian Hall on literature of the early twentieth century, and the imagery and iconography of the effects produced by the Egyptian Hall's magicians can also be identified in early film. The influence of the Egyptian Hall on two pioneering filmmakers is clear: Walter R. Booth (1869–1938), who had previously worked at the Egyptian Hall as a stage magician, and Georges Méliès (1888–1923), who while working in London was frequently in the audience (and would also go on to have a career as an illusionist), both employed ancient Egyptian imagery in their moving pictures.[175] Egyptian settings, themes and props feature in Booth's *Haunted Curiosity Shop* (1901), as well as several of Méliès's films: *Cléopâtre* (1899), *Les Infortunes d'un explorateur ou les momies récalcitrantes* (1900), *Le Monstre* (1903), *L'Oracle de Delphes* (1903), *La Prophétesse de Thèbes* (1907) and *Les Hallucinations du baron de Münchhausen* (1911). Devant, who knew Méliès, sold him two Paul Theatrographs in 1896, 'one of which [Méliès] converted to a camera', meaning that Méliès might have, at times, shot ancient Egyptian subject matter using former Egyptian Hall equipment.[176] Using emerging techniques that epitomised technological advancement in the era, Booth's and Méliès's conflation of ancient Egypt and magic reveals another means by which modernity and Egyptian antiquity were brought together in the period, and themselves contributed to the ongoing confluence of these concepts in the popular imagination.

That Méliès referred to one of his techniques as 'spirit photography' is revealing. The method of using double-exposure to give the illusion of translucency is the direct successor of a similar practice found in fake spirit photographs, whereby people or objects could be made to appear ghostly and indistinct.[177] Using the same vocabulary as those who supposedly photographed the spirit world, Méliès addressed the close relationship between science, illusion and the supernatural, and the techniques shared by both those investigating and those claiming to be able to produce occult images. That Méliès was familiar with Hopkins's *Magic: stage illusions and scientific diversions including trick photography* (1897) means that he would have known of the spirit photograph incorporating the face of Sichel's *Cleopatra*.[178] Several of Méliès's films explicitly imagined séance phenomena, including *Spiritisme Abracadabrant* (1900), *Le Portrait spirite* (1903), *Le Fantôme d'Alger* (1906) and *L'Armoire des frères Davenport* (1902), a film on the subject of the Davenport brothers made 'in tribute to Maskelyne' with whom he had struck up a friendship in the 1880s.[179] Indeed, there appears to have been a direct thematic conversation taking place not just between the world's imaging technologies, but in a variety of cultural contexts, including fiction.

While the illusions in these early films are often achieved through the use of well-timed cuts and dissolves (indicating film's inheritance from the magic lantern), their conceits make clear use of existing magic tricks, along with Egyptian themed props and scenery, exposing a direct line of influence from stage magic to the moving picture, the use of Egyptian iconography in stage-magic settings having been encouraged across the latter half of the nineteenth century by the success of the Egyptian Hall. Of these films, Méliès's *Cléopâtre* is now lost, though cursory descriptions of its plot reveal that it centres on a man who breaks into a tomb and dismembers a mummy found within, before going on to resurrect the ancient Egyptian woman. The basis for the narrative appears to be tricks involving dismemberment and restoration, and may have even provided a filmic counterpart to the 'sawing a woman in half' illusion.[180] Booth's *Haunted Curiosity Shop* also focuses on bodily transformations. Set against 'a painted backcloth decorated with a mummy case, statues, canopic jars, plinths, busts and figurines – a veritable Victorian fantasy of the Egyptian burial chamber', it features a bisected woman, along with a skull floating through the air (which wears something akin to a *nemes* headdress, making it reminiscent of Stodare's Sphinx).[181] Booth uses a cabinet as a means by which to effect stop tricks – also known as substitution splices, whereby 'two separate shots are carefully matched across a cut', usually with one or more changes between them, giving the impression of seamless transformations between a woman in blackface, a translucent white woman (presumably a ghost), a man in ancient Egyptian costume, a skeleton and an individual wearing a full suit of medieval armour.[182] These substitution splices underline that the entity responsible for the hauntings intends to torment the curiosity shop owner through its instantaneous jumping between racial, gendered and temporal identities.

In Méliès's *Les Infortunes d'un explorateur ou les momies récalcitrantes*, of which less than 20 seconds of footage survives, a sarcophagus is put to the same effect as Booth's cabinet. It, too, is a space in which actors in various costumes might be swapped, or used to suggest instantaneous materialisations or dematerialisations through substitution splices, of course also evoking the spirit cabinet of the spiritualist séance out of which spirit forms might emerge. The plot involves an explorer breaking into a tomb and finding a sarcophagus; a ghost manifests from within, which transforms into a goddess, and the goddess conjures up anthropomorphic animal-headed Egyptian monsters. Trapped within the sarcophagus, the explorer is tormented by the goddess, who sets the sarcophagus on fire before he escapes from the tomb. Méliès's *L'Oracle de Delphes* also makes use of substitution splices that make sphinxes guarding a temple transform into beautiful women and back again, along with a superimposition that allows the god of the temple to materialise slowly within its dark doorway.[183] Despite the film's title indicating that it is meant to be Delphi, this is clearly an ancient Egyptian setting – two temples are visible against a backdrop of pyramids. *Le Monstre* features the same backdrop, without the temple in the foreground, instead showcasing the enormous moonlit Sphinx of Giza. This narrative sees a magician torment a prince who has brought the skeleton of his lover to be revived so that he can see her one final time. While the magician does restore her to life, he first makes her skeleton dance, and transforms it into a ghoul (the throwing of a sheet over the body evoking the conventions of stage-magic transformation). Ultimately, the magician restores her to her skeletal state, casting her remains into the prince's arms. The description of *Le Monstre* in a catalogue of Méliès's films emphasises the moving picture's 'weird realism' and 'the perfect illusion of reality'.[184]

In *Les Hallucinations du baron de Münchhausen* (1911) the eponymous baron falls asleep only to have vivid nightmares of strange visions appearing in the large mirror by his bed. The mirror – with its enormous, ornate frame – has the appearance of a stage set. One of his visions features a bare-breasted Egyptian queen being presented to him before a temple. He steps over the mirror's threshold, falling to his knees before her in worship, but is cast out of the mirror only for the scene to change. Intriguingly, unlike in many of the other exotic and otherworldly scenes with which the baron is faced, there are no stop tricks: ancient Egypt is, in this visual medley, the only setting spectacular enough not to warrant an illusory effect. Alternatively, of course, it may be that the nudity in this scene – in place of magic – is the real spectacle.

That ancient Egyptian imagery was used so often by Méliès, in particular, is testament to the cultural impact of the Egyptian Hall as a centre of technological innovation, cloaked in the glamour and mystery of antiquity. In these short summaries, we see the moving picture as the successor to the magic lantern, facilitating effects that mimic the sudden switching between slides or slow dissolves. As with phantasmagorical displays, in nineteenth- and early twentieth-century stage-magic performances, and in literature that imagines transformations undertaken by ancient Egyptian bodies, there is an emphasis on the mummy, the skeleton and the beautiful young woman.

Of the full range of these filmic narratives of Egyptian magic *La Prophétesse de Thèbes* is of particular interest. Sadly, only a fragment of the film has survived – likely the reason why is it so rarely discussed by scholars. This moving picture is particularly intriguing in light of a broader understanding of ancient Egypt in illusory contexts, and especially given its role in the advent of film. The narrative is set in ancient Thebes, and the Theban king seeks knowledge of his future from an astrologer. The astrologer is not willing to provide the prophecy himself, but rather proposes to conjure a prophetess, whom he awakens by assembling several pieces of a statue. The prophetess uses a telescope through which, purportedly, can be seen the future. The view through the telescope is visualised between two richly painted columns, which provide the whole scene the appearance of an Egyptian temple. The angling of the telescope, which is replete with fabric cover to block out any light surrounding the viewer, and the circular view which appears as if projecting directly from it, recalls the Cinématographe or Theatrograph. The spinning abstract form emerging from the telescope, which changes into a depiction of the Theban king's assassination, is suggestive of pre-film animation devices including the Phenakistiscope and the Zoetrope, and, in the age of projection, the Zoopraxiscope. Ultimately, the ancient optical device depicted is at once scientific instrument and occult tool, a product of the ancient world but one that replicates the same modern technologies that allowed the capture and projection of this filmic narrative. The king, displeased with the prediction, seizes the prophetess, who promptly vanishes, and his attempts to murder the astrologer are in vain. The astrologer claims to have cursed the king, prompting him to part with a large sum of gold. The film's final scene sees the astrologer and prophetess gloating over their spoils. This ending suggests that they are charlatans, the telescope employed to deceive and the image of the future projected from it merely an optical trick. That Méliès creates this visual narrative through his own optical tricks underlines the film's metatheatricality. That Méliès – who often played key roles in his films – plays the part of the astrologer only serves to emphasise that *La Prophétesse de Thèbes* is as much about the process of filmmaking and projection as it is about ancient prophecy.

Antonia Lant addresses ancient Egypt's recurrence in early films, positing that it is its spectacular iconography that solidified Egypt's place in the early visual repertoire of the moving picture, before going on to claim that:

> The films celebrate the power of the present to animate the inert objects of the past ... It is as if the forces of industrial technology are so strong – the authority of the new, moving image – that the excavated, pre-industrial world must give up its secrets, be putty in the hands of modern masters. Its objects are reduced to props in the filmmakers' studio.[185]

While I agree with much of Lant's work on this subject, this, to me, is an over-simplification of a more complicated relationship between the filmmaker and their ancient Egyptian subject matter. Indeed, several such films visually depict the inability of the modern man to withstand ancient Egyptian horrors. Specifically, an interesting shift in power can be read between two of Méliès's works on ancient Egyptian subjects; the explorer who dismembers and then revives the ancient Egyptian female body in *Cléopâtre* in 1899 may represent the ultimate imperial fantasy of total domination of the Oriental woman (who is perhaps symbolic of Egypt itself), but this is reversed in *Les Infortunes d'un explorateur ou les momies récalcitrantes* of 1900. The latter might be read as a sequel, in which the ancient Egyptian feminine no longer waits passively for the penetration of her tomb and a violent bodily revival; instead, it is the explorer himself whose body is under threat, trapped, as he is, within a flaming sarcophagus.

Lant's assessment applies more comfortably to earlier illusory performances such as Stodare's Sphinx, in which the supposedly Egyptian entity is 'brought to life' by the modern magician, the tourist photographs in which a modern face looks out from a sarcophagus or sphinx statue, and perhaps some fictional works including 'The Paraschites', in which painted mummies are made to move when subjected to a photographic flash. This is certainly not the case in most of the literary texts encountered as part of this illusory and magical history, though. From Nesbit's children's novel to Haggard's historical romance and the supernatural fiction of Blackwood, ancient Egyptian magic is potent, at times even posing a deadly threat.

Indeed, what I would further add to Lant's position is the inextricability of the influence of stage magic on such depictions of the Egyptian occult, and specifically the Egyptian Hall's role in this transference. While the moving picture projector, the magic lantern, and even the spirit photograph, promised to visualise the 'objects' – and entities – 'of the past', this is not to say that they were always 'reduced to props'. Indeed, it is in literature that we see the language and imagery of such technologies used as a means to describe ancient powers in a way that only partially captures the mystical effects imagined by the likes of Haggard, Blackwood and Corelli. By its very nature, the simile only offers an approximation, a way for modern minds to conceive of something arcane for which they have no closer point of reference.

The use of projection imagery, glass and mirrors across the contexts considered in this chapter reinforces a link between imaging technologies and an Egyptian-flavoured Gothic. Even when the visual language of horror remains somewhat consistent – bats, skeletons and spirits being perpetually popular – references to the optical technologies that could manifest these projected images were being updated to reflect contemporaneous developments in image-making. Yet, this was not merely a superficial replication of ancient Egyptian symbols and tropes. As new optical techniques emerged, so did the possibility that they could allow unprecedented access to the past. There was, however, the possibility that, like the spirit of an 'unlucky mummy' or the antagonists of magical fiction, the ancient Egyptians being conjured up in the modern world would be vengeful and dangerous. With technologies that allowed these dangers to be captured on film or created fraudulently, they could be experienced more convincingly than ever before.

Windows to the past

The imaging technologies associated with the occult, theatrical and scientific spheres were frequently shared by their respective proponents. Within the broad range of pioneering visual technologies adopted by these magicians, mediums, photographers, showmen and filmmakers, there was a shared desire to revert to the ancient – to access antiquity through the new methodologies of modernity – whether this was predominantly for the purposes of education, spiritual enlightenment or deception. The yearning to depict the unseeable, or photograph the unphotographable, be that ancient Egypt or the ghosts of the dead, resulted in the construction of alternate realities captured on film or glass slides. The new technologies that produced these images were thought to have genuine occult applications yet to be discovered. Naturally, this relationship was paradoxical: technologies that were enabling their devotees to produce far more accurate and faithful images of reality than ever before were also used to create ever more convincing fantasies and illusions. Within this hazy mixture of suggestions of genuine supernatural manifestations and convincing optical effects, ancient Egypt emerged as deeply significant in embodying the points at which magic and illusion became indistinguishable. As a result, it was often depicted as surprisingly relevant to, or otherwise a fitting subject for, demonstrations of modern technological innovation, whether these technologies were put to use in uncovering – or themselves creating the impression of – ancient Egyptian presences in the modern world.

An attentiveness to the physical spaces in which these activities and displays took place is essential to an understanding as to why ancient Egypt was used in these contexts. The gloomy, red-lit séances and photographer's darkrooms, the dim theatre made spectral by increasingly kaleidoscopic lighting effects, the ancient tomb or temple cloudy with ceremonial incense, the darkened private rooms used for Masonic initiation ceremonies – all became indistinct as a result of the technological advances that facilitated such transformations of space. Lant has observed 'an association between the blackened enclosure of the silent cinema and that of the Egyptian tomb, both in theoretical texts and in the use of Egyptianate architectural style for auditoriums'.[186] With their eerie coloured lights, dramatic shadows, smoke and mirrors, the spaces in which the magical took place followed a specific set of conventions based upon thousands of years of ritual. Darkness is, and always has been, conducive to the creation and reception of imagery, whether the product of the scientifically explainable illusion or simply manifestations of the imagination. The more the sensory deprivation, the more we experience hallucinations of all varieties, imagining that we can sense things that do not exist. In these similar darkened spaces, it seems only natural that the experiences associated with each merge. The theatrical is brought out of the theatre and into the Masonic lodge, the paranormal occurrences of the séance find their way into the photographer's studio, and the secret rituals that took place in ancient Egyptian tombs and temples work their way into the modern imagination.

Egypt is particularly important in this exchange because it was given such spiritual significance, in many of the emerging alternative religious sects and in contemporary occultism. As a result, luminous, projected, and chemically developed images of ancient Egypt carry an additional weight. Their insubstantiality belies their illusory nature, and yet what they symbolise need not be in itself fictitious. In literature the confusion of tropes of illusion and magic from these extant visual cultures reveals something of the same effect taking place in the works of popular writers. These points of collision between reality and fantasy mirror the broader cultural desire to break down the barriers of the known world and reach out to make contact with the ancient world once considered 'lost' but perhaps, thanks to the windows to the past they promised to open up, within the modern grasp.

Notes

1. Clarke 1973, 21.
2. Lant 1992, 89.
3. Bell 2012, 1.
4. Bell 2012, 13.
5. Bell 2012, 6.
6. Saler 2012, 14.
7. *The Boy's Own Conjuring Book* 1859, 13.
8. Elliott 2012, 17; Richards 2009, 18; Bacon 1902, 298.
9. In London, the Great Eastern Hotel, the Horseshoe pub and Café Verrey all had rooms decorated with ancient Egyptian designs; Elliott 2012, 69.
10. Hornung 2002, 118.
11. Hoffmann 1894, 471–3.
12. Dickens 1999, 108 quoted in Pittard 2016, 295.
13. Lamb 1976, 106.
14. The image also appears at the front of *The Secrets of Ancient and Modern Magic: Or the Art of Conjuring Unveilled* [*sic*] c.1880, 8.
15. Evans 1906, 318. It is unclear whether the Egyptian Hall had been demolished by the time that Evans was writing this section of *The Old and the New Magic*. His use of the present tense may indicate that its composition predated the Hall's destruction.
16. Bacon 1902–3, 308.
17. 'The New and the Wonderful Professor Pepper Always at the Egyptian Hall' 1872. A grotesque sphinx features on an 1868 poster advertising the Egyptian Hall, demonstrating that such imagery was used on promotional materials earlier than Stodare's Sphinx; see 'Frederick MacCabe' 1868.
18. Herbert and McKernan 1996, 92; Mangan 2007, 4.
19. Wynne 2013, 42.
20. Podmore 1897, 13.
21. See, for instance, 'Egyptian Hall: England's Home of Mystery' 1879; 'Programme: Messrs Maskelyne and Cooke from England's Home of Mystery' 1887.
22. Colla 2007, 21; Hutton 1999, 178.
23. Ira Davenport (1839–1911) and William Davenport (1841–77).
24. Strobridge Lithographing Company c.1900.
25. These posters were based on an earlier depiction of the illusion produced by the same printing company, which does not feature ancient Egyptian iconography: Strobridge Lithographing Company 1894.
26. Carter would use ancient Egyptian imagery to advertise his shows for decades. A poster from the 1920s shows Carter – capitalising on the coincidence of his shared surname with the British archaeologist Howard Carter (1874–1939) – in the guise of an explorer, claiming that he 'sweeps the secrets of the sphinx and marvels of the tomb of old King Tut to the modern world'.
27. Strobridge Lithographing Company c.1914.
28. Thurston 1926, 12.

29. Nesbit 1907, 347.
30. Nesbit 1907, 348.
31. Nesbit 1907, 349.
32. Douglas 1896, 15.
33. Douglas 1896, 16, 19.
34. Nesbit 1907, 270.
35. Budge 1899, 78.
36. Nesbit 1907, 270 (emphasis in original). For the illustration, see Nesbit 1906, 111. Cyril's lit match evokes those of H. G. Wells's Time Traveller in *The Time Machine* (1895), which he uses 'to amuse' the Eloi and from which the Morlocks retreat.
37. Nesbit 1907, 280.
38. Dobson 'The Sphinx at the Séance' 2018, 83–4.
39. Nesbit 1907, 308, 309.
40. Nesbit 1907, 191. Nesbit likely knew Besant through the Fabian Society, which Nesbit co-founded in 1884.
41. Nesbit 1907, 367.
42. Nesbit 1907, 367–8.
43. Nesbit 1907, 371.
44. Only the second of the two images appears in *The Story of the Amulet* in novel form. Its original appearance in a periodical is indicated by the blank space at the top-left of the image, left for the inclusion of text in *The Strand Magazine* but unfilled in the novel edition.
45. Dobson 'The Sphinx at the Séance'.
46. Griffith 1906, 125.
47. Griffith 1906, 5, 119.
48. Griffith 1906, 129.
49. Lamont 2004, 906.
50. Oppenheim 1985, 26.
51. Saler 2012, 12; Bell 2009, 27.
52. Natale 'The Medium on the Stage' 2011, 249.
53. Parramore 2008, 96.
54. A 'weird spectacle entitled "She," … suggested by the Cave scene in H. Rider Haggard's celebrated novel' of the same name, was invented by the British magician R. D. Chater (1836–1913), who performed as 'Hercat'; Hopkins 1897, 72. The trick involved much of the same apparatus as Stodare's Sphinx, with a trapdoor concealed by angled mirrors. A beautiful woman would be concealed behind a curtain, and would ignite fireworks before escaping through the trapdoor, leaving a pile of bones behind her. Hercat performed this illusion at the Egyptian Hall in the 1880s.
55. Haggard 1894, 69.
56. Haggard 1894, 62, 69; Huckvale 2012, 151.
57. Haggard 1894, 69.
58. O'Byrne 2008, 291.
59. Haggard 1894, 258–9.
60. Haggard 1894, 111.
61. Haggard 1894, 111–12. Figures from antiquity were among the 'celebrity' spirits most often called forth in the séance, Cleopatra VII being the most common.
62. Haggard 1894, 112.
63. Lantiere 2004, 122.
64. Whymper's illustrated capitals originally accompanied Haggard's text as it was first serialised in *The Illustrated London News*.
65. Fleming and Lothian 2012, 124.
66. Lantiere 2004, 74; Fleming and Lothian 2012, 124.
67. The illustrated capital that opens the previous chapter also begins with a *t*, which similarly appears to depict the curve of a hippopotamus tusk; Haggard 1894, 94.
68. Wynne 2020, 695.
69. Douglas 1896, 20.
70. Douglas 1896, 185.
71. Douglas 1896, 185–6.
72. Warner 2006, 292. Palladino's séances, and specifically the spirit hands for which she was famous, had an impact on the Polish writer Boleslaw Prus (1847–1912). He attended

Palladino's séances in Warsaw in 1893, which influenced scenes in his novel *Pharaoh* (1895). In one, the protagonist explores a temple where he feels invisible hands on his head and back.

73. 'John Nevil Maskelyne … commenced his career by reproducing the Davenport cabinet and staging it as an illusion'; Wynne 2013, 41–2.
74. Douglas 1896, 92–3.
75. Luckhurst 2004, 203.
76. Ashley 2001, 35.
77. Punter and Byron 2006, 90.
78. Blackwood 1909, 212.
79. Warner 2006, 290.
80. Blackwood 1909, 218.
81. El Mahdy 1989, 175. Other texts featuring possession include E. and H. Heron's 'The Story of Baelbrow' (1898), which depicts an ancient Egyptian mummy possessed by an English ghost.
82. Blackwood 1909, 218.
83. Blackwood 1909, 219.
84. Lyons 2009, 107.
85. Blackwood 1909, 222.
86. Blackwood 1909, 235.
87. Ellis (n.d.).
88. Luckhurst 2012, 105.
89. Luckhurst 2012, 107.
90. Wolfe 2016, 1.
91. Wilson 1878, 96.
92. Wilson 1878, 103.
93. Blackwood 1912, 320.
94. 'All About the Magic Lantern' 1880, 127.
95. Evans 1907, 9–10.
96. Stafford 2001, 301–2.
97. Lant 1992, 91.
98. Warner 2006, 148.
99. Lant 1992, 93.
100. Barber 1989, 80.
101. Groth 2016, 289.
102. Natale 2012.
103. See, for instance, Rossell 1998; Askari 2014.
104. Mangan 2007, 123.
105. Warner 2006, 155.
106. Blackwood 1914, 306.
107. York & Son 1890s. Haggard's wearing of the ancient Egyptian scarab, which served as the inspiration for *She*, means that even the projection of Haggard's own image in late Victorian settings involved the luminous reproduction of Egyptian iconography. This ring is now in the Liverpool World Museum; see *Scarab Seal Finger Ring*, c.1186BC–715BC.
108. Haggard 1894, 58.
109. Haggard 1894, 58.
110. Lantern slides were even produced depicting Masonic initiations. T. H. McAllister's slide series 'How Jones Became a Mason', designed by the American illustrator Joseph Boggs Beale (1841–1926), is one such visual narrative that delights in the torturous scenes of the rituals. Jones enters a lodge decorated with hieroglyphs, the door of which is set into a pylon-shape topped with a winged solar disc. Egyptian temple architecture is visible in the background of many of the following slides, which combine cartoonish violence with typical phantasmagorical imagery including bats and skeletons.
111. Haggard 1894, 58.
112. Haggard 1894, 177, 190, 323.
113. Haggard 1894, 190.
114. In his autobiography, Haggard offered a personal account of seeing bats in Egyptian tombs, which inspired the spirit of the pharaoh in *Cleopatra*. When he revisited the same tombs years later, he found that the bats had dispersed after the installation of electric lights. '[I]n these new conditions [the tombs] did not produce quite the same effect upon me', Haggard related. He recalled the 'bats, weaving endless figures in the torchlight, dancers in a ghostly dance',

the Gothic element apparently adding to his enjoyment of witnessing the tombs of the pharaohs first hand; see Haggard 1926 I, 259–60.

115. Yoxall 1898, 11.
116. Plunkett 2007, 2.
117. 'The Lonely Pyramid' 1891, 707.
118. Yoxall 1898, 11.
119. Yoxall 1898, 12, 26.
120. Yoxall 1898, 43, 100.
121. Reviews of *The Lonely Pyramid* in *The Academy* and *The Athenæum* directly compare this text to Haggard's works. See 'The Lonely Pyramid. By J. H. Yoxall. (Blackie.)' 1891, 560; 'Christmas Books' 1891, 720.
122. Leadbeater 1912, i, 16
123. Leadbeater 1912, ii.
124. Leadbeater 1912, 52.
125. Leadbeater 1912, 55, 56.
126. Leadbeater 1912, 57.
127. Evans 1907, 199.
128. Rohmer 1924, 64.
129. Herbertson 1889, 79.
130. The Epigraphic Survey 2002.
131. Reid 2002, 89; Robinson and Picard 2009, 5.
132. 'Photographed as Sphinxes and Mummies' 1908, 429.
133. 'Photographed as Sphinxes and Mummies' 1908, 429.
134. Baedecker 1885, 235.
135. Lékégian 1906.
136. 'Mummy Photography' 1899.
137. Woodbury 1896, 28; Hopkins 1897, 437.
138. Sichel 1888, 649.
139. Hutschenreuther c.1900.
140. Ismail 2011, 397.
141. Addy 1998, 14; Ismail 2011, 398; Luckhurst 2012, 27.
142. Ismail 2011, 399.
143. Federico 2000, 6.
144. Corelli 1887, quoted in Federico 2000, 90.
145. For more on Corelli and her own perceived connection to ancient Egypt, see Dobson 2020, 62–96.
146. A.G. 1897, 552.
147. A.G. 1897, 552.
148. The American diplomat Frederic Courtland Penfield (1855–1922) suggested that Corelli, to whom he refers simply as 'the cynical writer of "Ziska,"' in listing the hotel's facilities, is 'quoting from a Mena advertisement'; Penfield 1899, 831.
149. Corelli 1897, 256.
150. C. S. M. 1898, 87.
151. C. S. M. 1898, 87.
152. C. S. M. 1898, 87. In referring to Corelli disparagingly as a 'biped' the poet echoes Corelli's critique of tourists in *Ziska*'s opening pages, as well as the language employed by the novel's psychical scientist Dr. Maxwell Dean, who observes tourists ascending the pyramids of Giza as 'mere protoplasm': '[t]he germ of soul has not yet attained to individual consciousness in any one of these strange bipeds'; Corelli 1897, 323.
153. Price 1933, 213.
154. Galvan 2003, 85.
155. Dobson 2020.
156. Corelli 1897, 164, 170.
157. Corelli 1897, 177.
158. Corelli 1897, 180, 254.
159. Corelli 1897, 177, 179, 254.
160. Corelli 1897, 57.
161. Corelli 1897, 86, 141, 151.
162. Corelli 1897, 234, 336.

163. Corelli 1897, 343.
164. Corelli 1890, 287.
165. Armstrong 2008, 259.
166. Douglas 1896, 141.
167. Douglas 1896, 175.
168. Douglas 1896, 271.
169. Taylor 1904, 59–60.
170. Haggard 1887, 142.
171. Haggard 1887, 293.
172. Georges Méliès's short film *Danse du feu* (1899) was based on the moment in *She* in which Ayesha steps into the fire. This film was released in the United Kingdom and the United States with the title *Haggard's 'She' – The Pillar of Fire*. See also n53.
173. Auguste Lumière (1862–1954) and Louis Lumière (1864–1948).
174. Herbert and McKernan 1996, 92; Elliott 2012, 42; Lamb 1976, 84.
175. Herbert and McKernan 1996, 28, 92; Mangan 2007, 117; Huckvale 2012, 7.
176. Booth 2019.
177. Mangan 2007, 132.
178. Ruffles 2004, 36.
179. Ruffles 2004, 36; Ezra 8.
180. The origins of the illusion are contested; see Steinmeyer 2004, 277–95.
181. Lant 1992, 104.
182. Rieser 2019, 114.
183. *Complete Catalogue of Genuine and Original 'Star' Films* 1905, 25.
184. *Complete Catalogue of Genuine and Original 'Star' Films* 1905, 26.
185. Lant 2013, 53, 60.
186. Lant 1992, 90.

2
Worlds lost and found: journeys through time and space

> To pass through the great Central Doorway and enter into the Temple of Sety I is like entering a 'Time Machine' of science fiction.[1]

As Bradley Deane asserts of the 'lost world' genre, at its peak between 1871 and 1914, its 'tales are set on every continent, and judge modern men against the imaginary remnants of almost every people of antiquity and legend', 'refiguring the frontier as an uncanny space in which the grand narrative of progress collapses', and 'br[inging] Victorian and Edwardian men face to face with their primitive past and challeng[ing] them to measure up'.[2] The genre's heyday, I would add, coincides with the period in which archaeology flourished. The lost-world genre, with its newly identified civilisations often living in subterranean spaces, appears indebted to the burgeoning academic discipline that sought to understand ancient traces excavated from beneath the feet of modern people.

Antiquarianism gave way to archaeology as practitioners turned increasingly to empirical methods in the final decades of the eighteenth century. Across the nineteenth century, landmark excavations stimulated public interest not only in the practice's discoveries but also in archaeology itself. The Italian archaeologist Giuseppe Fiorelli (1823–96), who oversaw the excavations at Pompeii from 1863, innovated the filling of voids left by bodies beneath the ash at Pompeii with plaster, making casts that replicated the forms of the ancient dead. A decade later, the German businessman and archaeologist Heinrich Schliemann (1822–90) made the remarkable discovery of the site of Troy. The first modern excavations of the Sphinx at Giza, meanwhile, were supervised by the Italian explorer Giovanni Battista Caviglia (1770–1845) in 1817, with the exposure of the Sphinx's chest and paws finally achieved in 1887.

We might read a literary echo of such events in narratives that hinge on modern Westerners' discovery of 'lost' civilisations in popular texts such as Edward Bulwer-Lytton's *The Coming Race* (1871) and H. Rider Haggard's *She* (1886–7). While these civilisations are not direct offshoots of ancient Egypt, they have key Egyptian features. The pyramidal structures beneath the ground and the beautiful sphinx-like features of Bulwer-Lytton's subterranean people – the Vril-ya – suggest that the author drew some inspiration from ancient Egypt. Meanwhile, Nicholas Daly describes *She* as 'in many respects a displaced Egyptian romance', identifying connections between the novel's Amahagger people and Victorian attitudes towards modern Egyptians, and between the ruins of Kôr and ancient Egyptian archaeological sites.[3] Later, civilisations depicted as explicitly ancient Egyptian in origin were imagined as living beneath the Earth's surface in several narratives that drew a less ambiguous line between Egyptian archaeology and texts it inspired. Subterranean Egyptian civilisations feature, for example, in Oliphant Smeaton's (1856–1914) adventure story *A Mystery of the Pacific* (1899) and Baroness Orczy's (1865–1947) *By the Gods Beloved* (1905).

Building from this starting point, in which archaeology is held to have made a particular impact upon the literary imagination at the *fin de siècle*, this chapter first addresses encounters with ancient Egypt in lost-world texts, in which offshoots of ancient Egyptian civilisation are imagined as spatially elsewhere, either underground or in another geographically remote location. Such works include Francis Worcester Doughty's (1850–1917) *'I': a story of strange adventure* (1887) and Jules Verne's *Le Sphinx des glaces* (1897). Next, it scrutinises tales in which ancient Egyptians are imagined existing on the planets closest to Earth, in the British writer and illustrator Fred T. Jane's *To Venus in Five Seconds* (1897) and the American astronomer Garrett P. Serviss's (1851–1929) *Edison's Conquest of Mars* (1898), in which ancient Egyptians are imagined as having found new homes even further afield. Finally, it turns to texts in which Egypt is not accessed by leaving the planet, but in which Egypt is encountered via time travel, focusing on H. G. Wells's (1866–1946) *The Time Machine* (1895) and E. Nesbit's *The Story of the Amulet* (1905–6), before examining the time-travelling ancient Egyptian Rames in William Henry Warner's (fl. 1919–34) novel *The Bridge of Time* (1919) and, finally, the astronomer Camille Flammarion's *La Fin du monde* (1894). I suggest that these stories of various Egypts, experienced by representatives of the nineteenth and twentieth centuries, sprang from a constellation of popular scientific interests in the latter half of the nineteenth century that crystallised around archaeology: namely, geology and astronomy. These sciences were themselves of intense fascination to occultists, who proposed new theories concerning the history of the Earth based upon findings of practitioners working in these fields, among them an influential hypothesis that Egyptian civilisation was an offshoot of the fabled utopia of Atlantis. Egypt, so often representative of the distant past, typically re-emerges as something futuristic in these texts, with its most recognisable monuments – the pyramids and the Great Sphinx – repeatedly called upon to imagine the distant future, and even the end of humanity itself.

Egypt elsewhere

While disproven in the eighteenth century, seventeenth-century geological theories of a hollow earth had a significant cultural afterlife in nineteenth-century literature, in which subterranean civilisations – often with an ancient Egyptian or Atlantean origin – proliferated. That these communities have ancient Egyptian links might be attributed in part to public fervour for archaeology, which, over the course of the nineteenth century, brought the remnants of this civilisation to light, often for public consumption in museums. That Egyptology was emerging as a late nineteenth-century science is discernible, for instance, in the regular inclusion of Egyptological pieces in journals such as the British astronomer Richard A. Proctor's (1837–88) *Knowledge: an illustrated magazine of science*, founded in 1881. Geological reassessments of the age of the Earth had monumental implications for the study of the ancient world, also suggesting a far greater span of time in which humankind had existed on Earth. Authors rose to the challenge of imagining alternate histories that challenged mainstream archaeological understandings of some of the oldest human civilisations celebrated in modern culture.

Indeed, archaeology seems to have directly inspired several 'lost world' stories featuring Egyptian or Egyptian-esque civilisations. Several such tales use frame narratives that foreground an ancient artefact or manuscript as in *She*, giving such narratives a distinct archaeological flavour.[4] The American writer Francis Worcester Doughty's *'I': a story of strange adventure* (1887), serialised under the pseudonym Richard R. Montgomery in *The Boys of New York*, is, for instance, evidently based on *She* in parts, and substitutes the ancient potsherd with its many scripts (including Egyptian hieroglyphs) for an ivory tablet on which Arabic script is picked out in gold.[5] The 'partly Egyptian, partly Assyrian' architecture of 'an ancient race' that the protagonists locate suggests a composite past made up of a hodgepodge of the kinds of collections filling European and North American museums, while the revelation that the ancient people themselves have been turned to stone by catastrophic weather conditions comprising eerie white clouds and thunder and lightning, suggests that Doughty was also inspired by the destruction of Pompeii.[6] The protagonists' pursuit of a version of the Old Testament that had been written in ancient Egypt, and their journey that sees them encounter peoples described by Herodotus, is reminiscent of the ambitions of early Egyptologists: the first excavations supported by the Egypt Exploration Fund (established in 1882), for example, sought proof of the biblical exodus. The Bible and classical writings were used as guides as to what one might look for, and where.

Baroness Orczy's short story, 'The Revenge of Ur-Tasen' (1900), meanwhile, is presented as a narrative rendered accessible by Egyptological processes. The tale's subtitle – 'Notes found written on some fragments of papyrus discovered in the caves of the Temple of Isis (the Moon) at Abydos' – immediately indicates the story's conceit as a product of antiquity brought to light not only through archaeological excavation (which had, in the final decades of the nineteenth century, as David Gange puts it, 'ma[de] leaps and bounds in the direction of scientific technique') but also through the decipherment of the ancient Egyptian language.[7] Meanwhile, in Charles Dudley Lampen's (1859–1943) *Mirango the Man-Eater* (1899), the opening of the narrative with the narrator purchasing a book containing 'lengthy descriptions of the country, its features, products and inhabitants' makes this work – upon the discovery that the civilisation is ancient Egyptian – a forerunner to the *Description de l'Égypte* (1809–29). This multi-volume work on Egypt produced by Napoleon's Bonaparte's (1769–1821) savants is often held as the first major milestone in the history of Western Egyptological scholarship.[8]

Many of these texts, of which Lampen's novel is a prime example, are, sadly, especially noteworthy today for their racist treatment of African and Arab people, who are used as a foil to ancient Egyptians. The similarities that these authors are keen to enforce, Egyptians being consistently presented as more akin to the Western travellers who encounter them, position modern Europeans as the rightful inheritors of ancient Egyptian culture. This ideology was evidently useful in the justification of the processes of Egyptology itself (and the removal of ancient Egyptian artefacts to museums overseas), as well as the British occupation of Egypt in 1882.

The pressure to establish a direct link between ancient Egypt and modern European culture may also go some way in explaining the emergence and perpetuation of hyperdiffusionist theories in the nineteenth and twentieth centuries, which posited that there was a single ancient civilisation from which all other civilisations emerged. Gange attributes to the British Egyptologist Peter le Page Renouf (1822–97) in 1878 the 'resurrect[ion of] the enlightenment idea ... that all of the world's civilizations sprang from a single source in a glorious imperial super-civilization that had known divine knowledge but in its decadence had been destroyed by the Noachic deluge'; Renouf speculated anew 'that ancient Egypt held memories, however vague, of a sophisticated and godly antediluvian civilization'.[9] Other Egyptologists, such as Grafton Elliot Smith (1871–1937), proposed ancient Egypt as the origin point of cultural sophistication. Less widespread among Egyptologists, although popular among occultists, particularly theosophists, was the theory that Egypt had inherited its wisdom from the lost continent of Atlantis and therefore might be considered a middleman between modern civilisation and an even more ancient society. Bulwer-Lytton, whose own writings proved so influential on theosophy, believed that all religions could be traced back to ancient Egypt as their original source, which is likely why the Vril-ya of *The Coming Race* have architecture that suggests Egypt as well as other ancient cultures.[10]

The later impact of hyperdiffusionist theories on literature can be read in 'The Green God' (1916) by William Call Spencer (1892?–1925?), in which an obelisk carved with hieroglyphs suggests a shared heritage between the ancient Egyptians, the Chinese and the Mexicans. Fiction written for children appears particularly to draw inspiration from these theories. In Oliphant Smeaton's *A Mystery of the Pacific*, a Pacific island is home to direct descendants of the ancient Romans and to a community of Black Atlanteans who live in a subterranean city. In this example, a rare exception to the rule, the Atlanteans, whose depiction is heavily Egyptianised, are imagined to be the more advanced civilisation.

A significant number of the texts considered in this chapter imagine ancient Egypt as having inherited its scientific learning from Atlantis, an idea that exploded in the popular cultural consciousness after the publication of the American politician Ignatius L. Donnelly's (1831–1901) *Atlantis: the antediluvian world* in 1882. Donnelly's understanding of Atlantis was derived from a fairly literal interpretation of Plato's mythological writings on this fabled civilisation. Donnelly's substantial volume makes several key claims in relation to Egyptian civilisation in its opening pages: first, '[t]hat the mythology of Egypt and Peru represented the original religion of Atlantis, which was sun-worship'; and, second, '[t]hat the oldest colony formed by the Atlanteans was probably in Egypt, whose civilization was a reproduction of that on the Atlantic island'.[11]

Donnelly's liberal quoting of renowned authorities such as the palaeontologist Richard Owen (1804–92), and some of the most famed archaeologists and Egyptologists of the nineteenth century – Giovanni Battista Belzoni (1778–1823), Jean-François Champollion (1790–1832), Karl Richard Lepsius (1810–84) and Reginald Stuart Poole (1832–95) – imbues his text, at times, with an air of learned authority. In other instances, his reverence for Egyptian civilisation, as being the closest one might get to Atlantis in the modern age, is expressed in passionate terms: 'Egypt was the magnificent, the golden bridge, ten thousand years long, glorious with temples and pyramids, illuminated and illustrated by the most complete and continuous records of human history'; nevertheless, he asserts, 'even this wonderworking Nile-land is but a faint and imperfect copy' of Atlantean civilisation.[12]

Donnelly's *Atlantis* was widely read and made a considerable impact not just on fiction but on contemporaneous esotericism, in particular theosophy. Charles Webster Leadbeater, whose writings we encountered in the first chapter of this book, claimed to have received Atlantean knowledge via 'astral clairvoyance', which in turn informed his fellow theosophist William Scott-Elliot's (1849–1919) publication *The Story of Atlantis* (1896). In Scott-Elliot's text, the author claimed that Atlanteans had such advanced technologies as airships, understanding Atlantean science and engineering to have been so sophisticated that modern civilisation was only just catching up to their achievements.

Such writings clearly informed depictions of lost worlds in which ancient Egyptians are encountered by modern individuals. As the inheritors of Atlantean knowledge, they are often depicted as magically and technologically advanced. Further, thanks to hyperdiffusionist theories, which saw occultists and Egyptologists alike seriously consider the idea that Egyptian (or an even older precursor) culture had spread across the globe, there came the possibility that archaeology would uncover evidence that such hypotheses were correct.

The idea is taken to the extreme in Jules Verne's (1828–1905) *Le Sphinx des glaces* (1897), which was translated into English as *An Antarctic Mystery* in 1898. In French, the novel's title and its illustrated title page depicting the monument prepare the reader for the discovery of an 'ice sphinx' in the Antarctic – perhaps the most surprising of Earthly locations for such a monument – while the English version, intriguingly, keeps these details concealed, perhaps in a bid to build up to a more thrilling climax. The French and English editions share an illustration by the French artist George Roux (1853–1929) of the sphinx with a skull-like face at the *dénouement*.[13] The accompanying description emphasises the sphinx's Grecian connotations, with Verne writing that the sphinx crouched *'dans l'attitude du monster ailé que la mythologie grecque a placé sur la route de Thèbes'* ('in the attitude of the winged monster that Greek mythology placed on the road to Thebes').[14] There is an Egyptian element, too, however; the original French edition of the text features a closer view of the sphinx not included in the English version, in which the sphinx's appearance is more noticeably Egyptian, similar to that depicted on the French edition's cover page.[15] The horizontal line of its back, and the flared shape of the rock from the top of its skull evoking a *nemes* headdress gives it a silhouette reminiscent of the Great Sphinx of Giza.

There is no explanation as to how this sphinx materialised at the South Pole, rendering an Egyptian presence in this most inaccessible of places a mystery. Conceived as a sequel to Edgar Allan Poe's *The Narrative of Arthur Gordon Pym of Nantucket* (1838) – Verne's characters attempting to discover the fate of Poe's eponymous protagonist – *Le Sphinx des glaces* concludes with a symbol of early human civilisation that cannot be deciphered. As Will Tattersdill observes, the poles in fiction of the 1890s offer up 'not only a blank space on the map ... but also an imaginative space in which science appears to be confounded'. Explorers who try to reach these points, he ascertains, 'encounter the uncanny folded alongside the scientifically explicable, the real alongside the fantastical'.[16] This is certainly the case in Verne's fiction: an archaeological reading of the images that accompany Verne's text tell us that this is an Egyptian sphinx, but the sphinx itself is a blank space: an unsolved riddle.

Tattersdill perceives a pattern in the scientifically informed adventure fiction of the *fin de siècle* that applies to narratives interested in displaced ancient Egyptian communities. Earth's poles, he discerns, function as 'a stepping stone to the stars, a place where spectrality and science, known and unknown, intersect with exploration and colonialism in a way which empowers a genre to leave the planet'.[17] As we shall see in the coming sections, ancient Egyptians are, at times, imagined to be space travellers, and in other contexts to wield magical powers that allow them to travel through time, no longer occupying the blank spaces on the map, but having escaped the map itself. If the poles offered up a blank canvas for the imagination of a scientifically informed fantastic, then so too might Earth's nearest neighbours: Venus and Mars. It is to the night sky, as another potential site of Egyptian knowledge and, therefore, Egyptian presences, to which we now cast our gaze.

Astronomy

As with archaeology, astronomy – once an elite pursuit – became increasingly accessible to the middle classes across the nineteenth century. With revolutions in printing, images depicting astronomy or astronomical phenomena also became more available. Among these were imaginative renderings of ancient astronomers.

The instalment of French scientist and writer Louis Figuier's (1819–94) five-volume *Vies des Savants illustres* (1866–70), devoted to '*Savants de l'antiquité*', features numerous engravings of the great 'scientists of antiquity' set against meticulously rendered ancient Egyptian architecture. Such images depict '*Pythagore chez les prêtres Égyptiens*' ('Pythagoras among the Egyptian priests') in an imposing temple space; '*Euclide présente a Ptolémée Soter ses Éléments de Géographie*' ('Euclid presenting to Ptolemy Soter his *Elements of Geography*') presumably in Ptolemy's palace; '*Apollonius dans le Musée d'Alexandrie*' ('Apollonius in the Alexandria Museum'), again in a building dominated by fine architectural detail; and *Ptolémée Soter fait construire le muséum d'Alexandrie* ('Ptolemy Soter building the Alexandria Museum').[18] In all of the aforementioned images, Figuier's work emphasises the Egyptian setting as one associated with the giants of ancient philosophy and science, and, elsewhere in this volume, a particular visual connection emerges between ancient Egyptian architecture and astronomy.

'*Hipparque à l'observatoire d'Alexandrie*' ('Hipparchus at the Alexandria observatory'), for example, depicts the eponymous astronomer surrounded by sizeable astronomical equipment and looking up into a starry sky over the city, recognisably Egyptian thanks to its pylon-shaped architecture along with a conspicuous obelisk.[19] A later image, '*Claude Ptolémée dans l'observatoire d'Alexandrie*' ('Claudius Ptolemy in the Alexandria Observatory') returns to this setting, albeit an alternative view, in which twin sphinxes flank the savant (figure 2.1).[20] Claudius Ptolemy (c.100–170 CE) studies a scroll before an enormous globe depicting the constellations, held aloft by seated ancient Egyptian figures that are, like the sphinxes, denoted as divine through their stylised beards. Such symbolism in these images reinforces an understanding of ancient Egyptian deities as guardians of knowledge.

The volume's final illustration, entitled '*Mort de la philosophe Hypatie, à Alexandrie*' ('Death of the philosopher Hypatia in Alexandria'), depicts a more frantic scene in front of rather than inside this impressive Egyptian architecture, as the philosopher and astronomer Hypatia (c.370–415 CE) is torn from her carriage (the carriage's high level of detail suggesting the consultation of genuine ancient Egyptian sources by the unnamed artist), moments before being beaten to death (figure 2.1).[21] While the image does not picture Hypatia with her scientific apparatus or in quiet contemplation as with the other astronomers, her learning is suggested by the image's composition: a tall pylon shape in the background

Figure 2.1 'Claude Ptolémée dans l'observatoire d'Alexandrie' and 'Mort de la philosophe Hypatie, à Alexandrie', in Louis Figuier, *Vies des Savants illustres: Depuis l'antiquité jusqu'au dix-neuvième siècle*, 3rd edn (Paris: Librairie Hachette et Cie, 1877), facing p. 406 and facing p. 458. Author's own.

divides the image vertically in two, with Hypatia herself occupying the central position at the bottom of the scene. With the pylon looming above her, inscribed with hieroglyphs, Hypatia is aligned with the hieroglyphic script as emblematic of mystical learning, and is thus marked out as the inheritor of – and contributor to – the lore of the ancients.

Around the same time as Figuier's *Vies des Savants illustres*, astronomical observation was becoming more widely practised in Egypt itself. The Khedivial Astronomical Observatory was founded in Cairo in 1868 and, just under half a century later, moved to a new site with better visual conditions at Helwan, built between 1903 and 1904. It was here, in 1909 and 1911, that photographic records of Halley's comet were first produced. The popular press also furthered an association between Egypt and astronomical phenomena, reproducing picturesque scenes of shooting stars streaking over Egyptian landscapes. In one example, from an 1882 issue of *The Graphic*, entitled 'The comet as seen from the pyramids from a sketch by a military officer' (figure 2.2), the comet leaves an impressive trail of light behind it, reflected in the waters of the Nile. As the accompanying article relayed, 'the comet is seen in Egypt in all its magnificence, and the sight in the early morning from the Pyramids (our sketch

Figure 2.2 'La grande comète vue des Pyramides d'Égypte, le 23 octobre 1882. (D'après le croquis d'un officier de l'armée anglaise.)', in 'La grande comète de 1882', *La Nature* 10 (2) (1882): 409.
Source: Cnum – Conservatoire numérique des Arts et Métiers.

was taken at 4 A.M.) is described as unusually grand'.[22] Earlier that year, one of the brightest comets on record was witnessed in Egypt; named Tewfik, after Mohamed Tewfik Pasha (1853–92), then Khedive of Egypt, the comet was seen – and photographed – during a solar eclipse that had brought a host of British astronomers to Egypt, cementing Egypt's reputation as an excellent location for modern astronomical enquiry.

The coming together of interests in astronomy and ancient Egyptian civilisation is of particular import to an understanding of the science fiction that emerged as the twentieth century approached. In the latter half of the nineteenth century, key individuals who were interested in astronomy – specifically in the planet Mars – were also occupied in archaeological study of ancient Egyptian sites; combining these two interests created the subdiscipline of archeoastronomy. Out of this context, and building on the ancient Egyptians' reputation as the stargazers who had imparted their knowledge to the Greek astronomers, emerges some of the earliest science-fiction works to imagine ancient Egyptians as space travellers. Fred T. Jane and Garrett P. Serviss – authors who have thus far attracted little attention from literary scholars – both wrote novels that sprang from this context, producing narratives in which ancient Egypt is not merely emblematic of the past but also of future civilisations and technologies. These speculative fictions can be seen to have been born of the space devoted in popular scientific works to imaginative speculations about the fate of the Egyptian monuments thousands of years into the future.

An intermingling of astronomical expertise and an interest in the Great Pyramid is best typified in the late nineteenth century by the British astronomer Richard Proctor.[23] Best known for his maps of Mars, Proctor understood the planet's dark patches to be oceans, and lighter patches to be land masses. This work built on images and observations by earlier astronomers, but Proctor's work would prove enormously impactful in designating some of these areas and in the diagrammatic act of mapping. In the 1880s he also published on subjects including the Great Pyramid as astronomical observatory, again using technical drawings, and details of precise measurements to support his hypothesis. Despite these features, Proctor's main ambition was to appeal to a popular rather than an exclusively scientific, scholarly audience, evident in the adornment of his work with images to capture the imagination. These illustrations included a rendering of what ancient Egyptian astronomers might have seen of the night sky from the Great Pyramid, which appeared in several astronomical publications from 1891 until at least 1912 (figure 2.3), designed by the French illustrator Louis Poyet,

Figure 2.3 [Louis] Poyet, 'Prêtres de l'ancienne Egypte observant les astres dans la grande Pyramide', in F. de Ballore, 'La grande Pyramide: Instrument des passages', *La Nature* 19 (1) (1891): 292. Source: Cnum – Conservatoire numérique des Arts et Métiers.

whose work appeared in an array of popularising scientific venues in the late nineteenth century.[24]

The Italian astronomer Giovanni Schiaparelli (1835–1910) built upon Proctor's mapping of Mars, his own diagrams going into more surface detail than Proctor's. Between the 1870s and 1880s an interesting change is detectable in Schiaparelli's images, in which some of the dark lines he could see on the surface of the planet were represented in much straighter, more regular ways. Continuing Proctor's work, Schiaparelli named these lines after rivers on Earth and mythological figures. These included the names of Egyptian gods: Anubis, Apis, Athyr (Hathor), Isis and Thoth. There was even a Martian Nile: Nilus.

Egyptian appellations entered into astronomy in the nineteenth century. Egyptian names had been given to asteroids from the 1850s, though the first of these, the naming of the asteroid Isis by the British astronomer Norman Robert Pogson (1829–91), was actually in honour of his daughter, Elizabeth Isis Pogson (1852–1945). Isis, as she was known, was an astronomer in her own right, who would go on to be the first woman nominated to be elected a fellow of the Royal Astronomical Society.[25] Subsequently, a meteor discovered by the Canadian-American astronomer James Craig Watson (1838–80) in 1876 was named Athor after the Egyptian goddess of motherhood, love, sexuality, music and dance. The German-American astronomer Christian Heinrich Friedrich Peters (1813–90) named a meteor that he discovered in 1889 Nephthys after the Egyptian goddess associated with mourning, protection and the night (Nephthys was the final meteor of the 47 discovered by Peters, who was at this stage likely running out of his preferred Classical names). In 1917, the German astronomer Max Wolf (1863–1932) discovered an asteroid which he named Aïda after the opera of the same name by Giuseppe Verdi (1813–1901), a work set in ancient Egypt, and the following year he named another asteroid Sphinx, likely an allusion to Greek mythology rather than Egyptian, but nonetheless with ancient Egyptian connotations.

Naming – and the misinterpretation of such labels – is crucial to what transpired next in scholarly work on Mars, and its representation in popular culture. It was Schiaparelli's terming of these lines as 'canali' – the Italian word for 'channels' – which famously led to the mistranslation of these patterns as 'canals' by the American astronomer Percival Lowell (1855–1916). This error implied that there was some kind of agency behind the creation of these features, rather than them simply being natural features on the planet's surface.[26] For these structures to have been artificially created, there had to be intelligent life on Mars.

While Lowell was by no means the first astronomer to suggest the prospect of civilised life on Mars, his understanding of these dark lines as canals (or other artificial structures) is enormously significant in its impact on the science and science fiction of the 1890s and beyond. Lowell's drawings of Mars suggest even more geometric, regular shapes than Schiaparelli's, and picture a planet covered – supposedly – in a complex web of waterways far more sophisticated than had been achieved on Earth.[27] The completion of the Suez Canal in 1869 and the attempts to construct the Panama canal across the 1880s and 1890s (which would not be successful until the early twentieth century), were proving – and would prove – world-changing in terms of international trade.[28] The imperialistic fanfare with which the opening of the French-controlled Suez Canal was celebrated on the cusp of the 1870s – in tandem with Lowell's work and others – may well have encouraged parallels in the minds of those who were interested in the supposedly superior efforts of Martian engineers; such subjects certainly dominated scholarly and popular discussion about the planet in the 1890s. It was perhaps only a small leap to see the pinnacle of canal engineering in Suez as if it were replicated – and superseded – in the 288 canals Lowell claimed to have documented on the surface of Mars.

Lowell was also fascinated by another considerable feat of human engineering: the Great Pyramid. Indeed, in 1912, heavily influenced by Proctor's work, he declared the Great Pyramid 'the most superb [observatory] ever erected', specifying that 'it had for telescopes something whose size has not yet been exceeded'.[29] While Lowell by no means asserts the overall superiority of the ancient Egyptian astronomers or their equipment over their modern counterparts, he does underline the unsurpassed scale of ancient Egyptian monumental construction. Lowell identifies one way, at least, in which ancient Egyptian achievements had not yet been overtaken by modern civilisation, an idea which had already proven influential in science fiction, by this time, for at least a couple of decades.

As if drawn directly from the debates of the 1890s, the naming of Martian features after Egyptian deities, and the parallels emerging between the Suez Canal and Martian structures, Garrett P. Serviss's 1898 novel *Edison's Conquest of Mars* features a textual and visual representation of the Great Sphinx of Giza as originally constructed by Martians rather than Egyptians, depicted in an image by an illustrator by the name of P. Gray (figure 2.4). Serviss himself was an astronomer, though his eclectic career also encompassed a period working for *The New York Sun* from 1876 to 1892. A sense of popular, journalistic writing is evident in his popular scientific works, as well as in his fictional output,

Figure 2.4 P. Gray, 'The Martians built the sphinx', in Garrett P. Serviss, 'Marvellous Discoveries', *New York Evening Journal*, 3 February 1898. Courtesy of Greg Weeks.

which comprises five novels and a short story. *Edison's Conquest of Mars* was Serviss's first foray into fiction, commissioned by *The Boston Post* as a sequel to an unauthorised and heavily edited version of H. G. Wells's 1897 novel *The War of the Worlds*, entitled *Fighters from Mars or the War of the Worlds*, which had been serialised in *The New York Evening Journal*.

In Serviss's text, a group of men are selected to venture to Mars by the American inventor Thomas Edison. Their aim is to destroy the Martians, who had previously made such a devastating attack on Earth, and they travel into space and to Mars itself to remove any future threat. That Mars is going to transpire to be connected to ancient Egypt in some way is foreshadowed in Edison's selection process. As Serviss's narrator relates, '[o]n the model of the celebrated corps of literary and scientific men which Napoleon carried with him in his invasion of Egypt, Mr. Edison selected a company of the foremost' scientists from a wealth of disciplines – 'astronomers, archaeologists, anthropologists, botanists, bacteriologists, chemists, physicists, mathematicians, mechanicians, meteorologists and experts in mining' – 'as well as artists and photographers'.[30] The flooding of Mars at the novel's conclusion means that these experts have little opportunity 'to gather materials in comparison with which the discoveries made among the ruins of ancient empires in Egypt and Babylonia', though it is clear in Serviss's comparison to Napoleon Bonaparte's invasion of Egypt 100 years before the publication of his novel that this is a mission of cultural imperialism as much as martial domination.

It transpires that there is indeed a historical connection between Mars and Egypt. A beautiful woman called Aina, whose ancestors hail from a utopian civilisation in Kashmir, tells the story of an ancient Martian invasion of Earth, which led to the construction of the pyramids and Sphinx. The Martians 'suddenly dropped down out of the sky … and began to slay and burn and make desolate'.[31] 'Some of the wise men', she relates, 'said that this thing had come upon our people because … the gods in Heaven were angry', this reference being the first of several that understands the arrival of the Martians in terms of the plagues in Egypt outlined in the Old Testament. Indeed, what follows is a blend of biblical narrative and pseudoarchaeology:

> they carried off from … our native land … a large number of our people, taking them first into a strange country, where there were oceans of sand, but where a great river … created a narrow land of fertility. Here, after having slain and driven out the native inhabitants, they remained for many years, keeping our people, whom

they had carried into captivity, as slaves … And in this Land … it is said, they did many wonderful works.[32]

Aina's language and syntax even shifts into a kind of biblical archaism as she recounts this story. While her people are from Kashmir rather than Atlantis, they function very much as Atlanteans do in the understandings of the origins of ancient Egyptian civilisation proposed by Donnelly and his adherents. Uprooted from their original home, the former inhabitants of this utopian civilisation are taken to Egypt, where the Martians assume the role of the ruling class, while they themselves – like the Israelites in the Bible – are enslaved. Aina communicates that the Martians, who had been so impressed with the mountains in Kashmir, erected 'with huge blocks of stone mountains in imitation of what they had seen', the blocks 'swung into their lofty elevation' not by 'puny man, as many an engineer had declared that it could not be, but … these giants of Mars'.[33] In keeping with biblical understandings of Egypt as emblematic of despotism and absolute power, the Sphinx is revealed to be 'a gigantic image of the great chief who led them in their conquest of our world'.[34] What follows is an allusion to Wells's *The War of the Worlds*, which concludes with the invading Martians overcome by pathogens, couched in biblical terms; it is only when 'a great pestilence broke out', interpreted as the 'scourge of the gods', that the Martians 'returned to their own world', taking with them the Kashmiri people.

The Great Sphinx was evidently of symbolic interest to Serviss. He would return to this monument in his story of a great flood (on Earth, rather than on Mars), *The Second Deluge*, serialised in *The Cavalier* in 1911 and then published in single-volume novel format in 1912 with illustrations by George Varian (1865–1923). Travelling the flooded world in a submarine named the *Jules Verne*, in a nod to his novel's inheritance from the French author, Serviss's protagonists accidentally collide with the Sphinx, causing a surface layer of the monument to fall away. This leaves 'an enormous black figure, seated on a kind of throne, and staring into their faces with flaming eyes' emitting 'flashes of fire'.[35] In the futuristic image of the sphinx provided by Varian, not only do we see light-emitting eyes that suggest advanced technology and also of a kind of occult potency, but the hieroglyphic symbols that adorn the sphinx evoke scientific diagrams. As we read on, we discover that this is a symbolic 'representation of a world overwhelmed with a deluge', under which is inscribed a hieroglyphic message reading 'I Come Again – | At the End of Time'.[36] The Great Sphinx is revealed to have been – all along – a record of a prophecy that a second flood would overwhelm the Earth.

While the direct influence of one on the other cannot be determined, it is striking that this scenario is suggested in Richard Proctor's article 'The Pyramid of Cheops', which appeared in *The North American Review* in March 1883. Proctor states that:

> Compared with the vast periods of time thus brought before our thoughts as among the demonstrated yet inconceivable truths of science, the life-time of such a structure as the great pyramid seems but as the duration of a breath. Yet, viewed as men must view the works of man, the pyramids of Egypt derive a profound interest from their antiquity. Young, compared with the works of nature, they are, of all men's works, the most ancient. They were ancient when temples and abbeys whose ruins now alone remain, were erected, and it seems as though they would endure till long after the last traces of any building now existing, or likely to be built by modern men, has disappeared from the surface of the earth. Nothing, it should seem, but some vast natural catastrophe ingulfing them beneath a new ocean … can destroy them utterly, unless the same race of beings which undertook to rear these vast masses should take in hand the task of destroying them.[37]

Returning to Proctor here is useful in showing how astronomers and scientific popularisers were themselves devoting part of their non-fiction texts to the kinds of speculation that we are more familiar with in genre fiction – imagining in this passage, in Proctor's case, a scenario similar to Serviss's, in which Egyptian monuments are subsumed beneath flood waters. Moreover, it offers up for examination intriguing linguistic nuances. Proctor credits the ancient Egyptians alone as having the power to remove their structures, referring to them as a 'race of beings'. In Proctor's use of the term 'beings' we are invited to imagine the ancient Egyptians as something other than human, chiming with depictions of them in science fiction. Even if in some of these fictions the Egyptians are still human, they are imagined as living an extraterrestrial existence.

The other work of science fiction of especial interest to us deals not with Mars but with Venus, though the planets are essentially interchangeable. Both written and illustrated by Fred T. Jane, his novel *To Venus in Five Seconds* imagines pyramids as landing and take-off sites for vehicles that move so fast that the movement is almost akin to teleportation, and ancient Egyptians (originally hailing from Mexico, suggesting Donnelly's theories) as effectively migrating to form a community of humans on Venus. There, they live alongside the indigenous intelligent species called the Thotheen, presumably named after Thoth, the ancient Egyptian god of wisdom. The Egyptians are inferior to the Thotheen in all sciences except medicine, and so they are permitted to remain on the planet in their capacity as superior physicians.

Jane's protagonist, a medical student called Plummer, encounters a fellow student named Zumeena, who seems to be romantically interested in him. While socialising, Zumeena takes Plummer into what appears to be a summer house, but that, once Plummer is inside, is evidently some kind of contraption. This is no ordinary structure, and within five seconds of the door having been closed Plummer is transported to Venus, an experience that he, at first, believes to be an illusion exceeding the feats of 'Maskelyne and Cooke', familiar to us from this book's previous chapter.[38] It is while there that Zumeena – as Aina does in Serviss's novel – provides the historical background detailing how ancient Egyptians came to be on another planet:

> The origins of the pyramids, which a later and more utilitarian age made into tombs, was really nothing more nor less than a convenient form for the system of transit we perfected some eight thousand years ago. You will find identical pyramids in Mexico and Egypt, and between these two points we carried on continual intercourse by means of argon-coated cars. By pure chance and accident a party of my ancestors, being in one of these cars upon a sandy plain, were suddenly transferred to this planet.[39]

The similarity between the pyramids of Mexico and Egypt reveals Donnelly as an influence on Jane's ideas, while the reference to argon, which had been first isolated from air just a few years before in 1894, underlines how the most up-to-date chemical knowledge was very much integrated into Egyptian technologies 8,000 years prior.

While such details serve to underscore the ancient Egyptians' vastly superior scientific advancement, ultimately, the superiority of the Thotheen and the humans on Venus is called into question in one regard: while they are more scientifically and technologically developed, they subscribe to problematic ethical systems. Once Plummer rejects Zumeena's advances, she resolves to vivisect him, along with the other earthlings that her people have abducted (the threat of the Thotheen and ancient Egyptians depicted in figure 2.5). Taking their captives through a utilitarian building whose pylon-shaped doors are a decorative nod to Egypt, the ancient Egyptians – now turned antagonists – ruthlessly pursue medical advancement at the expense of human life.

Figure 2.5 Fred T. Jane, 'Have you married him, female?', in Fred T. Jane, *To Venus in Five Seconds: an account of the strange disappearance of Thomas Plummer, pillmaker* (London: A. D. Innes, 1897), facing p. 111. Source: Internet Archive.

This was not the only occasion upon which Jane used ancient Egyptian imagery to represent technological modernity. While best remembered as an expert on warships and aircraft, and as a wargamer,

Jane was also a talented illustrator, who provided artwork for the science-fiction novels of George Griffith among others. He also produced a series of speculative images of the future commissioned by *The Pall Mall Magazine* in 1895, which included one design showing 'a dinner party AD 2000' in which servers dressed in ancient Egyptian costume distribute 'chemical foods' inside a building clearly inspired by an Egyptian temple.[40] This world appears at once ancient and futuristic, with the view outside showing the top of an obelisk, as well as hovering balloons projecting light downwards to illuminate the city below. The image also offers up a fascinating contrast between the people present. Jane pictures white Europeans being served by waiters in ancient Egyptian-inspired costume. There is clearly a hierarchy here, in which ancient Egypt is subservient, its feats of engineering appropriated for the modern world, along with, perhaps, its alchemical knowledge, which may be the basis of the 'chemical foods' consumed by the elite.

As Nathaniel Robert Walker observes, 'Jane placed a poetic signature that may contain a hint for decoding his Oriental futurism' amidst this image.[41] 'On the lintel is an inscription reading "Janus Edificator", below a winged, double-faced head', Walker notes, reading this as both an allusion to Jane himself, and 'also the Classical double-faced god of doorways, windows, and, appropriately, of time'. He reads in this image 'a unifying, evolutionary synthesis of all time and space'.[42] Walker is correct in his assertion, citing Edward Said, that 'the East' is often imagined in Western culture as 'an irrational, decrepit "Other"', and that at times 'the merging of Oriental and Occidental architecture was gleefully presented as an imperial appropriation of the former by the latter', such 'hybrid architectures ... calculated to express the tantalizing possibilities inherent in a world that was shrinking due to the proliferation of space- and time-annihilating technologies'.[43] I believe that there is something more nuanced in this illustration, however; certainly, ancient Egypt is imagined as subservient to the Westerners of the future, but this is not because they are the 'irrational, decrepit' denizens of the East. Rather, the subservience of a civilisation often held aloft in contemporaneous culture as sophisticated casts the image's Europeans as even more so.

Reading this image in the context of Jane's other work is also illuminating, establishing a kind of progression in his conception of ancient Egyptian cultural sophistication over time. By the time Jane wrote and illustrated his own narrative in *To Venus in Five Seconds*, published two years after this image, Egypt is no longer imagined as subservient to Western culture, but is a very real threat, embodying the 'vengeance theme' that Ailise Bulfin has identified in a body of Egyptian-themed fiction emerging in the 1860s and swelling at the *fin de siècle*.[44] Ancient Egyptians in Jane's text are very much the dominant people in terms of power and scientific advancement, and Plummer is lucky to escape with his life. The very opposite of service is depicted in Jane's own image of ancient Egyptians physically dominating the Westerners whom they have abducted.

Despite their differences, both Serviss's and Jane's texts relocate Egyptian presences to other planets, revealing that ancient Egyptian civilisation is not confined to earthly ruins, but lives on elsewhere. Both texts are noteworthy, too, for their imagination of Egyptian monuments as markers of extraterrestrial cultures, in the Martian origins of the Great Sphinx in Serviss's case, or, in Jane's, the pyramids reconfigured as transport devices between Earth and Venus. These sites, of archaeological and astronomical interest across the nineteenth century, cannot be comprehended by the practitioners of these disciplines, however, resisting conventional understanding. Instead, they highlight the work to be done in filling in the blanks left by advanced peoples, if not blank spaces yet to be filled in imperialist atlases, then in the scholarly tomes of archaeologists and astronomers.

Time travel

Time-travel stories as devised by various science-fiction pioneers in the nineteenth century were especially interested in accessing ancient Egypt and its future legacies. Mid-century narratives often used sleep as a device to conceptualise more rapid passing of time than the typical waking human experiences, exaggerated to the extreme (a literary device that stretches back to antiquity). The German Egyptologist Max Uhlemann's (d.1862) *Drei Tage in Memphis* (1856) and the British children's author Henry Cadwallader Adams's (1817–99) *Sivan the Sleeper: a tale of all time* (1857), both use sleep as a process whereby other eras are accessed. The former is an extended dream-like journey to the past, facilitated by the spirit of the deity Horus (a scrap of papyrus on which is written a hieroglyphic message being the 'proof' that it was no mere dream); the latter sees the eponymous ancient Egyptian protagonist use periods of sleep to make significant temporal jumps.[45]

Subsequent to these examples, ancient Egypt proved integral to several of the most innovative and influential time travel narratives in the decades that followed. The American minister and historian Edward Everett Hale's (1822–1909) 'Hands Off' (1881) – a short story first published anonymously in *Harper's New Monthly Magazine* – is a cosmic alternate history. While not, as Karen Hellekson asserts, 'the first example known to date of a work that deals with the time-travel paradox: a backward-traveling time traveler who causes the events [they] went back to study', 'Hands Off' does illustrate (well in advance of chaos theory) the concept of the 'butterfly effect', whereby one small change to events in the past is shown to have major consequences.[46] In 'Hands Off', with little in the way of explanation as to how they arrive in this state, Hale's narrator opens the story by describing being 'free from the limits of Time and in new relations to Space', privy to thousands of solar systems.[47] The narrator chooses to witness Joseph's journey towards Egypt, ultimately to be sold into slavery, as in the Bible's Book of Genesis. It transpires that there are other Earths amidst these duplicate solar systems, though, and the narrator witnesses a different version of the world, in which they themselves interfere. Killing a guard dog, the narrator allows Joseph to escape and to return to his father, Jacob. This action has significant repercussions: as Joseph never goes to Egypt, and never predicts years of plenty followed by years of famine, the Egyptian granaries are drained of their store. As a result, Egypt falls. Greek civilisation does not develop without Egyptian knowledge; in the end, there is '[n]o Israel ... no Egypt, no Iran, no Greece, no Rome', and the human race rapidly dies out.[48] There are no lasting ramifications, thankfully, this being a world of 'phantoms' – a duplicate of our world rather than the genuine article – and the narrator learns, ultimately, not to interfere. Hale's work is noteworthy (beyond its historical significance as, perhaps, the first example of the butterfly effect in fiction) for its imagination of multiple worlds, long predating the serious scientific consideration of this concept. As Paul J. Nahin asserts, the 'idea of a multitude of worlds ... (of which ours is but one) sounds very much like the many-worlds view of reality that many find implicit in theoretical quantum mechanics'.[49] Nahin dates the first earnest proposal of this idea in science to 1957, three-quarters of a century after Hale's short story, and over a century after the idea's first depiction in art in the French artist Jean-Ignace Isidore Gérard's (1803–47) *Un Autre Monde* (1844).

Egypt also contributes to other milestones in the history of time-travel fiction, performing a crucial role in Nesbit's *The Story of the Amulet*. This novel is, according to Somi Ahn, 'the first time-travel narrative written for children'.[50] This makes the children's first journey through space and time to predynastic Egypt the original spatiotemporal moment accessed by time travellers in children's literature. Indeed, it is not just the child protagonists who travel through time, but also the Egyptian priest

Rekh-marā who, like the children, harnesses the amulet's 'power to move to and fro in time as well as in space', meaning that an ancient Egyptian is the first independent time-travelling adult in children's fiction.[51]

Tales of time travel often function similarly to the lost-world genre, though instead of the text's protagonists being geographically displaced they are temporally so, usually (though not always) encountering Egyptian antiquity in Egypt itself rather than in an imagined alternative location. While archaeology and its relics likely offered up inspiration for lost-world narratives given how many of these texts begin with frame narrative based around a particular artefact, immersive simulacra of ancient Egypt in its glorious heyday that proliferated in metropolitan spaces – entertainment and education venues – suggested experiences of time travel.

As outlined in the previous chapter, the presence of ancient Egypt in London and other major cities was increasingly felt across the nineteenth century, as museums acquired and displayed Egyptian artefacts for their visitors, theatrical productions drew upon ancient Egypt's glamour, and metropolitan architecture incorporated ancient Egyptian elements. These fantastical pockets of ancient Egypt in the modern world crop up throughout this book, though one example of particular importance for our purposes here is the Egyptian Court at the Crystal Palace, a space that, for thousands of British people from the nineteenth century onwards, as Stephanie Moser records, provided 'their first visual encounter with ancient Egypt'.[52] The Egyptian Court was a new feature when the Crystal Palace, once occupying Hyde Park, was reassembled at Sydenham in 1854. The grandest rendering of ancient Egypt from the mid-nineteenth century until the destruction of the Crystal Palace by a fire in 1936, the Egyptian Court was unusual in that its statues were painted in dazzling polychrome, a level of detail conferring unprecedented authenticity (in Britain, at least) to this spectacle. Many of the finer details were based upon the notes and sketches of the Court's creators – the architect Owen Jones (1809–74) and the sculptor and artist Joseph Bonomi Jr (1796–1878) – made during independent excursions in Egypt, along with casts of relics in Europe's major museums. Despite this, the Egyptian Court did not resemble the ruins of ancient Egypt, but rather the great civilisation as it might be imagined at its cultural peak. The experience may well have suggested time travel (albeit to a composite ancient Egypt rather than any one distinct moment in ancient Egyptian history), and indeed, in *The Story of the Amulet*, one of the child protagonists, Anthea, expresses an interest in going back in time to ancient Egypt 'to see Pharaoh's house' as she 'wonder[s] whether it's like the Egyptian Court in the Crystal Palace'.[53]

The Egyptian Court was one of several zones at the Crystal Palace meant to reconstruct the art and architecture of various times and places: there was a court to represent Medieval Europe, and another for Renaissance Europe, along with the Alhambra, ancient Rome, ancient Greece and Pompeii. Experiences of far older times were complicated by the introduction of modern technologies into these spaces. A journalist writing for *The Illustrated London News* in 1892, for instance, commented on how '[i]n the Egyptian Court we can hear instrumental music and comic opera wafted ... from London, Birmingham, Manchester, and Liverpool'.[54] Just as sound technologies meant that recordings from various places could be played in settings far removed, and audio captured in the past could be replayed at a later time, so too did spaces like the Crystal Palace, in its very organisation, and in the introduction of such technologies into these interconnected zones, suggest the breakdown of conventional understandings of time and space. Indeed, the quick (and, indeed, non-linear) movement one might make between the various courts by visitors to the Crystal Palace might have offered itself up as an interactive predecessor to time-travel narratives that imagine their protagonists moving swiftly between several different societies of historical interest, as Nesbit's novel does.

That the Crystal Palace and the British Museum were favourite destinations of Nesbit in her own childhood implies the strong impact that these real spaces had on her conception of enchantment in her children's fiction.[55] The children in *The Story of the Amulet* only refer to the Egyptian Court by name, never actually venturing to the Crystal Palace in this novel, though they do visit the British Museum several times. As Joanna Paul notes of this text, 'the British Museum ... becom[es] the portal through which the children enter the future utopian London'.[56] While the titular amulet is how time travel is accomplished in Nesbit's novel, the British Museum itself also allows access to disparate times and places. Michel Foucault's (1926–84) understanding of the museum as the ultimate 'heterotopia of time' is a useful way of comprehending why museums suggest themselves as intriguing settings for such fiction. For Foucault as, apparently, for Nesbit, '[m]useums ... are heterotopias in which time never ceases to pile up', which hinge on 'the idea of accumulating everything ... the desire to contain all times, all ages, all forms, all tastes in one place, the idea of constituting a place of all times that is itself outside time and protected from its erosion'.[57] While *The Story of the Amulet* certainly casts the British Museum in such a light, this is by no means common to all time-travel narratives. The Palace of Green Porcelain in H. G. Wells's *The Time Machine* is recognisable as having been a museum akin to those of the Time Traveller's own era in its amassing of artefacts from the furthest reaches of the globe. The museum is, however, shown to succumb to the ravages of time, itself falling to ruin. Wells imagines a world in which even the museum has itself become a kind of archaeological site, with its 'inscription[s] in some unknown character' and its 'floor ... thick with dust'.[58] While Wells's Time Traveller does not venture to Egypt in any period of its history, that this future London with its ruined museum is watched over by a subtly smiling sculpture of a sphinx is a powerful allusion to ancient Egyptian iconography. It is to Wells's *The Time Machine*, and its relationship to *The Story of the Amulet*, that we now turn. In both texts, the line between London and Egypt, the past, present and future, is rendered indistinct, suggesting the temporal collapse encouraged by the cityscape itself.

The cultural pervasiveness of ancient Egypt in the city setting is exemplified in *The Time Machine*, in which Wells imagines the London suburbs in the year 802,701. The first landmark that the Time Traveller sees in this future moment is a statue of a sphinx, '[a] colossal figure, carved apparently in some white stone', while 'all else of the world was invisible'.[59] Made from marble, replete with spread wings and somewhat weatherworn, the sphinx is a guardian of sorts to the changed world in which the Time Traveller finds himself. The sphinx does not appear to the Time Traveller to be masculine or feminine and, as such, is referred to throughout by the neutral pronoun 'it', though the Time Traveller's repeated references to the sphinx's smile imbues the statue with an almost enchanted sentience. A hailstorm veils much of the Time Traveller's surroundings from his sight, and the hail falling harder and softer gives the 'winged sphinx' the appearance of 'advanc[ing] and reced[ing]' within this gloomy landscape, much like the visual effects of the phantasmagoria.[60] If we subscribe to David Shackleton's reading of the Time Traveller's view of the 'dreamlike and insubstantial' shifting landscape as he travels a mirroring of 'the magic lantern displays and phantasmagoria that geological lecturers used as visual aids' in their 'geological time travel' displays 'from the 1830s onwards', so too does the Time Traveller's encounter with the sphinx suggest the archaeological subject matter employed in magic lantern shows explored in this book's previous chapter.[61]

Just like the Time Traveller, the original readers of Wells's narrative as it was first published in the United Kingdom in novel format by William Heinemann in 1895 would, before opening the novella's first page, have been confronted by the sphinx.[62] Embossed in dark ink on the first UK edition's sandy-coloured covers (figure 2.6) – according to

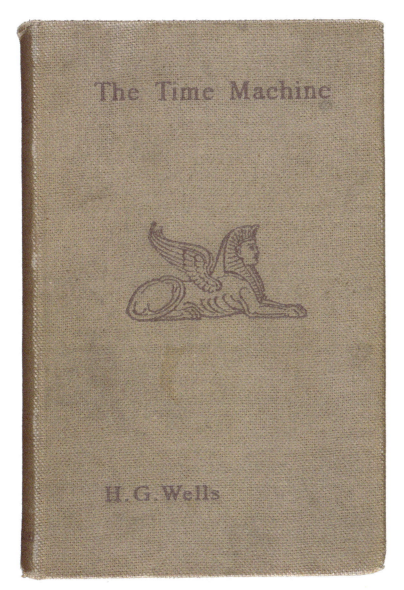

Figure 2.6 H. G. Wells, *The Time Machine* (London: William Heinemann, 1895). Courtesy of the Rare Book & Manuscript Library, University of Illinois at Urbana-Champaign.

Leon Stover '[a]t the author's insistence'[63] – is a simplistic line drawing of a sphinx couchant, informed by ancient Egyptian iconography. This sphinx, a design commonly attributed to one Ben Hardy, wears the distinctive *nemes* headdress of the pharaohs. Even in this hyper-futuristic setting, the Egyptianised elements infiltrating the London landscape are imagined not only to have continued to spring up, but to have survived. Embodying both the ancient past and the distant future, the sphinx symbolises (among other things) both the timelessness of the Egyptian fantastic and the metropolis's capacity to act as a gateway to the exotic.

Critics who recognise the sphinx's centrality or symbolic significance in Wells's imagined future have nonetheless often overlooked its Egyptianness, with Terry W. Thompson and Peter Firchow even declaring it (independently of one another) Greek rather than Egyptian.[64] Admittedly, any Egyptian qualities are not made verbally explicit, though Wells apparently requested that the sphinx appear on the cover of the Heinemann edition; one would hope that the sphinx as it appeared would have been drawn up to the author's specifications.

The judgements of earlier scholars have not stopped others, among them Margaret Ann Debelius, from recognising the cultural hybridity of Wells's sphinx, and Egypt's role in this hybridity, however. As Debelius asserts, alluding to Egypt and Greece respectively, the sphinx is 'a curious amalgam of eastern and western tradition'.[65] I would add that if the *nemes* headdress specifically codes Wells's sphinx as Egyptian, the wings mark it out as Greek or Assyrian (or both). In fact, Assyrian sphinxes – far more often than their Greek counterparts – are depicted with wings held aloft, rather than at their sides. My point is that while Wells's sphinx is not exclusively Egyptian, it does, in concrete ways, evoke something explicitly Egyptian in its design.

The component parts of Wells's sphinx as it appears on the Heinemann cover resemble pre-existing hybrid imagery that could be seen, for instance, in Wedgwood products. Sphinx ornaments produced by the pottery company from the late eighteenth century to at least around the 1880s feature these creatures in much the same pose, with *nemes* headdress and wings. Wedgwood wares often combined imagery from different ancient civilisations (pieces that were supposed to look Egyptian often featured Greek sphinxes, crouching female creatures who have adopted a *nemes* for the occasion), so the kind of iconographic hybridity that we see in the Heinemann motif echoes iconography that was then in circulation, not just in the elite products produced by Wedgwood but in cheaper alternatives targeting a less affluent consumer.[66] Such Wedgwood pieces are themselves reminiscent of genuine ancient Egyptian examples (aside from the wings), and were perhaps originally inspired by French Egyptian Revival designs, which also saw the introduction of wings onto otherwise fairly faithful reproductions.

Regardless of the source for this particular image, however, the sphinx's cultural hybridity indicates that the future of Wells's Time Traveller bears a particular resemblance to the ancient past. This ancient past combines several features to suggest a kind of composite Orientalised decadence, rather than simply reverting to one specific ancient culture.

While the first American edition published by Henry Holt (which predated the Heinemann edition in the United Kingdom by a matter of weeks) does not feature a specific design on the cover (the front's sole decoration being the publisher's emblem), it does include a frontispiece depicting the sphinx, created by illustrator W. B. Russell.[67] While Russell's sphinx wears a shorter headdress than that of the sphinx adorning the Heinemann cover, this nonetheless gives it an appearance more reminiscent of the Sphinx of Giza, the most famous Egyptian sphinx of all.

In fact, Debelius argues convincingly that Wells's original readership would have 'specifically' read the white sphinx in the context of 'Britain's military occupation of Egypt' and 'the Great Sphinx of Giza'; perhaps Russell was influenced by this context, too, in his visual representation of Wells's sphinx.[68] Indeed, Debelius claims that 'Wells' split society sounds even more like Cairo under British occupation' than it does the author's contemporary Britain.[69] Supporting Debelius's reading is the Time Traveller's repeated Orientalisation of the landscape; he observes that the archway into the 'colossal' building in which the Eloi sleep is 'suggesti[ve] of old Phœnician decorations', while at the crest of a hill he finds a seat with 'arm-rests cast and filed into the resemblance of griffins' heads', the earliest examples of the image of the griffin dating back to ancient Egypt and ancient Iran.[70] Looking over the vista, he observes 'here and there ... the sharp vertical line of some cupola' (evocative of minarets) 'or obelisk', features that encourage parallels that might be made between Cairo and the London suburbs of the future.[71] Aside from the industrial technologies of the Morlocks, this is an age where most of the trappings of the Time Traveller's civilisation – including knowledge of a written language – have slipped away, and so his encounter with this new world in which he finds himself unable to decipher traces of the written language across which he stumbles echoes European explorers' forays into Egypt before the decipherment of hieroglyphs.

Debelius also proposes the influence of H. Rider Haggard on Wells, 'as if the best-selling author of imperial adventure fiction had somehow left his ghostly signature on Wells' text'.[72] *The Time Machine* shares several features in common with Haggard's *She* of the previous decade, although one symbolic parallel stands out in particular. As Haggard's protagonists approach the landmass on which they will find the lost civilisation of

Kôr, their crossing of this boundary is overseen by 'a gigantic monument fashioned, like the well-known Egyptian Sphinx, by a forgotten people … perhaps as an emblem of warning'.[73] There is far more that might be said in drawing connections between these texts; suffice it to say that the sphinxes in both cases mark the shift from the known world into a fantastical space and that, whether this space exists in the present or in the future, it is imbued both with a sense of 'pastness' and 'primitive' dangers.

The Time Machine is interested in archaeology, geology, and their legacies, evident not just in the symbol of the sphinx, but in the Time Traveller's foray into the Palace of Green Porcelain. This is the largest surviving structure in this part of future London, sporting an 'Oriental' 'façade'.[74] Its original function as a museum leads the Time Traveller to declare it 'the ruins of some latter-day South Kensington'.[75] Patrick Parrinder interprets the Palace of Green Porcelain as a hybrid of the several museums in South Kensington that were funded by the Crystal Palace as it was originally conceived, along with the Crystal Palace as it was reimagined at Sydenham.[76] Robert Crossley proposes that 'Wells's Palace is … a composite of several English museums as they existed at the close of the nineteenth century: notably, the British Museum in Bloomsbury' in addition to 'the complex of museums in South Kensington' proposed by Parrinder.[77] For Crossley, 'Wells was accomplishing in fiction and in the future what was dreamed of by Prince Albert in the nineteenth century: a single grand institution that … would not separate "natural history" from human artifacts in the study of culture'. Its eclectic collections, the Time Traveller hypothesises, might incorporate 'a great deal more … than a Gallery of Palæontology … historical galleries … even a library'.[78] Unlike Crossley, I read the Palace of Green Porcelain as a reversion back to an earlier type of museum with less rigid differentiations between its different types of collections. Indeed, the eclectic exhibits of the Palace of Green Porcelain seem closer to the Wunderkammer out of which several nineteenth-century museums developed. The British Museum, which originated in the collections of the British physician Sir Hans Sloane (1660–1753), is one such example. The Palace of Green Porcelain's collections recall those of the British Museum before the creation of the Natural History Museum in 1881, as natural history exhibits give way to antiquities: walking through the museum, the Time Traveller observes '[a] few shrivelled and blackened vestiges of what had once been stuffed animals, desiccated mummies in jars that had once held spirit, a brown dust of departed plants', and shortly thereafter 'a vast array of idols – Polynesian, Mexican, Grecian, Phœnician, every country on earth'.[79] This is evidently a step backwards from the separate departments of the British

Museum, whereby artefacts were contextualised with other examples from the same civilisation of origin.

The Time Traveller himself even reverts to outdated forms of Egyptology in his encounter with the white sphinx, once he has realised that the Morlocks have secreted his time machine inside the pedestal upon which the statue stands. In a nod to the work of Giovanni Battista Caviglia, who was partially responsible for the excavation of the Great Sphinx in the 1810s and some of whose excavations at Giza involved the use of gunpowder, the Time Traveller speculates that had he found explosives in the Palace of Green Porcelain he would have 'blown Sphinx, bronze doors, and … my chances of finding the Time Machine, all together into non-existence'.[80] Far from the careful, meticulous archaeological processes of the 1890s, the methods considered by the Time Traveller in his desperation recall the destructive methods of Egyptology over half a century earlier. This appears to be part of the cultural degeneration that has not only taken place in the future, in which museum departments have collapsed back in on themselves – but takes place in the Time Traveller himself, in which he reverts to outdated science.

Intriguingly, *The Time Machine* may have impressed itself upon members of the scientific community interested in Egyptian archaeology and in the longevity of man-made structures over the course of millennia. The opening of astronomer Percival Lowell's article, 'Precession: And the Pyramids' in a 1912 issue of *Popular Science Monthly*, opens with the author imagining a 'tourist … transported back in time' to see the different view of the stars that would have existed 'five thousand years ago'.[81] It is tempting to read in Lowell's article, with its early allusion to time travel, the influence of Wells's text. Wells's Time Traveller, who journeys to a time far from his own (albeit a leap into the future rather than the past) also notes that despite the 'sense of friendly comfort' provided by the stars, '[a]ll the old constellations had gone'.[82] Lowell ends this piece with thoughts inspired by 'the pyramids … the enduring character of the past besides the ephemeralness of our day', which have their counterpart in the white sphinx of *The Time Machine*, a lingering Egyptian presence while most traces of nineteenth-century culture have decayed.[83] Although Lowell concedes that the Egyptians did not 'have printing', he counters that 'libraries are not lasting'. There is perhaps a whisper of Wells's crumbling books in the Palace of Green Porcelain here. While it is difficult to prove a direct line of influence from Wells to Lowell, they were very much thinking on the same wavelength.

More certain is the influence of Wells's time-travel fiction on Nesbit's *The Story of the Amulet*. One of the children's trips to the future takes them to the British Museum, perhaps in an allusion to the Time Traveller's visit to the Palace of Green Porcelain on his own journey. Like the landscape imagined in Wells's novella, at least at first glance, London of the future in *The Story of the Amulet* is a pastoral idyll: the Museum is surrounded by 'a big garden, with trees and flowers and smooth green lawns'.[84] The 'white statues' which 'gleamed among the leaves' even recall the white sphinx amidst this lush landscape. Here, in a far less distant future than Wells had imagined, the children encounter a boy called Wells, named 'after the great reformer' of the children's own time: Nesbit's 'friend and fellow Fabian socialist'.[85]

Nesbit's time-travel fiction is, despite these allusions to Wells's earlier work, enormously different to *The Time Machine*. Despite this, Nesbit's text, too, emphasises London's saturation with relics from the ancient past. The children's home in this story is that of their 'old Nurse, who lived in Fitzroy Street, near the British Museum'. The rooms of the 'learned gentleman on the top-floor' – an Egyptologist called Jimmy – are themselves filled with antiquities including a 'very, very, very big' mummy-case (an illustration of which appears both in the book and stamped in gold on the book's front cover). This means that the spaces that the children inhabit – even before their adventures through space and time – are heterotopic, whether on a macro or micro scale: London itself – a city that 'seems to be patched up out of odds and ends' – and the house in Bloomsbury, respectively.[86] Temporal collapses seem to define the spaces that the children occupy even when they are not travelling to distant civilisations. The aforementioned mummy case seems to change expression to something more benign over the course of the narrative 'as if in its distant superior ancient Egyptian way it were rather pleased to see them'.[87] This is certainly a less threatening presence than Wells's sphinx.

In Nurse's parlour, 'a dreary clock like a black marble tomb ... silent as the grave ... for it had long since forgotten how to tick' is an early symbolic indication that this is a space of no time, or else of all times.[88] The clock's morbid associations conjure up images of mausolea, very much in keeping with the supposedly 'dead' civilisations that the children go on to encounter. Another broken timepiece – 'part of the Waterbury watch that Robert had not been able to help taking to pieces at Christmas and had never had time to rearrange' – cements this sense that the children are destined to be outside-of-time.[89]

In fact, differences between the children's own time and the various civilisations they visit – accessed via portals to different places in time and space created by the amulet, which appear as keyhole-shaped doors – are often pared down. The first instance of time travelling in children's fiction sees the children, surrounded by 'the faded trees and trampled grass of the Regent's Park', catching a glimpse of 'a blaze of blue and yellow and red' within the archway opened up by the amulet.[90] Their first view of predynastic Egypt ('the year 6000 B.C.') is a sensory bombardment of primary colours suggesting, on the one hand, a kind of visual primitivism, but equally, on the other, of a vibrancy to which the children do not have access in modern London (aside from, one assumes, the technicolour Egyptian Court).[91] Nesbit's description of the 'faded' greenery of Regent's Park, suggests something tired and drab in contrast to the fresher colours of Egypt in the distant past. Despite this, the 'little ragged children playing Ring o' Roses' in the children's present are more suggestive of older pagan traditions than of any kind of cultural modernity, the circular formation of Ring o' Roses later taken up by the protagonists as they travel back to ancient Britain and by the children they witness there.[92]

Meanwhile, H. R. Millar's illustration of the corresponding moment (figure 2.7) depicts two settings that do not seem visually incongruous. Through the archway can be seen what appears to be the snaking curve of the Nile, edged by vegetation, with the horizon aligning fairly well with that of the scene outside of the arch, suggesting a visual continuation, at least, between modern and ancient worlds. To the right of the arch, in the distance, is what appears to be a Neoclassical structure featuring several columns topped by a pediment, redolent of Greek temples. Indeed, the inspiration appears to have been Decimus Burton's (1800–81) Grove Lodge (now Grove House), designed for the geologist George Bellas Greenough (1778–1855), geology working with far extremer timescales than those of human civilisation. Ultimately, the picture painted here is of temporal contradictions: despite their temporal and geographical distance, the ancient and modern worlds sit alongside each other comfortably; indeed, they blend in the children's present, supporting Somi Ahn's claim that the novel 'question[s] the ideal of linear progress'.[93]

This lack of easy differentiations between places and times continues throughout *The Story of the Amulet*. A British settlement in 55 BCE reminds the children of 'the old [predynastic] Egyptian town' they have previously visited.[94] The children's later visit to Egypt in the time of Joseph, which has them remarking that '[t]he poor Egyptians haven't improved so very much in their building', also contributes to this sense of cultural stagnation across times and geographies.[95] When the children encounter an Egyptian worker calling their 'comrades' to 'strike', one of the children, Robert, observes that he 'heard almost every single word of that … in Hyde Park last Sunday'; moreover, Egyptians who utter disparaging remarks similar to those of their modern counterparts at hearing

Figure 2.7 H. R. Millar, 'The opening of the arch was small, but Cyril saw that he could get through it', in E. Nesbit, *The Story of the Amulet* (New York: E. P. Dutton, [1907]), p. 78. Source: Internet Archive.

this call to action would 'nowadays … have lived at Brixton or Brockley', according to Nesbit's omniscient narrator.[96]

Nesbit's novel, as this tongue-in-cheek comment suggests, is one which treats its subject matter with humour, and Nesbit credits the children's adventures in the past with sparking major historical events that have lasting cultural repercussions, namely Julius Caesar's invasion of Britain, and the introduction of currency to ancient Egypt. Referring to the latter, the narrator jests, 'You will not believe this, I daresay, but really, if you believe the rest of the story, I don't see why you shouldn't believe this as well'.[97] Belief is, in fact, crucial to the amulet's magical facilitation of time travel. As various characters relate over the course of the novel, 'time is only a form of thought'. Think differently, Nesbit implies (and, if you are an adult reader, with the imagination of a child), and time travel is within easy reach. Joanna Paul reads the novel's magic as being the power of 'the written word' in granting the reader access to different points in space and time, an interpretation of the book itself as magical amulet or, indeed, time machine.[98]

Likewise, Nesbit treats magical and esoteric subjects with a wry smile. Jimmy, the 'learned gentleman' who lives on the top floor, believes that he is communicating details of antiquity to the children through 'thought-transference', at one point speculating 'perhaps I have hypnotised myself'.[99] Nesbit seems to enjoy the tension between the genuine supernatural or magical versus mythology, fakery, and illusion. One of Jimmy's friends ridicules 'thought-transference' as 'simply twaddle' before telling the novel's child protagonists about Atlantis – as a real historical place – a mere page later.[100] Indeed, encounters with the magical actually suggest the lack of truth to other phenomena, as if there can only be so much enchantment in the world; after visiting Atlantis, Jimmy 'ceased to talk about thought-transference. He had now seen too many wonders to believe that.'[101]

As U. C. Knoepflmacher records, Nesbit 'supported radical causes and esoteric cults such as the theosophy espoused by Madame Blavatsky', these interests manifesting in *The Story of the Amulet*. The novel hints, in the episode of the little girl called Imogen, who the children reunite with her mother in another time, that other forms of time travel – namely, reincarnation – feature in Nesbit's universe. Another humorous moment in which the queen of Babylon, transported to the children's present, is assumed to be the British theosophist and socialist Annie Besant, further suggests the indistinguishability between the cultures of the ancient past and modern present. Theosophy's influence can also be detected in the children's Atlantean excursion and in its incorporation of reincarnation into its mythology.[102] If we read Nesbit's novel as informed by esotericism, we can certainly perceive the influence of Ignatius Donnelly, whether first or second hand, in the novel's presentation of Atlantis as an origin point for human civilisation, and specifically in its suggestion of the Egyptians as the inheritors of Atlantean knowledge. As Joanna Paul observes, 'Nesbit's Atlantis is primarily the Atlantis of Plato', though unlike in Plato – but typical of nineteenth-century esoterica and pseudoscience – Atlantis is held aloft as the pinnacle of human civilisation.[103]

In *The Story of the Amulet*, Atlantis is a vibrant city of marble and precious metals, with 'temples and palaces ... roofed with what looked like gold and silver', both suggesting a material richness to this utopia, and the Atlanteans' potential alchemical knowledge.[104] The houses, meanwhile, are decorated with 'oricalchum', a metal mined in Atlantis, according to Plato.[105] Atlantis is also the origin of the stone from which the amulet is carved. During the catastrophic event that destroyed Atlantis, we learn, 'the stone ... fell on to a ship miles away that managed to escape and got to Egypt'.[106] Once in Egypt, the stone was sculpted into the shape of a *tyet*, or Isis knot, and inscribed with the hieroglyphic incantation which gives this artefact its magical qualities. That the Atlanteans recognise the hieroglyphic inscription as 'like our writing' again underscores Egypt's direct cultural inheritance from this mythological utopia.[107]

Nesbit's novel ends on an intriguing note, in which Jimmy the Egyptologist and Rekh-marā the ancient Egyptian priest agree to unite in one body. Rekh-marā desires '[a] learning greater and deeper than that of any man of my land and my time' and additionally to 'stay here, and be the great knower of all that has been'.[108] In choosing to stay in the children's present, having journeyed through time and space, and in willingly joining his soul with Jimmy's, Rekh-marā fulfils his dream of embodying the pinnacle of knowledge. Ancient Egypt may not have been acknowledged as the most advanced civilisation by the children's standards, Atlantis striking them as 'much more like *now* than Babylon or Egypt', boasting 'a far higher level of civilisation', but it is Egyptian knowledge – specifically Egyptian magical knowledge – that allows the children's travels through time and space at all.[109] Moreover, it is the ancient Egyptian priest himself who comes to stand as emblematic of the magical lore of the ancients and the science of early twentieth-century Egyptology, a man who, even after the children's adventure concludes, remains permanently out of time.

One further example of ancient Egypt featuring in a time-travel narrative seems pertinent here, and one in which, as in Nesbit's novel, an ancient Egyptian is imagined as travelling from their own time into the twentieth-century present. The American author William Henry Warner's novel *The Bridge of Time* (1919) sees the ancient Egyptian Rames pass through the millennia in the hope of being reunited with the woman he loved in ancient Egypt, Teta, who is killed by Assyrian invaders. To reach

Teta as she is reincarnated in the future, Rames must drink a potion that will accelerate time for him alone.

The high priest Hotep's warning that should the experiment go awry Ramses might 'lie in a perpetual state of suspended animation, a living mummy' appears to be a knowing nod to the (by this point somewhat clichéd) trope of a perfectly preserved female mummy ready to be awoken in the nineteenth or twentieth century.[110] Nolwenn Corriou has identified how the Egyptological process creates 'encounter[s]' between 'the ... bodies of the archaeologist and the mummy' that evoke temporal as much as geographical travel, reading mummy fictions as akin to time-travel narratives.[111] Unlike the female mummy who sleeps for thousands of years before her awakening in the modern age, however, Rames consciously experiences the rapid passing of time, very much akin to Wells's Time Traveller. The process of time travel, however, dances at the boundary between science and magic, not being a mechanical process, but instead being chemical, described in such enchanted terms that the storehouse of knowledge into which Rames and Hotep enter reads like an alchemist's laboratory.

Hotep presents Rames with 'two small phials of rock crystal, hermetically sealed, whose contents sparkled dazzlingly', 'one gleaming radiant and silver as an imprisoned moonbeam, the other, glowing and ardent as the clearest ruby, as though the precious stone itself had been melted and poured into it'.[112] The first liquid is suggestive of mercury, and the second of molten sulphur, these chemicals being '[t]he basic elements of the alchemist's art'.[113] Hotep decants the silver liquid into a golden goblet shaped like a lotus, at which 'the heart of the lotus bud became a lambent flame, weird, pulsing, restless, as with life', and it is after drinking this liquid that Rames hurtles through time, ending his journey in the same spot in the year 1914.[114] Even though Rames is confined to one location, the liquid's magical quality is such that it grants him visions of other times and places in the interim, including 'a glimpse of a cross raised on a barren hillside, on which hung a pathetic figure, which seemed mocked at and despised'.[115] Despite the magical language – and the highlighting of the crucifixion of Jesus as a moment of religious significance of which Rames must learn before entering the modern world – the process is consistently couched in scientific terms, however. As Warner relates, '[a]ll the might and energy of nature were concentrated on the mere atom of his being, every fiber was telescoped into itself with irresistible power, as though two worlds, rushing through space, had collided and caught his body between them'.[116] While Rames does not leave Earth, the language of 'space' and the 'telescope' paints his journey as one on a cosmic scale.

The metaphorical rebirth of a strapping, young, ancient Egyptian man is made explicit in Rames's 'com[ing] into the world as a babe, naked', paying (somewhat unusual) tribute to the young men who lost their lives in the First World War.[117] Lizzie Glithero-West has attributed a resurgence of interest in Egyptian revival jewellery in the 1920s to the widespread loss of life the decade prior, positing that scarabs and lotus flowers suggestive of rebirth offered particularly hopeful symbolism to the recently bereaved.[118] In a mirror image of this, drinking an alchemical concoction from the lotus cup, Rames emerges from the ground as if revived, going on to serve in the conflict.

The invasion of the Assyrians in the portion of the novel set in ancient Egypt is, in fact, shown to have a modern echo in the events of 1914; war is a consistent thread that runs directly between these two times, further emphasised in the novel's depiction of a kind of hereditary reincarnation whereby the same souls materialise throughout a bloodline. In fact, Rames is shown to travel through time by two means in *The Bridge of Time*: the first is executed through ancient Egyptian scientific knowledge, the second being his soul's linear travel through the ages via the more mystical process of reincarnation. That these two routes to the future are never reconciled is typical of the comingling of ideas of ancient Egyptian magical power and scientific might: one is impossible to divorce from the other.

Reading the sphinx

A particular presence rematerialises throughout the fictions considered here. In those that imagine lost worlds, where remnants of ancient Egyptian civilisation can be found underground (as in Haggard's *She*) or relocated to the Earth's poles (as in Verne's *Le Sphinx des glaces*), a sphinx lies waiting. In *Edison's Conquest of Mars*, space travel reveals a new archaeological history for the Great Sphinx of Giza, while in Wells's *The Time Machine*, a sphinx, again, heralds the crossing of the boundary into the future. Guardians of the temples where the most accomplished thinkers of the ancient world reached new intellectual heights, the sphinx suggests the reaches of scientific knowledge as much as it evokes the occult secrets of ancient Egypt.

To draw this chapter to a close, I would like to introduce one final example, that brings together most explicitly the esoteric and the scientific, and which offers a more hopeful image of the end of human life on Earth than the bleak picture presented by Wells. A year before the publication of Wells's novella, the French astronomer and author Camille Flammarion, who founded the Société Astronomique de France, published his *La Fin du monde*. In this work, Flammarion imagines the near end of humanity in the distant future. The last remaining humans on Earth – Omega and Eva – traverse the globe, stopping at the ruined base of the Great Pyramid, 'the only remaining monument of the earlier life of humanity'.[119] As in Wells's *Time Machine*, the landscape of the distant future is one marked by ancient Egyptian traces which, due to their survival, themselves become emblematic of futurity. It is here that they are greeted by the spirit of Cheops, a 'glid[ing]', 'self-luminous' 'white shadow'.[120] Cheops reveals to them the theosophically inflected reincarnatory system of the afterlife in which, once their souls have atoned for their past sins, they will move on to live eternally on other planets and their moons: 'Neptune, Ganymede, Rhea, Titan, Saturn, Mars, and other worlds as yet unknown to you'.[121] One is reminded of Alexander Copland's *The Existence of Other Worlds* (1834), 'a quasi-scientific speculation that Purgatory might lie in outer space, which he supported with a pair of mummy poems'.[122] While cosmic pluralism dates back to ancient Greece, entertaining the view that there may be life on other planets remained controversial in the nineteenth century, as the anonymous publication of *Of the Plurality of Worlds: an essay* (1853) by William Whewell (1794–1866) – the polymath who coined the terms 'scientist' and 'physicist' – suggests. By the end of the century, this idea had chimed with those involved in the Magical Revival, hence its re-emergence in Flammarion's work.

Cheops relates that Jupiter is now 'heir to all human achievement' and, 'shining majestically above them', this pharaoh-turned-psychopomp ascends with their souls, bearing them away from Earth and conveying them to their new home.[123] While Egyptian symbolism is therefore common to both Wells's and Flammarion's narratives, the ending of Flammarion's novel is vastly different. Informed as much by esotericism as by his scientific interests, Flammarion – a devoted theosophist and spiritualist, beliefs that he understood to be entirely compatible with contemporaneous science – presents a view of the afterlife that reconciles astronomy's potential for discovering seemingly countless new heavenly bodies with worldviews that imagined life (in some form) as continuing elsewhere.[124]

The novel's epilogue takes as its subject matter the cycle of death and rebirth, as individual stars and their planets die, new galaxies being born of their remnants in never-ending sequence. Underneath

Flammarion's final sentence – 'For there can be neither end nor beginning' – the rest of the page is filled with an image of a scholar pondering a sphinx atop an Egyptian-esque pylon, the novel's concluding symbol of eternity. The sphinx represents several things: the deep time illuminated by geology – the timescales in which we might conceivably imagine the human race coming to a natural end; the vestiges of the past unearthed by archaeology which, in Egypt's case, were often imagined to outlast any of the traces of the nineteenth or twentieth centuries; and the cosmic forces of the universe – the astronomical knowledge of the ancients, the prospect that there is no death, and that each of us might find a new home on another world. The sphinx is the ultimate traveller through time and space, guardian of scientific and esoteric knowledge of the deep past, the *fin-de-siecle* present, and the distant future. More so, and most importantly, the sphinx represents the alchemical points of intersection of such knowledge and stands proud as a symbol of Egypt itself as the locus where we might most readily imagine science and magic to co-exist.

Notes

1. Sety and El Zeini 1981, 71.
2. Deane 2014, 148.
3. Daly 1999, 106, 107. Simon Berington (1680–1755), a Catholic priest, is responsible for one of the first lost-world texts. His *The Memoirs of Sigr Guadentio di Lucca* (1737) imagines an African city populated by people implied to be ancient Egyptian in origin. The city's name in this text – 'Phor' – and its similarity to Haggard's 'Kôr', suggests Berington's precedent as a potential influence on Haggard.
4. See Malley 1997, for *She* as anthropological and archaeological adventure.
5. Montgomery 1902, 3.
6. Montgomery 1902, 25.
7. Orczy 1900, 558; Gange 2006, 1084.
8. Lampen 1899, 14.
9. Gange 2006, 1090, 1096.
10. Huckvale 2016, 81.
11. Donnelly 1882, 2.
12. Donnelly 1882, 361, 362.
13. Verne 1897, 419; Verne 1899, 321.
14. Verne 1897, 431.
15. Verne 1897, facing 432.
16. Tattersdill 2016, 168.
17. Tattersdill 2016, 172.
18. Figuier 1877, facing 64, facing 250, facing 268, facing 434.
19. Figuier 1877, facing 284.
20. Figuier 1877, facing 406.
21. Figuier 1877, facing 458.
22. 'The Comet from the Pyramids, Cairo' 1882, 477.
23. Before Proctor, astronomers including John Herschel (1792–1871) and Charles Piazzi Smyth (1819–1900) had placed significant weight on the Great Pyramid as monument which might embody divine measurements. See Schaffer 1997, 449–50.
24. Poyet's illustration of '*Prêtres de l'ancienne Egypte observant les astres dans la grande Pyramide*' ('Ancient Egyptian priests in the Great Pyramid observing the stars') was published in the

French popular science periodical, *La Nature*, in 1891. A streamlined version of this design would reappear in later astronomical publications, including Proctor's *Old and New Astronomy* (1892), in which it was given the rather less gripping title, 'The interior of the Grand Gallery, showing one fourth of its length; illustrating its astronomical character'; Proctor 1892, 27. This second version was also reproduced in Percival Lowell's 1912 article 'Precession: And the Pyramids', in which it was labelled 'The Grand Gallery. Vertical Section through'; Lowell 1912, 459.

25. Brück 2009, 157. Pogson's election attempt of 1886 was unsuccessful; she would go on to be elected a fellow of the Royal Astronomical Society in 1920.
26. Fayter 1997, 268.
27. Lowell 1906.
28. Weintraub 2020, 97.
29. Lowell 1912, 456.
30. Serviss 1947, 34.
31. Serviss 1947, 143.
32. Serviss 1947, 143.
33. Serviss 1947, 143, 146.
34. Serviss 1947, 143. For the sphinx to conceivably depict a Martian, the Martians must be humanoid; had Serviss been writing a sequel to Wells's *The War of the Worlds*, the Martians as Wells conceived them would not have been physiologically similar enough for this detail to make sense.
35. Serviss 1912, 303.
36. Serviss 1912, 306, 307.
37. Proctor 1883, 258.
38. Jane 1897, 28.
39. Jane 1897, 63.
40. Jane 1895, 96.
41. Walker 2015, 233.
42. Walker 2015, 233.
43. Walker 2015, 233, 234.
44. Bulfin 2011, 419.
45. An English translation of Uhlemann's *Drei Tage in Memphis* ('*Three Days in Memphis*') appeared in 1858.
46. Hellekson 2001, 13. The term 'butterfly effect' derives from Ray Bradbury's (1920–2012) short story 'A Sound of Thunder' (1952), which, like Hale's text, imagines the killing of an animal in the past significantly altering the future.
47. Hale 1895, 3.
48. Hale 1895, 30.
49. Nahin 2014, 37.
50. Ahn 2020, 349.
51. Nesbit 1907, 351.
52. Moser 2012, 81.
53. Nesbit 1907, 268.
54. Munro 1892, 314.
55. Paul 2015, 53.
56. Paul 2015, 52.
57. Foucault 1998, 182.
58. Wells 1895, 107, 108.
59. Wells 1895, 33.
60. Wells 1895, 34.
61. Shackleton 2017, 842.
62. *The Time Machine* was first published in *The New Review*, serialised between January and May 1895.
63. Stover 1996, 2.
64. Thompson 2001, 16; Firchow 2004, 130; Scafella 1981; Beaumont 2006.
65. Debelius 2000, 62.
66. Dobson *Writing the Sphinx* 2020, 105–6.
67. Little is known about Russell, other than that he was from Houston and that he had previously provided illustrations for *The Illustrated American*.

68. Debelius 2000, 61.
69. Debelius 2000, 76.
70. Wells 1895, 41, 49.
71. Wells 1895, 49.
72. Debelius 2000, 78.
73. Haggard 1887, 58.
74. Wells 1895, 87.
75. Wells 1895, 108.
76. Parrinder 1995, 43–4.
77. Crossley 1992, 211.
78. Wells 1895, 109.
79. Wells 1895, 110, 116.
80. Wells 1895, 117.
81. Lowell 1912, 449.
82. Wells 1895, 102.
83. Lowell 1912, 460.
84. Nesbit 1907, 297.
85. Nesbit 1907, 308; Zimmerman 2019, 78.
86. Nesbit 1907, 18, 22, 57, 136. For London as heterotopia, specifically regarding Egyptian presences, see Dobson 2021. Jimmy's first name and surname ('De Something' is all the children can recall of the latter) suggest that he may have been named after the Canadian novelist and academic James De Mille (1833–80), whose narratives also feature adventures in exotic locales. His posthumously published *A Strange Manuscript Found in a Copper Cylinder* (1888) is a lost-world tale recorded on 'some vegetable substance' that 'looks like Egyptian papyrus'; De Mille 1888, 9.
87. Nesbit 1907, 236.
88. Nesbit 1907, 21.
89. Nesbit 1907, 102.
90. Nesbit 1907, 77.
91. Nesbit 1907, 97.
92. Gomme 1898, 111; Nesbit 1907, 238, 243.
93. Ahn 2020, 348.
94. Nesbit 1907, 243.
95. Nesbit 1907, 72.
96. Nesbit 1907, 264, 266–7.
97. Nesbit 1907, 282.
98. Paul 2015, 49.
99. Nesbit 1907, 195.
100. Nesbit 1907, 206.
101. Nesbit 1907, 231.
102. Knoepflmacher 1987, 301–2, 320.
103. Paul 2015, 40, 41.
104. Nesbit 1907, 210.
105. Nesbit 1907, 216. That oricalchum is not mentioned by Donnelly suggests that Nesbit consulted Plato in the original, supported by additional theosophical reading.
106. Nesbit 1907, 230.
107. Nesbit 1907, 214. Atlantean writing is, likewise, first mistaken for ancient Egyptian hieroglyphs in C. J. Cutcliffe Hyne's (1866–1944) *The Lost Continent: The Story of Atlantis* (1899) due to 'the similarity of the inscribed character'; Cutcliffe Hyne 1900, 9, 11.
108. Nesbit 1907, 367.
109. Nesbit 1907, 219.
110. Warner 1919, 61.
111. Corriou 2021, 44.
112. Warner 1919, 65–6.
113. Materer 1995, 95.
114. Warner 1919, 67.
115. Warner 1919, 68.
116. Warner 1919, 332.
117. Warner 1919, 75.

118. Glithero-West 2020.
119. Flammarion 1894, 265. I refer to Flammarion's novel in the English translation by J. B. Walker, due to its better availability.
120. Flammarion 1894, 266.
121. Flammarion 1894, 266.
122. Day 2020, 26.
123. Flammarion 1894, 266, 268.
124. Keshavjee 2013. Flammarion would go on to serve as President of the Society for Psychical Research in 1923.

3
Weird physics: visible light, invisible forces and the electromagnetic spectrum

Electricity, the marvelous force that turned the wheels of this new world and seemed to be the means by which all its wonders were accomplished, could this be the same power the priests had harnessed for their mystic uses? He remembered their foreknowledge of victory or defeat for the Pharaoh's hosts, the instant transmission of messages from one temple to another, the tales of the magic lighting of certain places within the sanctuaries. Had the sages of ancient Kampt understood many of the wonders of this age and kept them secret, so as to strengthen their hold on the people?[1]

When the ancient Egyptian time traveller, Rames, in William Henry Warner's romance novel *The Bridge of Time* (1919) first sees electric lighting, he understands what he witnesses to be 'magic': 'a cluster of transparent balls ... suddenly burst into brilliance as he watched and when he looked closer he saw no flame, only a tiny glowing thread of quivering fire in their centre'.[2] Rames later encounters 'the skeletons of living men' captured 'by the magic of the *X*-ray'.[3] While these technologies at first seem supernatural to Rames, his encounters with the science of 1914 (when the action of the novel takes place) in fact cast light onto the supposed mystical powers of the priests of his own time. As the quotation that opens this chapter reveals, Rames's experiences of the future directly lead him to question the technologies of ancient Egypt, causing him to speculate as to the possibility that the priesthood had not only developed electric lights but also telegraphic communications. Moreover, when he hears of the discoveries of the Polish physicist and chemist Marie Curie that compel 'modern sages … to admit that there may have been something in those laughed-at ideas' involving the transmutation of one metal into another held by the 'old alchemists', he makes the connection between radium's chemical symbol – Ra – and the ancient Egyptian solar god of the same name (from whom Rames's own name is derived).[4] Rames realises that radium is in fact a substance dreamed about by his friend and mentor, the priest Hotep, and so even the scientific discoveries of the modern age had been conceived of or predicted by ancient Egyptian savants. Warner's text, while little known today, revolves around a plot that combines time travel with reincarnation, and which blends the scientific with the magical. Its ideas – about the knowledge and technologies it imagines as available to the ancient Egyptians – are by no means unique, however. As I go on to outline, the attribution of knowledge of electricity and its applications to the ancient Egyptians is very much a nineteenth-century concept. With the discovery of radioactivity and X-rays in the late nineteenth century, and the identification of new elements in the early twentieth century, an equivalent process took place, whereby this knowledge was imagined at the fingertips of the ancients.

The purpose of this chapter is twofold. I seek first to establish the myriad connections between ancient Egypt, electricity and the electromagnetic spectrum across the nineteenth century, emphasising how this ancient civilisation was imagined in tandem with the imagery and language intrinsic to scientific modernity. I probe works that use ancient Egypt as an imaginative springboard for an array of genre fiction that conveys the 'hidden wisdom' of ancient Egypt as simultaneously scientific and magical, from satire to science fiction, the Gothic to the detective novel: across these works, ancient Egypt and the most modern scientific discoveries pertaining to the electromagnetic spectrum sit comfortably alongside one another. Through engagements with art, literature and scientific publications, I show that this relationship was far from uncommon; from media dating to before Victoria's reign and continuing into the years after her death, ancient Egypt and electricity (and, later, X-rays and radiation) are brought into close alignment. These associations have various ends, put to uses that range from suggesting the magical potential of modern scientific discoveries to implying the scientific and magical supremacy of ancient Egyptian civilisation, an idea that dovetails rather neatly with *fin-de-siècle* fears of Western cultural decline. These sources speak to an appetite for imaginative narratives of the Egyptian past that explicitly bring this distant time and place into a close alignment with the present, suggestive of a desire to understand a civilisation that felt simultaneously familiar yet alien.[5] We might read in such instances a broader trend that saw the modern defined by its relationship to antiquity and *vice versa* – as I have suggested elsewhere, often a means to claiming the modern West's place as the rightful 'inheritors' of ancient Egypt's legacy, serving to strengthen Occidental imperial claims on Egypt and its antiquities.[6] Equally, though, several of these narratives imagine the modern West to occupy a rather more shaky position, in which ancient Egyptian forces refuse to be dominated or outdone, ultimately underlining ancient Egyptian supremacy.

The second claim that I make in this chapter relates to an innovative textual strand epitomised in works by Bram Stoker and H. Rider Haggard, which hammered home ancient Egyptian scientific advancement and (often) superiority. Growing out of an unshakeable association between ancient Egypt and electricity in the nineteenth century (through the illumination of monuments and artefacts, a fashion for Egyptianate lighting designs, and a fictional trend that saw mummies revived by electrical stimulation – examples central to this chapter), Stoker and Haggard both imagine worlds in which previously unknown parts of the electromagnetic spectrum are exploited by ancient Egyptians. These works – Haggard's *Ayesha: the return of She* (1904–5) and 'Smith and the Pharaohs' (1912–13), and Stoker's *The Jewel of Seven Stars* (1903; 1912) – differ from the corpus that forms the foundation of this chapter in their explicit alignment of alchemy with cutting-edge science: by the late nineteenth century, investigations into X-rays and radioactivity and the eerie glowing effects that such experiments produced in laboratories were consistently described in alchemical terms. The two are so inextricably linked, in fact, that across the final texts to which this chapter turns, we witness a peculiar exchange between the concepts of modern scientist and ancient god.

Ultimately, I suggest that the couching of modern scientific discoveries and exciting physical effects in magical terms led to their employment by popular authors for the conception or visualisation of ancient Egyptian supernaturalism. Thus, was see novel electrical phenomena, X-rays and radioactivity inserted into Egyptian scenarios. This is, more often than not, specific to Egypt. Fred Nadis records that towards the end of the nineteenth century 'imagining medieval times, exotic locales, or golden pasts' provided 'escapes from [technological] modernity'; when antiquity was evoked in relation to physical discoveries, it was in order 'to remind readers of how different the "modern" world was from the "ancient" world'.[7] Yet, as this chapter demonstrates, representations of Egypt did not always harmonise with these views of antiquity as scientifically or technologically distant. While narratives of mummy reanimation via electrical means had their roots in the early decades of the nineteenth century – Jane Webb's futuristic triple-decker *The Mummy!: a tale of the twenty-second century* (1827) features the galvanic resuscitation of the Egyptian pharaoh Cheops, heavily influenced by Mary Shelley's (1797–1851) *Frankenstein* (1818) – it was at the *fin de siècle* that ancient Egyptian characters seized electricity for themselves, usurping the Western scientist and asserting their own superior intellectual power. In a movement away from the reassuring Darwinian notion of progress over time, it was the fiction of the late Victorian era that saw modern electrical phenomena mastered by ancient hands: it was for modern science to rediscover these advanced ancient techniques. Resultantly, perceptions of *fin-de-siècle* degeneration are challenged; rather than singling out the criminal, the vampire, the dandy, the New Woman or the foreigner as emblematic of cultural decline, these narratives reveal a broader notion of societal degeneration that does not typecast or scapegoat a particular demographic. As Virginia Zimmerman states, '[f]ears of degeneration arose out of racist anxieties about contamination from already degenerate people (at home and abroad)'.[8] Yet the narratives I address, particularly those towards the end of the chapter, reveal a counterpoint to this fear that degeneration might occur or, indeed, had already occurred. They imagine that intellectual degeneration on a societal level had already transpired since a cultural and intellectual peak in antiquity, leaving modern science endeavouring to duplicate the technologies of the past, and the most ancient of civilisations, casting representatives of a foreign time and place as paragons of enlightenment. Most significantly of all, this belief was not confined to the pages of fiction – we have already seen some of the fictional forms in which such a scenario is presented in the introduction to this book, including works by Edgar Allan Poe, Grant Allen and Arthur Conan Doyle – but was entertained by some of the great scientific minds, and most influential cultural actors, of the age.

In the latter half of the nineteenth century, suggestions were indeed made, with varying degrees of sincerity, that the ancient Egyptians had not only known of electricity but had succeeded in harnessing its power. The eminent British astronomer Norman Lockyer (1836–1920) wrote about his experiences examining ancient Egyptian sites in *The Dawn of Astronomy: a study of the temple-worship and mythology of the ancient Egyptians* (1894). Looking for evidence that ancient Egyptian labourers had worked by torchlight, he notes that 'in all freshly-opened tombs there are no traces whatever of any kind of combustion having taken place, even in the inner-most recesses'.[9] Unable to explain the lack of evidence of more elementary light sources, Lockyer recounts how he and his companion joked of 'the possibility that the electric light was known to the ancient Egyptians', noting that the delicate paintwork on the walls of the tombs could not have been completed using natural light reflected from systems of mirrors, as others had previously proposed.[10]

The Russian occultist Helena Blavatsky, matriarch of the Theosophical Society, entertained the belief more seriously, writing of the accomplishments of ancient civilisations in her first major work *Isis Unveiled* (1877). Blavatsky claims that each new modern scientific revelation is overshadowed by the inevitable 'possibility, if not certainty, that the alleged discovery was not totally unknown to the ancients'.[11] The specific example she gives laments that abundant 'proofs to the contrary' had not altered the erroneous view that in ancient Egypt electricity was undiscovered and unharnessed.[12] Other notable figures who credited ancient civilisations with knowledge of electricity include the bestselling novelist Marie Corelli. Though outwardly contemptuous of modern occultism (or so she avowed), Corelli's views as to the mastery of electricity in antiquity echo Blavatsky's. '[T]he "Masters of the Stars" ... in Memphis', she claimed, in her non-fictional work *Free Opinions, Freely Expressed* (1905), used 'the electric light, the telephone, the phonograph, and many other modern conveniences' to produce '"miraculous" effects'; knowledge of electrical forces, she emphasised, was readily available to the ancients, and was only just being rediscovered by modern science.[13] Electricity, the 'epitome of the scientific and technological revolution during her lifetime', proved to be an effective symbol of the harmony between the spiritual and the scientific in her writing and her personal beliefs.[14] Corelli united a combination of concepts from Christian Science, spiritualism and Rosicrucianism that itself drew upon medieval alchemical traditions and ancient Egyptian theology, creating her own unique belief system that exalted electricity's occult possibilities; 'God', the Eastern magician Heliobas claims in Corelli's first novel, *A Romance of Two Worlds* (1886), 'is a Shape of pure electric Radiance'.[15]

The role that fiction played in encouraging this cultural association is key. In the previous chapter, we encountered Edward Bulwer-Lytton's Vril-ya in *The Coming Race* (1871), with their monumental architecture featuring 'huge heavy Egyptian-like columns', 'lighted from within' by a kind of energy termed 'Vril'.[16] Vril is evidently meant to suggest electricity: Bulwer-Lytton's narrator mentions several times experiencing this power source as akin to the sensation of an electric shock, compares its strength to lightning, and likens its healing powers to contemporaneous electrical medical therapies.[17] In their written language, the Vril-ya denote 'the Supreme Being' with 'the hieroglyphic of a pyramid'; Vril,

124   VICTORIAN ALCHEMY

meanwhile, is denoted by '[t]he letter V, symbolical of the inverted pyramid'.[18] 'V', of course, has its own electrical meaning, being an abbreviation of 'volt', the unit of electrical resistance, named as such in 1861 in recognition of the work of the Italian physicist Alessandro Volta (1745–1827). It requires just a small imaginative leap from the electrically adept fictional race of Bulwer-Lytton's text to envision ancient Egyptians wielding electrical power for themselves and, indeed, such a leap appears to have been made by some of the aforementioned personages of the latter half of the nineteenth century. Blavatsky has been found to have derived much of her material from the fiction of Bulwer-Lytton, through which he channelled information he had gleaned from various esoteric traditions.[19] Corelli's own familiarity with his *œuvre* is suggested in the plentiful contemporaneous reviews of her work that compared the two authors; one scathing review declared her fictional output 'erotic mysticism, clad in Lord Lytton's most gorgeous and falsely oracular colours'.[20]

With various luminaries of contemporary science and occultism suggesting, however teasingly, that ancient Egypt had access to electricity, the emergence and continuation of this theme in literature might be altogether expected, aligning antiquity with cutting-edge developments in physics. Novels such as Bram Stoker's *The Jewel of Seven Stars* see ancient Egyptians making use of electrical devices for their own purposes. In Stoker's novel, as we shall see, magnetism, electricity and radiation all contribute to a complex science developed by Queen Tera, who intends to use it to facilitate her own resurrection in the modern world. H. Rider Haggard, too, in his 'Smith and the Pharaohs', imbues his short story with concrete references to the application of X-rays to the mummified bodies of the ancient Egyptian dead, and his metaphorical reattribution of such power to the ancient Egyptians themselves further upsets notions of Western scientific superiority. In his *Ayesha*, similarly, the extreme forces that confer life or death controlled by the titular character are understood in terms of radioactivity and X-rays, positing Ayesha as both scientific pioneer and gifted alchemist. Stoker's and Haggard's allusions to groundbreaking research into radiation go far beyond any acknowledgements of such developments in the works of their contemporaries, and for this reason warrant a more detailed analysis later in this chapter. In fact, their raising aloft of ancient Egyptian scientific and magical power as supreme establishes, across their works, a rendering of the modern scientist as ancient god, and *vice versa*. With this, crucially, comes the inference that modern science is only just 'catching up' with a superior past, challenging narratives of linear progress, and reflecting *fin-de-siècle* fears of degeneration back onto their readers.

Egypt, illumination and electricity

The electric light played a crucial role in Britain's and France's imperial designs on modern Egypt. To illuminate Egypt was to dominate it: arc lights were used so that ships could navigate the Suez Canal by night, revolutionising international trade and facilitating increasing European colonisation of Africa. Bright arc lights had clear military applications: electricity lit up spaces that European powers sought to colonise. When the British invaded Egypt in 1882, for instance, electric lights were employed before the bombardment of Alexandria. We also see such devices used in imperialist propaganda of the late nineteenth century. In a trading card for Woodhouse and Rawson, to take one example, an electricity and engineering company based in London, produced in the early 1890s by the engraver Arthur Bartram Snell (1861–1942), the caption reads 'What is wanted in Darkest Africa is the Electric Light'.[21] The majority of the trading card is taken up with an image of a jungle scene, in which white European explorers are illuminated by a large hanging bulb; several Africans consigned to the peripheries look on, one shielding his eyes from the dazzling electric glare. The trading card's message is clear: electricity is emblematic of progress and civilisation, and it is this that white explorers are tasked with bringing to the depths of 'darkest Africa' and its 'unenlightened' inhabitants. That the trading card also sports a portrait of the Welsh-American explorer Henry Morton Stanley (1841–1904), famous after the Emin Pasha Relief Expedition (1886–9), cements its imperialistic thrust: Stanley's search for the source of the Nile on behalf of Belgium's King Leopold II (1835–1909) led directly to the Belgian occupation of the Congo. Egypt is present in this image, albeit in small vignettes tucked away in the top right corner. In the largest, a man sits astride a camel in front of a couple of pyramids. The smaller image is altogether more intriguing. A sphinx – presumably the Great Sphinx of Giza – is illuminated by an electric light that sits atop its headdress. Its facial expression is serene and haughty. On the one hand, it constitutes an example of imagery of the electric light specifically colliding with ancient Egyptian iconography – the focus of the first section of this chapter – in which symbols of ancient Egypt are aligned with electricity's power. On the other, the trading card's celebration of white imperial forces colours this vignette to suggest European domination of this particular monument as much as of the indigenous people in the jungle scene.

I open this section with this example to ascertain something of the heterodox imperialist thinking of the era, and as a useful starting place by which we might see various other cultural forms as working – to a greater or lesser degree – in contrast. In this section I take stock of the ways in which ancient Egyptian artefacts, spaces made up to look Egyptian, and even homewares drawing upon an Egyptian aesthetic, featured a more ambiguous collision between ancient Egypt and illumination as symbolic of technological modernity. In several of these examples, the electric light is not used as a point of contrast to suggest the 'savageness' of ancient Egypt, but instead – to use an appropriate metaphor – shines a new light on Egypt, and in the case of the statues and lamps to which I turn towards the end of this section, puts this light directly into ancient Egyptian hands. As this chapter progresses, we will see that this visual seizure of electrical power by ancient Egyptians infiltrates late nineteenth-century literature. The close alignment between ancient Egypt and electricity that emerged over the course of the nineteenth century might seem at first an unlikely one, but its prevalence – as detailed in this section and the next – may well have paved the way for understandings of ancient Egypt as an electrically advanced society in occultist and countercultural thought, and cemented the idea of modern scientific developments as being indivisible from alchemy and antiquity.

As noted in this book's introduction and suggested by the various Egyptian-themed entertainments covered its first chapter, throughout the nineteenth century, cities increasingly harboured fantasy spaces in which both accurate reconstructions and imaginative retellings of ancient Egypt could be engaged with and experienced, encouraged by technological developments that produced striking optical effects. It was also in these metropolises where electricity was well and truly making its mark. The West End, as London's central recreational hub, was a priority when it came to electrical embellishment. Its brightly lit entertainment venues dominated a landscape that facilitated night-time leisure like never before, and this dramatic electric light that had been used in theatres since the late 1840s appeared to be spilling out into the streets.[22] Thomas Edison's electric light bulbs, illuminated by carbon filaments, which had been invented in 1879, were displayed at the Paris Electricity Exposition in 1881.[23] The next year saw the first central electricity generation stations in London and New York, which were in turn replaced by more convenient power stations in the coming decades.[24] In London, major public buildings where gas lighting had been considered too dangerous – such as the British Museum – were being artificially illuminated for the first time. Meanwhile, in California, San José boasted an 'electric tower' in the shape of 'a four-sided pyramid' that cast a glow on the streets like 'the light of the moon on a very clear night'.[25] Scientists exploited new techniques to make electricity visible. Instead of being confined to the laboratory, electricity was firmly established as a spectacular crowd-pleaser in lecture halls. Electric light flooded all manner of recreational spaces.

This new variety of light revolutionised the methods by which ancient Egyptian relics and simulacra could be viewed and examined. If ancient Egypt was one of a variety of geographically and temporally exotic metropolitan fantasies, encouraged by the glitziness of spaces such as the West End, then the electric lustre that bathed such scenes must have permeated and disrupted this imaginary Egypt. As I detail in this section, the technological opulence of modernity and the antiquated glamour of a bygone era were fused in such spaces, which ranged from outdoor settings to museums, hotels to the home.

In Britain, France, the United States, and in Egypt itself, pioneering electric lighting effects were often demonstrated in spaces typified by their ancient Egyptian presences. For Britain and France, this was likely as a result of these spaces' perceived grandeur; open public spaces provided both the room required for large-scale demonstrations in the development of lighting technologies and, also, incidentally, were often the kinds of locale where Egyptian obelisks – typically erected as symbols of imperial might – were installed. In Paris in 1844, for instance, the French physicist Léon Foucault (1819–66) demonstrated a carbon arc lamp in Paris's Place de la Concorde. In an engraving depicting this event (figure 3.1), an intense beam of electric light can be seen emerging from the apparatus, falling at the base of the Luxor Obelisk. The obelisk, rather than the lamp itself (noteworthy for its obscurity in the surrounding darkness and its presumed positioning almost entirely outside of the illustration), is the focal point of the image, an imposing murky shape that looms in both the dark and illuminated sections of the picture, its face angled towards the lamp picked out in a streak of brilliant white. The ancient and the ultra-modern square up to each other in a composition in which they occupy opposing sides of the image. And yet, there is a coherence to the engraving, in which the angular shape of the Luxor Obelisk is echoed in that of the beam of light from the lamp. We might read in this scene the interrogation of an ancient Egyptian presence under the harsh arc lamp, or else we might see a kind of balance, in which two symbols of light – the obelisk representing the petrified solar ray, the light of the arc lamp itself often likened to the power of the sun – are united. `

In London, too, we witness the cultural collision of antiquity and technological modernity. The ancient Egyptian obelisk known as Cleopatra's Needle was erected on the Victoria Embankment in 1878. The Embankment proved an ambiguous location for the Needle, whose

Figure 3.1 'Première expérience publique d'eclairage par l'électricité sur la place de la Concorde faite par Deleuil et Léon Foucault (en décembre 1844)', in Louis Figuier, *Les Nouvelles Conquêtes de la Science*, vol. 1: *L'Électricité* (Paris: Librairie Illustrée, 1884), p. 9. Author's own.

situation was, for many years, the subject of extended debate. On its installation, the Needle was paradoxically both the oldest and newest monument in London (as the Luxor Obelisk had been in Paris when it was transported to the city earlier in the century). Having been completed eight years before the Needle's arrival, the Victoria Embankment provided the city with a modern sewerage system and, although gas lighting was restored in 1884 for financial reasons, within three months after the obelisk's installation it had become the first British street to feature permanent electric lighting. The sheet music of the composer Alphonse Cary's (1848–1922) 'The Electric Polka' (c.1879) features on its colour-printed cover a devil shining an electric light down on the Embankment, the luminous orb appearing directly above the Needle and casting a wide beam of brightness onto the scene below. The Embankment is itself studded with smaller versions of the devil's light in the lamps that line the street. The devil recalls the folkloric Lucifer, the 'light-bringer', aligned with the planet Venus, the morning star, and son of Aurora, the Greek goddess of the dawn; Lucifer's name was subsequently co-opted as a Christian epithet for Satan. The devil in this image thus brings with it connotations of antiquity but also of the Christian tempter, parading electricity's might, associations between electricity and occult sciences stretching back at least to the Renaissance.[26] The Needle was, therefore, a symbol of supreme antiquity in an area of London closely associated with cutting-edge modernity, but also – in sources such as Cary's printed image – one in which it is conceived of as magical in this electrically lit space.

Images of obelisks standing stark in otherwise electrically lit cityscapes proliferated. As electric lighting transformed outdoor spaces, obelisks (both genuine ancient Egyptian monuments and later reproductions) took on a more sinister appearance. Surrounded by bright electric streetlights or advertisements, they loom ominously as bold, dark reminders of the ancient world's endurance in an ever-changing landscape. To take one more example from the visual culture of the end of the long nineteenth century, the American journalist and urban planning theorist Charles Mulford Robinson (1869–1917) lamented 'the evil of black smoke and glaring advertisements' of British and North American cities in an article in *Harper's Magazine* of 1902, which featured obelisks in two of the article's eight illustrations.[27] In one of these images produced by the American illustrator Henry Sumner Watson (1868–1933), a rendering of one of the two obelisks that then stood at the centre of Ludgate Circus, the 'otherness' of the obelisk in the modern city is emphasised by its unparalleled darkness when set against the 'glaring advertisements' bemoaned by Robinson. The obelisk occupies the image's central space, severe and static, surrounded by the shimmering lights of advertisements that promote the ephemeral: 'potpie', 'American meals' and 'biscuits'. The obelisk is even partially obscured by the glow of the powerful electric light behind it, and its reflection in the fallen rain warps and mixes with those of the lights, the ancient merging with the modern.[28]

While in illustration, obelisks are usually conspicuous because of their lack of electrical illumination in otherwise brightly lit settings, the obelisk itself was symbolically connected to light. Almost all commemorating ancient Egypt's solar gods, obelisks were often topped with pyramid-shaped capstones called pyramidions, coated either in gold or the gold-silver alloy electrum.[29] Before the sun rose over the horizon, the polished metal of the pyramidion would reflect its rays, creating the appearance of a light source at the top of the obelisk. That ancient Egyptian obelisks and pyramids were often topped with materials that are effective at conducting electricity and, in the case of electrum, evoking linguistic connections to electricity, appears to have been a coincidence; gold and electrum seem to have been selected exclusively for their aesthetic qualities. Nevertheless, when nineteenth- and twentieth-century obelisks duplicated this feature, electrical conductivity was often taken into account when materials were selected for the tops of obelisks. The Washington Monument, a modern obelisk completed in 1884, was fashioned in the ancient Egyptian style including the metallic pyramidion at the apex. Rather than gold or electrum, the Washington Monument's pyramidion was fashioned from a distinctly modern metal, aluminium – an element only discovered earlier that century and whose potential functions were ill understood for some time – so cutting-edge that many Americans had not heard of it prior to the obelisk's completion.[30] The aluminium pyramidion served a dual function: first, to emulate the ancient Egyptian style; and, second, to act as a lightning rod in order to protect the obelisk from damage. Lightning struck the pyramidion just over six months later, and modifications had to be made; further lightning strikes did less damage but their regularity secured an association between the obelisk and the lightning rod that paralleled the popular literary device of the reanimation of mummies via the power of electricity, to which we shall later turn.[31]

On a larger scale, electric lighting enabled different – and later – encounters with cities' Egyptian traces. In 1879 the British Museum Library was electrically lit for the first time, making it one of the first buildings in London to install electricity. The Reading Room was described in *The Times* as being 'suddenly illumined as by a magic ray of sunshine'.[32] The likening of the light to the magical suggests optical trickery, stage effects and self-conscious drama. The readers' reaction to the illumination further emphasises the theatricality of the moment and the pervasive idea that electricity equalled spectacle; the light was met with 'a murmur of applause'.[33] With the Reading Room's reputation for attracting those with occult tastes in literature, from spiritualists to theosophists and members of the Golden Dawn, the 'magic ray of sunshine' becomes something more, a kind of literal enlightenment.[34]

A decade later, the Egyptian Sculpture Gallery – notorious for being particularly gloomy – was newly lit.[35] An engraving from the *Illustrated London News* depicts a private evening viewing (figure 3.2). A reporter for *Nature* makes clear the delicate balance that was struck between lighting the Museum's artefacts adequately and not overwhelming the eye: 'The light from glow lamps is more agreeable to the eyes than the more powerful light of arc illuminants; but these have been regulated with the utmost care.'[36] In the *Illustrated London News* image the electric light,

Figure 3.2 'Electric Lighting of the British Museum', *Illustrated London News*, 8 February 1890, p. 164. Courtesy of the Cadbury Research Library: Special Collections, University of Birmingham, f AP 4.I5.

more intense than the natural light previously relied upon to illuminate the museum's galleries, creates an increased contrast between light and dark, casting heavier shadows across the colossal artefacts, while causing the 'faces' of the sculptures to appear bathed in light. With the crowd contemplating the dramatically lit spectacle, the museum experience appears to shift sharply towards the theatrical. Before their electrical illumination, the 'dark color and block-like quality' of colossal Egyptian statues made them difficult to accommodate within the museum space, 'making them appear awkward and uneasy', at times even 'difficult to see properly'. This, as Stephanie Moser points out, served the Museum's purpose in suggesting the cultural superiority of Greece and Rome.[37] That the illustrator chose to focus on the Egyptian statuary as the focal point of the image, rather than Greek or Roman examples, suggests a significant shift towards the end of the century, whereby Museum visitors saw the Egyptian artefacts anew, no longer lesser than their Classical counterparts; the colossi foregrounded in the illustration meet the electric light as a symbol of technological advancement unflinchingly eye to eye.

The installation of electric lighting in the British Museum's galleries as well as the library marks a transition from illuminated encounters with scholarly material to those with the remnants of an ancient civilisation itself, and the opening up of the Museum at night to a broader public. The electric light, inherently theatrical and simultaneously symbolic of magical power and scientific advancement, proved an appropriate medium via which to view the relics of a civilisation that was renowned for its employment of the spectacular in order to glorify the divine. With new lighting methods in place, some parts of the museum were being kept open as late as 10 o'clock in the evening in the 1890s, transforming it from a daytime to a twilight venue and putting it in direct competition with London's theatres.[38]

Across the Atlantic, electric lighting was transforming engagements with Egyptianised spaces, too. The Western Electric Company's exhibit at the World's Columbian Exposition of 1893 included a mock Egyptian temple, featuring 'between 1,100 and 1,200 incandescent lamps … 700 of which [were] constantly burning'.[39] The first issue of *Electrical Industries* – the 'Weekly World's Fair Supplement' 'devoted to the electrical and allied interests of the World's Fair, its visitors and exhibitors' – showcased a view of the Western Electric Company's Egyptian temple on the front page, from which some delightfully creative details can be gleaned. The temple was created in a traditional pylon shape, its top edged with electric lamps, integrated into what appear to be stylistic sprays of lotus flowers. There is a degree of historical sensitivity here: the lotus flower opening its petals in daylight and closing them at night makes it a fitting solar symbol. As described in a contemporary guidebook, also gracing the outside of the temple were 'Egyptian figures and groups associated with electricity', including 'a group of Egyptian maidens, of the time of Rameses the Second, operating a telephone board, and another group of men of the same period laying telegraph lines'.[40] The anonymous author of the article in *Electrical Industries* reporting on the spectacle notes that 'the interior and exterior frescoing of the temple show' '[t]he lineman and wireman … at work'.[41] Elsewhere, several ancient Egyptian men appear to be working enormous dynamos; another Egyptian man is illuminated by an electric light bulb, bathed in a strong beam of light emerging from above him. 'The conceit' was, according to the guidebook, 'very popular'.[42] The article in *Electric Industries*, too, recorded that '[a]mong the large number of exhibits in the Electricity building none has attracted more attention from all classes of visitors than that of the Western Electric Company'.[43]

WEIRD PHYSICS 133

Inside the temple, the effect was even more dramatic. A couple of photographs held at Chicago History Museum show different views of the temple's interior (figure 3.3).[44] In this darkened space the lights appear all the more striking. Doorways are decorated with pylon-shaped surrounds topped with illuminated winged solar discs, and set into the temple walls are alcoves 'for the display of telegraph, testing, and other small instruments and brass work'.[45] Crowded together

Figure 3.3 W. H. Gardiner, photograph depicting the interior of the Western Electric Company's Egyptian temple exhibit at the World's Columbian Exposition, 1893. Chicago History Museum, ICHi-061755.

behind clear glass, these instruments produce a similar effect to quantities of small antiquities grouped in museum display cases.[46] The photographs capture imposing columns 'of heavy green glass illuminated by incandescent lamps placed within them', topped with elaborate capitals.[47] While the photographs only show these details in greyscale, sources record that the lights within the temple are all 'concealed behind translucent glass of many colors'; the intricate designs (which include more lotus motifs) suggest that the effect might have been akin to stained glass windows.[48]

The writer of the *Electrical Industries* article states that '[t]he combination of the ancient figures with the various applications of electricity, the most modern force, is certainly unique'.[49] This is surely true in the context of the world's fairs. In fact, the Western Electric Company's exhibit was not the only Egyptian temple constructed in Chicago at the World's Columbian Exposition that year. As was the case with previous world's fairs, a simulacrum of an Orientalist Cairene street had been constructed; 'the world's fairs' were intended to be, among other things, '"living" museums' whereby 'the visitor was meant to have an interactive experience that created the illusion that [they] had in some sense actually been transported to the culture in question'.[50] At the World's Columbian Exposition, as in events in previous years, representations of modern Egyptian life were juxtaposed with exhibits that served to enforce a contrast between Egypt's present and ancient civilisations. The Cairene street was home not only to various stalls, structures made out to look like mosques, the celebrated dancer 'Little Egypt', a conjuror, and camels and donkeys that visitors could ride, but also a replica of part of the Temple of Luxor that housed artificial mummies (so convincingly executed that some visitors assumed that they were real).[51] That Cairo and Luxor are separated by around 300 miles was of no importance, 'highlights' of Egyptian culture cherry-picked and condensed into a space that presented the hustle and bustle of modern Egypt sitting side-by-side with remnants of its ancient civilisation. As Eric Davis points out, in the case of Egypt, the country's 'glories were portrayed as relics of the past'.[52] That entry to the temple required an additional admission fee signified in and of itself the greater 'value' of what lay within compared to the immersive take on modern Egyptian life available outside. The World's Columbian Exposition of 1893 thus presented two Egyptian temples to its visitors: one that sought to represent a composite ancient Egypt whose constituent parts were, to greater or lesser extents, rooted in Egypt as it had actually existed, and one a more starkly alternative Egypt, with its multicoloured lights and array of electric devices. Encountering both must only have served to heighten the experience – and difference – of the other.

The juxtaposition of the ancient and the modern was palpable, too, in Egypt itself. Even in places that might otherwise look like 'a land unexplored', the British novelist Amelia B. Edwards (1831–92) observed in her landmark travelogue *A Thousand Miles up the Nile* (1877), one could discern 'the telegraphic wires stalking, ghost-like, across the desert'.[53] Cairo was, naturally, Egypt's most technologically advanced hub, its grand hotels capitalising on European and North American tourists' appetite for the glamour of antiquity and their expectations to be met with the most modern conveniences. Shepheard's Hotel in Cairo, for instance, was decorated in a style that mimicked restored ancient Egyptian tombs and temples, and was furnished with all of the gadgets associated with the luxury hotel experience, including electric lifts, lights and bells.[54] We have already encountered Shepheard's as referred to in Marie Corelli's *Ziska* (1897) in this book's first chapter, in which Corelli lists its modern amenities, including a darkroom for photography enthusiasts; beyond Corelli, Shepheard's, as Cairo's oldest and best-known accommodation, with its technological luxuries cloaked in pharaonic splendour, is often invoked in literature of the late nineteenth and early twentieth centuries as a space in which the real world and the fantastical blur.[55] Although the trappings of modernity suffused this space, it was disguised as a pharaonic fantasy, its entrance hall boasting lotus columns painted in vivid colours. The combination of ancient style – whose popularity among Westerners, ironically, also made it decidedly modern – and up-to-date functionality resulted in the hotel being described as 'Eighteenth Dynasty Edwardian' after the turn of the century.[56] As Britain's military presence in Egypt grew, Cairo became increasingly Westernised, and so the popular pharaonic style became more widely used. This style fused with cosmopolitan, European elements, such as public gardens, theatres, boulevards, museums and an opera house, creating a curious landscape where what looked to be ancient at first glance often turned out to be the most new.[57] The French novelist Pierre Loti (1850–1923) complained in *L'Égypte* (1909) of 'the blinding glare of the electric light' and the 'monstrous hotels [that] parade the sham splendour of their painted facades … a medley of all styles, rockwork, Roman, Gothic, New Art, Pharaonic'.[58]

Of particular interest for the purposes of this chapter is 'a pair of life-size bronze statues of bare-breasted women in pharaonic headdress' that stood in the hotel's entrance hall, at the bottom of the staircase (figure 3.4).[59] In a magic-lantern slide that reproduces this view, both statues hold aloft an electric light made to look like the flame of a

136   VICTORIAN ALCHEMY

Figure 3.4 T. H. McAllister, Lantern slide 'View 082: Egypt – Shepherd's [sic] Hotel, the Hall, Cairo' [n. d.], lantern slide 3.25 in × 4 in, Brooklyn Museum, New York.

torch, a prime example of the hotel's cutting-edge modern technological installations decked out to represent antiquity. That these twin pharaohs are light bearers suggests an association between enlightenment and ancient Egyptian civilisation, enlightenment having connotations ranging from the occult to the scientific. Their position flanking the staircase creates a sense of aesthetic grandeur whilst also extending this metaphor for the hotel guest: as one penetrates deeper into this temple-like space, granted entrance by the light bearers, one literally ascends into an atrium that, as the lantern slide reveals, appears flooded with natural light.

Similar lamps were installed outside Dublin's Shelbourne Hotel in 1867. Having been designed by the French sculptor Mathurin Moreau (1822–1912), advertised in the 1850s and subsequently mass produced, his 'Candélabre Égyptienne' is often accompanied by a 'Candélabre Négresse', representatives of North-East Africa and Sub-Saharan Africa respectively. While these torchbearers would have originally held aloft a gas flame, eventually the light sources were replaced with electrical mechanisms. Indeed, before the widespread introduction of electric light, gas light (or similar) was attributed to ancient Egyptians in imaginative narratives such as Grant Allen's burlesque, 'My New Year's Eve Among the Mummies' (1878), in which 'brilliant gas-lamps' illuminate the interior of a pyramid, or indeed in Bulwer-Lytton's *The Coming Race* where the Vril-ya's subterranean city with its Egyptianate features is lit by 'what seemed artificial gas-lamps placed at regular intervals'.[60] As gas gave way to electric lighting, so too did the lighting methods attributed to ancient Egyptians (or ancient Egyptian-esque civilisations) in speculative fiction evolve from one to the other.

There are several places where Moreau's 'Candélabre Égyptienne' can still be seen, besides the Shelbourne Hotel: in France, in the entrance to the town hall in Remiremont, and at one corner of the Place Louis Comte in Saint-Étienne (in the latter case, the ancient Egyptian light bearer is accompanied by a statue of a sphinx in a pharaonic headdress); examples can be found elsewhere in Europe in the Jardins do Palácio de Cristal in Porto, Portugal. In North America, a 'Candélabre Égyptienne' and a 'Candélabre Négresse' done out in gold flank the mausoleum of the architect Temple Hoyne Buell (1895–1990) in Denver, Colorado, in a rare instance of their incorporation into a modern design. The torch-bearers also seem to have been especially popular in South American mansions of the nineteenth century: they can be found in Chile's capital, Santiago, as well as at the Palacio la Alhambra and in the garden of the Museu do Estado do Pernambuco in Brazil.

From the 1860s to the 1890s, Britain's Coalbrookdale Company produced statues holding aloft lamps to represent 'Europe', 'America', 'Asia' and 'Africa'. 'Africa' is an ancient Egyptian woman, believed to have been designed by John Bell (1818–96). Full-size and miniature versions of this design were available, the latter being more suited to domestic spaces. Other nineteenth-century designs of ancient Egyptian-themed lamps produced for the home show a child (again, in pharaonic headdress) holding aloft the light, while further specimens incorporated obelisks (one example made in Manchester was directly inspired by Cleopatra's Needle, replicating its hieroglyphic inscriptions).[61] By 1923 the American inventor Louis Vincent Aronson (1869–1940) had brought out an electric light for the home whose electric bulb rested atop a hinged Egyptian sarcophagus. Opening the sarcophagus would reveal a nude ancient Egyptian woman luminous with gold, the electric light reflecting off her metallic body (contrasted against the dark interior of the sarcophagus) giving her the appearance of an entity composed of light. That

138   VICTORIAN ALCHEMY

this latest example appeared at a time when the electrical reanimation of Egyptian mummies had existed as a trope for nearly a century, and the decade before the 'light-bulb moment' first appeared in visual form in a Betty Boop cartoon,[62] suggests that we should read this example as a kind of opulent kitsch item, visually luxurious (and likely originally somewhat expensive) yet founded upon (often lurid, and often cheap) popular culture narratives. Speculative fiction and material culture was united in imagining ancient Egypt and electricity as often erotically combined; as we shall go on to see by the end of this chapter, it is often beautiful women who are imagined as electromagnetic alchemists. On the one hand, they are familiar subjects of Orientalist fantasy; on the other, they reflect the increasing opportunities available to women afforded by spiritualism, theosophy and the Golden Dawn, as well as by the sciences themselves.

Of all the light-bearing Egyptian women conjured up in the nineteenth- and early twentieth-century imagination, however, the forerunner to New York City's Statue of Liberty is the most monumental; due to the expense of the project, it also never progressed beyond a design on paper. 'Egypt Carrying the Light to Asia', designed by French sculptor Frédéric Auguste Bartholdi (1834–1904), was conceived as a lighthouse for the Suez Canal. Bartholdi's design takes the shape of an Egyptian woman with one arm low in a welcoming gesture and the other holding aloft a torch. While the figure is meant to suggest a modern Egyptian peasant woman, Bartholdi was also inspired by Egypt's ancient history; he was impressed by the 'kindly and impassive glance' of the sphinx, which 'seems ... to be fixed upon an unlimited future', and something of this welcoming character was seemingly intended to feature, too, in this guardian of the Canal.[63] Bartholdi's Egyptian woman stands atop a pylon-shaped plinth, in another nod to Egypt's ancient history. One version of Bartholdi's sketch shows the woman's headband as a light source, a feature that would find an afterlife in the Statue of Liberty, which itself functioned as a lighthouse from 1886 to 1901 (it was, also, the first lighthouse in the United States to be powered by electricity).[64] While the Statue of Liberty retained little of Bartholdi's original Egyptian design, Egypt remained intrinsically associated with the kinds of feats of engineering it represented. The legendary lighthouse of Alexandria known as 'Pharos', is represented in late nineteenth- and early twentieth-century illustrations as akin to a modern skyscraper.

An interesting juxtaposition thus emerges: the electric lighting surrounding artefacts and replicas including various cities' obelisks contributed to an association between ancient Egyptian imagery and that of modern scientific innovation. They co-existed side by side and may well have gone some way in uniting the two concepts in the cultural imagination. As museums and other recreational spaces became electrically lit, ancient Egypt was discovered anew, no longer the gloomy cousin of Greece and Rome but a vibrant civilisation in its own right. That lighting designs incorporated Egyptian figures holding aloft these symbols of enlightenment marks an ambiguous shift. In these spaces, ancient Egyptians – often individuals emblematic of royalty – become light bearers. On the one hand, they are servants to the Westerners using such spaces, literally objectified and fulfilling a menial function. On the other, they are imagined as guardians of knowledge, even as gilded immortal bodies, wielders of alchemical power. Certainly, what such complicated and at time contradictory meetings between the ancient and the modern ultimately established were ever-expanding opportunities for contact and for imaginative interpretation as to what this contact could mean. One key possibility would be that electricity might revive ancient Egypt, shocking its dead back to life, and allowing them to speak in the modern world.

Shocking mummies

Mummy reanimation in modern literature – and electricity's power to achieve this – has its roots in Mary Shelley's *Frankenstein* (1818). Referred to by its creator as more grotesque than 'a mummy again endued with animation', Frankenstein's creature is awakened through a scientific process that is left ambiguous.[65] Described simply as having been achieved through the use of 'instruments of life' designed to instil a 'spark of being into the lifeless thing', the reanimation process is not explicitly specified as electrical in nature.[66] Nevertheless, the novel's subtitle, *The Modern Prometheus*, echoes the German philosopher Immanuel Kant's (1724–1804) description of the American polymath and Founding Father Benjamin Franklin (1706–90) and his experiments with lightning; Franklin was, according to Kant, '*dem Prometheus der neuern Zeiten*' ('the Prometheus of modern times').[67] That the Shelleys were *au fait* with galvanism, which, as I go on to outline, is connected to mummy reanimation in several subsequent narratives, suggests a common scientific root to all of these early nineteenth-century texts.[68] Accordingly, the creature's awakening tends to be imagined through the use of galvanic equipment, and in retellings of Shelley's tale, is often powered by a bolt of lightning that strikes a lightning rod during a storm.[69] If Shelley's initial comparison of the creature to a reanimated mummy seems a fleeting one, she reaffirms the creature's mummy-like appearance towards the novel's close: the creature's hand, Robert Walton observes, 'was … in colour and apparent texture like that of a mummy'.[70]

The influence of *Frankenstein* and the possibility of implied electrical reanimation on later texts dealing with mummy revival cannot be underestimated. As Constance Classen points out, referring to mummies in nineteenth-century museum collections, '[c]ontemporary scientific experimentation made it possible to imagine such a revival occurring at any moment'.[71] It was not long after the arrival of Shelley's celebrated Gothic novel that the first reanimated Egyptian mummy in fiction appeared: Jane Webb's futuristic tale of a resuscitated Cheops was published in 1827. While Webb's heavy debt to Shelley's novel is undeniable – with reviewers commenting on how the resuscitation of Cheops 'would have been very fine, had not the conception, in some degree, been forestalled by Mrs. Shelley's Frankenstein'[72] – the scene in which the reanimation of the mummy takes place is described in far greater technological detail.[73] Webb's mummy reanimation – which is later revealed to be the work of God rather than that of the scientist – is first presented as being explicitly electrical in nature, achieved through the use of a galvanic battery:

> Worked up to desperation, he applied the wires of the battery and put the apparatus in motion, whilst a demoniac laugh of derision appeared to ring in his ears, and the surrounding mummies seemed starting from their places and dancing in unearthly merriment. Thunder now roared in tremendous peals through the Pyramids, shaking their enormous masses to the foundation, and vivid flashes of light darted round in quick succession. Edric stood aghast amidst this fearful convulsion of nature … Still, he stood immovable, and gazing intently on the mummy, whose eyes had opened with the shock, and were now fixed on those of Edric, shining with supernatural lustre.[74]

While the electrical current is applied solely to Cheops's body, it is as if the entire Giza Necropolis is suffused with electricity. Other mummies in the pyramid chamber appear to move as if they too have been shocked; Webb seems to take a particular pleasure in infusing the description of 'the surrounding mummies [which] seemed starting' with a kind of sizzling sibilance that mimics the sounds of the electric spark. It is not just this particular pyramid that is affected, but all of them, as if the force at work is an external thunderstorm rather than a battery (perhaps a clue as to divine intervention). As Sara Brio records, Edric as a representative of the England of 2126 employs galvanism as emblematic of 'scientific and technological advancement' to his own ends.[75] But hierarchies of power are immediately flipped with the application of the electric current; in the 'supernatural lustre' of Cheops's gaze can be read his unshakeable authority. Cheops, as 'a purveyor of mystical knowledge', is the British scientists' superior. Unlike Shelley's creature, who awakes as an innocent, only to be shunned by his creator, Cheops is experienced, adaptable and very quickly garners power in this futuristic setting. In his fixed gaze is the self-assuredness of a superior intelligence.

Less well documented than the influence of Shelley's text, though significant to an understanding of the influences on the first depiction of a reanimated mummy in literature, is Webb's friendship with the celebrated British painter John Martin (1789–1854), to whom Melanie Keene refers as 'the most famous geological artist', aligning him with contemporaneous scientific endeavours.[76] In illuminating electrical motifs in Martin's paintings of Egyptian settings, I hope to unearth another potential line of inspiration for Webb beyond Shelley's precedent. Martin's painting, *Seventh Plague of Egypt* (1823), for instance, depicts the cataclysmic biblical storm summoned by Moses, who stands holding his staff aloft like a magus. While the otherworldly light that almost connects the summits of the pyramids is not the typical jagged bolts of lightning of his other works, in watercolour studies and in subsequent engravings that saw the image popularised, sharp lines of electrical discharges are visible through the clouds (figure 3.5). The blue-tinted illumination that tears through the sky in the painting thus appears to be electrical light shining through stormclouds, lightning symbolising, as it did in many of Martin's paintings, divine wrath. Webb, orphaned in 1824, the year Martin's painting was exhibited in the Society of British Artists' inaugural exhibition in London, enjoyed a close friendship with Martin at this time.[77] Alan Rauch draws parallels between Webb's novel and Martin's painting *An Ideal Portrait of the Last Man* (1826), citing similarities in subject matter to a shared awareness of Shelley's novel.[78] If, as Rauch suggests, the pair discussed *Frankenstein* and harnessed its inspirational potential for their own works, then their mutual depiction of the pyramids and electrical forces implies that Martin's painting may have had its own influence on Webb, prefiguring the '[t]hunder' and 'flashes of light' *within* the Great Pyramid in her novel. Considered together, therefore, Webb and Martin present pictures of Egypt connected explicitly to electrical power, which laid the foundations for connections between electricity and ancient Egypt in the literary imagination later in the nineteenth century.

Figure 3.5   Henry Le Keux, *The Seventh Plague of Egypt*, after John Martin, c.1828, engraving, 7.3 cm × 10.5 cm, Victoria and Albert Museum, London, http://collections.vam.ac.uk/item/O692702/the-seventh-plague-of-egypt-print-le-keux-henry/ (accessed 7 April 2022) © Victoria and Albert Museum, London.

In turn, the British painter and printmaker J. M. W. Turner (1775–1851) may have provided inspiration for Martin's picture of an electrical storm over the pyramids. His *The Fifth Plague of Egypt* (1800) depicts the fabled tempest illuminating a pyramid and, as is the case with Martin's painting, bolts of lightning are more explicitly identifiable as the source of light in subsequent engravings of the image (figure 3.6). While Egypt's climate makes lightning relatively rare, the biblical story of the plagues of Egypt cemented the association between Egypt and storms, particularly at a time when the nascence of Egyptology meant that, culturally speaking, when British people thought of ancient Egypt they thought first of Joseph or Moses. Early nineteenth-century imagery of electrical storms in Egypt was yet more widespread: night-time views of Pompey's Pillar and Cleopatra's Needle painted in watercolours around the advent of the nineteenth century by one Private William Porter show Roman and Egyptian monoliths set against backgrounds of skies streaked with lightning.[79] Catriona Kennedy reads '[t]he shafts of light that illuminate both moments' in these watercolour paintings 'as celebrating the British expedition's

Figure 3.6 Joseph Mallord William Turner, *The Fifth Plague of Egypt*, 1808, etching and mezzotint, 20.6 cm × 29.2 cm, The Metropolitan Museum of Art, New York, https://www.metmuseum.org/art/collection/search/382982 (accessed 7 April 2022).

contribution to the scholarly understanding of Egypt'.[80] Kennedy discerns in these dramatic, stormy images 'the Old Testament Plagues of Egypt, and the Seventh Plague, a hugely destructive thunderstorm, in particular'.[81] Through his *Seventh Plague of Egypt*, Martin participated in this tradition, using lightning as symbolic of divine power in Egyptian settings again in his mezzotints that post-dated Webb's mummy reanimation novel, *The Destroying Angel* (1836) and *The Death of the First Born* (1836).

Electrical stimulation proved influential on other texts with ancient Egyptian subject matter, as in the little-known 'British theologian-turned-astronomer' Alexander Copland's 1834 poems 'The Mummy Awaked' and 'The Mummy's Reply'.[82] In the former, the poetic voice claims the ability to 'rouse the dead by a galvanic battery', insulting the mummy's appearance while boasting of the modern ability to 'transmute old rags to gold' by transforming material into banknotes.[83] In the latter poem, the mummy, while claiming to 'love to hear the changes which have been', mockingly retorts by inviting the voice to:

> Touch my poor frame, and make my body all
> Just as it was before grim Death stood by.

144   VICTORIAN ALCHEMY

> If you can do but this, then I'll believe,
> That you can all which you have said achieve.[84]

Merely being 'rouse[d]' by the instruments of modern science is not satisfactory for the mummy, who dreams rather of being as she was before death; for her, it is the restoration of her living beauty as well as her life – that is, through an act of *true* alchemy – that would demonstrate real scientific mastery. When the mummy explains that she will cease to speak 'To such as you, who know so much already', her tone is, as Jasmine Day points out, 'haughty' and 'chastising'.[85] In her rebuff of 16 stanzas (which feels somewhat curt after the 55 stanzas of 'The Mummy Awaked'), the mummy ultimately reinforces the limits of modern scientific progress, specifically ridiculing the inadequacies of galvanism. There are, of course, interesting gender and national dynamics at play here: the Western masculine scientist proposes to experiment on his Eastern feminine subject, who rebuffs him; later in the century, the Egyptian woman assumes the position of scientist and wields astounding alchemical powers.

References to electricity in relation to the ancient Egyptian dead continued throughout the century. The motion of the titular appendage in Théophile Gautier's 'Le Pied de momie' (1840) is likened to twitching muscles in receipt of an electric shock; the foot moves as if it were '*en contact avec une pile voltaïque*' ('in contact with a voltaic pile').[86] The '*pile voltaïque*' refers to the pile pioneered by Volta, which was a precursor to the battery and, according to Patricia Fara, 'often said to be the last Enlightenment instrument … mark[ing] not only a new century, but also the beginning of modern physics'.[87] Another simile likens the foot's movement to that of '*une grenouille effarée*' ('a startled frog'),[88] calling to mind Luigi (1737–98) and Lucia Galvani's (1743–88) experiments into static electricity and its effect on the nerves in frogs' legs: the application of electricity caused the muscles in the frogs' legs to twitch.[89] A scientific instrument called the 'frog galvanoscope' (essentially a skinned frog's leg with an exposed nerve, to which a conductor of electricity might be applied) invented by Galvani and used to detect voltage was still in use around the mid-nineteenth century.

Galvanism as a method of mummy revival was a concept borrowed by Edgar Allan Poe in his popular burlesque on the topic, 'Some Words with a Mummy' (1845). Poe's mummy – Allamistakeo – is revived by electricity generated by a 'Voltaic pile'; a 'wire' attaches the 'battery' to the 'temporal muscle', causing the mummy's eyelids to close.[90] The next point of application is 'the great toe of the right foot', through which they access the 'bisected nerves' of 'the *abductor* muscle'; stimulation, in this case, again recalls the Galvanis' experiments with frogs' legs: 'the mummy first drew up its right knee so as to bring it nearly into contact with the abdomen, and then, straighten[ed] the limb with inconceivable force'.[91] It is the third and final shock that ultimately revives the mummy, this time via 'a profound incision into the tip of the subject's nose'. The effect, Poe relates, was 'morally and physically – figuratively and literally … electric'.[92] Allamistakeo reveals that ancient Egyptian civilisation was far more advanced than that of the modern American men who restore him to life, observing disparagingly that he 'perceive[s] they are yet in the infancy of Galvanism, and cannot accomplish with it what was a common thing among us in the old days'.[93] While 'Some Words with a Mummy' is the earliest of the fictional texts examined in this chapter which specifically credits the ancient Egyptians with superior knowledge of electricity, reprints of Poe's tale in new editions – including the collection of Poe's works *Tales of Mystery, Imagination and Humour; and Poems* (1852) with its illustration of Allamistakeo, which Day has identified as 'the earliest known modern visual depiction of a living mummy'[94] – saw Poe's text repackaged for readers in the 1850s, 1860s, 1870s, 1890s and 1900s.

Other electrical reanimations of the early nineteenth century reappeared in new formats later in the century, including Webb's *The Mummy*, which was reprinted by Frederick Warne as a cheap edition in 1872, and which was subsequently serialised in *Dicks' English Library of Standard Works* in weekly instalments between April and June 1894. As such, this text had several moments of cultural currency long after its author's death, exposing new generations to the mummy awakened by electrical stimulation. Such conventions evidently transcended genre and form. George Day and Allen Reed's farce *The Mummy* (first performed in London in August 1896 before moving to Broadway later that year) also featured a titular mummy reanimated by a 'galvanic battery'.[95] The trope continued into the early twentieth century, where it can be seen, too, in silent films, including the Thanhouser Company's *The Mummy* (1911), in which a mummified ancient Egyptian princess is accidentally awoken from a death-like sleep, 'pop[ping] … out from her coffin' when her body comes into contact with a live electrical wire.[96] Electrification was used for comic effect a decade later in William Watson's comedy short *Tut! Tut! King* (1923), in which a team of scientists apply electric shocks to what they believe to be mummies in a bid to revive them, the joke being that the individuals subject to this treatment are actually a couple of unfortunate modern men hiding in the mummy cases. Richard Freeman observes that other than the supernatural methods used in Arthur Conan Doyle's short story 'Lot No. 249' (1892), fiction featuring mummy reanimation of the era employs either electricity or chemical stimulation, through the use of an elixir, as the technique by which the subject is awakened.[97] Aside from Doyle's tale, therefore, with its clearer indication of otherworldly powers, the key to reviving the ancient Egyptian dead is pervasively imagined as being rooted in science, albeit one that is often inflected with occult associations.

Tales such as these highlight the established connection between ancient Egypt and electricity in the broader cultural consciousness. Life was not only breathed into the mummies but into understandings of Egypt: this was a wider process of reanimation. Egypt's ancient monuments and relics, already associated with metallic conductors of electricity were being metaphorically revivified, illuminated by electric lights in public and in museums, and lit by increasingly dramatic lighting used in theatrical depictions of the civilisation. Amidst this context of increasing electrical encounters with ancient Egypt, stories of electrical reanimation through the use of galvanic batteries have an extensive history, these long-standing links harking back to before the beginning of Victoria's reign. As we shall go on to see, electrical demonstrations by eminent scientists in the latter half of the nineteenth century also proved suitable for transference onto scenes of ancient Egyptian occultism. Novel light effects were experienced as magical, mystical and arcane despite being the product of cutting-edge scientific knowledge, and so the transplantation of such scenes into depictions of Egyptian magic makes ancient Egyptian power appear timeless: simultaneously ancient and modern.

Electrical demonstrations

Beyond the epic storms of John Martin, and Webb's galvanic experiment in Cheops's tomb, electrical phenomena were reported in the vicinity of the pyramids of Giza. The German inventor Werner von Siemens (1816–92), whose company manufactured the tubes with which Wilhelm Röntgen (1845–1923) would go on to study X-rays and which supplied the carbon for the electric lights at the British Museum, recounted a peculiar experience in Egypt as he took some time away from laying telegraphic cable in the Red Sea. Standing at the summit of the Great Pyramid of Giza during a sandstorm, he notes in his *Personal Recollections* (1893) that he and his engineers could hear 'a remarkable hissing noise'.[98] Even more curiously, when one of his Egyptian guides lifted 'his outstretched finger above his head a sharp singing sound arose, which ceased as soon as he lowered his hand'.[99] Siemens raised his own finger and felt 'a prickling sensation', which he deduced was the result of an electrical phenomenon when he felt 'a slight electric shock' as he attempted to drink from a wine bottle.[100] In a moment of inspired ingenuity, Siemens fashioned the wine bottle into a rudimentary Leyden jar, which he charged by holding it aloft, producing 'loud cracking sparks'.[101] The Egyptians, believing the static electricity to be the result of 'magic' that might damage the pyramid, requested that Siemens and his men leave.[102] When he refused, one of the Egyptians attempted to forcibly remove him, provoking Siemens to use the wine bottle as an electrical weapon. Touching the man on the nose, Siemens felt a 'strong concussion', noting that his opponent must have had a much more 'violent shock' as 'he fell speechless to the ground, and several seconds elapsed … before with a sudden cry he raised himself, and sprang howling down the steps of the pyramid'.[103] Siemens adopts a role somewhere between the stage magician and the physicist. With theatrical execution, he harnesses the unusual electrical properties of the Great Pyramid, something which had been anticipated in earlier fiction featuring the reanimation of mummies, including Webb's tale in which the resurrection takes place within the pyramid itself. In a reversal of the mummy reanimation plot, bringing the lifeless subject to a state of consciousness, Siemens utilises electrical force to render the conscious subject cataleptic, at least for a few seconds.

By the closing years of the century, the image of the Westerner inspiring fear in Egyptians through demonstrations of electrical power made its way into fiction. In Richard Marsh's *The Beetle* (1897), the titular monster responds with terror to 'an electrical machine, giving an eighteen inch spark' controlled by the inventor Sidney Atherton, who himself 'occupies [the] ambiguous position between scientist and magician', which, as we have seen elsewhere, is often the domain of ancient Egyptian characters.[104] Here, the Egyptian monster is superstitious and degenerate rather than progressive and advanced. Marsh's character is a hybrid in every sense. Able to fluctuate between male and female, human and insect, its depiction as capable of adapting to its modern surroundings and yet fearful of modern technology suggests a blurring of stereotypes of the ancient and modern Egyptian. This is also implied by the way in which the creature, supposedly a devotee to the ancient Egyptian religion, 'salaamed down to the ground' at the sight of the electrical spark, aligning the eponymous monster with the modern Egyptians fearful of Siemens's power atop the Great Pyramid.[105] The image of the scientific showman, whether Siemens or Marsh's character Atherton, producing sparks and shocks for dramatic effect, is not limited to the Westerner, however. Indeed, these powers were often transcribed onto ancient Egyptian characters, Marsh's text in fact being something of an outlier.

The Bengali author Dinendra Kumar Roy, for instance, translated and adapted Guy Boothby's novel *Pharos the Egyptian* (1898; 1899), publishing *Pishach purohit* ('The Zombie Priest') in 1910. As Projit Bihari Mukharji outlines, in Roy's revised narrative the Bengali protagonist Naren Sen first encounters the ancient Egyptian villain Ra-Tai by the River Thames; this episode is a 'fairly faithful ... translation' of Boothby's original in which the British artist Cyril Forrester finds himself face to face with the eponymous Pharos. Roy makes a significant change to Boothby's text, however: the addition of a reference to electromagnetism. Mukharji elucidates that Naren recognises Ra-Tai's supernormal controlling abilities; Naren relates, 'upon the touch of this man, quite inexplicably, the state of my body became akin to the way one's hand becomes immobilized and insensible upon [accidentally] touching an electric battery'.[106] As such, Roy transforms the body of Boothby's antagonist into yet another electrically charged living mummy. Mukharji observes that Roy's employment of electricity originates in the works of several authors I have already mentioned in this chapter – Shelley, Bulwer-Lytton and Blavatsky (he records that Poe is also cited by early Bengali science-fiction authors as a common influence)[107] – while a fleeting reference to Marie Corelli and H. Rider Haggard in *Pishach purohit*'s preface suggests other sources – and, indeed, more complex chains of influence – that might have led Roy to augment the beginning of his reworking of Boothby's narrative in this particular way.[108]

Roy's intriguing revision of Boothby's text invites a consideration of the kinds of literature to which he claims to be indebted, and which encouraged the translocation of electrical powers into Egyptian hands. As this section goes on to show, inspired by the likes of Nikola Tesla, ancient Egyptians in texts by H. Rider Haggard and Bram Stoker master and manipulate the electrical with ease, drawing upon electrical showmanship on a far greater scale than Siemens's impromptu experiments atop the Great Pyramid. It may well be the case that such depictions of ancient Egyptians as master 'electricians' in works by these authors directly led to Roy's take on Boothby's electrically charged antagonist.

By the late nineteenth century, electricity had emerged as one of the most thrilling tools put to use by scientists whose demonstrations overlapped with the theatrical and were in direct competition with the metropolis' theatres, panoramas, dioramas and magic-lantern shows, among other visual spectacles.[109] Earlier in the century, lecture halls were filled by audiences desperate to witness evidence of the 'strange invisible forces' explored by Michael Faraday (1791–1867) in his presentations of electromagnetism.[110] By the late nineteenth century Nikola Tesla, a Serbian-American physicist and engineer, had emerged as one of Faraday's most glorified successors, stunning eager audiences with his extraordinary displays of electrical mastery. Tesla's demonstrations were not of wires moved by electromagnetism or even the simple shocks and sparks produced by the galvanic batteries of his predecessors that had been popular since the time of Faraday's mentor Humphry Davy (1778–1829), but were something more akin to wizardry.[111] Iwan Rhys Morus and Graeme Gooday both emphasise Tesla's flamboyant showmanship which helped transform his demonstrations into magical spectacles.[112] As Gooday notes, electricity was often anthropomorphised at the end of the nineteenth century, with personifications taking the form of goddesses and fairies if female, and wizards, genies, imps and infants if male.[113] Tesla appeared to encourage his own depiction as one of these types: the wizard, or a magical masculine embodiment of electricity itself, which had a striking impact on depictions of magical light effects in literature concerning ancient Egypt.

In 1892, Tesla's lecture on fluorescent lighting at the Royal Institution was celebrated as a 'dazzling theatrical display', securing his reputation as one of the great scientific showmen of the age.[114] Contemporary reports of Tesla's demonstrations vary in style, mainly in the degree to which they explain the science behind his impressive feats. They tend to be united, however, in a general sense of awe at the seemingly magical effects that Tesla produced. The British scientist Lord Rayleigh (1842–1919) – who would go on to win a Nobel Prize for Physics, and to become President of the Royal Society and President of the Social for Psychical Research – eulogised Tesla, commending his display, and making particular reference to how Tesla made his name appear 'in letters of fire'.[115] While an article reporting on the event published in *Scientific American* sticks mainly to the impartial terminology of scientific observation (a 'blue phosphorescent light' and 'sparks ... obtained over a distance of 1¼ inches', among other phenomena, are recorded), the author appears unable to contain an outburst of magical imagery towards the end: 'The lecturer took in his hand a glass wand, 3 feet long, and, with no special connection of any sort to his body or to the glass, when waved in the magnet field it shone like a flaming sword.'[116] The choice of the term 'wand' emphasises the enchanted aura of Tesla's performance, whilst also suggesting the scientific advancement of fantasy civilisations, including the electrically charged wands, staffs and 'rods' used by Bulwer-Lytton's Vril-ya. Crucially, magic was not just invoked in reports of Tesla's demonstrations such as this in the popular periodical press (or even the popular scientific press), but also in technical journals including the *Electrical Review* and *Engineering*.[117] It is evident that Tesla's displays could not be fully explained via the neat, impartial language of scientific description, as parallels are repeatedly drawn between his apparatus and magical implements, with Tesla represented a kind of sorcerer. That Tesla's work appears to have been a subject of great interest for the celebrated physicists and spiritualists William Crookes (1832–1919) and Oliver Lodge (1851–1940) suggests that its applications were perceived to have straddled the physical and the psychical.[118]

After his success in London, Tesla lectured for the French Physical Society and the International Society of Electricians in Paris, an event recorded by the French engineer Édouard Hospitalier (1852–1907) writing for *La Nature*. In his article, which is accompanied by two illustrations, Hospitalier introduces Tesla as *'un pionnier de la science électrique, l'un de ceux qui auront amorcé les progrès futurs par une transformation presque radicale des anciens procédés et des anciens errements'* ('a pioneer of electrical science, one of those who will have initiated future progress by an almost radical transformation of the old methods and the old errors').[119] *'Anciens'* can mean 'old', as the context here suggests, but it can also mean 'ancient'. The ambiguity as to how 'old' these 'old methods' really are makes it tempting to read Hospitalier as imagining Tesla as part of a scientific lineage that stretches back to antiquity. Much of Hospitalier's language, indeed, can be read in a way that casts Tesla's demonstrations as ancient or magical; he describes Tesla's *'expériences'* as *'magnifiques'*, *'remarquables'* and *'mémorables'*, *'expériences'* meaning 'experiences' as well as 'experiments', another interesting example of language's rich possibilities that suggests the scientific only as much as it skirts it.[120] The description of the event as a *'séance'* also has a pertinent dual meaning: Hospitalier uses the word to mean 'sitting', but the term had taken on supernatural connotations by the latter half of the nineteenth century with the fashionable rise of spiritualism. Hospitalier is impressed with *'la puissance et la grandeur des effets'* ('the power and magnitude of the effects'), the *'décharges lumineuses'* that *'traversent l'air'* ('luminous discharges' which 'pass through the air') and tubes that each shine with *'une vive lueur'* ('a vivid glow'), the hue depending on the gas inside.[121] Much of his account might describe effects produced in spiritualist séances, hovering at the boundary of the supernatural and the scientific. Tesla is reported as producing spectacles of biblical proportions. Hospitalier describes him as *'comme un apôtre'* ('like an apostle'), whose equipment produces *'décharges en forme de flamme'* ('flame-shaped discharges').[122]

The two illustrations that accompany the piece contrast in style. The first, by an artist called Gilbert, depicts Tesla during the lecture (figure 3.7). The second, by the French engraver and illustrator Louis Poyet, is of an alternator (through which high-frequency alternating currents might be produced). In Gilbert's image, Tesla brandishes illuminated tubes in front of his rapt audience. To the bottom left of the illustration, one member of the audience appears to have his mouth open in awe, while, to the bottom right, another man breaks into spontaneous applause. The perspective is such that the viewer is positioned as another audience member, further back than the first couple of rows visible in the image. Tesla makes direct eye contact with the viewer; his body language is one of confident mastery, and the eye is drawn to the scientist who, not needing to look at his equipment, seems to enjoy the self-conscious theatricality of the proceedings.

Tesla was consistently portrayed in such a way. In an 1895 article in *The Century Illustrated Magazine*, long-exposure photographs of Tesla's experiments with phosphorescent light bulbs take on an almost supernatural quality. These images present Tesla's indistinct features illuminated

Figure 3.7 Gilbert, 'Conférence de M. Tesla devant la Société de physique et la Société internationale des électriciens, le 20 février 1892', in E. Hospitalier, 'Expériences de M. Tesla sur les courants alternatifs de grande fréquence', *La Nature* 20 (1) (1892): 209. Source: Cnum – Conservatoire numérique des Arts et Métiers.

by a kind of spectral haze – one is reminded of séance photographs – while also captured is the American novelist Samuel Clemens (1835–1910), better known by his pen-name, Mark Twain.[123] Their friendship, based on reciprocal admiration for the one's technical abilities and the other's weaving of compelling fictions, is symbolically captured in images that are as much theatrical compositions as they are documentations of scientific experiments. It was around this time that Tesla inadvertently created the first X-ray image in America (in an attempt to capture a picture of Twain); he subsequently corresponded with and shared radiographs with Röntgen. Tesla's laboratory, in a poem that immediately follows the article written by *The Century*'s associate editor and close friend of Tesla, Robert Underwood Johnson (1853–1937), is further presented as a Gothic space. Johnson conceives of Tesla's '[t]houghts' as taking the form of 'blessèd spirits': these appear 'ghostly figures' 'in the dark'.[124]

In a later piece in *Pearson's Magazine* entitled 'The New Wizard of the West', Tesla's laboratory is described as a 'miracle-factory' and he himself is an 'audacious wizard'.[125] By heralding Tesla as 'The New Wizard of the West', M'Govern uses a moniker suggestive of that of Scottish stage magician John Henry Anderson (1814–74), the 'Wizard of the North'. Anderson was famed for his variety of 'quasi-scientific magic', 'blend[ing] illusion and science, heavily reliant on technological apparatus', and thus, M'Govern co-opts for Tesla a lineage rooted in performance magic heavily inflected with scientific enquiry.[126] Anderson cultivated an understanding of his work as operating simultaneously within categories of the genuine supernatural, illusory performance, and modern scientific demonstration – he was referred to in the press as a 'physicist', and was billed from 1840 onwards as 'Professor Anderson' (as Geoffrey Frederick Lamb observes, 'conjurors of the period freely awarded themselves professorships and doctorates').[127] Furthermore, Anderson explained his effects by positing himself as an inheritor of ancient technological feats: he 'claimed to "use the appliances and agencies resorted to by the Egyptian Magi"' (to which he gave mystical names such as 'the Casket of the Alchemists') with 'the assistance of the greatest mechanicians and the most scientific men of the age', all the while 'play[ing] to the perception of genuine magical ability'.[128] If, as Karl Bell claims, Anderson 'blurr[ed] distinctions between science and magic', then Tesla certainly continued this legacy.[129]

The interviewer lists a series of amazing demonstrations. Tesla summons 'a ball of leaping red flame' by simply 'snapping his fingers', he makes the darkened laboratory glow with 'a strange light as beautiful as that of the moon' but as powerful as sunlight, withstands powerful currents that instantly kill animals, and emerges from darkness with an illuminated 'halo ... formed by myriads of tongues of electric flame' that emerge from his own body.[130] Of course, it is not the snapping of Tesla's fingers that produces these effects, but the inclusion of this detail conveys Tesla's awareness of his own showmanship, taking pleasure in the act of misdirection that conceals how the effect is really produced.

One of the images accompanying the article, an illustration of Tesla by Warwick Goble (1862–1943), further enhances the connection that Tesla was cultivating between himself, as a modern scientist, and as a 'quasi-alchemical [master] of a hidden mystery'.[131] That this illustration was contributed by Goble, who had previously illustrated H. G. Wells's *The War of the Worlds* – originally serialised in Britain in *Pearson's Magazine* just two years prior – is suggestive of the generic fluidity of fiction and science writing that Will Tattersdill has observed in magazine publishing at the *fin de siècle* more broadly.[132] The illustration posits the account at the edge of credibility: a scientific romance. Tesla, masterfully occupying the central space, is the narrative's hero.

While the very image of the modern gentleman-scientist in Goble's portrait, the syntax of the image's caption, 'Nikola Tesla holding in his hands balls of flame', appears to be deliberately archaic – verging on biblical. Holding spectral light in each hand, Tesla, like the electric statues in Shepheard's Hotel – through both image and text – was meant to symbolise a kind of timeless enlightenment, simultaneously modern and ancient. This tension between the extremely old and the extremely new is captured, too, in the article's title. The now infamous photographs of Tesla sitting among seven-metre sparks in his Colorado Springs laboratory were part of the same scheme. The photos were actually exposed multiple times, creating the impression of the scientist, calm within the centre of the veritable thunderstorm that rages around him. As Gooday eloquently expresses, Tesla, 'magus-like', was encouraging an image of himself as 'manipulator of lightning and prophet of the most spectacular electrical technologies'.[133] The religious connotations are impossible to ignore. Holding orbs of light in his hands or emitting huge sparks from his own body that create the illuminative appearance of a halo, Tesla was only serving to further his depiction as 'a half-intoxicated god', one who, like the characters of early science fiction who sought to reanimate mummies, planned to perform miracles with his modern machines by waking the dead.[134]

Tesla was not alone in this practice. His rival and fellow inventor, Thomas Edison, was nurturing a similar image of himself as a maker of magic through his theatrical use of the electric light, employing the language of ancient occultism in order to further this persona.[135] Although

Tesla excelled at exemplifying contradictory roles, as simultaneously 'hypermodern' and 'archaic', common to both scientists was a desire to enrapture and beguile with scientific exhibition combined with grandiose ceremonious showmanship, one which presented the physical as the magical and the scientist as the enchanter.[136]

Tesla differed from many of his colleagues and competitors, however, in the eccentricity of his claims. From an early age he had been able to visualise complex machines that he could test in his mind; eventually he would state that the visionary ideas that suddenly came to him were being transmitted from Mars.[137] He also made fantastical assertions about electrical knowledge in the ancient world. Describing 'the history of electrical development' as 'a story more wonderful than any tale from the Arabian Nights' – immediately setting a tone of exoticism and fantasy – in an article written for *Manufacturers Record*, Tesla believed that 'Moses was undoubtedly a practical and skillful electrician far in advance of his time', and considered it 'very plausible to assume that the sons of Aaron were killed by a high-tension discharge'.[138] Such bold proclamations about the mastery with which the ancients handled electricity were far more often attributed to occultists such as Blavatsky, yet Tesla's reputation for genius resulted in the publication of these notions in respectable journals. That the editor of *Manufacturers Record*, a practical periodical focusing on developments in trade and industry, would introduce Tesla as 'inventor, physicist, electrical wizard and seer', suggests that Tesla's vision of Moses as educated among the palatial courts of Pharaoh and creating electrical weapons should be entertained more seriously.[139] As a modern 'electrician', Tesla considered himself an inheritor of the knowledge of these ancient forerunners.

Gooday stresses the influence of such scientific showmanship on the scientific romance literature of the period, which often combined electrical and supernatural themes.[140] H. Rider Haggard's short story 'Smith and the Pharaohs' makes an interesting case study, as it appears explicitly to draw upon descriptions of Tesla's impressive electrical performances, uniting contemporary concepts with ancient supernaturalism rather than the hypermodern. In Haggard's tale, Smith, an amateur Egyptologist, finds himself locked in the Cairo Museum overnight. Looking for a suitable place to sleep, he enters the central hall, boarded up while awaiting repairs. Here, in the darkness, the spirits of the museum's mummies convene with the gods, forming a 'great congregation'.[141] The phantoms stand in ranks facing the god Osiris, who stares out from the top of a flight of steps, emitting a spectral glow. The room is brightened by the 'pale and ghostly' light which, like the light Tesla summoned on stage, is described as having 'a blue tinge'.[142] As the light increases in intensity, it shoots out in 'long tongues … which joined themselves together, illuminating all that huge hall'.[143] Later, it takes the form of 'a blue spark' that transforms into 'upward pouring rays'.[144] The strange forms that the supernatural light appears to take are eerily reminiscent of descriptions of Tesla's fluorescent light, powered by an alternating current, and the positioning of Osiris and the spirits echo the set-up of the lecture hall, with Tesla at the front, and his eager audience facing him in rows. Indeed, much of the imagery and terminology is replicated from press reports of his demonstrations, particularly the 'tongues' of light, and the religious parallels between Tesla's and Osiris's light-producing bodies (Osiris 'radiat[es] glory').[145] Haggard elevates the scientist to the position of a god, standing in front of a worshipful audience. Simultaneously, the ethereal light symbolising ancient Egyptian magic is aligned with very modern ways in which electricity could be manipulated. Upon the discovery of Smith the pharaohs speak 'together, in a voice that rolled round the hall like thunder', and when the 'kings and queens' make judgement on Smith's fate they 'thundered an answer': their collective spectral voice is repeatedly compared to the effects of natural electrical phenomena.[146]

In an illustration captioned 'Cleopatra Lifted Her Hands and Stood Thus for a While' by the artist Alec Ball (figure 3.8), Haggard's evocations of Tesla's lectures are visualied; the bare-breasted Cleopatra, addressing the group after the departure of Osiris (and the goddesses Isis and Hathor who momentarily materialise and disappear) must have been the more obviously titillating choice than the presumably fully covered Osiris. As in images of Tesla standing before an audience, Cleopatra is met with rows of ancient Egyptian royals. She holds aloft a sceptre, similar to the 'staffs' or 'wands' brandished by Tesla (a detail that is not given in Haggard's text but which Ball evidently saw fit to include), and she appears surrounded by a halo of spectral light. This same illustration, in a full-colour version, was the artwork that graced the front of the issue of *The Strand Magazine* that included this second instalment in Haggard's three-part serial. Haggard's merging of the powers of the mortal scientist and immortal god, modernity and antiquity reveals the extent to which Victorian and Edwardian electrical display impacted upon visual culture, but also the reciprocity of this relationship: the supernatural was projected back onto the scientific, encouraged by scientific romances such as Haggard's that not only brought these threads together, but often rendered them indistinguishable. The city, with its electric lights, obelisks and wizard-like showmen, was inspiring the construction of factual and literary writing as part of the same discourse

Figure 3.8 Alec Ball, 'Queen Cleopatra lifted her hands and stood thus for a while', in H. Rider Haggard, 'Smith and the Pharaohs', *Strand Magazine* 45 (265) (1913): 2. Source: Visual Haggard.

that celebrated and explained science via the imagery of antiquity. This, however, was not restricted to electricity as visible light, but was apparent in discussions of other kinds of electromagnetic radiation, including invisible X-rays.

X-rays and radioactivity

In 1892 the celebrated physicist and chemist William Crookes commented on the existence of 'an almost infinite range of ethereal vibrations or electrical rays', which he believed could revolutionise telegraphic communications.[147] A few years later, and aided by Crookes's experiments with vacuums, the German physicist Wilhelm Röntgen successfully produced X-rays, a hitherto unrecorded form of electromagnetic radiation, which he tantalisingly described as 'a new kind of invisible light'.[148] Crookes was quick to speculate as to 'the possibility of links between roentgen rays and the cerebral ganglia', and that an undiscovered organ in the brain might be 'capable of transmitting and receiving ... electrical rays'.[149] X-rays, he thought, might prove a psychic counterpart to longer wavelength radio waves, allowing the transmission of messages telepathically (a biological counterpart to telegraphy), and even communication with the world of the spirits.[150] Crookes theorised that the parapsychological was intimately entwined with the findings of contemporary physics, occupying different zones of the same electromagnetic spectrum. An ardent spiritualist (who would go on to become president of the Society for Psychical Research in 1896), member of the Theosophical Society, and initiate of the Hermetic Order of the Golden Dawn, Crookes saw modern scientific developments and discoveries as illuminating aspects of his occult interests. He believed that the ether, the 'impalpable, invisible entity, by which all space is supposed to be filled' and which contained countless 'channels of communication' also sustained 'ghost-light ... invisible to the naked eye', and acted as a medium that allowed 'ethereal bodies to rise up'.[151] In other words, the matter through which light and electrical signals passed was envisaged as the same substance that allowed the spirits to fluctuate between visible and invisible forms. These links between the electromagnetic field and the occult, endorsed by Crookes and certain other high-profile scientists, anticipated turn-of-the-century associations between electricity, radiation and ancient Egypt, which, through its reputation as the birthplace of magic, was already central to Victorian conceptions of the supernatural and the magical.

Steve Vinson has recently read translations of ancient Egyptian texts in the late nineteenth century productively in the context of – as he terms it – the 'thoroughly-modern phenomenon' of 'Victorian/Edwardian esotericism', which responded not only to 'vastly more, and more varied, raw material to draw on than Western occultists had ever known' but also to 'modern ... science': 'invisible natural phenomena like electromagnetism and radioactivity'.[152] Vinson suggests that interpretations of genuine ancient Egyptian texts took on Gothic resonances in this age, whereby 'the supernatural', 'the exotic' and 'hidden wisdom' in the Egyptian source material was expanded upon to reflect late Victorian and Edwardian concerns. As this section of the chapter illustrates, original texts of the period are also receptive to these occult and scientific pressures and look back to ancient Egypt as much as they look forward to the promises of these discoveries.

Following their identification in the late nineteenth century, X-rays proved an even more mysterious phenomenon than static electricity and visible light effects. Higher frequency waves than the light of the visible spectrum, they were considered 'a new kind of invisible light', penetrating the flesh but not bone.[153] The ghostly images that they produced seemingly depicting the human body as it would appear after death and decay had strong supernatural connotations, and there was speculation by some, including Crookes (by this time President of the Society for Psychical Research), that they were related to the telepathic transmission of thoughts.[154] Their visual similarities to spirit photographs, with their translucent flesh, meant that as soon as the first X-ray radiographs were produced, they were regarded as new tools in the effort to prove the existence of the spirit world, and furthered the late nineteenth- and early twentieth-century fascination with spiritualism.[155] Indeed, X-rays became one of the implements of the psychical researcher, notably put to use by the Italian physician Cesare Lombroso (1835–1909) in his investigations into the ectoplasmic materialisations produced by fellow Italian and spiritualist medium Eusapia Palladino, an individual who allowed some of the most famous scientists in the world, including Marie and Pierre Curie (1859–1906), to examine her.[156] Simultaneously, X-ray radiographs were treated as modern spectacles, both in person via technologies such as Edison's fluoroscope, a device that created X-ray images that moved in real time, and in the still, reproduced images of the periodical press, thus, occupying a similar place in the cultural consciousness as that of electricity: spectacular, sensational and otherworldly.[157]

Just a few months after Röntgen's discovery, in March 1896, X-ray radiographs of mummified remains – of a cat and a human child – were produced for the first time, published in the German physicist Walter König's (1859–1936) booklet '14 Photographiën mit Röntgenstrahlen aufgenommen im Physikalischen Verein'.[158] Later that year, the Belgian botanist Henri Ferdinand van Heurck (1838–1909) produced a radiograph of an ibis, and British doctor Charles Thurstan Holland (1863–1941) – who would go on to specialise in radiology – 'obtained a radiograph of a mummified bird'.[159] The most striking early

X-ray radiograph of mummified remains is perhaps that published by the French medical researcher and photographer Albert Londe (1858–1917) in *La Nature* in 1897, accompanied by a black-and-white photograph for comparison (figure 3.9). The juxtaposition of these two images is one of their most intriguing qualities, making immediately apparent the benefits of X-ray imaging for the purposes of Egyptological examination: the mummy can be 'unwrapped' without any physical damage to the body. Equally, the radiograph of the ancient Egyptian remains reveals that the mummy, held to be a figure of horror in the cultural consciousness by this point for several decades, is, underneath its desiccated flesh, just like living subjects of radiography. The hand calls to mind the first published X-ray radiograph: that depicting the hand bones of Anna Bertha Ludwig (1839–1919), Röntgen's wife, which circulated internationally.[160] As Simon Avery establishes, radiographs '[d]irsupt[ed] the perceived boundaries between ... life and death', offering the living 'an image of what would remain after death and decomposition had taken place'.[161]

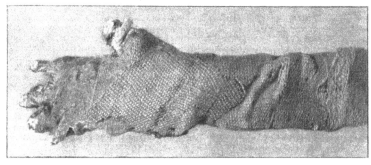

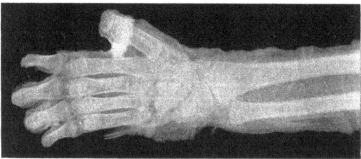

Figure 3.9 'Main de momie égyptienne (Photographie)' and 'Main de momie égyptienne (Radiographie négative)', in Albert Londe, 'Les rayons Röntgen et les momies', *La Nature* 25.2 (1897), 105. Source: Cnum – Conservatoire numérique des Arts et Métiers.

Equally, I would add, radiographs rendered living and dead bodies virtually indistinguishable from each other, imbuing X-ray radiographs of mummified bodies with the Gothic possibility of revival.

Londe worked at Paris's Salpêtrière Hospital, having been hired by the famed French neurologist Jean-Martin Charcot (1825–93) in 1878. His colleague, the French dermatologist Jean Alfred Fournier (1832–1914), Londe relates, '*mettre à notre disposition quelques pièces curieuses*' ('put at our disposal several curious pieces') that were X-rayed, but which could not be included in the article for reasons of space.[162] These included a mummy's skull, a mummified leg and arm, a small mummy, and a mummiform dog that Londe speculated was actually an ancient Egyptian toy (the implication being that there were no bones found within). The article's opening, not with details of these ancient Egyptian specimens but rather with an account of Londe's analysis of a 'Fiji mermaid' (a composite of primate and fish remains), adds a fantastical element to the piece, though the tone is one of scepticism: radiography allows Londe to declare the mermaid fake without having to dissect it. The potential for sensationalism remains, however, with Londe commenting on the possibility of discovering '*des surprises désagréables*' ('disagreeable surprises') when examining radiographs.[163]

The archaeological benefits of using this technique were immediately apparent, and as a result it proved popular with some of the era's most eminent Egyptologists. Among them were Flinders Petrie (1853–1942), who took plates of a mummy at the British Museum in 1897, and Gaston Maspero (1846–1916), who was the director of the Cairo Museum when its mummy of Thuthmose IV was examined using Egypt's only X-ray equipment in 1903.[164] With the aid of Howard Carter (1874–1939), the anatomist Grafton Elliot Smith transported the mummified body of Thuthmose IV to the premises of one Dr. Khayat, an Egyptian radiologist, where Khayat produced the first ever radiograph images of the mummified remains of a royal ancient Egyptian.[165] Several years later, Smith published a catalogue of the mummified bodies of ancient Egyptian royalty in the collections of the Cairo Museum, referring to features apparent in Khayat's X-ray radiographs.

Smith finds a fictional counterpart in Haggard's 'Smith and the Pharaohs', likely serving as inspiration for the tale's protagonist J. E. Smith. The similarities between the two men's names (Smith often published under his initials as G. E. Smith), the setting of the Cairo Museum, and a passing reference comparing the glare of the Egyptian spirits to 'a Röntgen ray' appear to indicate that Haggard was drawing upon true experiences to inspire his fiction.[166] Indeed, that 'Smith and the Pharaohs' opens with a paragraph that critiques scientists' beliefs 'that there is nothing in man which the dissecting-table will not explain' appears to be a joking nod to Smith's anatomical expertise. And, unlike in many mummy romances, the amateur Egyptologist does not unearth the perfectly preserved form of his ancient paramour; rather, nearly all that remains of the mummy are bones, as if most of her body is encountered as a radiograph image. Indeed, in a visual reversal of the first radiographs, many of which depicted skeletal hands (as in Röntgen's famous image of his wife's hand, in which the ring on her fourth finger appears bulky and opaque), the only body part to have survived from antiquity is her 'hand, broken off at the wrist' wearing 'two gold rings'.

Further evidence for the biological basis of Haggard's character lies in the similarities between Maspero and Haggard's unnamed director of the Museum: both are congenial, French, and willing to turn a blind eye to the discoverers of artefacts pocketing some of their more precious finds. The parallels are all the more striking considering that Maspero was still the Cairo Museum's director in 1912 when Haggard wrote the story, the same year as Smith's study of the Museum's mummies, which he had unwrapped with Maspero between 1881 and 1905.[167] Furthermore, as Roger Luckhurst records, the winter of 1912 saw Haggard's third trip to Egypt, which stimulated a wave of Egyptian themes in his subsequent works, 'Smith and the Pharaohs' among them.[168] Notably, the royal mummies that Haggard's narrator lists include Meneptah, whom Haggard and his daughter Angela (1883–1973) had privately inspected during this very visit, an opportunity facilitated by Maspero.[169] Haggard's familiarity with Smith's work – if not first-hand then second-hand in conversation with Maspero – is cemented when his narrator records that 'the doctors said he died of ossification of the arteries, and that the vessels of the heart were full of lime'.[170] Smith observes in his study of Meneptah's body that '[t]he aorta was in an extreme stage of calcareous degeneration, large bone-like patches standing out prominently from the walls of the vessel'.[171] 'Smith and the Pharaohs' was thus, while fantastical, also a receptacle for the most up-to-date Egyptological knowledge that X-ray radiography facilitated.

Rameses II is another pharaoh specifically mentioned in 'Smith and the Pharaohs', along with an anecdote about the pharaoh's unrolling that appears to be based on the real procedure undertaken by Maspero, in which the mummy's arm spontaneously lifted upon unwrapping. Haggard's narrator also refers to Seti II, whose mummy had been among the nine unwrapped by Smith in 1905.[172] Certainly, Haggard approved of X-raying techniques. His views were expressed in the 22 July 1904 issue of *The Daily Mail*. In something of a stark contrast to the sensational ways in which such bodies are treated in his fiction (which usually depicts the type of violence enacted on these bodies from ancient times to his present by those in search of valuables interred with the personage – including, crucially, by Egyptologists themselves), Haggard opined that, out of respect to the dead, mummies should be returned to their tombs after examination, rather than be installed behind glass in a museum: 'The mummies can first be unrolled, photographed, measured, weighted, Rontgen-rayed, etc. After that what more has science to learn from them?'[173] His opinion had not changed by 1923, towards the end of his life, when he wrote a similar letter to *The Times*, calling for experts to 'X-ray them; learn what we can of history from them … but then hide them away for ever, as we ourselves would be hidden away'.[174]

Haggard's tale, in which the spectral light that emerges from Osiris's body is described, tellingly, as 'penetrating', brings together the ancient Egyptian supernatural and the language and imagery of recent scientific developments.[175] Within the congregation, it is Khaemuas, 'the mightiest magician that ever was in Egypt', who first sees Smith, and this representative of the height of ancient Egyptian magical power to whom a power akin to that of the X-ray is attributed. Haggard writes, 'the eyes of that dreadful magician were fixed upon him, and that a bone had a better chance of escaping the search of a Röntgen ray than he of hiding himself from their baleful glare'.[176] The dual meaning of 'glare' makes it an interesting lexical choice to express both Khaemuas's fierce expression while simultaneously evoking the power of intense light. Intriguingly, the idea of X-rays emanating from eyes appears in Röntgen's interview for *McClure's Magazine* shortly after his discovery; the interviewer, H. J. W. Dam, uses X-rays as a metaphor for Röntgen's perceptiveness, commenting that '[t]he rays from the Röntgen eyes instantly penetrated the deeply hidden purpose'.[177] Haggard attributes this same metaphorical power to the eyes of his Egyptian magician, who assumes the place of the trailblazing scientist.

In 'Smith and the Pharaohs', the 'Röntgen ray' emanates not from the Egyptologist's equipment but from the very bodies he is supposed to be studying – literally in the case of Osiris and metaphorically in the case of Khaemuas – seeing the removal of agency from the Egyptologist. Haggard translates a kind of supernatural mastery of electromagnetic energy onto the gods and ghosts of ancient Egypt and, in a narrative twist of a decidedly theosophical character, we learn that Smith (himself based on a scientist familiar with radiography) is the reincarnation of an ancient Egyptian (implied to be the ancient predecessors to showmen such as Tesla). Thus, Haggard's tale is one in which the ancients wield anachronistic powers, reversing power dynamics of the active and the passive, in order to reassert themselves over cutting-edge techniques being put to use in Egyptology.

Haggard's veiled allusions to real practitioners with an interest in X-raying mummies correspond to Bram Stoker's reliance upon developments in theories of radiation when writing *The Jewel of Seven Stars*, an influence recorded by David Glover and Carol A. Senf.[178] Stoker first published his novel in 1903, the year in which scientific pioneers in the field of radioactivity, Marie Curie, Pierre Curie and Henri Becquerel (1852–1908), jointly received the Nobel Prize in Physics.[179] That same year, Ernest Rutherford (1871–1937) and Frederick Soddy (1877–1956) explained the concept of radioactive decay, and Crookes invented the spinthariscope, an instrument for the observation of the process.[180] Stoker alludes to a number of recent scientific discoveries to add a level of academic credence to his reimagining of the classic mummy reanimation plot, in which 'the exertion of magical will and radioactive particles coexist in the vanishing point between science and the occult'.[181] The experiment requires several magical items and the sarcophagus of Queen Tera to be arranged in a specific way to recreate the magnetic, electrical and radioactive conditions of Tera's original Egyptian tomb, forming 'a kind of magical nuclear device'.[182] If successful, the novel's fanatical Egyptologist Abel Trelawny hopes that they will 'be able to let in on the world of modern science such a flood of light from the Old World as will change every condition of thought and experiment and practice'.[183] Trelawny's chosen image of ancient Egyptian knowledge as 'a flood of light' is apt. Throughout the novel, otherworldly light symbolises the mysterious nature of ancient Egyptian power, which hovers at the nexus between science and sorcery. Trelawny believes that the ancient Egyptians possessed 'a knowledge beyond what our age has ever known', and as a result would revolutionise the modern world through its advancement of scientific understanding.[184]

The key to Tera's revival is a Magic Coffer, which 'glows from within' when exposed to starlight or the light of special lamps, but not to sunlight.[185] Stoker implies that the artefact responds to types of radiation listed by Trelawny, including 'Röntgen and Cathode and Becquerel rays'.[186] Trelawny also suggests that the newly discovered substances radium, helium, polonium and argon may be involved in contributing to its unusual properties, the aforementioned being an assortment of radioactive metals and noble gases (both radium and polonium having been discovered by the Curies in 1898).[187] Stoker's text, particularly towards the novel's climax, is dense with allusions to the work of the early Nobel Prize winners. 'Rontgen won the first Prize in Physics in 1901' and 'Becquerel and the Curies shared the Prize in Physics in 1903'; as Tania Anne Woloshyn points out, '[t]he mania for these rays … was only further fuelled by the prizes'.[188] Indeed, the linguistic emphasis on the word 'noble', which only occurs in the final third of Stoker's text, phonetically invokes both the noble gases, designated as such in 1898, and the Nobel Prizes, named after the Swedish chemist and engineer Alfred Nobel (1833–96). Margaret speaks of Tera's 'nobler dreams' and hopes of being revived in a 'nobler world'.[189] Speaking 'noble words' of Tera's plan, Margaret's face is 'lit from within by a noble light'.[190]

The special lamps that produce the unusual luminescence are explained to contain cedar oil (commonly used in mummy embalming), which is described as having a particular refractive effect on the light.[191] Their flames burn with 'a slow, steady light, growing more and more bright; and changing in colour from blue to crystal white'.[192] The light, already signified as unusual through its changes in hue and intensity, performs similarly to X-rays. When the light interacts with the Magic Coffer, it shines with 'a delicate glow' that increases in luminosity until it appears 'like a blazing jewel' that emits a 'faint greenish vapour'.[193]

A prototype of the radioactive artefact perhaps exists in the Irish palmist William John Warner's (1866–1936) *The Hand of Fate; or, A Study of Destiny* (1898), published under his aliases, Count Louis Hamon and Cheiro. This 'Strange Psychological Story' concerns three men trapped inside a singular Egyptian tomb. When their light source is nearly extinguished, one of the men discovers the key to their escape: 'a large ring' featuring 'a curious flat stone of a greenish colour' inscribed with hieroglyphs, which can be seen 'phosphorescent, emitting a pale uncertain shimmer' in the darkness.[194] The stone is suggestive of phosphorous paint, which was used to create glowing effects in séances,[195] or 'uranium glass', glass that has faint fluorescent qualities due to its uranium content. While uranium had been used in glassmaking since antiquity, it was at its fashionable peak in the late nineteenth and early twentieth centuries. The ring is equally evocative of the fluorescent screens that Röntgen observed glowing faintly green when exposed to X-rays, and which became staple tools in scientific investigations into radioactivity. When we consider, too, that the ancient Egyptian artefact in E. Nesbit's *The Story of the Amulet* (1906) also emits a 'green radiance' when magically activated in dark conditions, and the illuminated translucent archways opened up by the amulet as being visually depicted in such a way as to suggest light bulbs or even Crookes tubes (figure 3.10), we start

Figure 3.10 H. R. Millar, 'The word was spoken, and the two great arches grew', in E. Nesbit, *The Story of the Amulet* (New York: E. P. Dutton, [1907]), p. 342. Source: Internet Archive.

to build a picture of Stoker's glowing Egyptian apparatus as part of a wider trend.[196] Indeed, published the year after the first appearance of *The Jewel of Seven Stars*, Charlotte Bryson Taylor's *In the Dwellings of the Wilderness* (1904) features other glowing Egyptian artefacts discussed in terms that imply contemporaneous discussions of radioactivity. Taylor's protagonists break into a tomb only to find a 'perpetual lamp', an indefinite light source thousands of years old, the likes of which were of considerable interest to leading figures in the nineteenth-century magical revival, including Blavatsky, who claimed that 'the ancient Egyptians … used [perpetual] lamps far more than any other nation.[197] That the lamp is lit 'not [by] a flame' as in the examples given by Blavatsky, 'but a pale radiance as from some material highly phosphorescent' is the first indicator that the lamp is an artefact meant to conjure up images of contemporaneous scientific experiments in darkened laboratories.[198] Particularly telling is the language used to describe the light, 'a small atom of life, set in the midst of universal death' evoking the terminology associated with radioactive decay.[199] Writing in 1900, the American chemist Henry

Carrington Bolton (1843–1903), reflecting on 'New Sources of Light and of Röntgen Rays' in *Popular Science Monthly*, questioned, '[a]re we about to realize the chimerical dream of the alchemists?'[200] The recent discovery of 'mineral substances that apparently give out light perpetually without any exciting cause'– is exactly the apparatus that Taylor imagines, resituating it in the ancient context of the Egyptian tomb.[201] In Taylor's narrative, it is not modern scientists who 'realiz[e] the dream of the alchemists', but the ancient Egyptians themselves who harness the power of radioactive elements.[202] A fuller imagining of a conceptual collision between the ancient magic and contemporary science than Cheiro's fleetingly mentioned ring, then, and a forerunner to Nesbit's and Taylor's glowing artefacts, Stoker's Coffer typifies the ways in which ancient Egyptian technologies were imagined as quite literally outshining contemporary scientific equipment.[203]

Kate Hebblethwaite notes that the concept of transmutation also appears to have made an impression on Stoker's plot. Suggesting that Tera's resurrection is 'a spiritual version of Rutherford and Soddy's theory of the conversion of one chemical element into another through nuclear reaction', Hebblethwaite argues that in the text's original ending in which the queen vanishes, she has in fact taken possession of Margaret's body, her spirit moving from one medium to another.[204] While the theory of transmutation outlined in Rutherford and Soddy's 'Theory of Atomic Disintegration' (1902) was proposed in the year preceding the original publication of Stoker's novel, making this concept's influence on the text incredibly up to date, there is something much more ancient at work. At the time, both transmutation and X-rays were closely associated with alchemy.[205] Rutherford and Soddy's discovery was often illustrated in the press by ancient alchemical emblems, such as the ouroboros, a symbol first used by the ancient Egyptians, while the end of the nineteenth century saw an alchemical revival, during which there were numerous reports that common metals had been transformed into gold through the application of X-rays.[206] In Glasgow in 1904, a company was established whose aim was to modify lead into mercury and iron into copper, while '[i]n France, four alchemical societies and a university of alchemy were founded'.[207] As a legendary science with its origins in ancient Egypt, the transformation of one woman into another appears to be part of an alchemical mythology that also emphasises the permanence of the soul. Tera's ruby cut into the shape of a scarab, placed over her heart during the experiment, functions as the philosopher's stone, converting death to life by providing the queen's spirit with a younger body, mirroring contemporary depictions of radium as 'a miraculous healing agent, the elixir of life' or the legendary stone itself.[208] While other texts had imagined ancient Egyptians living forever, or instead with vastly elongated life spans – the best-known being Arthur Conan Doyle's 'The Ring of Thoth' (1890) and George Griffith's 'The Lost Elixir' (1903), in which the concoction is known as 'the tears of Isis', suggestive of divine power – Stoker's novel far more explicitly veils his alchemical agents in the language of contemporaneous science.[209]

It is clear that Stoker was drawing upon the latest scientific developments in his novel and, indeed, Clive Leatherdale has proposed that there is evidence to suggest that Stoker was keeping abreast of the publications of the great scientists of the age, including a particular paper co-authored by the French physician Albert Laborde (1878–1968) and Pierre Curie c.1900.[210] Like Haggard, who fashioned the Egyptian god Osiris as a kind of ancient Tesla, Stoker did not stop at scientific concepts, and drew upon real scientists as inspiration. The similarities between Marie Curie and the novel's ancient Egyptian Tera are striking. Curie was depicted romantically by the press; she was driven to discover forces that were enigmatic and hidden, which created 'beautiful and eerie effect such as luminescence, color changes in gems, and unexpected chemical reactions'.[211] The perceived disparity between Curie's unobtrusive and delicate demeanour and her phenomenal achievements as a pioneering female scientist only served to further public fascination with her and her work.[212] As women at the forefront of their respective – and, seemingly, closely related – sciences, Curie and Queen Tera appear to have much in common. While a number of critics have already identified the cryptic encoding of Tera's name within her English doppelgänger, Margaret Trelawny's,[213] linking the novel's female characters with Curie reveals yet another facet to Stoker's polysemic name-play; the similarities between 'Margaret' and 'Marie' – to say nothing of the linguistic echo of 'Tesla' and 'Tera' – point to a deliberate alignment of the novel's female characters and this contemporary scientist, both unique individuals who are exceptions to the rule that women were excluded from the 'technological sublime', a useful term coined by Leo Marx to describe the inspirational potential of technological advancement.[214]

It is possible, given these connections, that Curie's sudden celebrity catalysed the writing of *The Jewel of Seven Stars*. In around 1873, Stoker recorded an idea for a narrative in one of his early journals: 'Story of a man brought to life in a dissecting room by the application of a new power unexpected'.[215] If the novel emerged from this kernel – which resembles *The Jewel of Seven Stars* more than any other work in Stoker's *œuvre* – the alterations to the original concept 30 years later may be significant.

168   VICTORIAN ALCHEMY

Curie's remarkable discoveries certainly brought to light 'a new power unexpected' that captured the public imagination and, as such, would have provided a suitable foundation upon which Stoker could weave his scientific romance. The multiple ties to Curie and her work evident in the novel suggest that the change of the subject's sex from male in his original idea to female in his published work was also provoked by Curie and the fascination that she inspired as the first woman to receive a Nobel Prize. Stoker's translocation of this 'power' into ancient Egyptian civilisation certainly makes its reappearance and importance in the modern world all the more 'unexpected'. By channelling these neoteric concepts in *The Jewel of Seven Stars*, Stoker combined elements of the Gothic fantasy – so often preoccupied with antiquity – and the recent findings of contemporary science.

Haggard followed suit, retrospectively offering an explanation for the life-giving pillar of fire in *She* (1887) based on the discovery of radium in his sequel *Ayesha, the Return of She* (1905), a couple of years after the initial publication of Stoker's novel.[216] In a chapter entitled 'Ayesha's Alchemy', we are granted access to Ayesha's 'laboratory' with its 'metal flasks and various strange-shaped instruments', set within a volcano at the peak of which is an enormous stone *ankh*, the ancient Egyptian symbol of life.[217] While the geographical setting is Tibet rather than Egypt, and while Ayesha herself is not ethnically Egyptian, she is nevertheless a priestess of the ancient Egyptian goddess Isis (at times even suggested to be an incarnation of Isis herself).[218] As is the case with many of the Egyptian spaces encountered across this chapter, the laboratory is illumined by 'a gentle light' that does not radiate from a 'lamp or flame of fire' but an unnamed mysterious source.[219] Ayesha reveals the source of the light, a substance (later revealed to be gold) from which emanates 'blistering and intolerable' rays.[220] The narrative makes explicit that Ayesha 'held at her command the elemental forces of Nature, such as those that lie hid in electricity', and here we are presented with Ayesha mastering forces implied to be X-rays through their effect on her body: while the mortal protagonists experience symptoms akin to radiation burns even when wearing protective clothing, 'she … seemed a woman of molten steel in whose body the bones were visible', suffering no ill effects.[221] Equally, the 'Fire of Life' first encountered in *She* is speculated to have 'owed its origin to the emanations from radium, or some kindred substance'.[222] In both *She* and *Ayesha*, these mysterious forces have the power either to injure or destroy, or to reverse ageing and maintain youthfulness. At a time when X-rays' and radium's medical applications – and medical dangers – were only beginning to be understood,

'Ayesha was' as Haggard's 'editor' relays, 'familiar with' 'these marvellous rays or emanations' 'and their enormous possibilities'; 'our chemists and scientific men', he suggests, 'have, at present, but explored the fringe'.[223]

As a civilisation whose remnants and mortal remains were being re-examined in the light of revolutionary scientific techniques, ancient Egypt's association with the modern scientific process, and radical new media such as the X-ray radiograph, itself strongly associated with spiritualism, was inevitable. Marjorie C. Malley even suggests that spiritualism and occultism prepared society to accept the newly discovered invisible rays and the ghostly images they produced.[224] Credited with unparalleled aptitude in such magical sciences as alchemy, ancient Egypt seemed to be antiquity's counterpart to the incredible spectacles produced by modern trailblazing scientists, whose experiments offered tantalising possibilities of telepathy or communion with the spirit world. This concept was not merely confined to the realms of fiction but treated by some as an actual possibility. Soddy, for example, argued that the destruction of Atlantis had come about through the Atlanteans' inexpert attempts to use atomic energy.[225] The use of the imagery and theory behind contemporary science in these texts thus hints at a greater hope that continued study of antiquity might lead to similarly revolutionary advances in occult science, which would make accessible the ghosts of the past.

Scientists and gods

Unlike the scientifically inflected fantastical stories of the nineteenth and early twentieth centuries that, as Melanie Keene argues, 'demonstrate how, for many, the sciences came to replace the lore of old as the most significant marvel and wonder', this literature provides a counterpoint to perceptions of antiquity as inconsequential when confronted by modern developments.[226] Instead, this fiction posits science and antiquity in a dangerous embrace. Resultantly, it is clear that in the late Victorian and Edwardian consciousness, modernity did not necessarily equate to scientific or spiritual advancement. Alchemy, as the pinnacle of mythological science, was, by its very definition, ancient, foreign and teetering on the brink of the magical. As a result, modern scientific developments that appeared to approach the unreachable heights of alchemy were often best described in ancient terms. In ancient Egypt, the lapis lazuli blue hair and gold-plated skin on funerary masks signified the alchemical transformation from mortal into god, a miraculous process that could be undertaken only after death. In the late nineteenth century, equivalent acts which produced otherworldly colour changes, sparks and luminescence about the body of the scientist mimicked a similar process of deification. The more miraculous the scientific processes seemed to be, dramatised as sensory bombardments of glowing coloured tubes, blazing letters, glass wands, eerie luminosity and biblical tongues of flame, the closer the scientist became to a deity.

The city space is crucial to this coming together of the ancient and the modern. Its very fabric the product of multiple eras, London, in particular, with its obelisks standing stark against backdrops of electric lights, encouraged the blurring of the ancient and the modern. The city entertainment that often featured ancient or occult subject matter in its magic-lantern shows, immersive and exotic panoramas, spiritualist séances and early moving pictures, meant that science had to compete by becoming a similar kind of spectacle itself. The thrilling science of the lecture hall was growing ever more distant from the comparatively dry experiments of the laboratory. Science, like the city whose theatrical electrical lighting had emerged victorious in public and private spaces, had become a spectacular commodity.

Outside of the lecture hall, the fantastic imagery of scientific breakthroughs found its way into literature describing ancient powers. Most telling of all are the references to real scientists – most notably, in Haggard's and Stoker's veiled allusions to Nikola Tesla and Marie Curie. They align their ancient Egyptian characters with the modern scientists to give their literary magic modern relevance and potency. In doing so, they also ascribe some level of mysterious otherworldly qualities to these scientists, romantic notions that were already being nurtured by the scientists themselves, or by the journalists who detailed their experiments. As Perry Miller states of the technological sublime, 'the true sublime behind the obvious sublime of the immersive pageant of Technology … is mind itself'.[227] Visionaries like Tesla and Curie became godlike through their mental powers, which resulted in technologies that could produce such wonder, whose transcendence emulated ancient miracles and related back to alchemical tradition. Concurrently, ancient magic was given new significance within the realms of these new quasi-alchemical disciplines. In contrast to an evolutionary idea of linear progress over time, of a potentially threatening stream of unstoppable innovation, visionaries and their discoveries were imagined as inheritors of ancient practices, heirs to Egypt and recipients of alchemical lore.

While the imagination of ancient Egypt's scientific superiority had most frequently been employed as a satirical device in Victorian texts, downplaying modern achievements, the writings of Stoker and Haggard reveal a significant shift in tone, recasting the farcical as the solemn. With impressive visionaries such as Tesla proposing that the ancients had known of the forces only recently rediscovered, such claims took on a new gravitas. Accordingly, it became appropriate and potent for individuals breathing the same cultural air to explore Egyptian themes through novel physical concepts, and to describe demonstrations of these new marvels couched in language evoking antiquity. In opposition to the portrayal of modern literary scientists wielding god-like powers over their experimentees, *The Jewel of Seven Stars* and 'Smith and the Pharaohs' illustrate a transfer of agency from the experimenter to the subject. Ancient Egyptian bodies, once submitted to scrutiny, began to exert power over their investigators, manipulating the latest scientific phenomena with a fluency outdoing and overwhelming their modern counterparts.

Notes

1. Warner 1919, 310.
2. Warner 1919, 82.
3. Warner 1919, 232.
4. Warner 1919, 311.
5. See Duesterberg 2015, who compares ancient Greece, Egypt and Zimbabwe in nineteenth- and early twentieth-century British literature, concluding that Egyptian archaeology offered up a *'less familiar strangeness'* than Greek archaeology, yet nevertheless something more familiar to British writers than ancient Zimbabwe (emphasis in original).
6. Dobson, 'The Sphinx at the Séance' 2018, 85.
7. Nadis 2005, 11, 59.
8. Zimmerman 2008, 14–5.
9. Lockyer 1894, 180.
10. Lockyer 1894, 180.
11. Blavatsky 1877, 526.
12. Blavatsky 1877, 526.
13. Kershner 1994, 73; Corelli 1905, 57–8.
14. O'Byrne 2008, 231.
15. Stiles 2012, 163–5; Corelli 1886 II, 121.
16. Bulwer-Lytton 1871, 8.
17. Bulwer-Lytton 1871, 33, 35, 58, 114, 181, 258.
18. Bulwer-Lytton 1871, 88.
19. Franklin 2018, 29.
20. 'Art. II' 1898, 328.
21. Snell 1890–4.
22. Dennis 2008, 135; Sharpe 2008, 226; Morus 2011, 70.
23. Schivelbusch 1995, 58.
24. Schivelbusch 1995, 65.
25. Hospitalier 1883, 438.
26. Darvay 2016, 159–86.
27. Robinson 1902, 788.
28. Watson 1902, 789.
29. Curran, Grafton, Long, and Weiss 2009, 14.
30. Binczewski 1995.
31. Binczewski 1995.
32. 'Electric Light at the British Museum' 1879, 9.

33. 'Electric Light at the British Museum' 1879, 9.
34. Luckhurst 2012, 176; Gange 2013, 263.
35. Moser 2006, 196.
36. 'The Electric Light at the British Museum' 1890, 301.
37. Moser 2006, 223.
38. Black 2000, 101.
39. 'The Western Electric Company's Exhibit in the Electricity Building' 1893, 1.
40. White and Igleheart 1893, 314.
41. 'The Western Electric Company's Exhibit in the Electricity Building' 1893, 2–3.
42. White and Igleheart 1893, 314.
43. 'The Western Electric Company's Exhibit in the Electricity Building' 1893, 1.
44. These images, among the collections of the Chicago History Museum have the designations ICHi-013685 and ICHi-061755.
45. 'The Western Electric Company's Exhibit in the Electricity Building' 1893, 2.
46. 'The Western Electric Company's Exhibit in the Electricity Building' 1893, 2.
47. 'The Western Electric Company's Exhibit in the Electricity Building' 1893, 2.
48. 'The Western Electric Company's Exhibit in the Electricity Building' 1893, 2.
49. 'The Western Electric Company's Exhibit in the Electricity Building' 1893, 2–3.
50. Davis 2002, 349.
51. Gilbert 1991, 112, 114.
52. Davis 2002, 350.
53. Edwards 1877, 469.
54. Humphreys 2011, 84.
55. Dobson 'A Tomb with a View' 2018.
56. Brendon 1991, 232.
57. Mitchell 1988, 17; Gange 2013, 166.
58. Loti 1910, 26.
59. Humphreys 2011, 82.
60. Wilson 1878, 101; Bulwer-Lytton 1871, 5.
61. Stayton 1990, 8.
62. Professor Grampy's 'thinking cap' consists of a mortar board with a light bulb integrated on top. The bulb illuminates when he has an idea. The character's earliest appearance is in *Betty Boop and Grampy* (1935). See Bowen and Evans 2019, 246–7.
63. Moreno 2000, 32, quoted in Kollin 2010, 15.
64. Kollin 2010, 15, 16.
65. Shelley 1823, 101.
66. Shelley 1823, 97.
67. Carlo 2012, 125–7.
68. Rauch 1995, 241–2; Fara 2003, 168–9.
69. Morus 2011, 37.
70. Shelley 1823, 267.
71. Classen 2017, 53.
72. 'The Mummy' 1827, 330.
73. Hopkins 2003. Lynn Parramore credits 'a mummy unwrapping' held in a Piccadilly Circus theatre in 1821 with inspiring Webb's novel; Parramore 2008, 80.
74. Webb 1828, 218–9.
75. Brio 2018, 333.
76. Keene 2015, 35.
77. Rauch 2001, 63.
78. Rauch 2001, 222.
79. Kennedy 2018, 215.
80. Kennedy 2018, 216.
81. Kennedy 2018, 216.
82. Day 2020, 26.
83. Copland 1834, 172, 174.
84. Copland 1834, 190, 193.
85. Day 2020, 26.
86. Gautier 1872, 405.
87. Fara 2003, 153.

88. Gautier 1872, 405.
89. Fara 2003, 148–51.
90. Poe 1845, 364.
91. Poe 1845, 365.
92. Poe 1845, 365.
93. Poe 1845, 367.
94. Day 2020, 20.
95. 'Through the Opera Glass' 1896, 358.
96. Lant 2013, 61; 'The Mummy' 1911, 454.
97. Freeman 2009.
98. Von Siemens 1893, 186.
99. Von Siemens 1893, 186.
100. Von Siemens 1893, 186–7.
101. Von Siemens 1893, 187.
102. Von Siemens 1893, 187.
103. Von Siemens 1893, 188.
104. Marsh 1907, 130–1; Rebry 2016, 11.
105. Marsh 1907, 131.
106. Roy 1910, 30, translated by and cited in Mukharji 2019, 114.
107. Mukharji 2019, 102.
108. Mukharji 2019, 106, 117.
109. Morus 2005, 88.
110. Parramore 2008, 91; Lyons 2009, 1.
111. Morus 1998, 70; Morus 2004, 38; Morus 2005, 160.
112. Morus 2004, 214–5; Gooday 2008, 58–9.
113. Gooday 2008, 19, 208.
114. Gooday 2004, 251.
115. 'Tesla at the Royal Institution' 1892, 168.
116. 'Tesla at the Royal Institution' 1892, 168.
117. Carlson 2013, 135, 148.
118. Noakes 2019, 107 n42.
119. Hospitalier 1892, 209. The article – with both illustrations – later appeared in English in the 26 March 1892 issue of *Scientific American*.
120. Hospitalier 1892, 209, 210, 211.
121. Hospitalier 1892, 210.
122. Hospitalier 1892, 210, 211.
123. Martin 1895, 922, 923.
124. Johnson 1895, 933.
125. M'Govern 1899, 470–1.
126. Bell 2009, 30, 31.
127. Bell 2009, 31; Lamb 1976, 6, 88.
128. 'Art Treasures Exhibition, 1857' 1857, 1, quoted in Bell 2009, 40; Bell 2009, 43, 45.
129. Bell 2009, 47.
130. M'Govern 1899, 470–1.
131. Gooday 2008, 58.
132. Tattersdill 2016. *The War of the Worlds* was first published in the United States in *Cosmopolitan*, serialised from January to December 1897.
133. Gooday 2008, 59.
134. M'Govern 1899, 476.
135. Willis 2006, 176–7, 200.
136. Nadis 2005, 66.
137. Klein 2008, 378.
138. Tesla 1915, 37.
139. Tesla 1915, 37.
140. Gooday 2008, 58.
141. Haggard 1921, 44. I cite *Smith and the Pharaohs* as it was first published in a single volume (1921) for ease of referencing.
142. Haggard 1921, 44.
143. Haggard 1921, 44.

144. Haggard 1921, 51.
145. Haggard 1921, 44.
146. Haggard 1921, 55, 61.
147. Crookes 1892, 174.
148. Dam 1896, 413; Warner 2006, 256; Lyons 2009, 105.
149. Lyons 2009, 105; Crookes 1892, 176.
150. Lyons 2009, 105; Noakes 2019, 174–5.
151. Crookes 1892, 176; Owen 2004, 70; Oppenheim 1985, 347; Warner 2006, 253–6.
152. Vinson 2018, 57.
153. Dam 1896, 413.
154. Lyons 2009, 105.
155. Natale, 'The Invisible Made Visible' 2011, 353; Natale, 'A Cosmology of Invisible Fluids' 2011, 272; Malley 2011, 8.
156. Luckhurst 2002, 229; Noakes 2019, 288.
157. Mussell 2007, 78; Tattersdill 2016, 97; Natale, 'The Invisible Made Visible' 2011, 348.
158. Eladany 2011, 122.
159. Adams and Alsop 2008, 21; Van Tiggelen 2004, 11.
160. Avery 2015, 65, 69.
161. Avery 2015, 62.
162. Londe 1897, 105.
163. Londe 1897, 105.
164. El Mahdy 1989, 75; Eldany 2011, 126.
165. Adams and Alsop 2008, 21; Chhem 2007, 5.
166. Haggard 1921, 54.
167. Eladany 2011, 126.
168. Luckhurst 2012, 196.
169. Addy 1998, 22.
170. Haggard 1921, 38.
171. Smith 1912, 67. Smith uses an alternative spelling of the pharaoh's name, 'Menephtah'.
172. Brier 2001, 173.
173. Addy 1998, 52. While Haggard amassed ancient Egyptian artefacts, his personal collection does not seem to have included human remains. The mummified body of a priest named Nesmin was sent to Haggard by one of his brothers, Andrew Haggard (1854–1923) in 1886; that Haggard put Nesmin's body in storage that year, before sending his remains to Norwich Castle Museum, suggests that Haggard was not comfortable keeping human remains in his own home. His opinion on mummified remains being kept in museums versus being re-interred evidently changed sometime between 1886 and 1904. In Haggard's fiction, the violation of the mummified body is treated with horror, as in the burning of mummies in *She*, and Cleopatra's penetration of the pharaoh's body to remove jewels secreted within in *Cleopatra*.
174. Haggard 1923, 13.
175. Haggard 1921, 44.
176. Haggard 1921, 54.
177. Dam 1896, 413.
178. Glover 'Introduction' 1996, xvii; Senf 2002, 84. That one of the mummies proposed to have inspired Stoker's novel was X-rayed in the following decades is an apt coincidence; see Sitch 2013.
179. Hebblethwaite 2008, xxviii.
180. Hebblethwaite 2008, xxviii.
181. Luckhurst 2012, 175.
182. Luckhurst 2012, 174.
183. Stoker 1904, 252.
184. Stoker 1904, 269.
185. Stoker 1904, 211.
186. Stoker 1904, 228.
187. Stoker 1904, 228.
188. Woloshyn 2017, 142.
189. Stoker 1904, 223, 227.
190. Stoker 1904, 224, 267, 286.
191. Brier 2001, 43.

192. Stoker 1904, 306.
193. Stoker 1904, 306.
194. Cheiro 1898, 152.
195. Lyons 2009, 95.
196. Nesbit 1907, 68.
197. Taylor 1904, 111; Blavatsky 1877, 226. Several legends of perpetual lamps found in various ancient cultures exist, foremost among them the lamp supposedly found burning within the Roman tomb of Tullia, the daughter of Marcus Tullius Cicero. See Blavatsky 1877, 224.
198. Taylor 1904, 39.
199. Taylor 1904, 39.
200. Bolton 1900, 322.
201. Bolton 1900, 318.
202. Bolton 1900, 318.
203. Malley 2011, 89.
204. Hebblethwaite 2008, xxx.
205. Morrisson 2007, 4.
206. Morrisson 2007, 114; Malley 2011, 11, 51.
207. Malley 2011, 51.
208. Malley 2011, 209; Morrisson 2007, 118.
209. Griffith 1903, 163. The October issue of *The Pall Mall Magazine* in which 'The Lost Elixir' appeared also, incidentally, featured an article on the Curies; see Lees 1903.
210. Leatherdale 1996, 194n19.
211. Malley 2011, 209.
212. Malley 2011, 209–10.
213. Byron 2007 provides the fullest linguistic assessment.
214. Marx 2000; Nye 1994, 31.
215. Stoker 2012, 66.
216. Morrisson 2007, 27; Burdett 2004, 227.
217. Haggard 1905, 294.
218. Haggard 1905, 59, 236.
219. Haggard 1905, 294.
220. Haggard 1905, 295.
221. Haggard 1905, 290, 295. Pierre Curie related symptoms of reddened skin after having tested the effects of radium on his own body; Lees 1903, 201.
222. Haggard 1905, 303 n2.
223. Haggard 1905, 303 n2.
224. Malley 2011, 17.
225. Morrisson 2007, 164.
226. Keene 2015, 19.
227. Miller 1965, 321.

4

Occult psychology: dream, trance and telepathy

> In Egypt ... there was a regular class of dream-interpreters, men who undertook to *explain* what was prefigured by dreams. No one doubted that the phenomena were supernatural.[1]

As this anonymous author observes in an 1861 issue of Charles Dickens's weekly magazine *All the Year Round*, popular nineteenth-century views of ancient Egypt attributed the belief in dreams imbued with encoded meanings to this civilisation, along with an understanding that these symbolic visions might be interpreted by magical means. The well-known episode in the Bible's Book of Genesis in which Joseph predicts the future by interpreting the dreams of the Egyptian pharaoh (and others) was enormously significant in entrenching these long-standing associations not just in Christian culture but across the Abrahamic religions. While elsewhere in the Bible Egypt was depicted as a mysterious country, whose wise men boasted oracular abilities rivalling those of divine origin, Joseph's remarkable mind powers, in contrast, were temporarily bestowed upon him by God, facilitating his rapid rise to power in Egypt.[2] These God-given gifts saw Joseph surpass even the mystical might of 'all the magicians of Egypt, and all the wise men thereof' who cannot interpret Pharaoh's dreams in Genesis.[3]

On 11 January 1913, a dramatic retelling of the story of Joseph in Egypt – entitled *Joseph and His Brethren* – opened in New York's Century Theatre on Broadway. This play is noteworthy for an interesting digression from the scriptural story familiar to the Victorians and Edwardians, however, in its juxtaposition of Joseph's divine interpretative abilities with the occult mind powers of Potiphar's wife, the bewitching Zuleika who, in the Bible, is not even given a name, let alone powers akin to Joseph's. Both her physical attractiveness and keen intellect (specifically, her knowledge of the occult arts) are remarkable enough to inspire 'strange tales'.[4] In Zuleika's room, smoky with incense and decorated with 'curious instruments of magic', she sits before 'a great globe of crystal in which weird changing lights and colours dimly come and go as she speaks'.[5] Zuleika 'stares fixedly' at the crystal ball as if in a trance, a stage direction reproduced by the original actress to assume the role, Pauline Frederick (1883–1938), in a photographic portrait sold as postcards (figure 4.1).[6] Far from the nameless seductress renowned only for her bodily temptations, Zuleika is reimagined as a powerful sorceress whose beauty is matched by her cerebral power, and whose occult abilities rival Joseph's own.

Joseph and His Brethren was written by the prolific British playwright Louis N. Parker (1852–1944). The play enjoyed a successful run in New York – directed by Parker himself – with another production opening in London later that year, premiering on 2 September 1913 at His Majesty's Theatre.[7] As Angie Blumberg has shown, the minor biblical figure of Potiphar's wife was fleshed out by mid-Victorian writers, coming to portend the 'complex, sexually aware female character[s]' imagined as hailing from ancient Egypt at the *fin de siècle*.[8] Blumberg reads in earlier examples of this character the 'mediati[on of] her sensuality through an elevated intellect'.[9] Parker's reinterpretation of the wife of Potiphar follows suit, the playwright granting her knowledge in such spheres that associate her with sometimes controversial topics in late nineteenth- and early twentieth-century psychology. Zuleika attempts to read the present and the future from the crystal ball 'without moving; speaking as if unconsciously'.[10] It is clear that it is the power of Zuleika herself – her 'soul's sight' – and not that of the orb that reveals the images.[11] At one point she declares that 'the storm in [her] soul' is making the mystical pictures cloudy and indistinct; it is her own emotional volatility and inability to maintain the calm of the trance that renders the crystal ball nothing more than a 'useless toy' on this occasion.[12] Nevertheless, such an instance is presented to us as anomalous; in the photograph of Frederick in role, Zuleika, at her crystal-gazing apparatus, is seated and elevated, indicating tranquillity and a sense of authority. The crystal ball's positioning atop the head of a decorative serpent recalls the snake's place in mesmeric and hypnotic writings as an example of an animal that could induce a trance state in its prey.[13] Zuleika's outstretched palms and her fixed gaze indicate the calm stillness required for divination, emphasising both the significance of the hand and the eye, the locus of the transferral of power for the mesmerist and the fixed point of concentration for the hypnotist.

Figure 4.1 'Pauline Frederick – Potiphar's Wife', Bain News Service, c.1913. Source: Library of Congress, Prints & Photographs Division, LC-DIG-ggbain-12499.

Zuleika's alignment with medical and psychical science is also emphasised in Parker's script. Her later command to Joseph during her attempted seduction of him parallels the typical instructions of a stage mesmerist or hypnotist, rather than the biblical *femme fatale*. Instead of '[l]ie with me' – her order in Genesis – she instead directs him to '[l]ook into mine eyes'.[14] While this revision is, on the surface, less sexually threatening, Zuleika's command is still put to the purposes of her attempted seduction of Joseph. The playwright clearly differentiates his version of the story from others through the embellishment of the character of Potiphar's wife, however, bestowing upon her – as far as I can ascertain, for the first time – parapsychological abilities. Parker's reimagining of the Egyptian seductress sees her aligned with contemporaneous popular representations of ancient Egyptian characters who wield the kinds of mind powers that were theorised, tested and described by medical doctors, psychologists and occultists in the nineteenth and early twentieth centuries. Rather than elaborating as to Joseph's abilities, or else those of the famed 'wise men' of Egypt, Parker transfers a rival power to the ancient Egyptian woman, transforming Zuleika's character from a two-dimensional, spurned would-be adulteress into an adversary to be reckoned with. The significant role of women in the magical revival along with women's increasing – if somewhat slower – infiltration into the medical profession makes Zuleika a provocative, and thoroughly modern, choice of hypnotist in Parker's play; Zuleika can be read as part of a sisterhood of ancient Egyptian sorceresses who populate literature of the late nineteenth and early twentieth centuries.

By the *fin de siècle*, trance, hypnosis, telepathy, along with other forms of potentially troubling mind powers, were common themes in popular literature, with these abilities regularly imagined as being put to immoral ends.[15] Pamela Thurschwell suggests H. Rider Haggard's *She* (1886–7), George du Maurier's (1834–96) *Trilby* (1894), Bram Stoker's *Dracula* (1897) and Richard Marsh's *The Beetle* (1897) as prime examples of such narratives.[16] While these novels' antagonists are all coded as 'Eastern' to some extent, it is noteworthy that one of the four – Marsh's Beetle – is Egyptian, with Haggard's Ayesha, though of Arab descent, having lived, thousands of years prior to the novel's events, in ancient Egypt. It is here, according to the novel's sequel – *Ayesha: the return of She* (1904–5) – that she had been trained in the art of clairvoyance (also known as 'second sight' in both occult and stage-magical contexts) by 'a famous magician' in 'the court of the Pharaoh', 'half charlatan and half seer'.[17] By the final decades of the nineteenth century, ancient Egypt had indeed come to represent matchless cerebral faculties, especially those which trespassed into supernatural territory. As Roger Luckhurst notes, ancient Egyptian characters in Gothic fiction of the *fin de siècle* tend to be blessed with superior mental abilities which not only grant prophetic dreams, but also the power to access higher planes of being, to induce trance states in themselves and others, and to communicate via telepathy.[18]

While it was in the literature of the late nineteenth century that such ideas proliferated, we have already encountered earlier tales such as Edgar Allan Poe's 'Some Words with a Mummy' (1845) that made comparisons between the ancient Egyptians and modern notions of remarkable mind powers. In Poe's burlesque, a reanimated mummy imparts 'that the manœvres of Mesmerism were really very contemptible tricks when put in collation with the positive miracles of the Theban *savans*'.[19] Mesmerism – named after German physician Franz Anton Mesmer (1734–1815), who theorised that disruptions to the flow of an invisible fluid from one body to another caused all manner of illnesses – dates to the eighteenth century. Mesmer believed that he could transfer electrical or magnetic energy through 'passes' ('long, sweeping movements of the hands'), 'stares, and pointing with charged wands', all of which purportedly exerted power to alleviate the subject's symptoms.[20] While Mesmer's theory was widely rejected by his fellow scientists, 'it nonetheless was to flourish throughout Europe as a medical treatment and cultural phenomenon', formalised by a network of societies based on the structure of Freemasonry.[21] Part of mesmerism's appeal was its occult flavour: as Nicholas Goodrick-Clarke observes, 'Mesmer himself enhanced the cultic atmosphere of his sessions with an aura of mystery; the rooms were bathed in a soft light, and he wore robes embroidered with occult symbols', clearly fostering an atmosphere of ancient arcane knowledge at the expense of cutting-edge medical science.[22] It followed, in the final decades of the eighteenth century, that individuals put into a trance state through this process were alleged to have demonstrated powers beyond normal human faculties: among them were the ability to 'read thoughts', along with 'prophecy and clairvoyance'.[23]

Mesmerism had a wide following at the time of Poe's text, though it diminished as a popular interest towards the end of the nineteenth century as scepticism regarding its authenticity increased.[24] This coincided with the rise of hypnotism, a mid-nineteenth-century 'medical response to mesmerism' as Alison Winter puts it, which understood the power to slip into trance states as belonging to the subject themselves, rather than an external mesmerist; '[d]ivested of its fluidist explanation … animal magnetism' (as 'mesmerism' was also termed) 'was ushered … as hypnosis into the realm of modern psychology'.[25] It was in 'the 1880s and 1890s' – 'the "golden age" of hypnotism research' – that 'hypnotism enjoyed an unprecedented medico-scientific legitimacy', which necessitated that its practitioners acknowledge the perceived continuation between mesmerism and hypnotism while clearly enforcing the boundaries between the two practices.[26] Nevertheless, hypnotism could not entirely escape the 'supernatural light' in which *fin-de-siècle* scientific enquiry was so often 'cast'. [27] According to Martin Willis, '[t]he scientist added to this increasing paranormality; professionalisation was creating a scientific culture that was more and more unintelligible for a lay audience'. '[W]ith a lack of understanding', Willis asserts, 'comes a sense of mystery and occult'. [28]

Mesmerism's legacy continued among occult and supernatural enthusiasts too, whose interests were also transferred onto spiritualism and, later, theosophy. [29] Spiritualism inherited much from mesmerism: both the mesmeric séance and the spiritualist séance were understood to have relied upon trance states for the manifestation of their desired effects. Both also benefitted from a shared sense of occult lineage; '[t]he phenomena of modern spiritualism demonstrate[d] interesting similarities with ancient theurgy (mediums, trance states, altered voices, spirit communication)' as, of course, did mesmerism before it. [30] Retrospective understandings of mesmerism to have originated in antiquity secured its appeal to those invested in occult power, and deterred those with an aversion to notions of pagan magic; the astronomer Frances Rolleston (1781–1864) claimed to be 'afraid of mesmerism, for it has been employed in the service of idols and evils; the magicians of Egypt … evidently used it'. [31] Just as spiritualism built upon the success of mesmerism, so too theosophy and other esoteric groups branched off from the spiritualist movement. This evolution goes some way in explaining the continuation of interest in trance states across the nineteenth century, which was then made all the more tantalising by its investigation, in the century's closing decades, by a new breed of scientific professional: the psychologist. [32] Whether a subject for study by the physicist, psychologist, or psychical researcher, telepathy, trance and hypnosis provoked popular fascination, encouraged by promises made by alternative religious groups that used ancient Egypt as evidence that esoteric mental abilities were within reach. [33] At the end of the nineteenth century, the Golden Dawn adept Florence Farr commented 'that a great part of Egyptian Magic', which Golden Dawn initiates and other occult devotees hoped to be able to access, 'lay in a species of Hypnotism, called by later magicians, Enchantment, Fascination, and so forth'. [34]

Thus, when we attend to the image of Zuleika at her crystal ball, we read in her outstretched hands – not touching the ball itself but hovering over it as if making 'passes' – a cultural echo of mesmerism. Yet we also see, in her fixed gaze, Zuleika bringing about a trance state in herself rather than anyone else, aligning her occult activities also with hypnotism. While distinctions were made between the practices (most vehemently, at the turn of the century, by medical practitioners), it was not uncommon for the two practices and terminologies to be conflated. Of the texts mentioned by Thurschwell as typical *fin-de-siècle* novels involving mind powers, for instance, *The Beetle* – with its ancient Egyptian antagonist – uses the terms 'mesmerism' and 'hypnotism' interchangeably. In Parker's play, Zuleika likewise appeals to an intermingling of the two; she is equally suggestive of the mystical mesmerist, increasingly denigrated by modern scientists, and of the skilled hypnotist, a champion of medical advancement, albeit one that hinted at (at least in the popular imagination) occult power.

This chapter uses Zuleika as a springboard for an exploration of extraordinary mind powers attributed to or stimulated by ancient Egyptian characters in late nineteenth- and early twentieth-century literature. Theosophy and other forms of Eastern-inspired occultism contributed to the imagination of Egyptian characters' supernormal mental abilities, aligning them with contemporaneous esotericism, but also the modes of modern scientific enquiry that sought to interrogate the powers of the mind that such practices claimed to develop. Haggard's *She* and *Cleopatra* (1889), Marsh's *The Beetle* and Stoker's *The Jewel of Seven Stars* (1903; 1912) have attracted plentiful scholarly attention, and bringing these well-discussed texts into conversation with lesser-known writings – including Florence Carpenter Dieudonné's *Xartella* (1891), Lucy Cleveland's short story 'Revelations of a Moorish Mirror' (1896), and Thomas Jasper Betiero's *Nedoure, Priestess of the Magi: an historical romance of white and black magic* (1916) – suggests the prevalence of such themes across a wide range of literature, from novels to short stories, and in publication venues that range from mainstream periodicals to more specialist occult imprints.

In discussing these texts and contexts, this chapter focuses on the eye as the bodily organ central to depictions of abnormal powers (itself one of the most widely reproduced Egyptian symbols). The eye is both mystical hieroglyph, and site of occult power, but also a vulnerable point of potential psychological penetration exploited by the ancient Egyptian antagonists of *fin-de-siècle* fiction. I investigate links between snakes, cats and the occult eye in fiction, before examining how mirrors, crystals and flames are used as surfaces that aid in the production of trance states. Beyond the eye, ancient Egyptian bodies are repeatedly imagined across this fiction to be dangerously seductive, inspiring passive, automatic states in their victims. This chapter culminates in a reading of the British writer Sax Rohmer's *The Brood of the Witch-Queen* (1918), informed by the theories and practices of famed psychoanalyst Sigmund Freud (1856–1939), who understood nightmares of ancient Egypt as representative of sexual threat. The sexual depravity that the ancient Egyptian antagonists invite across the fictions considered in this chapter – from adultery in *Joseph and his Brethren* to the non-consensual interspecies sexual activity in *The Beetle* – highlights an unresolved tension that characterises these figures at the *fin de siècle*: while wielding parapsychological powers far in advance of those of their potential victims, they are also symbolic of sexual and moral degeneracy, afflictions of particular interest to late nineteenth- and early twentieth-century psychology.

Egyptian mind powers

As Richard Noakes observes, 'many of the architects of the academic discipline of psychology – notably Granville Stanley Hall [1846–1924] and William James [1842–1910] – were involved in psychical research', and 'in many quarters, mesmerism, spiritualism and psychical research were pursued as new forms of psychology or sciences of the mind'.[35] Psychological pioneers, including Freud, collected antiquities and employed archaeological metaphors when describing the mind in their publications.[36] This was the case, too, in spiritualist contexts; in séances and in fictional representations of spiritualist activity, whether they are understood to be 'born of the deepest stratum of the psyche' or the true spirits of the ancient Egyptian dead, in the context of the séance 'Egypt's ghosts claim to develop the brain's supernatural sensitivities'.[37] The Egyptian spirit in such contexts is often 'akin to the modern psychologist, penetrating the depths of the subject's mind and bringing to light relics hitherto hidden', meanwhile enhancing the individual's parapsychological abilities: 'Egyptian artefacts and spirits encourage clairvoyance and psychometry'.[38]

Beyond spiritualism, other communities key to the magical revival – the theosophists and the Golden Dawn foremost among them – were devoted to 'exploring the hidden reserves and dissociated states of consciousness revealed during magical rites'. As with nineteenth-century psychologists, occultists 'ma[de] sense of such phenomena' by 'conceiv[ing] the mind as a series of levels or strata, an analogy legitimated by the scientific prestige of Victorian archaeology [and] geology'.[39] By the end of the nineteenth century the word 'Egyptology' had come to be synonymous with 'esotericism' or 'occultism' in some contexts;[40] Egypt had 'emerg[ed] as the locus associated with the deepest depths of the mind' and 'symboli[sed] the darkest depths of a universal psyche', something as evident in fiction as in the metaphors employed by psychologists, psychical researchers and occultists.[41]

184   VICTORIAN ALCHEMY

Maria Fleischhack indeed records that 'Egyptian characters' in Edwardian fiction, 'through trance states, possession, and other psychically inflected psychological means' 'reveal layers of the cultural and psychological strata of the Western protagonists'.[42] As she points out of Stoker's *The Jewel of Seven Stars*, 'all Western characters in the novel … suffer from symptoms of psychosis – a loss of physical and mental control, hallucinations, delusions, and catatonia' – 'reflect[ing] anxieties specific to the context of contemporary psychological and theosophical research'.[43] Fleischhack also identifies that in several such stories the act of falling asleep 'denot[es] a narrative shift into the realm of the unconscious', a device that predates Edwardian examples, being evident, too, in some of the earliest mummy fiction including Théophile Gautier's 'Le Pied de momie' (1840).[44]

A triad of interests evidently existed in the nineteenth century, and spilling over into the twentieth, that encouraged imaginative leaps from medical study of the mind to studies of the occult and to studies of ancient Egypt. When the British physician T. W. Mitchell (1869–1944) assumed the position of President of the Society for Psychical Research in 1922, such subjects were evidently so interwoven for him to declare in his presidential address that:

> If we try to tell how modern medicine has arisen from the therapeutic practices of primitive peoples, a great gap in our knowledge must be admitted. The scientific medicine of to-day has a more or less uninterrupted history which we can trace back to Greek medicine in the fifth century B.C.; but beyond that all is darkness. The transition from the highest development of thought in savage races to the beginnings of Greek culture forms an almost blank page in the history of mental evolution; but it is probable that progress from the practice of the Magic Age to the practice of scientific medicine has taken place by way of religion, and the priest-physician of early Egyptian and European civilization may be regarded as the connecting link between the medicine man as magician and the physician of to-day.[45]

We see authors eager to fill this 'almost blank page in the history of mental evolution' in a wealth of fictions in the decades prior to Mitchell's statement, though ancient Egyptians are often depicted as outshining the modern physician in their magical-medical powers rather than simply functioning as a missing link in a narrative of linear progress. Ancient Egyptians in the now little-known author Marie Hutcheson's novel *Taia: a shadow of the Nile* (1890) – published under the pseudonym Mallard Herbertson – boast abilities that mark them out as remarkably parapsychologically attuned, for instance. Despite 'not [being] deeply versed in the lore of the diviners of dreams', and drawn to 'the practical' far 'more than the mystic', the priest Phanes experiences preternatural dreams.[46] One of these dreams, which reveals the scheming Atet sitting on the royal throne, is implied to be a glimpse of current events at a significant geographical distance (a power encompassed in the broader category of 'second sight' and which would come to be known as 'telegnosis' once this more medically inflected term was coined in 1911). This may seem a subtle shift from biblical understandings of the ancient Egyptians as using dreams to interpret the future that predate this example by millennia, though it is a crucial one: rather than predicting events to come, ancient Egyptians are understood, by the late nineteenth century, to use periods of unconsciousness to enjoy far broader psychical access to other times and places: not just to the future, but also to the past and present. We have already seen ancient Egyptians travel through time and space via scientific and magical means in this book's second chapter, and fictions such as Hutcheson's saw ancient Egyptians facilitate such journeys exclusively through the power of their own minds, without need of external apparatus. The unconscious mind, and the potent abilities accessed during dream states, renders the brain (usually of an ancient Egyptian but occasionally the mind of a subject in whom an ancient Egyptian awakens latent powers) occult device *par excellence*.

To take a better-known example, in Stoker's *The Jewel of Seven Stars*, dreams appear to enhance characters' natural telepathic abilities. The novel begins with the protagonist, Ross, dreaming of the day that he and his love interest Margaret first met, reliving the details of the memory only to be awoken by a message from Margaret herself. This may indicate that Margaret – who, unknown to her at the beginning of the novel, has a physical and psychical double in the ancient Egyptian queen Tera – has already had some kind of unusual psychic effect on Ross, awakening in him a previously latent parapsychological power to mirror her own visions 'beyond mortal sight'.[47] Margaret's own dreams, she later reveals, allow her access into Tera's world, seen through 'sleeping eyes'.[48] The present, as well as antiquity, is accessible to Margaret in her sleep. At one point, she awakens 'suddenly', sensing that her father is 'in great and immediate danger'.[49] Thus, in Stoker's novel, dreams break down barriers of time and space, allowing Margaret the ability to visualise or at least detect current and past events separate from her immediate surroundings.

Dream-like visions in Stoker's novel also reveal the normally invisible spiritual world. Although Ross has no recollection of 'being asleep or waking', he is aware of the astral body of the tiger that Tera keeps as a pet.[50] Ross describes thinking that 'all the real things had become shadows – shadows which moved'.[51] He sees the tiger's silhouette, and is aware that the creature 'had sentience', hearing it 'mew'.[52] Although this scene does not appear to be a dream in the traditional sense, to Ross it feels like a 'nightmare', having all of 'the horror of a dream within a dream, with the certainty of reality added'.[53] The tiger's astral body is not evident while Ross or any of the other characters are fully conscious; it is instead only in this semi-conscious state that enhances clairvoyant abilities that the spiritual becomes visible. The conscious sight of the open eye and the dream-visions of the closed eye become indistinct while under a supernatural ancient Egyptian influence.

Conceptions of such powers of the mind during unconsciousness were bolstered by historical evidence provided by a wealth of ancient Egyptian texts, newly translatable since the decipherment of hieroglyphs. After major breakthroughs by scholars including the French philologist Jean-François Champollion (1790–1832) in 1822, modern Europeans began to read the ancient Egyptian language for the first time.[54] Archaeological sources revealed that trance states were used in healing, and in these conditions and others, including sleep and coma, the *ka* (the part of the soul believed by the ancient Egyptians to depart the body in death) was considered to be liberated.[55] It is likely that the insights that newly translatable Egyptian texts offered to modern Egyptological enthusiasts, along with the interest taken in mind powers by groups central to the magical revival, and in contemporaneous science, led to individuals reassessing their understandings of the significance of Egyptian-inflected dreams or visions. While key cultural figures such as Thomas De Quincey (1785–1859) had recorded their drug-induced visions of ancient Egyptian iconography earlier in the nineteenth century, by its close such experiences were understood to be far more meaningful than symbolically empty hallucinations brought about by intoxication.

After the novelist Marie Corelli's death, for example, her lifelong companion Bertha Vyver (1854–1941) published Corelli's memoirs, which included an account of 'a curious happening': a mysterious clairvoyant encounter with an ancient Egyptian entity during sleep.[56] Corelli had been given a necklace made (in part) of Egyptian beads by Sir John Aird (1833–1911) likely in the closing years of the nineteenth century, and had promised to lend it to the actress Constance Collier (1878–1955), who was to play the part of the Egyptian queen in a 1906 production of

Shakespeare's *Antony and Cleopatra*.[57] Vyver recalled that Corelli was contacted by the necklace's original owner in a dream, warning her against the necklace being used in the production. A document dating to around 1910 held at Kresen Kernow suggests that Corelli interpreted this figure not simply as a ghost of an ancient Egyptian woman, but Corelli's own former self as she had existed in a past life in ancient Egypt.[58] Corelli made her excuses, and Collier wore a substitute necklace. Sure enough, 'Cleopatra, in a passionate scene with Anthony, tore the necklace she then wore from her throat and it fell in fragments on to the stage'.[59] With the spectral cautioning in this account clearly credited with the survival of Corelli's necklace, it is that Corelli attached considerable meaning to experiences within dreams, perhaps even believing that those regarding ancient Egypt had more significant truths to impart than others.

Corelli was not the only writer who contemplated their receptiveness to the supernatural – and to communications from past selves – during states of unconsciousness. Vivid dreams with Egyptian elements experienced by H. Rider Haggard led him to consider that he had mental access to scenes from past lives.[60] Describing the scenes as 'dream-pictures' or 'mind-pictures', Haggard claimed to have experienced these visions 'between sleeping and waking'.[61] Although he professed to believe they were the product of 'subconscious imagination and invention', he nevertheless considered the possibility that they were in reality 'memories of some central incident that occurred in a previous incarnation' or 'racial memories of events that had happened to forefathers'. Haggard described one of these scenes as set in ancient Egypt, in which he saw himself 'in quaint and beautiful robes … walking at night up and down some half-enclosed and splendid chamber' in 'a great palace'. He was startled to see an attractive young woman who, although frightened (probably at the prospect of the pair being discovered together), embraced him in a moment of passion. Haggard seemed fairly eager to establish his position in this account as sceptical, though he did note that when he related these visualisations to the eminent physicist and ardent spiritualist Oliver Lodge, Lodge seemed to attribute more significance to them (nevertheless, also reminding Haggard of his imaginative gifts as a novelist).[62] Even without any definitive conclusion as to the significance of these dreams on Haggard's part, it remains noteworthy that he at least entertained the notion that during sleep he was receptive to images and scenes from the past, inherited from his ancestors or experienced during a previous incarnation.[63] With Corelli and Haggard reporting similar dreams, visions of ancient Egyptians (with implications for these individuals' understandings of potential previous incarnations) were shared by two of the most popular authors of the late nineteenth century.

Theosophy was certainly responsible for the proliferation of narratives in which modern individuals are proposed to be reincarnations of ancient Egyptians (both fictional and purportedly factual as in Corelli's and Haggard's cases),[64] a truth supposedly often realised during trance or dream states. With its emphasis on ancient Egyptian and Indian mysticism, theosophy revitalised concepts of unusual Eastern mind powers in the late nineteenth century. Helena Blavatsky professed that powers of 'astral travel, mesmerism, or various forms of psychic sensitivity' perfected by the ancients could be harnessed through specific programmes of study.[65] It was in a theosophical publication, in fact, where the term 'parapsychology' appeared for the first time, coined by Max Dessoir (1867–1947), the German psychologist, amateur magician, and member of the Society for Psychical Research. Dessoir first used the term in 1889, in a German theosophical periodical called *Die Sphinx*, which ran from 1886 to 1896. Featuring an Egyptian sphinx with luminous eyes on its cover – glowing eyes being a popular visual shorthand for occult powers of the mind around this time – *Die Sphinx* was published by various theosophical organisations over its decade in print. Nonetheless, for several years it was run by the Munich Psychological Association, rooting it in medicalised understandings of the mind as much as in the occult (its other contributors included the French physician and psychological pioneer Pierre Janet [1859–1947]).

Theosophy has been understood to have made a significant impact on Haggard.[66] Diana Basham argues that in *She* – one of the most iconic novels of the late nineteenth century to deal with the possibilities of heightened powers of the mind – Haggard draws upon theosophical doctrine, specifically Blavatsky's *Isis Unveiled* (1877). Robert Fraser, meanwhile, reads Ayesha as a figure directly inspired by Blavatsky.[67] Blavatsky herself evidently thought highly of the novel. In *The Secret Doctrine* (1888) she asks, 'has the rising novelist Mr. Rider Haggard also had a prophetic, or rather a retrospective, clairvoyant dream before he wrote *She*?'[68] Blavatsky clearly felt that Haggard's novel subscribed to the same fundamental ideologies as theosophy, but she also implies that *She* was based on historical events, the details of which, lost to all but Haggard, were accessed through his singular clairvoyant abilities. Haggard revealed how he had written the novel in a six-week period, so fast that his process appeared to be a kind of automatic writing, recalling spiritualist techniques endorsed by the eminent spiritualist, member of the Society for Psychical Research, and co-founder of the London

Spiritualist Alliance William Stainton Moses (1839–92), who gave this process the name 'psychography'. Through 'psychography', 'automatic writing', or 'spirit writing' as it was also known, spiritualist mediums would purportedly convey written messages from the other side during séances.[69] Psychologists countered with the suggestion that such textual productions might be derived from the subconscious, rather than from the spirits;[70] the novel made a considerable impact upon the thinking of Sigmund Freud in relation his understanding of his dreams, and thus his subconscious.[71] Nevertheless, Haggard's novel was, according to Blavatsky, a text *about* telepathy and written *via* telepathy. It is noteworthy that Blavatsky speculated that Haggard received this secret history in the form of a dream, during a state of unconsciousness. Speculating that '[o]ur best modern novelists, although they are neither Theosophists nor Spiritualists, nevertheless begin to have very psychological and suggestively Occult dreams', Blavatsky suggested that Haggard's telegnosis was the result of ancient methods of unconscious clairvoyance.[72]

Intriguingly, Blavatsky was not alone in suggesting that Haggard received the story via supernatural means. Describing Haggard and himself as 'only telephone wires', the author Rudyard Kipling (1865–1936) told his friend, '*you* didn't write "She" you know … something wrote it through you!'[73] Kipling, somewhat ambiguously, suggested a higher power channelled the novel through Haggard by means of a telepathic communication. Kipling makes much the same claim as Blavatsky, though his invocation of the mechanics of the telephone cloaks his occult suggestion in the language of science and technology. Kipling's metaphor was, however, one common to spiritualist and other esoteric contexts. In describing Haggard in mechanical terms, he refers to the modern technologies imagined – both literally and figuratively – in narratives of entranced bodies, and the mind powers that bring about automatic states. This, as we shall see, featured not just in Haggard's work on Egyptian minds and bodies, but across the writings of his contemporaries.

Bodies and machines

She was dedicated to Haggard's friend, Andrew Lang (1844–1912), who would later go on to serve as President of the Society for Psychical Research, and features the term 'telepathy' to describe Ayesha's powers, a word coined by the Society for Psychical Research's founder Frederic Myers (1843–1901) just four years prior to the publication of the final instalment of *She*, as it was originally serialised in *The Graphic*.[74] Indeed, in the early volumes of the Society for Psychical Research's *Proceedings*, articles on clairvoyance, telepathy and trance far exceed those dedicated to other subjects, such as spirit manifestations.[75] Stories of telepathic communication travelled back from the furthest corners of the British Empire, including Egypt, which had been under British control since 1882. Telepathy was seen as closely related to mesmerism and its more respectable successor, hypnotism, along with trance states entered into by psychic mediums, and was a particularly contentious subject in late nineteenth-century science. Often theorised as akin to communication via radio waves, some considered telepathy a mysterious way of transferring information that would one day be fully understood and put to productive ends, like the technologies that shared its etymology: the telegraph and the telephone. Certainly, scientists as eminent as Lodge, William Crookes and Nikola Tesla entertained this view. The mind powers attributed to Haggard's ancient and formidable Ayesha are thus expressed with the up-to-date terminology used in scientific investigations of seemingly supernatural powers, and to abilities that were speculated to be conceivably integrated into medical understandings of the mechanics of the mind in future. As *She* aptly demonstrates, the ancient and modern were being united through Haggard's use of sources relating to enquiries into parapsychological powers; he contextualises such allusions both in relation to historical details gleaned from Egyptological texts, and new scientific terms to describe paranormal phenomena.

In *She*, Ayesha can project images that are accessed telepathically from the minds of others, or of places with which she is familiar as they currently exist, onto the surface of water within a 'font-like vessel'.[76] Although Haggard's use of water as a surface for scrying is historically accurate in that it was a genuine ancient Egyptian magical practice, Horace Holly, the novel's narrator, describes the image on the water's surface as a 'photograph'.[77] Such a descriptor aligns the picture only not with technologies that promised the impartial processes of scientific observation, but which, as we have seen in this book's first chapter, was ripe with occult possibilities, being a technology employed in both spiritualist image-making and in psychical research. The likening of the magical image to a photograph situates it within distinctly mechanical contexts, emphasising the imagery of modernity to align the text – and Ayesha's supposedly ancient magic – with the contemporary world of Haggard's readers.[78] The overall implication is that such practices are by no means supernatural to Ayesha: as telepathy itself might one day be understood in terms of the brain's mechanics, so are her telepathic powers described, in this instance, in strikingly technological terms.

The British writer C. J. Cutcliffe-Hyne's (1866–1944) short story 'The Mummy of Thompson-Pratt' (1898) literalises the use of technologies in attempting to access the minds of others. Set at the University of Cambridge – the same university where Holly works in *She* – with its reputation as a place of cutting-edge scientific innovation, and also the birthplace of the Society for Psychical Research, the variety of occult enquiry it draws upon is gentlemanly and scientifically rigorous. Cutcliffe-Hyne's narrative centres on the Egyptologist Gargrave, who attempts to learn of ancient Egypt by hypnotically connecting a mummy to its living descendant, the titular Thompson-Pratt. Gargrave's methods involve the employment of modern technologies including the phonograph, which he uses in tandem with 'a hypnotic influence' produced via a technique vaguely described as involving 'something more' than 'the usual way', in order to manifest – and, crucially, to capture – his results.[79] Although his method utilises up-to-date equipment and a more reputable variety of trance from a medical perspective – hypnotic rather than mesmeric – there is clearly an element of the ancient to his technique, gleaned, one assumes, from his Egyptological studies: he uses a mysterious green powder that produces a flame when mixed with water to bring an end to Thompson-Pratt's unconscious state. Along with Thompson-Pratt's assertion that 'I've a notion those old Egyptians were a lot ahead of us in some branches of chemistry', and his entreaty that if his ancient Egyptian ancestor 'let slip something in the natural science line which is strange to us to-day' he might be informed after the fact, the overall presentation of the experiment is one in which modern and ancient knowledge are brought to bear on each other.[80] With the mummy and its hypnotised descendant laid out on the floor, the unconscious face of the living Thompson-Pratt appears 'dead', while the mummy's reveals 'some flicker of life'.[81] When the mummy begins to speak of his earthly experiences, it is with Thompson-Pratt's voice, suggesting a psychical borrowing of the mechanics of Thompson-Pratt's vocal cords, channelled through the mummy's mouth as if via telephone. The ancestral link between the two individuals is paramount. It is not simply the hypnotic trance that allows the mummy to speak, but a deeper connection, one that is suggested to be more prosaically scientific in nature: hereditary, rather than spiritual. Perhaps drawing upon theories of organic memory which, according to advocates such as Henry Maudsley (1835–1918), allowed 'past impressions' to be passed down through families, and calling to mind Haggard's speculations that his dreams of ancient Egypt had been experiences of a direct ancestor, shared bloodlines appear to be vital to the success of the experiment.[82] That the telephone is also evoked in Ernest Richard Suffling's

'The Strange Discovery of Doctor Nosidy' (1896), with which I opened *Victorian Alchemy*, suggests this device as one often imagined as having occult applications in a broader span of Egyptian-themed fiction of the 1890s. While the electrical instrument is unnamed in Suffling's tale, the illustration by Paul Hardy shows the equipment to resemble a telephone, albeit one that also requires a hypnotic – as well as electrical – connection.

The contemporaneity of 'The Mummy of Thompson-Pratt' is emphasised by the employment of a phonograph to capture the mummy's message; the significance of this piece of equipment is stressed by its positioning in the foreground of an accompanying image by the illustrator T. W. Holmes (1872–1929). Through the phonograph recording, the experiment might theoretically be verified, although as the mummy speaks both in Thompson-Pratt's voice and in English, such a record would surely be read by anyone not in attendance at the original demonstration as a hoax. The phonograph was associated with both occult and scientific contexts; as Steven Connor records, both 'the telephone and the phonograph' 'quickly entered the language of spiritualism', as had telegraphy before them.[83] Indeed, in this case, the phonograph is used to record a message relayed by the dead, an uncanny task made even more unnatural by the contrast between the antiquity of the mummy and the newness of the apparatus. The tale evokes Thomas Edison's original speculations as to how his invention would be put to use: to record 'the sayings, the voices, and the last words of the dying member of the family'.[84] It also foreshadows Edison's efforts to create apparatus to converse directly with the deceased in the early 1920s.[85] Tales such as Cutcliffe-Hyne's, but also those as early as Poe's 'Some Words with a Mummy', were the precursors to the design, if not the realisation, of electrical machines that would make the dead speak. Like the physical body, which seemed to have been reduced to its mere mechanics by the hypnotist or mesmerist, leaving the entranced brain free for higher – potentially occult – functions, machines become increasingly important in facilitating access to ancient minds in these literary contexts, encouraging a sense of scientific innovation and impartial observation when it comes to measuring and recording occult phenomena.

Crucial to a historical understanding of the parallels drawn between bodies and machines in such contexts is the British physician William Benjamin Carpenter's (1813–85) criticism of supernatural explanations for 'a range of abnormal mental phenomena including hysteria, somnambulism, "trance" behaviour, mesmerism … and table turning'.[86] Carpenter held that such states and their seemingly occult productions were exclusively the result of external suggestion, which rendered the individual who was 'subjected to such involuntary actions' little more than an automaton.[87] The effects of mesmerism and hypnotism were often described in similar terms of 'automatism' and mechanics, which were likewise employed by spiritualists and psychical researchers.[88] Victorian spiritualists 'sought to defend the conventions of the spirit circle by appealing to analogies between séance bodies and scientific instruments'.[89] The American spiritualist medium Leonora Piper (1857–1950), to take one striking example, would describe herself, when in a trance state entered into via hypnosis, as 'the Machine'.[90] As Noakes has established, such language was used by those who investigated such phenomena; the Society for Psychical Research 'appropriated physiologists' and psychologists' language of mental machinery', nonetheless 'le[aving] a place for spiritual agencies'.[91] Thus when we encounter bodies rendered little more than shells by trance states in nineteenth-century fiction, the automaton is a decidedly ambiguous figure, as much suggesting hypnotic suggestibility as conceptualised by modern medicine as it does a genuinely occult state in which the passive brain and body might be entered into by another entity.

This ambiguity is certainly at play in Richard Marsh's 1897 novel, *The Beetle*. Marsh's eponymous villain initially establishes control over its first victim, Robert Holt, with the power of its voice alone. Holt is disgusted by his own 'passivity' and 'impotence' while under the Beetle's influence.[92] He reports that he moves 'mechanically' and 'automatically', and he and the novel's other characters consider him to be 'more like an automaton than a man'.[93] The unmanned entranced subject is left powerless to resist when the Beetle enters his body through his mouth in a moment that reads like an act of possession: 'horror of horrors! – the blubber lips were pressed to mine – the soul of something evil entered into me in the guise of a kiss'.[94] It is through this forced oral penetration that Holt's body is controlled when it is outside of the Beetle's immediate vicinity. In this state, the Beetle can direct Holt through London's streets without losing its power over him, maintaining constant physical as well as mental dominance. Another male character describes how the Beetle transforms Holt into a 'fibreless, emasculated creature', not just underscoring how the androgynous Beetle itself troubles gender, but equally suggesting that men are transformed by its powers of possession into the passive, receptive bodies of (usually female) spiritualist mediums.[95] The Beetle manipulates its victims by overwhelming their psychological selves, leaving them little more than physical machinery. Likewise, Josephus, who falls under the hypnotic influence of the Horus Stone in George Griffith's novel *The Mummy and Miss Nitocris* (1906), moves 'with the motions of a mechanical doll'.[96] Such descriptions are common to depictions of the mesmeric or hypnotic trance, though their employment in relation to the mind powers of Isis worshippers and the parapsychological effects of ancient Egyptian relics see modernity and antiquity collide.

It is perhaps unsurprising that at a time when ancient Egyptian mind powers – whether used by ancient Egyptian characters or modern Egyptologists – were imagined as bringing about 'automatic' states, reanimated mummies were themselves being conceptualised as simply bodily mechanisms controlled by external powers, at odds with earlier depictions of reanimated ancient Egyptians who retain their identity from when they were alive. The foremost of these texts is Arthur Conan Doyle's (1859–1930) short story 'Lot No. 249' (1892). Crucially, it is ancient Egyptian knowledge and not any more modern scientific discovery, recorded on 'an old yellow scroll of papyrus', which 'contains wisdom … nowhere else to be found', that allows the tale's antagonist – Edward Bellingham – to 'use the creature as an agent'.[97] '[W]ield[ing] a weapon such as no man had ever used in all the grim history of crime', Bellingham revives the mummy in order to guide it to commit murder on his behalf.[98] We can read Doyle's reanimated mummified individual, known only by its auction number – the 'Lot. 249' of the story's title – as a body emptied of its soul, and therefore at risk of being controlled by external forces. As Noakes records, 'spiritualism's controversial claims' included the idea 'that the spiritual body survived the death of the natural body which was itself a mere "machine"'.[99] Doyle had attended séances and participated in telepathic experiments as early as 1887, and was to join the Society for Psychical Research the year after the publication of this short story, having founded the Hampshire Society for Psychical Research in the interim. Doyle's mummy is all machine. Its 'blazing eyes' visible through the dark as it pursues the tale's protagonist – this luminance pictured as narrow beams of light in an illustration by the American artist William T. Smedley (1858–1920) – marks it out as an occult body, but instead of suggesting the power of this particular individual, the light symbolises the psychical connection between it and Bellingham that transforms it into aggressor.[100] While the method of Bellingham's control of the mummy is never made clear, the implication is that it is derived from Bellingham's Egyptological study, rather than any modern scientific knowledge. As we shall see in the next section of this chapter, the light-emitting eye is usually emblematic of mind powers: mesmerism, hypnotism and telepathy, and so might conceivably indicate a telepathic link between Bellingham and the mummy, in a similar vein to the Beetle's control of its victims. With Doyle's mummy, however, there is little suggestion that any of its original individuality is retained.

Less well-known, but predating Doyle's text in its imagination of mummified bodies as automata, is the American writer Florence Carpenter Dieudonné's *Xartella* (1891). This short, fantastical text opens with a mysterious 'old stranger' asking the narrator whether he believes in the titular Xartella, 'a deathless creature … who had been seen, for centuries, in the vicinity of [the] pyramid' that they are visiting.[101] The stranger speaks of events that took place 12 years ago, which he believes will convince the narrator that Xartella really existed. In the stranger's account, the eponymous character is 'more than human'; '[h]e might be a thousand years old; ten thousand years old', with a face that 'might have borrowed its repose from the Sphynx'.[102] That Xartella has remarkable mind powers is soon apparent in the stranger's assertion that '[w]hen the gaze of those wondrous deep eyes struck mine I could not move'.[103] The stranger is only able to breathe again once eye-contact is broken. Xartella uses his powers (speculated by the stranger to be hypnotic in nature) to coerce a young woman, Artossa, into fleeing her home with him; that she is entranced is indicated in the lack 'of expression in her fixed blue eyes', and her falling to the floor 'like an inanimate object' 'in a stupor of unnatural slumber'.[104] The stranger recounts how Xartella commands '[a] bevy of beautiful slave girls' to tend to Artossa, and as they approach he 'notice[s] how singular was their step, their feet click[ing] like machines'.[105] Such descriptions illustrate how those under Xartella's control are robbed of their individuality, the clicking sound made by the repetitive movements of their bodies suggestive of the telegraph or typewriter. '[R]eturned [to] the somnambulistic state', Artossa walks with 'the same clicking step'.[106] As in Doyle's 'Lot No. 249', in *Xartella* mind powers dating back to ancient Egypt are used to exert total control over the bodies of others, which offer little resistance when confronted with such arcane forces.

Xartella's heinous plan is revealed in the interior of a pyramid, where he conducts experiments on the dead in an attempt to bring them back to life. All that he has been able to achieve, however, is the reanimation of their bodies; without a soul, the bodies are mere biological mechanisms. The stranger recalls the horrifying sights of the experiment: 'a living mummy' that 'moved its eyes and head but did not speak', and 'a beautiful youth' – a former mummy restored to perfect physical health – with 'great vacant eyes' that 'stared' 'sightlessly', who Xartella 'drop[s] like a limp doll upon an inanimate collection of the same sort of humanity'.[107] Some of these beautiful automata are evidently selected to serve Xartella: we retrospectively recognise the slave girls with their clicking feet to be reanimated mummies, as are Xartella's dancers who 'mov[e], in a mechanical accord, with discordant music' until Xartella releases his control over them and '[l]ike dolls they ... drop in their places'.[108] The repetition of the doll simile underscores Xartella's total physical control of these bodies, the sinister way in which he 'plays' with them, and their disposability. Artossa's true purpose is made clear at this point: under Xartella's hypnotic influence she must sacrifice herself in exchange for souls to inhabit the bodies of the reanimated dead. The scheme is foiled by Xartella's spurned wife (restored to life by the stranger), who brings about both her and Xartella's deaths, drawing the tale to a close.

Across these fictions, mechanical bodies and passive minds rendered malleable through mesmeric or hypnotic trance states find counterparts in modern machines – the telegraph, telephone, typewriter and the phonograph – while a figurative precursor is suggested in Haggard's envisaging of telepathically transferred pictures as photographs, in which thoughts are visualised as mechanically reproduced images. Automatic bodies can be controlled like machines once ancient Egyptian mind powers are used to infiltrate the brains of these experimenters' subjects: with its wire-like neurons and electrical impulses, the brain suggests itself as yet another piece of technology, at present incomprehensible by modern science in its seemingly supernatural abilities, but fully within the understanding of the ancient priests, whose knowledge is either encoded on scrolls or else still known to ancient Egyptians who have survived for millennia. Across these fictions, and in culture more broadly, as we shall see, it is the eye that is often conceived as the point at which mind and body might be simultaneously penetrated, and the occult site from which occult mind powers are most often imagined as emanating.

Serpents, cats and the occult eye

In *She*, Ayesha's mysterious mind powers are imagined as embodied in her unusual eyes. As in mesmeric demonstrations, which often involved prolonged, continuous eye-contact between the mesmerist and their subject, Ayesha exerts control through the power of her stare, which incapacitates and restrains 'more strongly than iron bonds'.[109] The mesmeric trance, understood to be the result of electrical or magnetic forces, clearly impacted upon Haggard's depiction of his ancient character. Her ability to 'blast' her opponents is described as being the result of 'some mysterious electric agency', one which seems to be expressed corporeally when her eyes blaze with 'an awful light ... almost like a flame'.[110] Indeed, the physical sensation of meeting her gaze in direct eye-contact is described as if experiencing 'some magnetic force' or a kind of electric current.[111] The unusual way in which Ayesha's eyes produce light (perhaps itself of an electrical variety) is in keeping with a broader late nineteenth-century literary trend whereby the strange eyes of the 'criminal hypnotist' were emphasised as a physical marker of the danger they posed.[112] This, however, is a trait common not just to the hypnotist or mesmerist, but to the telepath and the clairvoyant. The literary characters most commonly held aloft as examples of the embodiment of anxieties surrounding psychological forces, but particularly those connected to occultism in the late nineteenth century – Svengali, Dracula, Ayesha, the Beetle – all have eyes that are in some way marked out as abnormal. Living inside her tomb-like cavern, surrounded by mummies, and herself ancient and swathed, Ayesha is mummy-like, with her dark eyes imbued with magical power calling to mind the enlarged eyes painted onto sarcophagi in stylised representations of the dead.

Beyond contemporaneous parapsychology, Haggard drew upon classical and Egyptian mythology concerning the power of the eye, particularly that involving snakes. Ayesha's gaze is described as 'more deadly than any Basilisk's'.[113] Reptilian, and often depicted as a variety of snake, the basilisk is just one of the serpentine creatures to which Ayesha is connected, in a series of references that go well beyond the traditional trope of the snake as symbolic of feminine evil. Lucy Hughes-Hallett notes that the word 'basilisk' comes from the Greek meaning 'little king', used to refer to the ancient Egyptian *uraeus* or the cobra, symbolic of royalty, which the Greeks thought could kill with a single glance.[114] The Egyptian goddess Wedjat, who was both the cobra worn by royalty and the personification of the symbol more commonly known as the Eye of Horus, was one of two Egyptian snake goddesses who were said to kill with the power of their gaze.[115] Both Wedjat and another female snake deity, Renenutet, were often represented in the form of a snake with a woman's head or a woman with a snake's head.

Indeed, a snake with a woman's head appears in Haggard's later work of fiction *The World's Desire* (1890), which he co-authored with Lang, and is perhaps a feature derived from Haggard's Egyptological reading. In this sequel to Homer's *Odyssey*, Haggard and Lang imagine an evil sorceress queen, Meriamun, who awakens an occult embodiment of her own sin to magnify her power. Taking a jewel carved into the shape of a serpent, Meriamun breathes life into the amulet and awakens a creature with a snake's body and her own face. In this context, while the snake has the appearance akin to that of the goddesses Wedjat and Renenutet, and is described as emitting 'from its eyes … a light like the light of a flame', suggestive of her powerful occult gaze, this is by no means a holy light.[116] In fact, that the luminance is described as 'witch-light', along with various references to evil, establishes that this entity is as much biblical serpent as it is Egyptian deity.[117] Meriamun already has impressive psychical powers before invoking the serpent – she has dreams that reveal the past and future, and she claims to 'know of the magic of … Queen Taia', a real ancient Egyptian monarch (whose name is now most frequently spelled in English as 'Tiye') who is invoked in several texts dealing with the Egyptian occult.[118] Haggard and Lang cast Meriamun – and, implicitly, Tiye before her, as a psychic medium; she poisons one of her ladies in waiting who catches the eye of the pharaoh before boasting that she can 'drag her spirit back ere she be cold, from where she is, and … force knowledge from its lips', a chilling claim which she goes on to fulfil.[119] While the novel was not especially well received – likely due to its archaic style – Robert Louis Stevenson (1850–94) praised the text in his correspondence with Lang, noting in particular that 'he is "thrilled and chilled" by Meriamun'.[120]

While the text was first serialised in *The New Review* between April and December 1890, a single-volume novel edition of the text being published in autumn of the same year, it was not until 1894 that an edition of the text appeared that featured illustrations. This later version of the text captured Meriamun in an image by Maurice Greiffenhagen (1862–1931) that saw Haggard and Lang's villainess become part of a broader group of Egyptian snake-women in *fin-de-siècle* visual culture, which included the American artist Charles Allen Winter's (1869–1942) painting *Fantasie Égyptienne* (1898). Greiffenhagen's illustration (figure 4.2) captures an erotic view of the sorceress, in which she gazes into the eyes of the snake bearing her own face. Meriamun's and the serpent's eyes appear white as if lacking pupil and iris, conveying an occult quality to this gaze – a suggestion of the glowing 'witch-light' to which Haggard refers. That Meriamun reads as a kind of successor to Ayesha is underlined in this image. Not only are Ayesha and Meriamun both women whose occult power is imagined both in terms of their luminous eyes and in their connection with snake imagery, but the coiling of the snake around Meriamun's waist evokes the 'double-headed snake of solid gold' that secures Ayesha's diaphanous drapery about her body in *She*.[121] With her predatory gaze, 'hissing' tone and sinuous form partially concealed in white, filmy gauze adorned with serpents, Ayesha's association with snakes – particularly when contextualised alongside Meriamun – functions in more complex symbolic ways that convey a sense of serpentine eroticism and imply deadly power expressed through unblinking eyes.[122] As a woman whose

Figure 4.2 Maurice Greiffenhagen, 'And they whispered each to each', in H. Rider Haggard and Andrew Lang, *The World's Desire* (London: Longmans, Green and Co., 1894), new edn, facing p. 192. Author's own.

200 VICTORIAN ALCHEMY

eyes can kill, or else render the onlooker powerless to move, she is a Medusa-like figure.[123] Medusa herself, sometimes also depicted wearing a belt of two intertwined snakes, seems a likely source of inspiration for Haggard's semi-divine adversary with a fatal gaze.[124]

Snakes were also of particular interest to understandings of mesmerism across the nineteenth century. The cover of the occult novel, *The Hand of Fate; or, a study of destiny* (1898) by the Irish palm-reader William John Warner – more commonly known as Cheiro – combines imagery of ancient Egyptian architecture with electrical forces emerging from a giant hand, evocative of the visualisations of mesmeric force (figure 4.3), which was customarily depicted as emerging in lightning bolts from the practitioner's fingertips. The snake in one of the lower corners, struck by electricity, reflects the novel's imagining of a family curse manifesting as a venomous snake growing out of a man's abdomen, but also, even before the novel is opened, denotes content associated with animal magnetism. Snake charming was often cited as evidence of the veracity of the mesmerist's ability to induce trance states in non-human animals. Snakes were also credited with their own mesmeric powers, which they supposedly used to entrance their prey.

While snake charming was especially popular with Western tourists travelling to Egypt and India in the nineteenth century, in Britain experiments into the possibility of mesmerism between humans and other animals in medical contexts often made use of domesticated species. The physician John Wilson's (d.1858 or 1859) *Trials of Animal Magnetism on the Brute Creation* (1839) outlines how he performed his experiments on cats, all of which (in his account, at least) seemed especially susceptible to his mesmeric techniques. The year prior, on 24 April 1838, the physician John Elliotson (1791–1868) had performed an experiment to see whether a young girl could be mesmerised by a cat. While it transpired that the cat did not have mesmeric powers, the occasion was still historically significant; when the anatomist Herbert Mayo (1796–1852) reported on the afternoon's experiments in *The London Medical Gazette*, one of his accounts featured the first use of the word '"trance" to describe the mesmeric sleep'.[125]

The trope of the 'magnetised' animal was reversed in the 1890s for comic effect in a cartoon published in *Punch* (figure 4.4), imagining the 'Horrible Result of Using the "Egyptian Fur-tiliser".' The image illustrates the effects of using '180,000 mummified Cats … as Manure', the ground-up mummified cat bodies having been used to fertilise farmland in Britain.[126] The feline remains in the *Punch* cartoon have evidently been worked into the soil, and the ghosts of the mummified cats emerge out

Figure 4.3 Cheiro, *The Hand of Fate; or, A Study of Destiny* (New York: F. Tennyson Neely, 1898), cover design by T. Di Felice. Source: Internet Archive.

Figure 4.4 Edward Tennyson Reed, 'Horrible result of using the "Egyptian fur-tiliser"', *Punch* 98 (2536) (15 February 1890): 81. Author's own.

of the ground to face the farmers who have employed their sacred bodies for so mundane a purpose. Their spirits maintain the appearance of their mummified bodies, some with pharaonic headdresses to add a further comic element, these being reserved for Egyptian royalty. In fact, their tightly wound bodies and the way in which they rear up gives them a serpentine appearance. Most noteworthy of all, for the purposes of this chapter, are the beams of light that appear to emerge from the eyes of the spectral cats. The light appears to mimic depictions of occult forces working between the bodies of mesmerist or hypnotist and their subjects; here, this is no longer a power exerted by one human over another, or by one human over a non-human animal. Ancient Egyptian animals are imbued with sophisticated psychical powers, which they use to strike terror into the farmers, most of whom fall backwards in fear, while one sprints off into the distance.

The French writer Anatole France's (1844–1924) short story 'M. Pigeonneau' (1887), rarely discussed in Anglophone scholarship, is one in which, converse to the mesmeric experiments earlier in the century, a cat is used successfully as a hypnotic agent. In this text, an Egyptologist is hypnotised, and again the eye is highlighted as the sight of the transference of power.[127] Dedicated to his friend Gilbert-Augustin Thierry

(1843–1915), who was heavily involved in the Occult Revival in France and who had recently published his own text on the subject of hypnotic suggestion,[128] France's tale opens with an Egyptologist – the eponymous Pigeonneau – delivering a lecture on the beauty regime depicted in an ancient image of an Egyptian woman. As he speaks, his view alights upon a man in the audience whose beard lends him an Assyrian appearance, and Pigeonneau is struck by the fixed gaze of the man's green eyes. He finds that '*malgré le plus violent effort, je ne parvins pas à arracher mes regards des deux vivantes lumières auxguelles ils étaient*' ('despite the most violent effort, I did not manage to tear my eyes from the two living lights to which they were mysteriously riveted'), the description of the eyes as lights immediately establishing the man's occult power.[129] Pigeonneau finds himself working '*[s]ous l'influence d'une force étrangère, inconnue, irrésistible*' ('[u]nder the influence of a strange, unknown, irresistible force') as he speaks, deviating from his paper and passionately improvising on the subject.[130] The man – later revealed to be a physician called Diaoud – is introduced as employing '*le magnétisme, l'hypnotisme et la suggestion*' in order to cure ailments, and accompanies the beautiful Annie Morgan, who also has striking green eyes and to whom Pigeonneau similarly finds himself drawn. Pigeonneau himself seems to be more psychically intuitive after this event and when, after three days of productive work, the bell rings announcing a visitor, his now keen senses pick up that '*la secousse imprimée au cordon avait quelque chose d'impérieux, de fantasque et d'inconnu*' ('there was something about the shock imprinted on the cord that was imperious, whimsical, and unknown').[131] The bell announces Morgan's arrival, and she relates that she and Pigeonneau were both ancient Egyptians in previous incarnations (a claim that is never verified). She had attended his lecture in the hopes of making an Egyptian costume that she desires to wear at a fancy-dress ball as historically accurate as possible. Inviting him to her home to consult with her on the costume, Morgan's revelations are so eccentric that Pigeonneau plans not to attend, and when he is surprised to find himself compelled to, Morgan reveals that '*j'ai des secrets pour me faire obéir*' ('I have secrets by which I make myself obeyed').[132] Having received Pigeonneau's advice as to the historical authenticity of particular details, Morgan makes one more unexpected request: that Pigeonneau write her a story. This he does, after receiving from her a gift of '*un petit chat*' ('a little cat') whose name is Porou, '*fort ressemblant … à ceux de ses congénères dont on trouve en si grand nombre, dans les hypogées de Thèbes, les momies enveloppées de bandelettes grossières*' ('very similar … to those of his species which one finds in such great number, in the burial chambers of Thebes, the mummies wrapped in coarse strips').[133]

With Porou in attendance, Pigeonneau finds himself distracted and unable to work, until the deadline for the story approaches when, he relates, suddenly '*j'écrivis tout le jour, avec une prodigieuse rapidité*' ('I wrote all day long, with amazing speed').[134] The Egyptologist becomes automatic writer, and when he finishes the tale he observes that '*la chambre n'était éclairée que par les yeux phosphorescents de Porou*' ('the room was lit only by Porou's phosphorescent eyes'). The cat's luminous eyes – all that is visible in the dark once the automatic writing is complete – is a direct link back to the luminous gaze of Diaoud and, indeed, the occult light-giving eye so common to individuals who sport parapsychological abilities in *fin-de-siècle* fiction were anticipated by the belief, centuries prior, that cats' eyes emitted light at night that they had captured during daylight hours, an 'unsettling' quality that only reinforced their perceived connections to demons at this time.[135] The revelation, at the story's end, that Pigeonneau wrote the story for Morgan under Diaoud's influence, purely so that she could ridicule him, emphasises the remarkability of Diaoud's powers, as well as the trivial ends to which his abilities are put:

> *Ni Bernheim, ni Liégeois, ni Charcot lui-même n'ont obtenu les phénomènes qu'il produit à volonté. It produit l'hypnotisme et la suggestion … par l'intermédiaire d'un animal … il suggère un acte quelconque a un chat, puis il envoie l'animal … au sujet sur lequel il veut agir. L'animal transmet la suggestion qu'il a reçue, et le patient, soul l'influence de la bête, exécute ce que l'opérateur a commandé … Miss Morgan … fait travailler Daoud àson profit et se sert de l'hypnotisme et de la suggestion pour faire faire des bêtises aux gens, comme si sa beauté n'y suffisait pas.*[136]

Neither Bernheim, nor Liégeois, nor Charcot himself have obtained the phenomena that he produces at will. He produces hypnosis and suggestion … through an animal … he suggests some action to a cat, then he sends the animal … to the subject on whom he wants to act. The animal passes on the suggestion it has received, and the patient, under the influence of the beast, does what the operator commanded … Miss Morgan … makes Daoud work for her profit and uses hypnotism and suggestion to make fools of people, as if her beauty was not enough.

France compares Diaoud's abilities to those of several high-profile medical practitioners: Hippolyte Bernheim (1840–1919), remembered for his contributions to the understanding of hypnotic suggestion; Jules Liégeois (1833–1908), who worked on hypnotic suggestion and sleepwalking in relation to criminal activity; and Jean-Martin Charcot, who believed that susceptibility to hypnosis went hand in hand with hysteria. That Diaoud's powers exceed those of the most famous French doctors investigating hypnosis is one thing; for the effects that he produces to be achieved through a suggestive cat renders the scenario ridiculous and provides France's story with its comic *dénouement*.

As Kim M. Hajek points out, '"pigeon" in French can denote a gullible person, someone easily swindled'.[137] That Pigeonneau – whose surname is the term for a baby pigeon – has been mastered by a cat also imbues the tale with a fabular quality and recalls medical hypnotism's indebtedness to the more spurious animal magnetism. While cats had been used in mesmeric experiments earlier in the century, likely due to their ready availability and tameness, the cat is suitable for introduction into tales of the supernatural because of its longstanding association with witchcraft (Tera's tiger cat in *The Jewel of Seven Stars* is even referred to as her 'familiar') and its sacred status in ancient Egypt.[138] In 'M. Pigeonneau', the cat's name, 'Porou', suggests the porousness of Pigeonneau's psyche, and its susceptibility to external suggestion, but equally the cat's openness to suggestion, which it can then pass on to others. Porou's eyes glowing in the dark heavily indicate the eye as the site of such porousness.

Through the serpent's eye to the cat's eye, these texts imbue the mesmeric or hypnotic gaze with qualities that invoke the powers of Egyptian deities or sacred animals, but which, intriguingly, also replicate something of the materiality of Egyptian statuary. Ancient Egyptian statues and figurines depicting both people and cats often convey a haunting lifelike quality in the materials selected for inlay into the eyes. Rock crystal is used in many cases, behind which is conventionally painted a dark pupil. The translucent crystal iris catches and reflects light in a way that sets these artefacts apart from other ancient statuary in major European collections in the nineteenth century, from the British Museum to the Louvre, along with the teaching collections held at various universities, as Egyptology became formalised as a subject of study. Crystals, and other reflective surfaces – the mirror and the flame – also suggest themselves as enabling hypnotic trance, and themselves proliferate in fictions that imagine Egyptian mind powers.

Crystals, mirrors and flames

The image of the occult ancient Egyptian eye – so powerful in *She*, *The World's Desire* and 'M. Pigeonneau' – is also central to *The Mummy and Miss Nitocris* (1906). In Griffith's novel, trance is induced through the use of a hypnotic emerald that has the appearance of a light source.[139] Like the mystical ruby in Stoker's *The Jewel of Seven Stars* that, significantly, is likened to 'that fabled head of the Gordon Medusa' (another connection between Haggard's and Stoker's texts), the emerald has magical properties signified by hieroglyphic 'characters carved in the stone'.[140] The German chemist and gemologist Karl von Reichenbach's (1788–1869) 1850 *Physikalisch-physiologische Untersuchungen über die Dynamide des Magnetismus, der Elektrizität, der Wärme, des Lichtes, der Krystallisation, des Chemismus in ihren Beziehungen zur Lebenskraft* ('Physico-Physiological Researches on the Dynamics of Magnetism, Electricity, Heat, Light, Crystallisation, and Chemism, in their relation to Vital Force') was promptly translated into English for British and American editions. Von Reichenbach's early relation of a case of a young woman whom he had mesmerised includes the employment of a crystal 'which made her very sleepy', the crystal apparently being the final catalyst for the woman being 'put ... to sleep by the gaze'.[141] He refers to his patients whose sensitivity to crystals is useful in attaining such states of unconsciousness as 'crystallic-sleepers'.[142] The mesmerist's employment of crystals clearly worked its way into texts that feature the ancient Egyptian supernatural; just as the forces supposedly emanating from the mesmerist's body during 'passes' with the hands gave way to the idea of the particular power of the fixed point central to hypnotism, so too did the crystal or the gemstone become associated with this new locus of hypnotic power.

In Griffith's text, the jewel has distinctive physiological effects both on the Egyptian magician Phadrig, and his unsuspecting Jewish subject Josephus. Drawing upon the emerald's power, Phadrig's voice becomes 'slow' and 'penetrating', his eyes widen and, like Ayesha's fiery eyes in *She*, '[glow] with a fire that made them look almost dull red'.[143] Josephus feels Phadrig's eyes 'look into his brain' and is unable to move, save for 'trembling' and shaking.[144] He is only able to speak when asked a direct question, and then his speech is fragmented: 'I should think not—I should think—I should—oh, beautiful—glor—glorious—splendid—did—splen—oh, what a light—li—light—li—oh——!'[145] These dramatic effects of bodily shaking and disjointed speech appear to echo the stock tropes of stage hypnotism, although the emission of light from the eyes adds a supernatural element to a passage that otherwise reads as essentially theatrical. Yet, like Haggard and Stoker, Griffith draws upon genuine mythology to combine the symbolism of contemporary mind powers with their ancient antecedents. To Josephus, the emerald, named the Horus Stone, appears 'like a great green-blazing eye glaring into the utmost depths of his being'. This links it directly to the Eye of Horus as a magical hieroglyphic symbol.

A magical device frequently used for funerary amulets, and thus in Victorian archaeology frequently encountered in close proximity to the dead, the Eye of Horus is also connected to the sun as a divine light-giving eye.[146] With this cluster of connotations, the Eye of Horus was ripe for appropriation by occultists. In a famous photograph of Aleister Crowley (1875–1947) who, incidentally, used the name of Ayesha's reincarnated lover in *She* – Leo Vincey – as a *nom de plume*, the Eye of Horus embellishes Crowley's pyramid-shaped hat. This situates a mystical third eye in a central position at the top of his head (figure 4.5). A third eye in the centre of the forehead was theorised by some, including Blavatsky, to be an organ of supernatural sight that the human race had lost over time, an ethereal organ that the influential theosophist Charles Leadbeater would later claim took the form of a snake with an eye at the end.[147] Crowley also chose the Eye of Horus enclosed within a pyramid and emitting light to appear on the cover of *The Equinox*, the official periodical of a magical order he founded called the A∴A∴ after the fracturing of the Golden Dawn. In *The Mummy and Miss Nitocris*, the Eye of Horus recalls these varied associations, being both symbolic of the occultist's power and, through its common use as a funerary amulet, foreshadowing Josephus's death as he commits suicide under its hypnotic influence.[148]

The occult jewel that encourages parapsychological states also features in William Henry Warner's novel *The Bridge of Time* (1919). It is when 'gaz[ing] into [the ring's] smouldering depths' that the protagonist's modern love interest, Iris, first recovers some memories of her past life as the ancient Egyptian Teta: as 'strange visions of unfamiliar things and places seemed to rise mistily before her, like the half-forgotten memory of a dream'.[149] Other gemstones gifted to her by Rames further connect her to her past: '[a]s light seen through the windows of some distant fairy castle, the gems flowed and sparkled with alluring, mystic fire … again those vague, formless pictures half-fancy, half-memory, struggled for expression'. Such descriptions mimic the methodologies of self-hypnosis, Iris focusing on the gems as a fixed point to enter this enlightened state. When she does so, '[t]he room about her seemed

Figure 4.5 Aleister Crowley c.1909. Courtesy of Ordo Templi Orientis Archives.

to fade away and she saw once more those enchanting vistas of palm-shaded gardens and the gleam of that majestic river'.[150] That it is not, in fact, any property innate to the gems themselves – though it is enhanced by them, as in von Reichenbach's accounts – is suggested by her other moments of clarity concerning her past life, which occur when looking in a mirror or staring into a fire. Nonetheless, that Rames's ring is specifically marked out as producing magical effects is suggested in the reputation that it garners through the ages. Rames's ring exists in two states: in its well-preserved form, having passed through ancient Egypt directly to the modern day as Rames himself travels through time, and in its aged form, in which it has been handed down through count-less generations, eventually coming into the possession of Richard Lackland (simultaneously Rames's direct descendant, and reincarna-tion). Lackland reveals that the ring 'is supposed to mirror the future', meaning that as an occult device it is credited with the kinds of pow-ers that ancient Egyptians had long been aligned with in the cultural consciousness.[151]

Mirrors and flames, in fact, have similar effects in other texts with ancient Egyptian subject matter, in keeping with nineteenth-century understandings of these rituals to encourage clairvoyance in ancient Egypt. George Eliot (1819–1880) began her first novel *Adam Bede* (1859) with such an image: 'With a single drop of ink for a mirror, the Egyptian sorcerer undertakes to reveal to any chance comer far-reaching visions of the past.'[152] This practice is depicted as still in use by modern Egyptians in the British writer and archaeologist E. F. Benson's (1867–1940) 'A Curious Coincidence' (1899). With references to Frederic Myers and the Society of Psychical Research, the protagonists approach the story's visions (seen either in ink or black fabric) from a rational, sci-entific perspective, and thus understand them to be genuine with some authority.[153] So too, mirrors are used for parapsychological revelation in venues with a readership interested in mental powers, and scientific and occult understandings of such abilities. Lucy Cleveland's (1850–?) mysti-cal romance story 'Revelations of a Moorish Mirror' (1896), published in an American occult periodical, *The Metaphysical Magazine*, is a beauti-fully written though little-known example.[154] Cleveland's narrator falls in love with Neferu Ahsoon, a modern woman who, it transpires, is the reincarnation of the Egyptian queen Taia. Her 'electric eyes' and the nar-rator's pondering whether she is 'reading my thoughts' mark her out as having particular psychical abilities.[155] Together, in an antique shop in New York, the protagonists encounter the mummified head and foot of Taia and, as the narrator spies Taia's head reflected in the antique mirror of the story's title, it appears to him as Neferu's. He resolves to purchase the mirror, interpreting '[i]ts sharp, white glance at me across the dim curio shop [as] an omen of some future revelation'.[156] In such a personi-fied description, Cleveland emphasises how the mirror is not merely to be looked at, but looks back, imbuing it with a kind of occult agency. It certainly expands his understandings of his own psychology: 'What depths of sub-consciousness had tipped my brushes with light-sparkles as of glints from the restless jewel-hearts of crowned Pharaohs?', he asks. 'How was it that I had understood her so well, as I painted from this awful, sublime palette of the sub-consciousness …?'[157] As the narrator looks into the mirror he observes that visions of the ancient past 'swept luminously across my consciousness' and, when he holds an image of the pharaoh Amenhotep up to the mirror, he realises that he himself was Taia's husband in a past life.[158] While such narratives' revelations in the reflective surfaces of jewels and mirrors suggests the practice of scrying in ancient Egypt their repeated emphasis on reincarnation grounds them, also, in modern occultism, specifically in theosophical doctrine. Nonetheless, ancient rituals were of renewed significance to occultists at the *fin de siècle*: magicians of the Golden Dawn used mirrors for the purposes of perceiving mystical images.

Beyond Cleveland, these tropes appear in other occult publications, which have received less critical attention than mainstream fiction of the time, and which cement the contemporaneous inextricability of psychological enquiry and occult pursuits. Thomas Jasper Betiero's *Nedoure, Priestess of the Magi: an historical romance of white and black magic* (1916) promises to be 'A Story That Reveals Wisdom of the Ancient Past', and follows its protagonist, Althos, the usurped rightful ruler of Kashmir, initiated into the Egyptian mysteries.

Betiero was a devotee of science and the occult; the Chicago Masonic Temple published his *Practical Essays on Hypnotism and Mesmerism* in 1897, establishing at this early stage in his career a careful crafting of his professional persona as a man well-versed in scientific subjects of interest to 'eminent physicians' but also in 'the deepest mysticism'.[159] He founded the Society of Oriental Mystics in 1902, placing great emphasis on his knowledge of the Tarot. In the early twentieth century, he ran a 'School of Oriental Mysticism' that offered courses in 'Hypnotism, Magnetism, Practical Occultism, Astrology, Palmistry, Metoposcopy and all branches of Occult Science'. In an advertisement placed in an occult magazine in 1903 Betiero claimed to have been 'educated in Europe (University of Barcelona)', and to have been 'born in Egypt', the latter presumably included so as to convey some kind of mystical authority.[160] These details also, sadly, suggest an invented personal history for Betiero that would aid him in attempting to sidestep late nineteenth- and early twentieth-century racial prejudices. Betiero, a mixed race man, wrote to the American scholar and activist W. E. B. Du Bois (1868–1963) communicating that he had met with violence on account of being assumed to have been African-American;[161] his claim to be Spanish and to have been born in Egypt served the purpose of providing him with a backstory more palatable to white occultists, rooted both in European systems of knowledge and in an Eastern mysticism that had been subsumed into Western traditions for millennia.

Betiero's novel abounds with scenes of trance, the taking of drugs and the inhalation of intoxicating perfumes, references to magic mirrors, prophetic dreams, reincarnation, alchemy, animal magnetism, and characters whose eyes suggest telepathic or hypnotic abilities. Althos's path to his occult education in Egypt is sparked when his psychical abilities are awoken by the sight of an enormous diamond suspended from the Maharaja's neck by 'a unique chain of gold so wrought as to represent a serpent'.[162] As Althos looks at the gemstone, which danced and sparkled … like a ball of fire', he finds that 'it held me spellbound'. In this trance state the diamond appears to transform into 'a huge eye, so large indeed that I could see my own image or reflection therein', 'as if gazing into the depths of a placid pool'.[163] In this series of images, which moves rapidly from snake to jewel, eye to mirror, Betiero bombards his readers not just with occult iconography, but also with the paraphernalia of scientific enquiry into the subconscious: creatures associated with animal magnetism or used in trance experiments, materials speculated to encourage hypnotic states, and the optical organ conceived as a point from which psychical power might both emanate and penetrate.

Once in Egypt, Althos studies in 'the most perfectly appointed alchemical laboratory in the known world', '[u]nder the tutelage of the world-famed Pheros', an occult master whose name evokes the lighthouse of Alexandria, and with it a sense of unsurpassed metaphorical illumination.[164] Indeed, the architectural feats of Egypt are crucial to Althos's development as a magus, and towards the novel's end he is confronted by a counterpart to the Maharaja's diamond on a far greater scale, inside Egypt's largest pyramid. Inside an observatory at the peak of the Pyramid of Cheops is 'the largest and brightest crystal I had ever beheld'.[165] This precious gem, to which the magi refer as the 'Glittering Eye', is a magical apparatus, which calls forth 'astral image[s]' fuelled by the psychical powers of the initiated.[166] Like the Maharaja's diamond before it, the crystal transforms to take on 'the appearance of a glowing ball of fire', before fading to a 'glow', intriguingly described as 'photographic'.[167] Betiero's use of the term self-consciously evokes modern imaging technologies as much as it recalls the linguistic components of the term: *phōtós* meaning 'light', and *graphê* meaning drawing. The giant crystal, from within which can be seen realistic images of other times and places, ultimately functions as Ayesha's pool of water does in *She*, acting as a surface on which occult images appear, far surpassing the technological achievements of the modern world.

By 1916, when Betiero's novel was published, Haggard had in fact elaborated on Ayesha's use of a variety of occult imaging surfaces in his sequel, *Ayesha: The Return of She*. The eponymous sorceress makes images appear on a 'curtain of fire' produced by a volcano, 'pictures[s] ... form[ing] as it forms in the seer's magic crystal'.[168] These images are of ancient Egypt, and that they come directly from Ayesha's mind is suggested by Haggard's description that 'confused pictures flitted rapidly to and fro across the vast mirror of the flame, such as might be reflected from an intelligence crowded with memories of over two thousand years'.[169] The reliability of these images is undercut, however, by the suggestion that although these scenes were 'founded on events that had happened in the past', they were 'vapours' of Ayesha's 'brain', twisted versions of the past altered so as to manipulate the protagonists.[170] The collision of images here – the brain, the mirror, the crystal – suggests a wide range of imaging devices ranging from the mind's eye through to the occultist's apparatus. Ayesha's power is later imagined in relation to her eyes, too, a 'radiance upon her brow' which illuminates her forehead suggesting the pineal gland, linked by Blavatsky to the third eye, which sees what normal sight cannot. Ayesha's eyes reflect this light, 'bec[oming] glowing mirrors'.[171] That Ayesha is conducting alchemical experiments with a substance 'fashioned ... to the oblong shape of a human eye', from which 'poured' a light more intense than '[i]f all the cut diamonds of the world were brought together and set beneath a mighty burning-glass' emphasises the significance of the eye as occult mechanism but equally the significance of lenses – crystals, jewels and other reflective surfaces – as enhancing parapsychological powers.[172] In *The Jewel of Seven Stars*, Margaret, the double of the ancient Egyptian queen Tera, is noteworthy for her striking dark eyes, which are also described with religious and alchemical imagery; Ross, the narrator, relates that looking into Margaret's eyes is 'like gazing at a black mirror such as Doctor Dee used in his wizard rites' or, as relayed to him by another man – 'a great oriental traveller' – 'as looking at night at the great distant lamps of a mosque through the open door'.[173] The latter simile evokes Egypt, reinforcing a sense of Margaret's psychical heritage, while both – as with Ayesha's luminous eyes – emphasise light or reflection to conjure up an image of occult power.

Already associated with divine power and prophetic dreams, the ancient Egyptian eye had a long history as a symbol of occult potency. To this was added the threat of inescapable hypnotic effects which simultaneously implied connotations of the atavistic, degenerate, reptilian and animalistic, alongside the modern and highly evolved. These contradictory associations, of an ancient degeneracy and psychological modernity, were not limited to the eye, however, but instead can be seen to pervade the entire body. As this chapter's next section shall discuss, ancient Egyptian bodies manifested hypnotic potential beyond their enigmatic eyes, seeing the power to entrance migrate from its traditional locus and reveal itself in sensual and nightmarish ways.

Hieroglyphic nightmares

As I have established elsewhere, 'in the final decades of the Victorian era ... ancient Egyptian artefacts – specifically the bodies of the ancient Egyptian dead – began to be held as objects which might trigger moments of psychological disturbance'.[174] One can read in mummy fiction in particular, in texts ranging from Doyle's 'Lot No. 249' to Guy Boothby's *Pharos the Egyptian* (serialised in 1898 and published in novel form in 1899), how ancient Egyptian antagonists – with their (literally) physically degenerating bodies – trigger a kind of psychological degeneration in modern characters. Their bodies are often either 'asexual and corpse-like' or 'hermaphroditic and alluring', their 'sexual indistinctness' chiming with the pathologisation of gender nonconformity by influential physicians including Havelock Ellis (1859–1939) and Max Nordau (1849–1923).[175] I have shown how these troubling bodies are often depicted as inciting hysteria in (usually) white, male, British characters. In some cases, as in *Pharos the Egyptian* and *The Beetle*, psychological deterioration comes about not just through the unsettling power of ancient Egyptian bodily remains, but also through such individuals' ability to dominate the wills of their victims. Across a range of such texts, ancient Egyptian characters repeatedly upset 'masculine identity and patriarchal norms'.[176]

David Trotter notes the startling frequency with which male protagonists fall in love with reanimated ancient Egyptian women in late nineteenth-century fiction.[177] This, I suggest, is not only due to their often idealised beauty – female mummies are often imagined in a much better state of preservation than their male counterparts[178] – but also due to the supernatural and entrancing allure intrinsic to their occult bodies. The romantic gaze becomes the hypnotic stare, as beautiful bodies become the mechanism through which entrancing effects are achieved. The ancient Egyptian female body is often represented as seductive, exerting a particular kind of sexual control. Haggard's ancient Egyptian queen in *Cleopatra* is one such example. Initially clad in the robes of Isis in a demonstration of her esoteric authority, her body is partly exposed and partly tantalisingly concealed beneath a transparent 'garment that [glistens] like the scaly covering of a snake'.[179] Drawing upon the rich tradition of ancient

Egyptian women associated with serpents that we have already seen with Haggard's Ayesha, Cleopatra exhibits both her supernatural sympathies and her destructive allure. Like the biblical character of Joseph, she too has prophetic dreams, and yet it is her body and not her mind that can 'match' the magical prowess of sorcerers.[180] Terrence Rodgers perceives something supernatural in her voluptuousness, labelling her 'a sexual vampire' and, in doing so, likens her to a typical *fin-de-siècle* mesmeric monster.[181] Her body certainly has an entrancing effect; the protagonist Harmachis is left 'gazing after her like one asleep'.[182] His body is left as if in a state of unconsciousness, 'wrapped ... closer and yet more close in her magic web, from which there [is] no escape'.[183] Again, as in the immobility that Haggard's Ayesha inspires, the language of physical restriction is used to describe the victim of Cleopatra's mesmeric influence.

In a publicity photograph for *Cleopatra* (1917), a silent film based on Haggard's novel of the same name, now lost save for under 20 seconds of footage, the combination of the alluring body and penetrating occult gaze is made clear (figure 4.6). The American star of stage and screen who played the title role, Theda Bara (1885–1955), raises her flat palms above her eyes in a pose that recalls the use of the straightened hand in mesmerism, and directs attention to her cranium as the seat of her

Figure 4.6 Theda Bara in a promotional photograph for *Cleopatra* (1917). Source: The Cleveland Press Collection. Special Collections, Michael Schwartz Library, Cleveland State University.

power. Her concentrated frown and direct eye-contact with the camera lens suggests that this is no quick glance but a long, still stare. Her dark, eyes, exaggerated with Egyptian-style makeup, are implied to see more than just the normal faculties of sight can provide, exerting their force on the viewer. Although not visible in this image, a surviving still from the film shows her using a crystal ball, further drawing upon powers of supernatural envisioning.

Dressed in the most famous of the film's selection of elaborate and erotic costumes, which would later contribute to the film being declared too obscene to be shown according to the standards of the Motion Picture Production Code, there is also a continuation of the snake imagery associated with the mesmerist.[184] The snakes that adorn her breasts adumbrate Cleopatra's method of suicide while suggesting a hypnotic effect to her body; the positioning of the snakes' bejewelled heads over her nipples makes the link between entrancement and eroticism explicit. Meanwhile, her snake crown, placed at her third eye, functions as a symbol of Egyptian royalty, as well as evoking the coiled serpents of Medusa's hair. There is also a suggestion – in this image and beyond, in the emphasis on the reptilian, cold-blooded serpent – that Cleopatra draws upon primitive and atavistic sources of power to control those who meet her gaze. As Suzanne Osmond asserts, towards the end of the late nineteenth century, stage Cleopatras cast aside their distinctly Victorian corsets and began adopting costumes that embraced the exotic and erotic, emphasising their power through their sexual and racial difference.[185] In the early twentieth century, inspired by Haggard's Cleopatra rather than Shakespeare's, Bara took this visual 'otherness' to the extreme. This Orientalised take on the *femme fatale* was, however, not just a character cultivated before the cameras, but also off-screen. The Fox publicity department constructed an exotic backstory for Bara (whose real name was Theodosia Goodman, and whose stage name is an anagram of 'Arab Death'). Claiming that her birth at the foot of the Sphinx had been prophesised on the walls of an ancient Egyptian tomb, Fox asserted that Bara would lead men to debauchery and ruin. She was, purportedly, reared not on milk but on vipers' venom.[186] Bara thus assumed the role of Cleopatra, bringing a whole host of dangerous, serpentine associations to the character, blurring the boundary between Cleopatra as ancient queen and Bara as modern twentieth-century woman. Like the character of Potiphar's Wife, Cleopatra is a character not usually granted supernormal mind powers. Yet, as this image suggests, by the early twentieth century, ancient Egypt had become so closely connected to imagery of mesmerism, supernatural eyes, hypnotic snakes and entrancing bodies as they proliferated in the modern cultural imaginary that these historical and mythological characters were being recast in light of these associations.

The power of Cleopatra's body has particular Freudian resonances, both in the 1917 film adaptation of Haggard's 1889 novel and in the original text itself. Akin to Ayesha's and Tera's paralysing bodies and evoking the myth of Medusa, Cleopatra's physical form, in Haggard's text, leaves male onlookers frozen in desire. Freud, a self-proclaimed fan of Haggard's novels, characterised the terror evoked by Medusa as castration anxiety, a fear of being unmanned or rendered passive.[187] Cleopatra, likewise, renders Harmachis 'womanish weak', unable to use the phallic dagger with which he has been entrusted to murder her.[188] It is through this process of emasculation that the subject is reduced to inertness, existing simply as (yet another) uncanny automaton.

It is to a Freudian understanding of the hieroglyphic nightmare and sexual threat that we now turn. Freud's impact on fiction is especially evident in the works of Sax Rohmer (1883–1959), in which sensual bodies promise nightmarish sexual experiences and, as in Haggard's fiction in the decades prior, the potentially dangerous blurring of established gender lines. Rohmer's supernatural novel *Brood of the Witch-Queen* (1918) is something of a composite of several Egyptian-inflected and sexually troublesome tales by other writers which predated it. The antagonist, Antony Ferrara, physically resembles Dracula, while other clues as to Rohmer's indebtedness to earlier texts in a similar vein include chapter titles: 'The Beetles' evoking Marsh's 1897 novel and 'The Ring of Thoth' echoing a short story by Doyle of the same name (1890). There is a kind of literary invocation at work here, in which Rohmer conjures up something of the works of his predecessors, weaving these earlier texts into a larger nightmarish patchwork. Other elements can be traced to Marie Corelli's *The Sorrows of Satan* (1895) and *Ziska* (1897), Stoker's *The Jewel of Seven Stars*, Doyle's 'Lot No. 249', and Guy Boothby's *Pharos the Egyptian*. The novel is also an Egyptological composite as well as a fictional one: among the Egyptologists to whom Rohmer refers are François Chabas and his *Le Papyrus Magique Harris* (1860), Flinders Petrie, Auguste Mariette (1821–81) and Gaston Maspero, while the witch queen herself bears more than a passing resemblance to Hatshepsut, Egypt's longest reigning female pharaoh, whose tomb was discovered by Howard Carter in 1902.[189]

A 'Prefatory Notice' preceding the novel proper relates that '[t]he strange deeds of Antony Ferrara, as herein related, are intended to illustrate certain phases of Sorcery as it was formerly practised … in Ancient Egypt'.[190] Furthermore, '[i]n no case do the powers attributed to him exceed those which are claimed for a fully equipped Adept'. Rohmer immediately establishes that the 'powers' within are not only historically accurate, but that such abilities in ancient Egypt were by no means rare. Nevertheless, Ferrara is yet another villain who, like those examined in the first chapter, has magical abilities that recall showmanship rather than arcane rites: his 'theatrical affectation' is such that the protagonists claim that he 'should have been a music-hall illusionist', while his ability to make his disembodied hands appear in the dark to strangle his victims evoke the spiritualist séance more than they do ancient Egyptian magic as described in historical sources.[191]

The main threat posed by Ferrara, however, is one intimately bound up in dangerous and perverse sexuality, and its powerful psychological effects: he is so 'popular with the women' that 'there have been complaints' at his Oxford college.[192] His room, 'pungent' with '*Kyphi* – the ancient Egyptian stuff used in the temples', is described as 'a kind of nightmare museum' full of '[u]nholy things'.[193] The protagonist, Robert Cairn, relates that:

> There was an unwrapped mummy there, the mummy of a woman – I can't possibly describe it. He had pictures, too – photographs. I shan't try to tell you what they represented. I'm not thin-skinned; but there are some subjects that no man is anxious to come into contact with.[194]

Cairn refers to these photographs again as 'monstrosities' and 'outrages,' and notes another distinct collection of pictures 'which [Ferrara] has taken himself,' predominantly of 'girls', to which Cairn refers as a 'photographic zenana'.[195] Roger Luckhurst speculates that the undisclosed subject of the photographs is related to 'some unholy miscegenate sexual interest', implying paedophilic attraction on Ferrara's part.[196] And when, as Luckhurst continues, Ferrara 'establishes himself as a leading medical specialist in women's nerves in London, where his rooms in Piccadilly … are filled with mummies and Eastern trinkets', the implication is that his female patients are vulnerable in his care. Not only do the nervous disorders with which they are afflicted suggest that their minds will be threatened (and, in a weakened state, overcome) by Ferrara's hypnotic abilities, but that – particularly if suffering from a perceived psycho-gynaecological disorder such as hysteria – their reproductive organs are also at risk.[197] The unwrapped mummy of a woman in his room at Oxford stands in for and anticipates the prostrate patient, divested of clothing and passively awaiting treatment whilst surrounded by the collection of antiquities: the patient's body, under Ferrara's control, becomes part of this collection. Whatever Ferrara has done to this mummy, subsequent to unwrapping, it is so horrible that the narrator dares not repeat it.

While there is little concrete evidence that Rohmer was actively drawing upon an image of Freud in this moment, the parallels between Ferrara and Freud are striking. Take, for instance, this passage from Hilda Doolittle's (1886–1961) letter to her partner Bryher (1894–1983) and Kenneth Macpherson (1902–71) describing her first session with Freud:

> I shook all over, he said I must take off my coat, I said I was cold, he led me around room [*sic*] and I admired bits of Pompeii in red, a bit of Egyptian cloth and some authentic coffin paintings. A sphynx faces the bed. I did not want to go to bed, the white 'napkin for the head' was the only professional touch, there were dim lights, like an opium dive.[198]

Of course, Rohmer would not have had access to this private material, but it is not implausible that details of Freud's consultations might have created a similar, sinister image in his mind, particularly when considering the availability of Freud's case study concerning a patient known by the pseudonym Dora, *Fragments of an Analysis of a Case of Hysteria* (1905). Freud believed that Dora harboured feelings of sexual desire towards him, and Dora terminated her treatment. Both Freud and Ferrara coax women supposedly suffering from hysteria into consultation rooms crowded with ancient relics; minds and bodies are equally vulnerable under the doctors' care. Unlike Freud's analysands, however, Ferrara's victims end up dead.

While the sexual danger that Ferrara poses is never made explicit (only ever referred to in terms of its unspeakability), one of the victims and the protagonist's love-interest, Myra Duquesne, is magically endangered in a scene in which the symbolism is unapologetically Freudian. Having acquired some of Duquesne's hair and somehow introduced these strands into a bulb of 'a species of the extinct sacred lotus', Ferrara arranges for the plant to fall into the hands of an orchid enthusiast with ties to the protagonists, under the pretence that it is a rare specimen.[199] A powerful symbol in Egyptian mythology, art and iconography, the lotus grows to produces 'huge, smooth, egg-shaped buds' that 'seem on the point of bursting at any moment', denoting (rather transparently) powerful sexual fecundity.[200] Duquesne, who, unlike most visitors, is allowed among the orchid collection, seems susceptible to the seductive atmosphere created by the orchids and the masquerading lotus, admitting that she has 'felt their glamour'.[201] While the protagonists brand orchids 'parodies of what a flower should be', 'products of feverish swamps and deathly jungles' that look like 'distorted unholy thing[s]', Duquesne is drawn to them, a psychological attraction that is implied to be the result of the presence of material from her own body secreted inside the developing lotus.[202] As the plant matures, its magic clearly manifests: Duquesne's health deteriorates. When the lotus is destroyed, the full extent of its threat becomes apparent: it is 'severed just above the soil', its 'soft tentacles' and 'swelling buds' crushed, resulting in '[a] profusion of colourless sap ... pouring out upon the floor' releasing 'a smell like that of blood'.[203]

The danger that Ferrara poses is also evident in his collection of antiquities which includes the mummified corpses of a variety of creatures, including (female) human remains. Among his preserved animal bodies are mummies of 'snakes and cats and ibises', which the Egyptians gave as offerings to the gods, as well as a particularly morbid collection of beetles.[204] These, Ferrara relates, hatched and grew inside the brain of an Egyptian priestess, whose head is also contained within Ferrara's cabinets. 'Those creatures never saw the light', he reveals, and refers Cairn to a case containing 'nearly forty' of 'these gruesome relics'.[205] Cairn '[finds] something physically revolting in that group of beetles whose history had begun and ended in the skull of a mummy'.[206] They are not only horrors in and of themselves, but emerge and perish within the brain like nightmarish thoughts, physical embodiments of the monstrous images that ancient Egypt could call forth within the mind, anticipating the beetles that would later manifest in the dreams of the Swiss psychoanalyst Carl Jung (1875–1961) and his patients.[207] These beetles make a psychical appearance later that very day, when Cairn sees 'darker patches' 'in the shadowy parts of [his] room'.[208] He attempts to convince himself that the beetles are products of his imagination and, relating the events to his father, declares that 'either I am mad, or to-night my room was filled with things that *crawled*'.[209] Cairn 'describ[es] Ferrara's chambers with a minute exactness which revealed how deep, how indelible an impression their strangeness had made upon his mind'.[210] The unsettling relics of Ferrara's rooms affect Cairn's mental state: as his father identifies, Ferrara is attempting to achieve the 'destruction of [Cairn's] mind, and of something more than mind' through a psychical attack.[211] His father confronts Ferrara, and discovers the cause of Cairn's torment: '[a] square of faded linen lay on the table, figured with all but indecipherable Egyptian characters, and upon it, in rows which formed a definite geometrical design, were arranged a great number of little, black insects.'[212]

These beetles, positioned on top of Egyptian hieroglyphic script, function as a monstrous form of writing, physically resembling the beetle hieroglyph that existed as part of the ancient Egyptian writing system and, as such, the spell that Ferrara casts is one that is textually layered: 'beetle shapes' on top of other Egyptian letters.[213] Freud referred to Egyptian hieroglyphs as 'a way of imagining dream-language',[214] and described his *The Interpretation of Dreams* (1899) as an 'Egyptian dream book', casting himself as a modern Joseph upon whom the gift of dream interpretation had been bestowed.[215] That he continued to use this metaphor is made probable by H.D.'s relation that Freud 'had first opened the field to the study of' 'the *hieroglyph of the unconscious*'.[216] Rohmer's beetles certainly manifest as if emerging from Cairn's subconscious: they are 'thought-things', disembodied, 'magnified doubles—glamours—of ... horrible creatures' that, when the spell is broken, '[fade] like a fevered dream'.[217] Rohmer's Gothic employment of the beetles gestures towards Marsh's *The Beetle*, which famously features an antagonist who can fluctuate between a variety of forms: male and female, human and insect. Marsh's Beetle is a sexually complex aggressor; torturing and killing women, and forcibly penetrating men, its bisexual predilections – troubling by mainstream nineteenth-century standards – are entirely typical of *fin-de-siècle* horror. It even leaves one female victim, Marjorie Lindon, in a prolonged state of psychological disturbance; at *The Beetle*'s conclusion, we learn that 'she was for something like three years under medical supervision as a lunatic', presumably treated for the effects of trauma by Freud-like practitioners.[218] Freud had studied with Bernheim and Charcot, the physicians devoted to hypnosis and mentioned by name in 'M. Pigeonneau', and had used hypnotic techniques early in his career. While Marjorie Lindon recovers, the neurologists' powers could evidently be put to various ends, whether good or evil.

Correspondingly, Cairn wonders what Harley Street doctors would make of his account, and his father speculates as to the unknowable number of victims that Ferrara has 'sent to the madhouse'.[219] When the novel's action shifts from London to Egypt, Ferrara appears in costume mimicking that of the Egyptian gods and their corresponding hieroglyphs: 'rising hideously upon his shoulders was a crocodile-mask, which seemed to grin – the mask of Set, Set the Destroyer, god of the underworld'.[220] Ferrara's donning of a crocodile mask and, at a later point a 'black robe' that lends him 'the appearance of a gigantic bat', suggests that he too, like Marsh's Beetle, is a kind of human–animal hybrid, making his inner monstrosity externally visible, and physically mimicking the hieroglyphs that depicted the ancient Egyptian hybrid gods.[221] When Ferrara is wearing the crocodile mask, '[t]he gruesome mask seemed to fascinate' Cairn, who 'could not take his gaze from that weird advancing god'.[222]

Rohmer describes how Cairn 'felt impelled hypnotically to stare at the gleaming eyes set in the saurian head', emphasising a kind of dinosaur-like ultra-antiquity to Ferrara in this flamboyant moment.[223] When not sporting these unsettling costumes, moreover, Ferrara is described as having 'basilisk eyes' (evoking Haggard's Ayesha) and an androgynous appearance: 'a slim and strangely handsome young man' with 'a womanish grace expressed in his whole bearing and emphasised by his long white hands', and in whose gait is 'something revoltingly effeminate; a sort of cat-like grace which had been noticeable in a woman, but which in a man was unnatural, and for some obscure reason sinister'.[224] Ferrara even admits that 'in common with all humanity I am compound of man and woman'.[225] Of all of the novel's characters, Ferrara is the sole individual who really blurs the boundaries between masculine and feminine, very much conforming to psychosexual understandings of androgyny as symbolic of sexual degeneracy.

Evolution versus degeneration

Ferrara and other androgynous ancient Egyptian villains complicate our understanding of ancient Egypt as representing advanced knowledge in the decades bookending the turn of the twentieth century, with their captivating and unsettling bodies promising decadent sexual experiences, while their superior mental abilities penetrate and dominate the minds of their victims. Paradoxically, towards the end of the nineteenth century, visions including dreams and hallucinations, and supernatural mind powers were seen as a reversion to the savage – Roger Luckhurst claims that 'the psychology of dreams, hallucinations, hypnotic susceptibility, and supernatural belief still constituted markers of primitive regression to the majority of psychologists' – and yet also, to eminent scientists such as Myers, were 'signs of evolutionary modernity'.[226] A *fin-de-siècle* poster advertising the talents of a hypnotist by the name of George Andre shows 'The Progress of Hypnotism' (figure 4.7). There is something that anticipates the oft-parodied 1965 illustration 'The Road to Homo Sapiens' in the image's suggestion of a kind of linear inheritance from antiquity.[227] In some regards, it is unusual that the Egyptian Priest is presented as a primitive ancestor of the modern hypnotist; this seems at odds with many of the associations of ancient Egypt with great sophistication and modernity elsewhere. Nonetheless, it does make visual a degenerate quality to ancient Egyptian mind powers, which chimes with the sinister purposes to which these powers are put. The Egyptian Priest, cast in

Figure 4.7 David Allen & Sons, 'The Progress of Hypnotism', c.1890–1910?. Source: John Johnson Collection, Bodleian Library, University of Oxford, Entertainments folder 11 (13).

shadows and hunched over, progresses through increasingly erect and illuminated figures – the Witch, Merlin, the Fakir – until we reach modern individuals – first Mesmer, and then George Andre. Andre, who was often billed with the title 'Dr', performed shows including one entitled 'The Dark Continent'.[228] His performances evidently capitalised upon imperialistic views of Africa as primitive. Thus, while hypnotism was understood as a modern scientific marvel, which promised 'new modes of being' and the retrieval of forgotten knowledge, whose realisation would impact upon modern medicine and methods of communication, it was nonetheless simultaneously marked out as inherited from a fallen empire emblematic of a kind of cultural decadence.[229]

The dual status of these concepts as ancient and modern made them particularly well suited for use in literature that introduced characters from antiquity into the modern world, or to add interest to tales of the ancient world by alluding to subjects of interest to contemporary audiences. Returning to the play with which this chapter opened, when Louis N. Parker utilised trance, hypnosis and clairvoyance to add depth to the character of Potiphar's wife in his version of the story of Joseph, he was not only adapting the story in a way that responded to modern interests, but also situating her within a tradition of Eastern mind powers that had been an especially popular literary subject for the past few decades. This increased cerebral and occult power does not come at the expense of Zuleika's eroticism but serves to complement and accentuate it. Her body and mind are made equal weapons of seduction, a threat embodied by several of the Egyptian characters examined in this chapter.

There is a genealogy at play here. Nina Auerbach and David Glover both read Stoker's Tera as indebted to Haggard's Ayesha.[230] The legacies of both – indeed, of a still broader group of women wielding ancient Egyptian mind powers in media of the *fin de siècle* – is evident in Parker's Zuleika, whose clairvoyant abilities during states of trance inspire gossip among the other characters. Zuleika, as with antagonists including Rohmer's Antony Ferrara, is certainly morally degenerate by *fin-de-siècle* standards – seeking an extramarital affair with an enslaved man purchased for her husband – and yet, her highly developed (and modern) powers of the mind make her a dangerous and highly evolved adversary. Joseph's resistance is all the more admirable given the ease with which Ayesha and Tera enchant those who gaze upon them and the bodily passivity that their minds and forms inspire. Of course, Parker was working with an established story, with a fixed end to the narrative. Zuleika's failure is inevitable, which raises the question, why did Parker elaborate upon this aspect of the story, and in this way? Ultimately, Zuleika is transformed into much more of a psychologically threatening opponent. As with Ayesha and Tera, it is not simply their enticing bodies that ensnare in a physical sense, but the mind powers that lie behind these tempting exteriors. As an antagonist, Zuleika is empowered by her physique, but particularly through her eyes. In the image of Pauline Frederick in role, her eyes are emphasised by heavy black makeup similar to that depicted on ancient Egyptian funerary masks, or the Eye of Horus motif. Zuleika, too, stares unblinking, and it is to her eyes as symbolic of her remarkable power that she directs Joseph in Parker's retelling because, although the female body still holds its erotic appeal, the eye is the true source of the occultist's influence.

Notes

1. 'Magic and Science' 1861, 565 (emphasis in original).
2. Muhlestein 2004, 139.
3. Genesis 41:8.
4. Parker 1913, 27.
5. Parker 1913, 69–70.
6. Parker 1913, 70.
7. A similar image to that of Frederick as Zuleika was taken of Maxine Elliott (1868–1940), who played this part in the London production. See Findon 1913.
8. Blumberg 2020, 70.
9. Blumberg 2020, 77.
10. Parker 1913, 70. The crystal ball was not used in ancient Egypt, although similar performances of clairvoyance did take place with the use of liquids. By the nineteenth and early twentieth centuries, however, the crystal ball was associated with Egyptian occult practices. As Ronald Pearsall records of the mid-Victorian era, '[i]n London, crystal balls were all the rage, and the "original" was bought by Lady Blessington from an "Egyptian magician", though she admitted that she never got the hang of it'; Pearsall 2004, 34.
11. Parker 1913, 70.
12. Parker 1913, 70.
13. Gilman and Marcuse 1949, 152.
14. Genesis 39.7; Parker 1913, 80.
15. Grimes 2011, 80; Luckhurst 2000, 150.
16. Thurschwell 2001, 37.
17. Haggard 1905, 306.
18. Luckhurst 2012, 213.
19. Poe 1845, 369.
20. Winter 1998, 2; Goodrick-Clarke 2008, 175.
21. Goodrick-Clarke 2008, 178.
22. Goodrick-Clarke 2008, 177.
23. Goodrick-Clarke 2008, 179.
24. Winter 1998, 5.
25. Franklin 2018, 30; Winter 1998, 184, 185; Goodrick-Clarke 2008, 184.
26. Hajek 2017, 126.
27. Willis 2006, 173.
28. Willis 2006, 173.
29. Goodrick-Clarke 2008, 183.
30. Goodrick-Clarke 2008, 188.
31. Rolleston 1867, 320.
32. Warner 2006, 253, 268; Luckhurst 2002, 106.
33. Montserrat 2000, 150.
34. S. S. D. D. 1896, 11.
35. Noakes 2019, 11.
36. See Johnson 2018.
37. Dobson 'The Sphinx at the Séance' 2018, 98.
38. Dobson 'The Sphinx at the Séance' 2018, 98–9.
39. Glover *Vampires, Mummies and Liberals* 1996, 85.
40. Harper 1987, 71.

41. Dobson 'The Sphinx at the Séance' 2018, 85, 87.
42. Fleischhack 2017, 259, 268.
43. Fleischhack 2017, 262.
44. Fleischhack 2017, 267.
45. Mitchell 1922, 3.
46. Herbertson 1890, 79.
47. Stoker 1904, 223.
48. Stoker 1904, 223.
49. Stoker 1904, 47.
50. Stoker 1904, 41.
51. Stoker 1904, 41.
52. Stoker 1904, 41.
53. Stoker 1904, 43.
54. See El-Daly 2005 for an account of Arab scholars' understanding of the ancient Egyptian language.
55. El Mahdy 1989, 12.
56. Vyver 1930, 186.
57. Vyver 1930, 186. Vyver misremembers the date. The opening night of Herbert Beerbohm Tree's revival of the play was 27 December 1906, not 1903.
58. Dobson 2020, 81.
59. Vyver 1930, 187. As I have explored elsewhere, Corelli and Haggard both used Egyptian jewellery to suggest in their fictions (and, in Corelli's case, the stories she told about her own life), to symbolically represent, or as evidence of, reincarnation; see Dobson 2020, 60–86; 199–206. Lesser-known writers to employ this trope include Nellie T. Sawyer, whose theosophically inflected romance *The Egyptian Ring* features a scarab in a gold setting that once belonged to the historical Cleopatra VII and is now in the possession of her reincarnation in the modern world. That the ring is at one point stolen by a character with the surname Flamel hints at connections between this item of jewellery and the philosopher's stone, purported to have been discovered by the French scribe Nicolas Flamel (c.1330–1418).
60. Hutton 1999, 151–2; Burdett 2004, 217.
61. Haggard 1926 ii, 168.
62. Haggard 1926 ii, 168–71.
63. Dobson 2020, 62.
64. Blavatsky's assertion that the cycle of reincarnation usually takes at least 1,500 years may well have suggested that individuals should look to antiquity for their previous identities; Goodrick-Clarke 2008, 222.
65. Luckhurst 2012, 215.
66. Brantlinger 2011, 172; Burdett 2000, 217.
67. Basham 1992, 187; Fraser 1998, 43. Blavatsky's eyes were often noted to be particularly striking, for their large size, bright colour and piercing, hypnotic quality; Meade 1980, 24–5. Ayesha shares these features.
68. Blavatsky 1921, 331.
69. Mazlish 1993, 731n14.
70. See Flournoy 1911, for example.
71. See Mazlish 1993.
72. Blavatsky 1921, 331.
73. Kipling 1965, 100 (emphasis in original).
74. Grimes 2011, 29; Haggard 1887, 216.
75. Oppenheim 1985, 120.
76. Butler 2011, 45; Haggard 1887, 215.
77. Haggard 1887, 216.
78. O'Byrne 2008, 169.
79. Cutcliffe-Hyne 1898, 247.
80. Cutcliffe-Hyne 1898, 247.
81. Cutcliffe-Hyne 1898, 247.
82. Otis 1994, 5.
83. Connor 1999, 212; Satz 2013, 37.
84. Edison 1878, 533, quoted in Enns 2006, 72.
85. Enns 2006, 65.

86. Noakes 2002, 137.
87. Noakes 2002, 137.
88. Pick 2000, 106.
89. Noakes 2002, 126.
90. Tompkins 2019.
91. Noakes 2002, 139.
92. Marsh 1907, 17, 30.
93. Marsh 1907, 227.
94. Marsh 1907, 23.
95. Marsh 1907, 255.
96. Griffith 1906, 219.
97. Doyle 1892, 530, 542, 544.
98. Doyle 1892, 539.
99. Noakes 2002, 127.
100. Doyle 1892, 540.
101. Dieudonné 1891, 4.
102. Dieudonné 1891, 6, 7.
103. Dieudonné 1891, 6.
104. Dieudonné 1891, 12, 13.
105. Dieudonné 1891, 15.
106. Dieudonné 1891, 16.
107. Dieudonné 1891, 15, 16.
108. Dieudonné 1891, 21, 22.
109. Winter 1998, 31, 139.
110. Haggard 1887, 156–7, 227.
111. Haggard 1887, 156.
112. Hurley 2012, 172.
113. Haggard 1887, 189.
114. Hughes-Hallett 1997, 142.
115. Hart 2005, 135, 161.
116. Haggard and Lang 1894, 191.
117. Haggard and Lang 1894, 192.
118. Haggard and Lang 1894, 77. Tiye was the wife of Amenhotep III, and mother of the pharaoh Akhenaten (formerly Amenhotep IV), the monarch famous for introducing monotheistic religion to Egypt. Akhenaten's reputation as a visionary appears to have coloured how Tiye was received in *fin-de-siècle* fiction: while Tiye was a powerful queen who 'appear[ed] more prominently in official monuments than any other queen consort before her', there is little to suggest that she was particularly renowned in her own time as a student of the occult; Montserrat 2000, 31. Haggard was likely inclined to refer to Tiye specifically as he owned a ring that once belonged to her; see Dobson *Writing the Sphinx* 2020, 119, 121.
119. Haggard and Lang 1894, 79.
120. Haggard 1926, ii, 7. Lang, in contrast, found that the character 'bored' him; Lang 1990, 118.
121. Haggard 1887, 155.
122. Haggard 1887, 164.
123. Mazlish 1993, 734.
124. Ogden 2013, 96.
125. Moore 2017, 127.
126. Day 2006, 25. Contemporaneous articles on the subject reported that some of the mummified cats had been used as fertiliser on farms in Egypt, that, once reaching the United Kingdom, some had ended up in the Liverpool Museum, and that the remaining quantity had been won at auction by 'a local fertiliser merchant'. According to a writer for *The Northampton Mercury*, '[t]he broker knocked the lot down with one of the cats' heads for a hammer'. See 'Nineteen Tons of Mummified Cats' 1890, 12.
127. 'M. Pigeonneau' was published in France's collection of short stories, *Balthasar* in 1889. This collection was translated into English by Anna Eichberg Lane (1856–1927) in an edition published by the Bodley Head in 1908, bringing this narrative to Anglophone readers.
128. Hajek 2017, 134.
129. France 1889, 49.

130. France 1889, 49.
131. France 1889, 53.
132. France 1889, 59.
133. France 1889, 64.
134. France 1889, 67.
135. Serpell 2013, 96–7.
136. France 1889, 69.
137. Hajek 2017, 134.
138. Serpell 2013, 89, 94–5.
139. Budge 1899, 42–3.
140. Stoker 1904, 142; Griffith 1906, 285.
141. Von Reichenbach 1851, 18.
142. Von Reichenbach 1851, 38.
143. Griffith 1906, 214–16.
144. Griffith 1906, 215–16.
145. Griffith 1906, 216.
146. Ulmer 2003, 2, 5.
147. Morrisson 2007, 74.
148. Griffith may have consulted Egyptological sources in imagining this jewel. In *Egyptian Magic* (1899), E. A. Wallis Budge describes an amulet called the 'ring of Horus', a 'beetle … carved out of a precious emerald', which bears some resemblance to the 'Horus Stone'; Budge 1899, 42. After the correct rituals were performed and words spoken, the ring would grant the wearer magical powers.
149. Warner 1919, 237. Iris's name seems symbolic: its similarity to 'Iras' gives is an Egyptian inflection, while also evoking part of the human eye and, therefore, sight.
150. Warner 1919, 350.
151. Warner 1919, 371.
152. Eliot 1859, 1. For a reading of Eliot's novel as informed by Egyptian mythology, see Bastawy 2020.
153. Benson 1899. This short story was later republished under the title 'At Abdul-Ali's Grave' in *The Room in the Tower and Other Stories* (1912).
154. Lucy Cleveland was the daughter of the classicist and abolitionist Charles D. Cleveland (1802– 69). Little is known about her beyond her parentage, though her participation in occult fora is evident in her publication of a poem and two short stories in *The Metaphysical Magazine*, between 1895 and 1896. The short stories, 'More than Minerva's: A Studio Experience' (1895) and 'Revelations of a Moorish Mirror' (1896), share themes of art and the otherworldly. Her writing career extended to poetry collections – including *Lotus-Life and Other Poems* (1893) – places and dates given after a couple of the poems indicating that she spent the winter of 1892–3 in Egypt – and *The Scarlet-Veined and Other Poems* (1897). The former led to a short piece commenting favourably on her work and its ancient Egyptian themes in New York's *The Sun and Erie County Independent*; Holland 1893, 6.
155. Cleveland 1896, 128, 129.
156. Cleveland 1896, 131.
157. Cleveland 1896, 131. While by no means a new coinage by the time of Cleveland's story, the term 'sub-consciousness' is noteworthy for its use predominantly in psychological works, the word in its hyphenated form appearing, for instance, in Eliot's partner George Henry Lewes's (1817–1878) multi-volume *Problems and Life and Mind* (1874–9).
158. Cleveland 1896, 132.
159. Betiero 1897, 5.
160. Betiero 1903, 26.
161. Betiero 1907; Demarest 2015.
162. Betiero 1916, 11.
163. Betiero 1916, 11.
164. Betiero 1916, 49. The fabled library of Alexandria is also conjured up by association.
165. Betiero 1916, 184.
166. Betiero 1916, 185.
167. Betiero 1916, 185, 186.
168. Haggard 1905, 222.
169. Haggard 1905, 225.

170. Haggard 1905, 225.
171. Haggard 1905, 287.
172. Haggard 1905, 295.
173. Stoker 1904, 28.
174. Dobson 'Emasculating Mummies' 2018, 397.
175. Dobson 'Emasculating Mummies', 2018, 398, 399.
176. Dobson 'Emasculating Mummies' 2018, 406.
177. Trotter 2001, 149.
178. See Dobson 2017.
179. Haggard 1894, 85, 90.
180. Haggard 1894, 118.
181. Rodgers 1997, 54.
182. Haggard 1894, 130.
183. Haggard 1894, 161.
184. Golden 1996, 135.
185. Osmond 2011, 56, 64.
186. Hughes-Hallett 1997, 330–1.
187. Freud 1963, 213.
188. Haggard 1894, 210. For more on Cleopatra as masculine in the nineteenth century, see Dobson 2019.
189. Luckhurst 2012, 95; Irwin 2015, 29. After the discovery of Tutankhamun's tomb 20 years later, *Brood of the Witch-Queen* was republished under a different title, *It Came Out of Egypt* (1923), capitalising upon the so-called 'supernatural events' plaguing the excavations.
190. Rohmer 1924, v.
191. Rohmer 1924, 38.
192. Rohmer 1924, 3.
193. Rohmer 1924, 7, 8 (emphasis in original). Rohmer purportedly made kyphi himself, according to ancient instructions; see Van Ash and Rohmer 1972, 35.
194. Rohmer 1924, 8.
195. Rohmer 1924, 9.
196. Luckhurst 2015, 8.
197. See Grimes 2011, 94. Freud himself did not attribute hysteria to gynaecological dysfunction; nevertheless, the (long-held) association proved difficult to shake; see Micale 2008, 240.
198. *Analyzing Freud*, p. 34.
199. Rohmer 1924, 213. Orchids also feature in Rohmer's 'The Haunted Temple' (1916). Orchids were among Freud's favourite flowers. As H.D. records, a friend wrote to her stating that 'the florists told me that Professor Freud liked orchids and that people always ordered orchids for his birthday'; see H.D., *Tribute to Freud*, pp. 9, 11.
200. Rohmer 1924, 203, 217.
201. Rohmer 1924, 202.
202. Rohmer 1924, 202.
203. Rohmer 1924, 217, 218. H.D. too recognised the sexual potency inherent in lotus symbolism, describing Egyptian columns as having a 'bulbous upper portion that was swollen like the outswelling of some giant river-bud'; see H.D. 1926, 303. 'These bulbous buds, enormous, pregnant, seemed endowed after these four thousand years with some inner life; to still hold that possibility of sudden bloom-burst. They became again … just the columns, tall, though with that illusion of squatness that was brought about chiefly by the swelling toward the roof into these heavy sodden buds'; 303–4.
204. Rohmer 1924, 39.
205. Rohmer 1924, 42.
206. Rohmer 1924, 42.
207. Jung records one of his own dreams that featured a giant Egyptian scarab beetle; see Jung 1993, 203. In *Synchronicity*, Jung reflects on the appearance of a beetle at the window at the moment one of his patients recounts 'a dream in which she was given a golden scarab'; see Jung 1985, 31.
208. Rohmer 1924, 52.
209. Rohmer 1924, 52 (emphasis in original).
210. Rohmer 1924, 54.
211. Rohmer 1924, 55.

212. Rohmer 1924, 61. Rohmer refers to these insects as 'Dermestes beetles', although – judging from his description of their black and orange hair – they appear to be based upon khapra beetles (*Trogoderma granarium*), whose name, coincidentally, evokes that of the ancient Egyptian scarab god, Khepri; Rohmer 1924, 41.
213. Rohmer 1924, 64.
214. Bergstein 2009, 187.
215. O'Donoghue claims that Freud was not alluding to ancient Egyptian papyri in this comparison, but rather contemporary dream interpretation guides that harnessed the aforementioned biblical association between Egypt and dream analysis; O'Donoghue 2009, 217–18.
216. H.D. 1985, 93 (emphasis in original). See also Colby 2009, 110–11.
217. Rohmer 1924, 61, 64.
218. Marsh 1907, 348.
219. Rohmer 1924, 63.
220. Rohmer 1924, 110. Rohmer demonstrates a somewhat unsteady grasp of the ancient Egyptian deities: he describes the god Set's face as being that of a crocodile, either Sobek the crocodile-headed god for Set (Sobek's father), or else the goddess Ammit, who is depicted as a composite of lion, hippopotamus and crocodile. The latter is more likely, given that Ammit inhabited the underworld.
221. Rohmer 1924, 179.
222. Rohmer 1924, 110.
223. Rohmer 1924, 110.
224. Rohmer 1924, 130, 231, 262.
225. Rohmer 1924, 223.
226. Luckhurst 2002, 104, 214.
227. There are some similarities between this illustration and Thomas Huxley's (1825–95) frontispiece to *Evidence as to Man's Place in Nature* (1863).
228. 'Public Amusements' 1892, 4.
229. Luckhurst 2002, 204.
230. Auerbach 1982, 25; Glover 1996, 85.

Conclusion: afterlives

The vogue for all things Egyptian – 'Egyptomania' as it has come to be known – resulted in popular understandings of ancient Egypt being both projected onto and receptive to other modern interests in the broader cultural consciousness across the nineteenth and early twentieth centuries. Among these, as we have seen, were dazzling displays of scientific showmanship, public and private séances, stage magic, theatre and immersive simulacra, which transported their visitors thousands of years back in time to the magnificent Egyptian past, along with strange sciences that promised to probe the depths of the human psyche or that looked to the stars with a mind to finding alien civilisations. This array of practices, by their very currency and popularity, were emblematic of modernity and yet were often conceived of through allusions to antiquity. Thus, ancient Egypt was aligned with – and was sometimes even a byword for – Victorian and Edwardian novelty. Modern theories and discoveries were related in terms that evoked Egyptian antiquity, be that the past as it was then understood according to Egyptological evidence, a fantastical reimagining of this civilisation, or – most often – occupying the tantalising space in between.

As I have shown in *Victorian Alchemy*, this fascinating cultural phenomenon gained traction throughout the nineteenth century, making an enormous impact on speculative fiction, especially science fiction and fantasy, that continued into the twentieth century. The sheer quantity of twentieth- and twenty-first-century material that inherited tropes and plot points from the sources considered in the body of this book warrants attention in its own right. While impossible to do full justice to it here, it is certainly useful to observe, as this volume draws to a close, some of the particular legacies of this stimulating corpus of material.

We can trace in a variety of media from the past century including fiction, pseudo-archaeological works, graphic novels, television and film, the afterlives of the uses of ancient Egypt to represent the aspects of modernity that have been the focus of this book, to say nothing of the adaptations of these nineteenth- and twentieth-century sources that have brought these stories to new audiences. The ways in which we understand and encounter ancient Egypt today are heavily indebted to the nineteenth-century imagination, as academic criticism is beginning to illuminate. Julie Chajes, for instance, has recently outlined how the New Age movement of the 1960s and 1970s owes much to Helena Blavatsky and theosophy, while Frederick Krueger demonstrates the inheritance of narratives of ancient aliens – discourse in which ancient Egypt is key – from the same theosophical sources.[1] Only when we recognise theosophy as part of a much broader interconnected cultural web – as appealing to a more widespread 'magical imagination', and both informed by fiction and informing fiction – do we realise that theosophy itself is just a small piece of the puzzle, and that the reach of the discourse surrounding Egypt's magic, science and technology is far more widespread.

We might, for instance, see echoes of the association between ancient Egypt and illusory technologies in the British horror film *The Mummy's Shroud* (1967), directed by John Gilling (1912–84). As Basil Glynn records, the mummy in this film is 'less brutal monster than apparition, appearing to his intended victims as a series of distorted images'.[2] That the mummy appears 'mirrored in a crystal ball' and 'reflected in a tray of chemicals' neatly aligns the film's antagonist with both magical and chemical enquiries (themes of mummy fiction since its nineteenth-century origins), while also evoking ancient Egyptians as they were represented in Victorian illusory contexts: this mummy may well be a physical being, but its filmic representation reflected on various surfaces makes it part Stodare's Sphinx, part Pepper's Ghost.

The same year saw the release of an episode of *Star Trek* entitled 'The City on the Edge of Forever' (1967),[3] an instalment that features a time portal known as the 'Guardian of Forever', constructed by an ancient alien civilisation. This time-travel device is encountered amidst ruins that evoke classical civilisation rather than ancient Egypt; nevertheless, through the portal can be witnessed various scenes of the past, including views of an Egyptian plateau and a monumental pyramid.[4] Such glimpses through the portal directly recall the illusory effects of projection technologies and Egypt's presence in some of the earliest moving pictures – particularly the moment in which an ancient Egyptian tableau materialises within an enormous mirror in Georges Méliès's *Les Hallucinations du baron de Münchausen* (1911). It also speaks to Egypt's importance in the history of time-travel narratives. The coming decades saw such illusory Egypts transplanted into virtual reality worlds: simulations of Egypt feature in Raymond Harris's (1953–) *The Schizogenic Man* (1990) and Tad Williams's (1957–) novel *City of the Golden Shadow* (1996), paralleling the immersive experiences offered to nineteenth-century audiences – the panorama, diorama and phantasmagoria – as the turn of the millennium approached.

Time travel – the effects of which is mimicked through access to the aforementioned virtual worlds – remains one of the most popular legacies of nineteenth-century narratives influenced by ancient Egypt. In Samuel Bavli's children's adventure book *The Secret of the Sphinx* (2016), a sphinx encountered in a museum – perhaps an allusion to the sphinx which confronts H. G. Wells's Time Traveller in the distant future – transports the protagonist back to ancient Egypt. In Tim Powers's *The Anubis Gates* (1983), the ancient Egyptians themselves are time travellers; what they achieve with magic, modern scientists are only just beginning to replicate. Outside of published fiction, apocryphal stories have circulated for decades that the Egyptian-inspired mausoleum in London's Brompton Cemetery holding the remains of Hannah Courtoy (1784–1818) and her daughters is a time machine and, more recently, a teleportation device. In a meticulous study tracking these urban legends, David Castleton has identified such fantastical speculations as deriving from a 1998 news article and a 2011 blog post, respectively.[5] Evidently, these narratives are not confined to literature and film, but still infuse city spaces with their own kind of mythology.

Ancient Egyptians have consistently been imagined as space travellers or as themselves extraterrestrials. H. P. Lovecraft's (1890–1937) Nyarlathotep, an alien entity that 'came out of Egypt' and 'looked like a Pharaoh', is read by Will Murray as perhaps inspired by Nikola Tesla.[6] Appearing in Lovecraft's 1920 prose poem of the same name, Nyarlathotep is Tesla-like in his having 'heard messages from places not on this planet', as well as in his scientific demonstrations with 'strange instruments of glass and metal'.[7] Notoriously xenophobic, Lovecraft presents an antagonistic 'tall, swarthy man' from the East as an unknowable alien being. Around the same time, the writer and painter Wyndham Lewis (1882–1957) worked on – but never completed – a satirical narrative entitled *Hoodopip*, whose 'futuristic setting … is a kingdom called "O", located on a distant planet which has developed a culture at least superficially inspired by ancient Egypt'.[8] That such themes were of interest both to writers producing genre fiction for pulp magazines and to those working within an emerging avant-garde modernist tradition is testament to the widespread reach of the original narratives. Evidently, the texts considered in this book's second chapter sowed the seeds of what would come to be familiar tropes in the coming decades.

John Scott Campbell's novel *Beyond Pluto* (1932) also imagines the ancient Egyptians to have been 'much more sophisticated ... than was generally accepted', having access to technologies that allow them to travel through time and space.[9] Ancient Egyptians are themselves cast as aliens in the French comic artist and film director Enki Bilal's (1951–) series of graphic novels *La trilogie Nikopol* (1980–92), its loose film adaptation *Immortel, ad vitam* (2004) and in Roland Emmerich's film *Stargate* (1994). Extraterrestrial mummies appear in the science-fiction television series *The Phoenix* (1982) – in which the ancient Egyptian in question has telepathic, telekinetic and clairvoyant abilities – as well as in the science-fiction horror film *Time Walker* (1982), in which an alien in a dormant state is found within the tomb of Tutankhamun. In this latter example, the application of X-rays stimulates a fungus on the alien's skin, leading to the alien's reanimation, demonstrating how, the best part of a century after the technique was pioneered, X-rays were still imagined as having alchemical applications.

Douglas Sladen's (1856–1947) novel *The Crystal and the Sphinx: a romance of crystal-gazing in Egypt* (1925) credits ancient Egypt with knowledge of atomic power, while the unnamed mineral in *Stargate* needed to produce advanced alien technologies is akin to how the applications of radium and other newly discovered elements had been imagined in texts such as Bram Stoker's *The Jewel of Seven Stars* (1903; 1912). Meanwhile, once the dangers of radiation were better understood, radiation poisoning was proposed as the scientific means behind the mummy's curse. Many modern texts on supernatural phenomena repeat an unverified statement from an individual named Louis Bulgarini (often described as a nuclear scientist), who purportedly speculated in 1949 'that the Ancient Egyptians used atomic radiation to protect their holy places. The floors of the tombs could have been covered with uranium. Or the graves could have been finished with radioactive rock'.[10] A source is never given, so Bulgarini's postulations are likely yet another work of fiction. An individual called Louis Bulgarini did exist, working as a science-fiction illustrator around the middle of the twentieth century, so it may be the case that his expertise as a scientist was invented, even if he did propose theories about radioactivity being behind the untimely deaths of certain excavators.[11]

Other familiar pseudoarchaeological premises, for example that extraterrestrials built the pyramids, can also be charted back to the nineteenth century, in this instance to the American astronomer Garrett

P. Serviss's science-fiction novel *Edison's Conquest of Mars* (1898), via keystones of fringe theory such as Erich von Däniken's (1935–) *Chariots of the Gods?* (1968). Modern landmarks in media representations of such concepts include an episode of the acclaimed science-fiction television series *Doctor Who* entitled 'Pyramids of Mars' (1975), which, like Serviss's novel before it, imagines iconic ancient Egyptian structures on the surface of the red planet. Similarly, *Stargate*'s planet Abydos, reached by travelling through the titular stargate, has a distinctly Egyptian appearance, and, further suggesting Serviss's text or its offshoots as inspiration, its occupants are descended from the ancient Egyptian people – in Serviss's work the humans on Mars are not originally Egyptian, though the Martians relocate them to Egypt from their original home. In Terry Pratchett's (1948–2015) *Pyramids* (1989), meanwhile, an enormous pyramid warps space-time so that the kingdom of Djelibeybi (based on ancient Egypt) falls out of alignment with the rest of the world.

Equally significant to the fantastical cultural afterlives of pyramids in the second half of the twentieth century is the American clairvoyant Edgar Cayce (1877–1945), whose speculation that the Pyramids of Giza were erected in 10,500 BCE – far earlier than most scholarly assessments – still provides an imaginative launchpad for alternative theories as to who constructed them. Aliens and Atlanteans are popular suggestions as to the original architects (both of which have direct ancestors in nineteenth-century science fiction), hypotheses that *Stargate*'s protagonist Daniel Jackson is mocked as subscribing to at the beginning of the film.[12] '[T]he promise of treasure at the end of the quest, the treasure of lost ancient knowledge that somehow will be of value for humankind' which Garrett G. Fagan observes in pseudoarchaeological texts and television shows is by no means a new phenomenon; we have seen it time and time again in late nineteenth-century speculative fiction, in the treatises of esotericists, and in the theories of scientists. Krueger has convincingly charted a path from the 'ancient astronaut theories' of pseudoarchaeology back to Blavatsky via Lovecraft, and has made the case for particular pseudoarchaeologial sources impacting directly upon *Stargate*'s minutiae.[13] While the influence of pseudoarchaeology on Hollywood frustrates (some) Egyptologists, as Scott Trafton posits, 'for the level of cultural capital it has been able to maintain professional Egyptology owes as much to what it considers the fantastic tradition as it does to its more controlled rhythm of decades of slow excavation punctuated by periodic Eurekas'.[14] Narratives imagining a connection between ancient Egyptians and extra-terrestrials are by no means a twentieth-century New Age phenomenon: they have been selling to receptive publics for well over a century.

The attribution of knowledge of electricity to ancient Egyptians is a trope with particular longevity. Sax Rohmer's novel *The Bat Flies Low* (1935) imagines this knowledge as being concealed within the 'Book of Thoth', invoking the ancient Egyptian god of science and magic, and alluding to alchemical lore.[15] According to Rohmer's biographer Cay Van Ash (1918–94) and Rohmer's wife Rose Ward (1886–1979), the electric lamp in this text:

> had [really] existed, and an American company had employed a research team on the project. The factual outcome – bleakly different from Sax's story – was that, after a year's work the researchers … reported that they believed a further few months of study would enable them to reproduce this long-forgotten system. Thereupon, belatedly, the sponsors woke up to the fact that, if they did, they would create a thing which would outdate all their profitable stock lines of electrical equipment. The research team was hastily disbanded.[16]

Rohmer himself may well have contributed to the mythology of ancient Egyptian knowledge – and technological employment – of electric power, both through his fiction and in the stories of occult sciences he shared with his friends and family. The term 'outdate' even suggests that not only did the ancient Egyptians produce their own electric lamps, but that this technology was further advanced than American equipment of the early twentieth century, reinforcing the idea of superior scientific advancement on the part of the ancient Egyptians when held up against the achievements of the modern Western world.

The most famous fringe archaeological theories involving electrical technologies supposedly used by the Egyptians include light bulbs claimed to be depicted in stone reliefs at the Temple of Hathor in Dendera, an interpretation which von Däniken justified with the same observation that the astronomer Norman Lockyer made in the 1890s: there is no soot from open flames on the walls or ceiling of the temples.[17] The so-called bulbs resemble nineteenth-century technologies – Crookes tubes or arc lamps – more than they do modern examples, providing them with an aesthetic that is at once retro (by contemporary standards), and futuristic (in comparison to non-expert perceptions of other ancient Egyptian iconography). Other speculations as to Egypt's electrical advancement includes an original use for the pyramids as enormous generators, an image which is now familiar in steampunk universes, as is a brief glimpse of the pyramids put to industrial purposes in *Avril et le monde truqué*

(2015). The pyramid spaceships of *Stargate* – an example of which is first seen landing during an electrical storm, when it is struck by lightning several times – are intriguing descendants of early nineteenth-century apocalyptic paintings of biblical Egypt, and *fin-de-siècle* novels such as Fred T. Jane's *To Venus in Five Seconds* (1897), in which, rather than transportation devices, pyramids are landing sites for mechanical craft.

The electric pyramid is no longer confined to fantastical narratives. The Louvre Pyramid is a glass and metal pyramidal structure designed by the Chinese-American architect I. M. Pei (1917–2019) installed in one of the courtyards of Paris's Musée du Louvre. When illuminated at night, the Pyramid appears both translucent and suffused with a golden electric glow. With its combination of the ancient structure and modern materials, the Louvre Pyramid might have come directly from fantastical *fin-de-siècle* narratives about ancient Egypt. Completed in 1988, this pyramid is one of the two most famous modern pyramids in the world. The other, the Luxor Las Vegas Hotel, which mimics the Great Pyramid in structure, followed not long after, in 1993. More ostentatious than its Parisian cousin, it emits the strongest beam of light in the world. Called the Luxor Sky Beam, this intense shaft of light shines from the top of the pyramid (though only half of the lamps have been used since 2008 in a bid to save energy). The Luxor Sphinx, which accompanies the pyramid, also houses mechanisms for the production of striking light effects, projecting laser beams from its eyes, the offspring of narratives in which the eyes of ancient Egyptian characters symbolise potent hypnotic powers. Margaret Malamud connects this spectacular architecture to older '[s]imulations of Egypt in America for the purposes of mass entertainment and consumerism', noting in particular the World's Fairs that 'celebrated American and European imperialism, commerce, and technological progress'.[18] Malamud's comparison is a pertinent one; the Egyptian Temple at the World's Columbian Exposition of 1893 combined ancient Egyptian structures with dazzling electric lighting effects nearly a century earlier. When Malamud observes that 'the Luxor capitalizes on … New Age interest in ancient Egyptian religion in which pyramids are thought to be containers of cosmic energy and power', boasting its own trilogy of specially commissioned adventure films that are shown in this setting, these ideas – including the notion that the pyramids are advanced technologies no longer understood – are already familiar to us from *fin-de-siècle* science fiction.[19]

The illuminated eyes of the Luxor Sphinx are part of a similarly long tradition of ancient Egyptian powers symbolised by uncanny eyes. Karl Freund's horror film *The Mummy* (1932) features an iconic shot in which can be seen the mummy's illuminated eyes and, as Basil Glynn records of mummies in film and television subsequently, '[t]here have been Mummies with blacked-out eyes, Mummies with glowing eyes, Mummies with flashing eyes and Mummies with eyes that shoot laser beams'; he cites *The Mummy's Hand* (1940), *Archie's Weird Mysteries: curse of the mummy* (1999), *El Latigo Contra Las Momias Aesinas* (1980) and *Ultraman: cry of the mummy* (1966) respectively, as providing examples of each of these ocular peculiarities.[20] Speaking of Freund's *The Mummy*, but perhaps equally applicable to these other examples, is Grizelda Pollock's understanding that the 'technical wizardry' of this film 'feed[s] our Egyptomaniac fantasies'.[21] 'Technical wizardry' is, in fact, a highly appropriate term to describe how, even at the advent of moving pictures, ancient Egypt made itself known through technological tricks that emulated stage magic. Moreover, in films such as Freund's *The Mummy* we see the collision of a fixation on the ancient Egyptian's eyes and filmic trickery to produce effects heretofore reserved for fiction.

As we have seen, illuminated eyes are often used as a shorthand for hyper-developed psychological powers. In venues such as *Weird Tales* magazine, stories of reincarnation, memories of an ancient past, dreams or visions of Egyptian antiquity proliferated across the 1920s and 1930s – in stories such as Frank Belknap Long Jr's 'The Dog-Eared God' (1926) and Seabury Quinn's 'The Dust of Egypt' (1930). Hypnotism is used as a means to channel an ancient Egyptian individual into the body of a living man in Arlton Eadie's 'The Scourge of Egypt' (1929), while ancient Egyptian hypnotic powers are explored in Quinn's 'The Jewel of Seven Stones' (1928), a story heavily indebted to Stoker's *The Jewel of Seven Stars* in its title and in its attacking feline, and to *Iras: a mystery* (1896) in its necklace with seven pendants and mysterious materialising hands. Ancient Egyptian figures wielding abilities such as hypnotism, telepathy and mind control can still be seen in the figures of Osira (an alien who comes to Egypt and is worshipped as a goddess) in the *Wonder Woman* comics (1977; 2006; 2007), in Stephen Sommers's (1962–) film *The Mummy* (1999) and in the 2017 film of the same name directed by Alex Kurtzman (1973–). In *Stargate*, Ra's inhabitation of the body of a young man is akin to spirit possession, seeming both otherworldly yet scientific, as he maintains the youth of this new physical form in a sarcophagus-*cum*-regeneration chamber. The glowing eyes in the mechanical masks of *Stargate*'s aliens suggest scientific rationales for these kinds of power; Ra explains to Jackson that 'I chose your race' because 'your bodies [are] so easy to repair', suggesting that even biological structures are valued for how straightforward they are to maintain.[22] The aliens' weapons, meanwhile, which fire electrical discharges, evoke those of Edward Bulwer-Lytton's Vril-ya who inhabit a subterranean, Egypt-like world. Ra's own eyes, which illuminate with a menacing flash when threatening or enacting violence, nonetheless offer a more mystical counterpart to his species' technological sophistication. The illuminated ancient Egyptian eye is a physical manifestation of mental powers – both scientific and magical – beyond normal human reach. Across the sources considered in this study, illuminated eyes are alchemical organs, unsurpassed in their perspicacity, born of the past and looking to the future, at once ancient and modern.

As an example of the reception of nineteenth- and early twentieth-century narratives about ancient Egypt, *Stargate* appears particularly responsive to its forebears. Indeed, it is striking that within this body of more modern material, there often appears to be a longing not only to access a fantastical ancient Egyptian past, but also a version of the nineteenth- or early twentieth-century world from which a wealth of speculative fiction invested in ancient Egypt sprung. A selection of these narratives are themselves set in the past (or a future that evokes the past), against which ancient Egypt is contrasted as even further removed. While *Stargate* harks back to fictional archaeological discoveries of the 1920s rather than the Victorian or Edwardian eras, the decoding of Egyptian hieroglyphs alongside constellations is suggestive of Bram Stoker's influential Edwardian horror novel *The Jewel of Seven Stars*. Jackson's disparaging comment about other scholars translating hieroglyphs by using the publications of E. A. Wallis Budge (1857–1934) – a joke added to the script by Stuart Tyson Smith (1960–), the Egyptologist who consulted on the film to ensure linguistic authenticity – makes a point about the outdatedness of late nineteenth and early twentieth-century understandings of the ancient Egyptian language, underlining the progress that has been made since. In addition, Lynn Meskell reads a kind of Victorian aesthetic in the costumes worn by Jaye Davidson, playing the alien Ra: '[t]he sort of tight bodice or corset we see Davidson in, emphasizing the chest and waistline, is more reminiscent of erotically charged Victorian porn' rather than anything perceptibly ancient Egyptian in style.[23] Although *Stargate* is in no part set in the nineteenth century, the nineteenth century is still perceptible, whether that is in modern scholarship's inheritances (favourable or unfavourable) from Victorian Egyptology, or in the representation of Egypt itself, with its alchemical symbols, and its Orientalised, exoticised, sexualised bodies.

For other stories, the Victorian and Edwardian eras are central to their setting. The *Doctor Who* episode 'Pyramids of Mars' (1975) is set in 1911, gesturing back to an age in which narratives combining ancient Egypt and space travel was beginning to gather steam. A far more recent episode, 'Dinosaurs on a Spaceship' (2012), sees the Egyptian queen Nefertiti taken from her own time to the twenty-fourth century, travelling forwards thousands of years, just as her kin had been doing in fiction since the *fin de siècle*. That she decides at the episode's conclusion not to return to her own time, but to begin a new life in 1902, likewise suggests the early twentieth century as an apposite time for the Egyptian queen. Despite being predominantly set in the future, Luc Besson's action blockbuster *The Fifth Element* (1997), meanwhile, opens in an Egyptian temple in 1914. Inside a sarcophagus secreted within a hidden chamber is the fifth element, an addition to the four classical elements (earth, air, fire and water). When the fifth element is nearly destroyed, technology allows the recreation of the sarcophagus's inhabitant from the remaining small biological sample. In this film, the sarcophagus is represented as a kind of stasis chamber as in the earlier *Stargate*, a technology not understood in 1914, and which thus reads as 'advanced' in the film's original early twentieth-century context. The short stories that comprise the collection *Clockwork Cairo: steampunk tales of Egypt* (2017) use an alternative nineteenth-century past for many of their settings, while certain of the stories' authors – Gail Carriger and P. Djèlí Clark – have adopted steampunk versions of the past elsewhere, in *Timeless* (2012) and *A Dead Djinn in Cairo* (2016), respectively. Tiffany Trent's contribution to this collection, 'The Lights of Dendera', even features Tesla transported back in time from early twentieth-century New York to the ancient Egyptian past by the god Anubis. The magic used by Anubis to achieve the time travel is, in Tesla's words, 'technology yet to be discovered'.[24] It transpires that Tesla has been summoned to provide wireless electric lighting as a warning signal for the Egyptians to prepare for the onslaught of the god Set. Tesla's technological abilities are a counterpart to the gods' magic, and it is his success as a scientist that allows Anubis to open a portal for him to return his modern life.

Of these more recent media that seem more self-aware of their nineteenth- and twentieth-century narrative roots, however, it is the French adventure film *Les Aventures extraordinaires d'Adèle Blanc-Sec* (2010), based on comics by Jacques Tardi (1946–), that comes closest to reproducing the alchemical intersection between magic and science that typifies earlier works. Written and directed by Luc Besson (who had previously directed the *The Fifth Element*), the film opens in 1911. We are privy to an Egyptologist, Marie-Joseph Espérandieu – the author of a book entitled *Y-a-t-il une vie après la mort* ('*Is there Life after Death*') – practising a kind of telepathy or astral projection in order to enter into the mind of an unhatched pterodactyl, which proceeds to break free of its shell and to wreak havoc in Paris. Adèle enlists Espérandieu's aid in reanimating the ancient Egyptian Patmosis, in the hope that he can help her sister, who is in a catatonic state after a brain injury. The same psychical process that brings to life the pterodactyl, when worked on the ancient Egyptian mummy, makes ancient objects levitate and rotate around the professor, who also floats in the air. Their anticlockwise movement suggests a rapid temporal movement backwards, and a clock showing the minute hand going rapidly backwards and the hour hand forwards indicates the collision of two separate worlds separated by vast swathes of time. That Patmosis describes the Egyptologist's power as radiating outward as 'waves' establishes a scientific basis for a process that seems at first magical but is retrospectively coded in physical terms, and suggests Egyptology as a discipline as uniting magical and scientific understanding.[25] Such forces are evidently familiar to the ancient Egyptians; Patmosis has telekinetic powers that can open locks, and can cause other people to fall unconscious at will (a power shared by the aliens in the scene inside the Egyptian temple in *The Fifth Element*). Several of the reanimated mummies in the Louvre can move objects telekinetically, revealing that these powers are widespread among ancient Egyptians, in contrast to the relatively rare psychical powers among the modern French characters (with the exception, of course, of the Egyptologist). Egypt is understood to be magically sophisticated in a way that supersedes modern understanding.

This magical erudition is evidently accompanied by scientific knowledge far in advance of their time. Upon his reanimation, it transpires that Patmosis is not a doctor but a nuclear physicist. There is comedy in his relaying to the reanimated pharaoh Ramses II that twentieth-century France is primitive in comparison to ancient Egypt, echoing the message delivered by the restored mummy Allamistakeo to mid-nineteenth-century Americans in Poe's 'Some Words with a Mummy' (1845). Patmosis's sneeze upon awakening is certainly a wry nod to this text. Additionally, Adèle's published account of one of her adventures glimpsed earlier in the film – *Le Monstre des glaces* – is evidently meant to evoke Jules Verne's novel *Le Sphinx des glaces* (1897), referred to in the second chapter of this book. Besson's film is evidently interested in paying homage to its nineteenth-century roots, and to rewarding viewers who pick up on such references.

As in Poe's precedent, ancient Egypt is here revealed to have been more scientifically advanced than the modern world; in this and in other examples of media wherein ancient Egypt and steampunk collide,

Madeleine Chawner observes, 'ancient Egyptian science, technology, magic, superstition' is 'used to solve situations that modern technology or science could not'.[26] While Patmosis is not a doctor, he does aid Adèle in finding another ancient Egyptian – Nosibis – who can help. The medical procedure is decidedly alchemical. In a golden vessel, the pharaoh's entrails are mixed with an unnamed fluid, releasing light and smoke. This is applied to Adèle's sister's wound, and she is awoken from a death-like existence, much like the mummies of nineteenth-century fiction. It is the narrative reversal of the trances common to *fin-de-siecle* texts, brought about by ancient Egyptian antagonists. A newspaper's headline – '*La Malediction des pharaons s'abat sur Paris*' ('The Curse of the Pharaohs Strikes Paris') misinterprets the revived Egyptians as evil-doers rather than heroes and, crucially, beings with purely occult powers rather than the magically coded scientific knowledge they exhibit.

In fact, the very act of misunderstanding is at the heart of this project, and the imagined narratives it investigates. The media on which the various chapters of *Victorian Alchemy* have focused have in common the conceit that we somehow do not fully comprehend the ancient past, and specifically the knowledge and powers wielded by the ancient Egyptians. While modern scientists may use new technologies in an attempt to interrogate this world, they may find those very techniques already in the hands of an ancient people whom they have underestimated. Rather than dying out, this conceit has survived for over a century, retaining some of its original currency. A byword for magic, illusion, otherworldly power, technological advancement and alien civilisations since the nineteenth century, ancient Egypt as it is imagined and consumed to this day continues to stand on a foundation established by Victorian appetites.

Notes

1. Chajes 2019, 2; Krueger 2017.
2. Glynn 2020, 159.
3. I am grateful to Christian Langer for drawing this episode to my attention.
4. '[F]ootage seen … through the time portal is, for the most part, lifted from old Paramount Pictures and RKO Pictures films'; 'Guardian of Forever' (n.d.).
5. Castleton 2020.
6. Lovecraft 2011, 121; Murray 1991.
7. Lovecraft 2011, 121.
8. Chaney 2020, 68.
9. McLaren 2013, 27.
10. Beynon 2011, 201.
11. The earliest reference I can find to Bulgarini's supposed statement dates to 1997.
12. Fagan 2003.
13. Krueger 2017.
14. Trafton 2005, 31.

15. Rohmer also refers to the 'Book of Thoth' in his earlier novel *Brood of the Witch-Queen* (1918).
16. Cay and Rohmer 1972, 234–5.
17. Feder 2018, 194.
18. Malamud 2000, 32.
19. Malamud 2000, 35.
20. Glynn 2020, 2.
21. Pollock 2007, 63.
22. *Stargate* 1994.
23. Meskell 1998, 71.
24. Trent 2017, 90.
25. *Les Aventures extraordinaires d'Adèle Blanc-Sec* 2010.
26. Chawner 2021.

Bibliography

Adams, Judith E., and Chrissie W. Alsop. 2008. 'Imaging in Egyptian Mummies'. In *Egyptian Mummies and Modern Science*, edited by Rosalie David, 21–42. Cambridge: Cambridge University Press.

Addy, Shirley M. 1998. *Rider Haggard and Egypt*. Accrington: A. L. Publications.

A.G. 1897. 'Alive Again'. *The Sketch* 17 (21 April): 552.

Ahn, Somi. 2020. 'National Regeneration Through Childhood in Edith Nesbit's *The Story of the Amulet*'. *Children's Literature in Education* 51: 348–60.

Alder, Emily. 2020. *Weird Fiction and Science at the* Fin de Siècle. Cham: Palgrave Macmillan.

'All About the Magic Lantern'. *Young England*, 2.52 (24 December 1880): 127.

Armstrong, Isobel. 2008. *Victorian Glassworlds: glass culture and the imagination, 1830–1880*. Oxford: Oxford University Press.

'Art. II. 1. *A Romance of Two Worlds*. And other Works. By Marie Corelli. London, 1886–1897. 2. *The Christian*. By Hall Caine. London, 1897'. *Quarterly Review* 188 (July 1898): 306–37.

'Art Treasures Exhibition, 1857'. *Manchester Times* 789 (2 May 1857): 1.

Ashley, Michael. 2001. *Starlight Man: the extraordinary life of Algernon Blackwood*. London: Constable.

Askari, Kaveh. 2014. *Making Movies into Art: picture craft from the magic lantern to early Hollywood*. London: Bloomsbury.

Auerbach, Nina. 1982. *Woman and the Demon: the life of a Victorian myth*. Cambridge, MA: Harvard University Press.

Avery, Simon. 2015. '"A New Kind of Rays": gothic fears, cultural anxieties and the discovery of x-rays in the 1890s'. *Gothic Studies* 17 (1): 61–75.

Bacon, Gertrude. 1902–3. 'The Story of the Egyptian Hall'. *The English Illustrated Magazine* 28 (October 1902 to March 1903): 298–308.

Baedeker, Karl, ed. 1885. *Egypt: handbook for travellers*, 2nd edn. Leipsic: Karl Baedeker.

Barber, X. Theodore. 1989. 'Phantasmagorical Wonders: the magic lantern ghost show in nineteenth-century America'. *Film History* 3 (2): 73–86.

Basham, Diana. 1992. *The Trial of Woman: feminism and the occult sciences in Victorian literature and society*. New York: New York University Press.

Bastawy, Haytham. 2020. '*Adam Bede*: an ancient Egypt book of Genesis'. In *Victorian Literary Culture and Ancient Egypt*, edited by Eleanor Dobson, 43–67. Manchester: Manchester University Press.

Beaumont, Matthew. 2006. 'Red Sphinx: mechanics of the uncanny in "The Time Machine"'. *Science Fiction Studies* 33 (2): 230–50.

Bell, Karl. 2009. 'Remaking Magic: the "Wizard of the North" and contested magic mentalities in the mid-nineteenth century magic show'. *Magic, Ritual, and Witchcraft* 4 (1): 26–51.

Bell, Karl. 2012. *The Magical Imagination: Magic and Modernity in Urban England, 1780–1914*. Cambridge: Cambridge University Press.

Benson, E. F. 1899. 'A Curious Coincidence'. *The Graphic* 1543 (24 June): 793–5.

Bergstein, Mary. 2009. 'Freud's Uncanny Egypt: Prologomena'. *American Imago* 66 (2): 185–210.

Besson, Luc, dir. 1997. *The Fifth Element*. Gaumont Buena Vista.

Besson, Luc, dir. 2010. *Les Aventures extraordinaires d'Adèle Blanc-Sec*. Europacorp.

Betiero, T. J. 1903. 'Occultism'. *Ye Quaint Magazine* 3 (4) (June): 26.

Betiero, T. J. Letter from T. J. Betiero to W. E. B. Du Bois, 14 March 1907, W. E. B. Du Bois Papers (MS 312), Special Collections and University Archives, University of Massachusetts Amherst Libraries.

Betiero, T. J. 1916. *Nedoure, Priestess of the Magi: an historical romance of white and black magic*. Seattle: W. F. Wohlstein & Co.

Beynon, Mark. 2011. *London's Curse: murder, black magic and Tutankhamun in the 1920s West End*. New York: The History Press.

Bilal, Enki, dir. 2004. *Immortel, ad vitam*. UGC Distribution.

Binczewski, George J. 1995. 'The Point of a Monument: a history of the aluminium cap of the Washington Monument'. *JOM* 47 (11), http://www.tms.org/pubs/journals/jom/9511/bin czewski-9511.html (last accessed 12 April 2022).

Black, Barbara J. 2000. *On Exhibit: Victorians and their museums*. Charlottesville, VA: University Press of Virginia.

Blackwood, Algernon. 1909. *John Silence, Physician Extraordinary*. Boston: John W. Luce & Co.

Blackwood, Algernon. 1912. *Pan's Garden: a volume of nature stories*. London: Macmillan.

Blackwood, Algernon. 1914. *Incredible Adventures*. London: Macmillan.

Blavatsky, H. P. 1877. *Isis Unveiled: a master-key to the mysteries of ancient and modern science and theology*, I: *Science*. New York: J. W. Bouton.

Blavatsky, H. P. 1893. *The Secret Doctrine: the synthesis of science, religion, and philosophy*, II: *Anthropogenesis*. London: The Theosophical Publishing House (rev. edn, repr. 1921).

Blumberg, Angie. 2020. 'Remembering Mrs Potiphar: Victorian reclamations of a biblical temptress'. In *Victorian Literary Culture and Ancient Egypt*, edited by Eleanor Dobson, 68–89. Manchester: Manchester University Press.

Bolton, Henry Carrington. 1900. 'New Sources of Light and of Röntgen Rays'. *The Popular Science Monthly* 57: 318–22.

Booth, Toni. 2019. 'Magic and Early British Cinema'. *Science and Media Museum* (13 February), https://blog.scienceandmediamuseum.org.uk/magic-early-british-cinema/ (last accessed 12 April 2022).

Booth, Walter R., dir. 1901. *The Haunted Curiosity Shop*. Paul's Animatograph Works.

Bowen, Tracey, and M. Max Evans. 2019. 'Shedding Light on "Knowledge": identifying and analyzing visual metaphors in drawings'. *Metaphor and Symbol* 34 (4): 243–57.

The Boy's Own Conjuring Book: being a complete handbook of parlour magic. New York: Dick and Fitzgerald, 1859.

Brantlinger, Patrick. 2011. *Taming Cannibals: race and the Victorians*. Ithaca, NY: Cornell University Press.

Brendon, Piers. 1991. *Thomas Cook: 150 years of British tourism*. London: Secker & Warburg.

Brier, Bob. 2001. *Egyptian Mummies: unraveling the secrets of an ancient art*. London: Brockhampton.

Brio, Sara. 2018. 'The Shocking Truth: Science, Religion, and Ancient Egypt in Early Nineteenth-Century Fiction'. *Nineteenth-Century Contexts* 40 (4): 331–44.

Brück, Mary. 2009. *Women in Early British and Irish Astronomy: stars and satellites*. Dordrecht: Springer.

Budge, E. A. Wallis. 1899 *Egyptian Magic*. London: Kegan Paul, Trench, Trübner & Co.

Bulfin, Ailise. 2011. 'The Fiction of Gothic Egypt and British Imperial Paranoia: the curse of the Suez Canal'. *English Literature in Transition, 1880–1920* 54 (4): 411–43.

[Bulwer-Lytton, Edward.] 1871. *The Coming Race*. Edinburgh: William Blackwood and Sons.

Burdett, Carolyn. 2004. 'Romance, reincarnation and Rider Haggard'. In *The Victorian Supernatural*, edited by Nicola Bown, Carolyn Burdett and Pamela Thurschwell, 217–35. Cambridge: Cambridge University Press.

Butler, Alison. 2011. *Victorian Occultism and the Making of Modern Magic: invoking tradition*. Basingstoke: Palgrave Macmillan.

Byron, Glennis. 2007. 'Bram Stoker's Gothic and the Resources of Science'. *Critical Survey* 19 (2): 48–62.

Carlo, Danielle. 2012. 'Delivering Prometheus: a critique of enlightenment from Benjamin Franklin to Los Alamos'. Unpublished PhD thesis, New York University.

Carlson, Bernard. *Tesla: inventor of the electrical age*. Princeton, NJ: Princeton University Press, 2013.

Castleton, David. 2020. 'Brompton Cemetery's Time Machine – a Victorian Contraption Hidden in a London Tomb?'. *The Serpent's Pen* (25 November), https://www.davidcastleton.net/bromp ton-cemetery-time-machine-courtoy-tomb-egypt-victorian-london-bonomi/ (last accessed 12 April 2022).

Chajes, Julie. 2019. *Recycled Lives: a history of reincarnation in Blavatsky's theosophy*. Oxford: Oxford University Press.

Chaney, Edward. 2020. '"Mummy First: Statue After": Wyndham Lewis, diffusionism, mosaic distinctions and the Egyptian origins of art'. In *Ancient Egypt in the Modern Imagination: art, literature and culture*, edited by Eleanor Dobson and Nichola Tonks, 47–74. London: Bloomsbury.

Chawner, Madeleine. 2021. 'The Extraordinary Adventures of Ancient Egypt in a Steampunk World'. *YouTube* (6 August), https://www.youtube.com/watch?v=NY33d_jr2RE&ab_channel=DigitalHammurabi (last accessed 12 April 2022).

Cheiro. 1898. *The Hand of Fate; or, A Study of Destiny*. New York: F. Tennyson Neely.

Chhem, Rethy K. 2007. 'Paleoradiology: history and new developments'. In *Paleoradiology: imaging mummies and fossils*, edited by Rethy K. Chhem and Don R. Brothwell, 1–14. Berlin: Springer.

'Christmas Books'. *The Athenæum* 3344 (28 November 1891): 719–20.

Clarke, Arthur C. 1973 (rev. edn). *Profiles of the Future*. London: Harper & Row.

Classen, Constance. 2017. *The Museum of the Senses: experiencing art and collections*. London: Bloomsbury.

Cleveland, Lucy. 1896. 'Revelations of a Moorish Mirror'. *The Metaphysical Magazine* 4 (2): 125–35.

Colby, Sasha. 2009. *Stratified Modernism: the poetics of excavation from Gautier to Olson*. Bern: Peter Lang.

Colla, Elliott. 2007. *Conflicted Antiquities: Egyptology, Egyptomania, Egyptian modernity*. Durham, NC: Duke University Press.

'The Comet from the Pyramids, Cairo'. *The Graphic* 26 (675) (4 November 1882): 477.

Complete Catalogue of Genuine and Original 'Star' Films. Paris: Georges Méliès, 1905.

Connor, Steven. 1999. 'The Machine in the Ghost: spiritualism, technology, and the "direct voice"'. In *Ghosts: Deconstruction, Psychoanalysis, History*, edited by Peter Buse and Andrew Stott, 203–25. Basingstoke: Macmillan.

Copland, Alexander. 1834. *The Existence of Other Worlds, Peopled with Living and Intelligent Beings, Deduced from the Nature of the Universe*. London: J., G. & F. Rivington.

Corelli, Marie. Letter from Marie Corelli to George Bentley, 16 March 1887, Corelli-George Bentley Correspondence, Beinecke Rare Book and Manuscript Library, Yale University.

Corelli, Marie. 1886. *A Romance of Two Worlds: a novel*, 2 vols, ii. London: Richard Bentley and Son.

Corelli, Marie. 1890. *Wormwood: a drama of Paris*. New York: National Book Company.

Corelli, Marie. 1897. *Ziska: The Problem of a Wicked Soul*. London: Simpkin, Marshall.

Corelli, Marie. 1905. *Free Opinions, Freely Expressed on Certain Phases of Modern Social Life and Conduct*. New York: Dodd, Mead & Co.

Corriou, Nolwenn. 2021. 'Through Time and Space: traveling bodies in archaeological fiction'. In *Mobility and Corporeality in Nineteenth- to Twenty-First-Century Anglophone Literature*, edited by Jaine Chemmachery and Bhawana Jain, 43–60. Lanham, MD: Lexington.

Crookes, William. 1892. 'Some Possibilities of Electricity'. *Fortnightly Review* 51 (302): 173–81.

Crossley, Robert. 1992. 'In the Palace of Green Porcelain: artifacts from the museums of science fiction'. In *Styles of Creation: aesthetic technique and the creation of fictional worlds*, edited by George Slusser and Eric S. Rabkin, 205–20. Athens, GA: University of Georgia Press.

C. S. M. 1898. 'An Offending Novelist', *Photographic Times* 87.

Curran, Brian A., Anthony Grafton, Pamela O. Long and Benjamin Weiss. 2009. *Obelisk: a history*. Cambridge, MA: Burndy Library.

Cutcliffe-Hyne, C. J. 1898. 'The Mummy of Thompson-Pratt'. *Cassell's Magazine* 26 (3) (August): 244–9.

Cutcliffe Hyne, C. J. 1900. *The Lost Continent*. New York: Harper & Brothers.

Daly, Nicholas. 1999. *Modernism, Romance and the* Fin de Siècle: *popular fiction and British culture, 1880–1914*. Cambridge: Cambridge University Press.

Dam, H. J. W. 1896. 'The New Marvel in Photography'. *McClure's Magazine* 6 (5): 403–15.

Darvay, Daniel. 2016. *Haunting Modernity and the Gothic Presence in British Modernist Literature*. Cham: Palgrave Macmillan.

Davis, Eric. 2002. 'Representations of the Middle East at American World Fairs 1876–1904'. In *The United States and the Middle East: cultural encounters*, edited by Abbas Amanat and Magnus T. Bernhardsson, 342–85. New Haven, CT: Yale University Press.

Day, Jasmine. 2006. *The Mummy's Curse: mummymania in the English-speaking world*. London: Routledge.

Day, Jasmine. 2020. 'Allamistakeo Awakes: The earliest image of an ambulatory mummy'. In *Victorian Literary Culture and Ancient Egypt*, edited by Eleanor Dobson, 20–42. Manchester: Manchester University Press.

[De Mille, James.] 1888. *A Strange Manuscript Found in a Copper Cylinder*. New York: Harper & Brothers.

Deane, Bradley. 2014. *Masculinity and the New Imperialism: rewriting manhood in British popular literature, 1870–1914*. Cambridge: Cambridge University Press.

Debelius, Margaret Ann. 2000. 'The Riddle of the Sphinx at the *Fin de Siècle*'. Unpublished PhD thesis, Princeton University.

Demarest, Marc. 2015. 'Reliable Advertisements: the life and death of Thomas Jasper Betiero'. *Chasing Down Emma* (12 March), http://ehbritten.blogspot.com/2015/03/reliable-adverti sements-life-and-death.html (last accessed 13 April 2022).

Dennis, Richard. 2008. *Cities in Modernity: representations and productions of metropolitan space, 1840–1930*. Cambridge: Cambridge University Press.

Desmares, Christian, and Franck Ekinci, dirs. 2015. *Avril et le monde truqué*. StudioCanal.

Dickens, Charles. 1999. *The Letters of Charles Dickens*, 12 vols. xi: 1865–1867, edited by Graham Storey. Oxford: Clarendon.

Dobson, Eleanor. 2018. 'A Tomb with a View: Supernatural Experiences in the Late Nineteenth Century's Egyptian Hotels'. In *Anglo-American Travelers and the Hotel Experience in Nineteenth Century Literature: nation, hospitality, travel writing*, edited by Monika Elbert and Susanne Schmid, 89–105. London: Routledge.

Dobson, Eleanor. 2018. 'Emasculating Mummies: gender and psychological threat in *fin-de-siècle* mummy fiction'. *Nineteenth-Century Contexts: an interdisciplinary journal* 40 (4): 397–407.

Dobson, Eleanor. 2018. 'The Sphinx at the Séance: literature, spiritualism and psycho-archaeology'. In *Excavating Modernity: physical, temporal and psychological stratification in literature, 1900–1930*, edited by Eleanor Dobson and Gemma Banks, 83–102. London: Routledge.

Dobson, Eleanor. 2019. 'Cross-Dressing Scholars and Mummies in Drag: Egyptology and queer identity'. *Aegyptiaca: journal of the history of reception of ancient Egypt* 4: 33–54.

Dobson, Eleanor. 2020. 'Oscar Wilde, Photography and Cultures of Spiritualism: "The most magical of mirrors"'. *English Literature in Transition, 1880–1920* 63 (2): 139–61.

Dobson, Eleanor. 2020. *Writing the Sphinx: literature, culture and Egyptology*. Edinburgh: Edinburgh University Press.

Dobson, Eleanor. 2021. 'Deciphering the City: ancient Egypt in Victorian london and psychogeographical archaeology'. In *Writing Remains: New Intersections of Archaeology and Literature*, edited by Josie Gill, Emma Lightfoot and Catriona McKenzie, 119–43. London: Bloomsbury.

Donawerth, Jane. 1997. *Frankenstein's Daughters: women writing science fiction*. Syracuse, NY: Syracuse University Press.

Donnelly, Ignatius. 1882. *Atlantis: the antediluvian world*. New York: Harper.

Douglas, Theo [Henrietta Dorothy Everett]. 1896. *Iras, A Mystery*. London: William Blackwood and Sons.

Doyle, Arthur Conan. 1890. 'The Ring of Thoth'. *Cornhill Magazine* 14: 46–61.

Doyle, Arthur Conan. 1892. 'Lot No. 249'. *Harper's Magazine* 85 (September): 525–44.

Duesterberg, Susanne. 2015. *Popular Receptions of Archaeology: fictional and factual texts in 19th and early 20th century Britain*. Bielefeld: Transcript.

Edison, Thomas. 1878. 'The Phonograph and Its Future'. *North American Review* 126 (262): 527–36.

Edwards, Amelia B. 1877. *A Thousand Miles up the Nile*. London: Longmans, Green and Co.

'Egyptian Hall: England's home of mystery'. 1879. Evan 31, *British Library*, http://www.bl.uk/cat alogues/evanion/Record.aspx?EvanID=024-000002021 (last accessed 13 April 2022).

El-Daly, Okasha. 2005. *Egyptology: the missing millennium: ancient Egypt in medieval Arabic writings*. London: UCL Press.

El Mahdy, Christine. 1989. *Mummies, Myth and Magic in Ancient Egypt*. London: Thames and Hudson.

Eladany, Abeer Helmy. 2011. 'A Study of a Selected Group of Third Intermediate Period Mummies in the British Museum'. Unpublished PhD thesis, University of Manchester.

'Electric Light at the British Museum'. *The Times*, 24 November 1879, 9.

'The Electric Light at the British Museum'. *Nature* 41 (301) (30 January 1890): 301.

Eliot, George. 1859. *Adam Bede*, I, 3 vols. London: William Blackwood & Sons.

Elliott, Chris. 2012. *Egypt in England*. Swindon: English Heritage.

Ellis, Markman. n.d. 'The Spectacle of the Panorama', *British Library*, https://www.bl.uk/pictur ing-places/articles/the-spectacle-of-the-panorama (last accessed 13 April 2022).

Emmerich, Roland, dir. 1994. *Stargate*. MGM/UA Distribution.

Enns, Anthony. 2006. 'Mesmerism and the Electric Age: from Poe to Edison'. In *Victorian Literary Mesmerism*, edited by Martin Willis and Catherine Wynne, 61–82. Amsterdam: Rodopi.

The Epigraphic Survey, Oriental Institute. 2002. 'Lost Egypt: photography and the early documentation of Egyptian monuments', *Fathom Archive*, https://fathom.lib.uchicago.edu/1/77777 7190176/ (last accessed 13 April 2022).

Evans, Henry Ridgely. 1897. 'Introduction: the mysteries of modern magic'. In Albert A. Hopkins, *Magic: stage illusions and scientific diversions, including trick photography*, 1–26. London: Sampson Low, Marston and Co.

Evans, Henry Ridgley. 1906. *The Old and New Magic*. Chicago, IL: The Open Court Publishing Company.

Evans, Henry Ridgely. 1907. *The House of the Sphinx: a novel*. New York: The Neale Publishing Company.

Ezra, Elizabeth. 2000. *Georges Méliès: the birth of the auteur*. Manchester: Manchester University Press.

Fagan, Garrett G. 2003. 'Seductions of Pseudoarchaeology: far out television'. *Archaeology: a publication of the Archaeological Institute of America* 56 (3), https://archive.archaeology.org/0305/abstracts/tv.html (last accessed 13 April 2022).

Fara, Patricia. 2003. *An Entertainment for Angels: electricity in the enlightenment*. Cambridge: Icon.

Fayter, Paul. 1997. 'Strange New Worlds of Space and Time: late victorian science and science fiction'. In *Victorian Science in Context*, edited by Bernard Lightman, 256–80. Chicago, IL: University of Chicago Press.

Feder, Kenneth L. 2018. *Frauds, Myths, and Mysteries: science and pseudoscience in archaeology*, 9th edn. Oxford: Oxford University Press.

Federico, Annette R. 2000. *Idol of Suburbia: Marie Corelli and late-Victorian literary culture*. Charlottesville, VA: University Press of Virginia.

Figuier, Louis. 1877. *Vies des Savants illustres: Depuis l'antiquité jusqu'au dix-neuvième siècle*, 3rd edn. Paris: Librairie Hachette et Cie.

Findon, B. W. 1913. 'Story of the Play'. *The Play Pictorial* 12 (135): 101–20.

Firchow, Peter. 2004. 'H. G. Wells's *Time Machine*: In Search of Time Future – and Time Past'. *The Midwest Quarterly* 45 (2): 123–36.

Fitzsimons, Eleanor. n.d. 'The Life and Loves of E. Nesbit'. *Books Ireland*, https://booksirelandm agazine.com/the-life-and-loves-of-e-nesbit/ (last accessed 13 April 2022).

Flammarion, Camille. 1894. *Omega: the last days of the world*, translated by J. B. Walker. New York: The Cosmopolitan Publishing Company.

Fleischer, Dave, dir. 1935. *Betty Boop and Grampy*. Paramount Pictures.

Fleischhack, Maria. 2017. 'Possession, Trance, and Reincarnation: Confrontations with Ancient Egypt in Edwardian Fiction'. *Victoriographies* 7 (3): 257–70.

Fleming, Fergus, and Alan Lothian. 2012. *Ancient Egypt's Myths and Beliefs*. Rosen: New York.

Flournoy, Theodore. 1911. *Spiritism and Psychology*, translated by Hereward Carrington. New York; London: Harper & Brothers.

France, Anatole. 1889. *Balthasar*. Paris: Calmann-Lévy.

Franklin, J. Jeffrey. 2018. *Spirit Matters: occult beliefs, alternative religions, and the crisis of faith in Victorian Britain*. Ithaca, NY: Cornell University Press.

Fraser, Robert. 1998. *Victorian Quest Romance: Stevenson, Haggard, Kipling and Conan Doyle*. Plymouth: Northcote House.

'Frederick MacCabe'. 1868. *British Library*, Evan 2785, https://www.bl.uk/catalogues/evanion/Record.aspx?EvanID=024-000004913 (last accessed 13 April 2022).

Freeman, Richard. 2009. '*THE MUMMY* in context'. *European Journal of American Studies* 4 (1), http://ejas.revues.org/7566 (last accessed 13 April 2022).

Freud, Sigmund. 1963. *Sexuality and the Psychology of Love*, edited by Philip Rieff. New York: Collier Books.

Freund, Karl, dir. 1932. *The Mummy*. Universal Pictures.

Foucault, Michel. 1998. 'Different Spaces', translated by Robert Hurley, in Michel Foucault, *Essential Works of Foucault 1954–1984*, 3 vols, II, 175–85. London: Penguin.

Galvan, Jill. 2003. 'Christians, Infidels, and Women's Channeling in the Writings of Marie Corelli'. *Victorian Literature and Culture* 31 (1): 83–97.

Gange, David. 2006. 'Religion and Science in Late Nineteenth-Century British Egyptology'. *The Historical Journal* 49 (4): 1083–103.

Gange, David. 2013. *Dialogues with the Dead: Egyptology in British culture and religion, 1822–1922*. Oxford: Oxford University Press.

Gautier, Théophile. 1872. 'Le Pied de momie'. In Théophile Gautier, *Romans et contes*, 397–414. Paris: Charpentier et Cie.

Gilbert, James. 1991. *Perfect Cities: Chicago's utopias of 1893*. Chicago, IL: University of Chicago Press.

Gilling, John, dir. 1967. *The Mummy's Shroud*. Warner-Pathé.

Gilman, Thelma T., and F. L. Marcuse. 1949. 'Animal Hypnosis'. *Psychological Bulletin* 46 (2): 151–65.

Glithero-West, Lizzie. 2020. 'Tutankhartier: death, rebirth and decoration; or, Tutmania in the 1920s as a metaphor for a society in recovery after World War One'. In *Ancient Egypt in the Modern Imagination: art, literature and culture*, edited by Eleanor Dobson and Nichola Tonks, 145–60. London: Bloomsbury.

Glover, David. 1996. 'Introduction'. In Bram Stoker, *The Jewel of Seven Stars*, edited by David Glover, ix–xxii. Oxford: Oxford University Press.

Glover, David. 1996. *Vampires, Mummies and Liberals: Bram Stoker and the politics of popular fiction*. Durham, NC: Duke University Press.

Glynn, Basil. 2020. *The Mummy on Screen: orientalism and monstrosity in horror cinema*. London: Bloomsbury.

Golden, Eve. 1996. *Vamp: the rise and fall of Theda Bara*. Vestal, NY: Empire Publishing.

Gomme, Alice Bertha. 1898. *The Traditional Games of England, Scotland and Ireland*, 2 vols, ii. London: David Nutt.

Gooday, Graeme. 2004. 'Profit and Prophecy: electricity in the late-Victorian periodical'. In *Science in the Nineteenth-Century Periodical*, edited by Geoffrey Cantor, Gowan Dawson, Graeme Gooday, Richard Noakes, Sally Shuttleworth and Jonathan R. Topham, 238–54. Cambridge: Cambridge University Press.

Gooday, Graeme. 2008. *Domesticating Electricity: technology, uncertainty and gender, 1880–1914*. London: Pickering & Chatto.

Goodrick-Clarke, Nicholas. 2008. *The Western Esoteric Traditions: a historical introduction*. Oxford: Oxford University Press.

Griffith, George. 1903. 'The Lost Elixir'. *Pall Mall Magazine* 31 (126) (October): 154–65.

Griffith, George. 1906. *The Mummy and Miss Nitocris: a phantasy of the fourth dimension*. London: T. Werner Laurie.

Grimes, Hilary. 2011. *The Late Victorian Gothic: mental science, the uncanny and scenes of writing*. Farnham: Ashgate.

Groth, Helen. 2016. 'Mediating Popular Fictions: from the magic lantern to the cinematograph'. In *New Directions in Popular Fiction: genre, distribution, reproduction*, edited by Ken Gelder, 287–307. London: Palgrave Macmillan.

'Guardian of Forever'. n.d. *Memory Alpha*, https://memory-alpha.fandom.com/wiki/Guardian_of_ Forever (last accessed 13 April 2022).

Haage, Bernard D. 2006. 'Alchemy II – Antiquity–12th Century'. In *Dictionary of Gnosis & Western Esotericism*, edited by Wouter J. Hanegraaff, 16–34. Leiden: Brill.

Haggard, H. Rider. 1887. *She: A History of Adventure*. London: Longmans, Green and Co.

Haggard, H. Rider. 1894. *Cleopatra*. London: Longmans, Green and Co.

Haggard, H. Rider. 1905. *Ayesha: the return of She*. New York: Doubleday, Page & Co.

Haggard, H. Rider. 1921. 'Smith and the Pharaohs'. In H. Rider Haggard, *Smith and the Pharaohs and Other Tales*, 1–68. New York: Longmans, Green and Co.

Haggard, H. Rider. 1923. 'King Tutankhamen', *The Times*, 13 February 1923, 13.

Haggard, H. Rider. 1926. *The Days of My Life*, 2 vols. London: Longmans, Green and Co.

Haggard, H. Rider, and Andrew Lang. 1894. *The World's Desire*. London: Longmans, Green and Co.

Hajek, Kim M. 2017. ' "A portion of truth": demarcating the boundaries of scientific hypnotism in late nineteenth-century France'. *Notes and Records* 71: 125–39.

Hale, Edward E. 1895. *Hands Off*. Boston: J. Stilman Smith & Co.

Hammer, Olav. *Claiming Knowledge: Strategies of epistemology from theosophy to the new age*. Leiden: Brill, 2004.

Harper, George Mills. 1987. *Yeats's Golden Dawn: the influence of the Hermetic Order of the Golden Dawn on the life and art of W.B. Yeats*. Wellingborough: Aquarian.

Hart, George. 2005. *The Routledge Dictionary of Egyptian Gods and Goddesses*. London: Routledge.

H.D. 1926. *Palimpsest*. Paris: Contact Editions.

H.D. 1985 (rev. edn). *Tribute to Freud*. Manchester: Carcanet.

Hebblethwaite, Kate. 'Introduction to Bram Stoker'. In *The Jewel of Seven Stars*, edited by Kate Hebblethwaite, xi–xxxviii. London: Penguin, 2008.

Hellekson, Karen. 2001. *The Alternate History: refiguring historical time*. Kent, OH: Kent State University Press.

Herbert, Stephen, and Luke McKernan, eds. 1996. *Who's Who of Victorian Cinema: a worldwide survey*. London: British Film Institute.

Herbertson, Mallard [Marie Hutcheson]. 1889. 'The Paraschites', *Belgravia* (July): 77–87.

Herbertson, Mallard [Marie Hutcheson]. 1890. *Taia: a shadow of the Nile*. London: Eden, Remington & Co.

Hoffmann, Professor. 1894. *Modern Magic: a practical treatise on the art of conjuring*, 9th edn. London: George Routledge and Sons.

Holland, Theo. 1893. 'In New Lines'. *The Sun and the Erie County Independent*, 22 December 1893, 6.

Hopkins, Albert A. 1897. *Magic: stage illusions and scientific diversions, including trick photography*. London: Sampson Low, Marston and Co.

Hopkins, Lisa. 2003. 'Jane C. Loudon's *The Mummy!*: Mary Shelley meets George Orwell, and they go in a balloon to Egypt'. *Cardiff Corvey: reading the Romantic text* 10: 5–15.

Hornung, Erik. 2002. *The Secret Lore of Egypt: its impact on the West*, translated by David Lorton. London: Cornell University Press.

Hospitalier, E. 1892. 'Expériences de M. Tesla sur les courants alternatifs de grande fréquence'. *La Nature* 20 (1) (5 March): 209–11.

Hospitalier, E. 1883. *The Modern Applications of Electricity*, translated by Julius Maier, 2nd edn, 2 vols. London: Kegan Paul, Trench & Co, I: Electric Generators: Electric Light.

Hroncek, Susan. 2017. 'From Egyptian Science to Victorian Magic: on the origins of chemistry in Victorian histories of science'. *Victorian Review* 43 (2): 213–28.

Huckvale, David. 2012. *Ancient Egypt in the Popular Imagination*. Jefferson, NC: McFarland.

Huckvale, David. 2016. *A Dark and Stormy Oeuvre: crime, magic and power in the novels of Edward Bulwer-Lytton*. Jefferson, NC: McFarland.

Hughes-Hallett, Lucy. 1997. *Cleopatra: histories, dreams and distortions*. London: Pimlico.

Humphreys, Andrew. 2011. *Grand Hotels of Egypt in the Golden Age of Travel*. New York: The American University in Cairo Press.

Hurley, Kelly. 2012. 'Science and the Gothic'. In *The Victorian Gothic: an Edinburgh companion*, edited by Andrew Smith and William Hughes, 170–85. Edinburgh: Edinburgh University Press.

Hutschenreuther, c.1900. *Cleopatra (after Nathaniel Sichel)*, Artnet, http://www.artnet.com/artists/hutschenreuther/cleopatra-after-nathaniel-sichel-U-AzMoszkqWU09JUxiEKtQ2 (last accessed 13 April 2022).

Hutton, Ronald. 1999. *The Triumph of the Moon: a history of modern pagan witchcraft*. Oxford: Oxford University Press.

Irwin, Robert. 2015. 'Orientalism, Fu Manchu, Arabophilia'. In *Lord of Strange Deaths: the fiendish world of Sax Rohmer*, edited by Phil Baker and Antony Clayton, 19–39. London: Strange Attractor Press.

Ismail, Matthew. 2011. *Wallis Budge: magic and mummies in London and Cairo*. Kilkerran: Hardinge Simpole.

Jane, Fred T. 1895. 'Guesses at Futurity. No. 8: A Dinner Party A.D. 2000. Menu of Chemical Foods'. *The Pall Mall Magazine* (May): 96.

Jane, Fred T. 1896. *The Incubated Girl*. London: Tower.

Jane, Fred T. 1897. *To Venus in Five Seconds: being an account of the strange disappearance of Thomas Plummer, pillmaker*. London: A. D. Innes.

Johnson, George M. 2018. 'Excavating the Psyche as Constructed by Pre-Freudian Pioneers'. In *Excavating Modernity: physical, temporal and psychological strata in literature, 1900–1930*, edited by Eleanor Dobson and Gemma Banks, 9–25. New York: Routledge.

Johnson, Robert Underwood. 1895. 'In Tesla's Laboratory'. *The Century Illustrated Monthly Magazine* 49: 933.

Jung, C. G. 1985. *Synchronicity: an acausal connecting principle*, translated by R. F. C. Hull. London: Routledge.

Jung, C. G. 1993. *Memories, Dreams, Reflections*, edited by Aniela Jaffé, translated by Richard Winston and Clara Winston. London: Fontana Press.

Keene, Melanie. 2015. *Science in Wonderland: the scientific fairy tales of Victorian Britain*. Oxford: Oxford University Press.

Kennedy, Catriona. 2018. 'Military Ways of Seeing: British soldiers' sketches from the Egyptian campaign of 1801'. In *Militarized Cultural Encounters in the Long Nineteenth Century*, edited by Joseph Clarke and John Horne, 197–221. Basingstoke: Palgrave Macmillan.

Kennedy, Tom, dir. 1982. *Time Walker*. New World Pictures, 1982.

Kershner, R. B. 1994. 'Modernism's Mirror: the sorrows of Marie Corelli'. In *Transforming Genres: new approaches to British fiction of the 1890s*, edited by Nikki Lee Manos and Meri-Jane Rochelson, 67–86. Basingstoke: Macmillan.

Keshavjee, Serena. 2013. 'Science and the Visual Culture of Spiritualism: Camille Flammarion and the symbolists in *fin-de-siècle* France'. *Aries* 13: 37–69.

Kipling, Rudyard. 1965. *Rudyard Kipling to Rider Haggard: the record of a friendship*, edited by Morton Cohen. London: Hutchinson.

Klein, Maury. 2008. *The Power Makers: steam, electricity, and the men who invented modern America*. New York: Bloomsbury.

Knoepflmacher, U.C. 1987. 'Of Babylands and Babylons: E. Nesbit and the reclamation of the fair tale'. *Tulsa Studies in Women's Literature* 6 (2): 299–325.

Kollin, Susan. 2010. '"Remember, you're the good guy": *Hidalgo*, American Identity, and Histories of the Western'. *American Studies* 51 (1/2): 5–25.

Krueger, Frederic. 2017. 'The Stargate Simulacrum: ancient Egypt, ancient aliens, and postmodern dynamics of occulture'. *Aegyptiaca: Journal of the History of Reception of Ancient Egypt* 1: 47–74.

Lamb, Geoffrey Frederick. 1976. *Victorian Magic*. London: Routledge & Kegan Paul.

Lamont, Peter. 2004. 'Spiritualism and a Mid-Victorian Crisis of Evidence'. *The Historical Journal* 47 (4): 897–920.

Lampen, Charles Dudley. 1899. *Mirango the Man-Eater: a tale of central Africa*. London: Society for Promoting Christian Knowledge.

Lang, Andrew. 1990. *Dear Stevenson: letters from Andrew Lang to Robert Louis Stevenson with five letters from Stevenson to Lang*, edited by Marysa Demoor. Leuven: Uitgeverij Peeters.

Lant, Antonia. 1992. 'The Curse of the Pharaoh, or How Cinema Contracted Egyptomania'. *October* 59: 86–112.

Lant, Antonia. 2013. 'Cinema in the Time of the Pharaohs'. In *The Ancient World in Silent Cinema*, edited by Pantelis Michelakis and Maria Wyke, 53–73. Cambridge: Cambridge University Press.

Lantiere, Joe. 2004. *The Magician's Wand: a history of mystical rods of power*. Oakville, CT: Joe Lantiere Books.

Leadbeater, C. W. 1912. *The Perfume of Egypt and Other Weird Stories*, 2nd edn. Adyar: The Theosophist Office.

Lees, Frederic. 1903. 'The Discoverers of Radium'. *Pall Mall Magazine* 31 (126) (October): 199–202.

Lékégian, G[abriel]. 1906. 'Studio portrait of a man with a head-through-the-hole foreground prop of a mummy case', *Luminous Lint*, http://www.luminous-lint.com/app/image/2265477122 779213498949938/ (last accessed 13 April 2022).

Lockyer, J. Norman. 1894. *The Dawn of Astronomy: a study of the temple-worship and mythology of the ancient Egyptians*. London: Cassell and Co.

Londe, Albert. 1897. 'Les rayons Roentgen et les momies'. *La Nature* 25: 103–5.

'The Lonely Pyramid. By J. H. Yoxall. Illustrated. (Blackie and Son.)'. *The Spectator* 67 (3308) (21 November 1891): 707.

'The Lonely Pyramid. By J. H. Yoxall. (Blackie.)'. *The Academy* 1024 (19 December 1891): 560.

Loti, Pierre. 1910. *Egypt*, translated by W. P. Baines. New York: Duffield & Company.

Lovecraft, H. P. 2011. *The Complete Fiction*. New York: Barnes & Noble.

Lowell, Percival. 1906. *Mars and its Canals*. New York: Macmillan.

Lowell, Percival. 1912. 'Precession: and the pyramids'. *Popular Science Monthly* 80 (May): 449–60.

Luckhurst, Roger. 2000. 'Trance Gothic, 1882–97'. In *Victorian Gothic: literary and cultural manifestations in the nineteenth century*, edited by Ruth Robbins and Julian Wolfreys, 148–67. Basingstoke: Palgrave.

Luckhurst, Roger. 2002. *The Invention of Telepathy: 1870–1901*. Oxford: Oxford University Press.

Luckhurst, Roger. 2004. 'Knowledge, Belief and the Supernatural at the Imperial Margin'. In *The Victorian Supernatural*, edited by Nicola Bown, Carolyn Burdett and Pamela Thurschwell, 197–216. Cambridge: Cambridge University Press.

Luckhurst, Roger. 2012. *The Mummy's Curse: the true history of a dark fantasy*. Oxford: Oxford University Press.

Luckhurst, Roger. 2015. 'Sax Rohmer's Egyptian Intoxication'. In *Lord of Strange Deaths: the fiendish world of Sax Rohmer*, edited by Phil Baker and Antony Clayton, 1–17. London: Strange Attractor Press.

Lyons, Sherrie Lynne. 2009. *Species, Serpents, Spirits, and Skulls: science at the margins in the Victorian age*. Albany, NY: Suny Press.

M'Govern, Chauncy Montgomery. 1899. 'The New Wizard of the West'. *Pearson's Magazine* 1 (3): 470–6.

[Mackay, Charles.] 1887. *The Twin Soul; or, The Strange Experiences of Mr. Rameses*, 2 vols. London: Ward and Downey.

'Magic and Science'. *All the Year Round* 4 (100) (1861), 561–6.

Malamud, Margaret. 2000. 'Pyramids in Las Vegas and in Outer Space: ancient Egypt in twentieth-century American architecture and film'. *Journal of Popular Culture* 34 (1): 31–47.

Malley, Marjorie C. 2011. *Radioactivity: a history of a mysterious science*. Oxford: Oxford University Press.

Malley, Shawn. 1997. 'Time Hath No Power Against Identity'. *English Literature in Transition, 1880–1920* 40 (3): 275–97.

Mangan, Michael. 2007. *Performing Dark Arts: a cultural history of conjuring*. Bristol: Intellect Books.

Marsh, Richard. 1907. *The Beetle: a mystery*. London: T. Fisher Unwin.

Martin, Thomas Commerford. 1895. 'Tesla's Oscillator and Other Inventions: an authoritative account of some of his recent electrical work'. *The Century Illustrated Monthly Magazine* 49: 916–33.

Marx, Leo. 2000. *The Machine in the Garden: technology and the pastoral ideal in America*. New York: Oxford University Press.

Materer, Timothy. 1995. *Modernist Alchemy: poetry and the occult*. Ithaca, NY: Cornell University Press.

Mazlish, Bruce. 1993. 'A Triptych: Freud's *The Interpretation of Dreams*, Rider Haggard's *She*, and Bulwer-Lytton's *The Coming Race*'. *Comparative Studies in Society and History* 35 (4): 726–45.

McLaren, Kevin. 2013. 'The Marriage of Science Fiction and Egyptology'. *The Forum: journal of history* 5 (1): 21–34.

Meade, Marion. 1980. *Madame Blavatsky: the woman behind the myth*. New York: G.P. Putnam's Sons.

Méliès, Georges, dir. 1900. *Les Infortunes d'un explorateur ou les momies récalcitrantes*. Star Film Company.

Méliès, Georges, dir. 1903. *Le Monstre*. Star Film Company.

Méliès, Georges, dir. 1903. *L'Oracle de Delphes*. Star Film Company.

Méliès, Georges, dir. 1907. *La Prophétesse de Thèbes*. Star Film Company.

Méliès, Georges, dir. 1911. *Les Hallucinations du baron de Münchausen*. Pathé.

Meskell, Lynn. 1998. 'Consuming Bodies: cultural fantasies of ancient Egypt'. *Body & Society* 4 (1): 63–76.

Micale, Mark S. 2008. *Hysterical Men: the hidden history of male nervous illness*. Cambridge, MA: Harvard University Press.

Miller, Perry. 1965. *The Life of the Mind in America: from the revolution to the civil war*. New York: Harcourt Brace.

Mitchell, T. W. 1922. 'Presidential Address: delivered at a general meeting of the Society on May 10th, 1922'. *Proceedings of the Society for Psychical Research* 33 (85) (June): 1–22.

Mitchell, Timothy. 1988. *Colonising Egypt*. Berkeley, CA: University of California Press.

Montgomery, Richard R. [Francis Worcester Doughty]. 1902. '"I": a story of strange adventure'. *Pluck and Luck: complete stories of adventure* 217 (30 July): 1–29.

Montserrat, Dominic. 2000. *Akhenaten: history, fantasy and ancient Egypt*. London: Routledge.

Moore, Wendy. 2017. *The Mesmerist: the society doctor who held Victorian London spellbound*. London: Weidenfeld & Nicolson.

Moreno, Barry. 2000. *The Statue of Liberty Encyclopedia*. New York: Simon and Schuster.

Morrisson, Mark S. 2007. *Modern Alchemy: occultism and the emergence of atomic theory*. Oxford: Oxford University Press.

Morus, Iwan Rhys. 1998. *Frankenstein's Children: electricity, exhibition, and experiment in early-nineteenth-century London*. Princeton, NJ: Princeton University Press.

Morus, Iwan Rhys. 2004. *Michael Faraday and the Electrical Century*. Cambridge: Icon.

Morus, Iwan Rhys. 2005. *When Physics Became King*. Chicago, IL; London: The University of Chicago Press.

Morus, Iwan Rhys. 2011. *Shocking Bodies: life, death and electricity in Victorian England*. Stroud: The History Press.

Moser, Stephanie. 2006. *Wondrous Curiosities: ancient Egypt at the British Museum*. Chicago, IL: University of Chicago Press.

Moser, Stephanie. 2012. *Designing Antiquity: Owen Jones, ancient Egypt and the Crystal Palace*. New Haven, CT: Yale University Press.

Muhlestein, Kerry. 2004. 'European Views of Egyptian Magic and Mystery: a cultural context for the Magic Flute'. *BYU Studies* 43 (3): 137–48.

Mukharji, Projit Bihari. 2019. 'Hylozoic Anticolonialism: archaic modernity, internationalism, and electromagnetism in British Bengal, 1909–1940'. *Osiris* 34 (1): 101–20.

'The Mummy'. *John Bull*, 22 October 1827, 330.

'The Mummy'. *Moving Picture World* 8 (9), 4 March 1911, 454.

'Mummy Photography'. *The Photographic News* 43 (181), 16 June 1899.

Munro, J. 1892. 'Electricity at the Crystal Palace'. *Illustrated London News*, 26 March 1892, 394.

Murray, Will. 1991. 'Behind the Mask of Nyarlathotep'. *Lovecraft Studies* 24: 25–9.

Mussell, James. 2007. *Science, Time and Space in the Late Nineteenth-Century Periodical Press*. Aldershot: Ashgate.

Nadis, Fred. 2005. *Wonder Shows: performing science, magic, and religion in America*. New Brunswick, NJ: Rutgers University Press.

Nahin, Paul J. 2014. *Holy Sci-Fi!: where science fiction and religion intersect*. New York: Springer.

Natale, Simone. 2011. 'A Cosmology of Invisible Fluids: wireless, x-rays, and psychical research around 1900'. *Canadian Journal of Communication* 35: 263–75.

Natale, Simone. 2011. 'The Invisible Made Visible: x-rays as attraction and visual medium at the end of the nineteenth century'. *Media History* 17 (4): 345–58.

Natale, Simone. 2011. 'The Medium on the Stage: trance and performance in nineteenth-century spiritualism'. *Early Popular Visual Culture* 9 (3): 239–55.

Natale, Simone. 2012. 'A Short History of Superimposition: from spirit photography to early cinema'. *Early Popular Visual Culture* 10 (2): 125–45.

Nesbit, E. 1906. 'The Amulet: a story for children'. *The Strand Magazine: an illustrated monthly* 31: 107–15.

Nesbit, E. 1907. *The Story of the Amulet*. New York: E. P. Dutton.

'The New and the Wonderful Professor Pepper Always at the Egyptian Hall'. 1872. *British Library*, Evan 151, https://www.bl.uk/catalogues/evanion/Record.aspx?EvanID=024-000002035 (last accessed 13 April).

'Nineteen Tons of Mummified Cats'. *The Northampton Mercury* 169 (8829), 8 February 1890, 12.

Noakes, Richard. 2002. '"Instruments to Lay Hold of Spirits": technologizing the bodies of Victorian spiritualism'. In *Bodies/Machines*, edited by Iwan Rhys Morus, 125–63. Oxford: Berg.

Noakes, Richard. 2019. *Physics and Psychics: the occult and the sciences in modern Britain*. Cambridge: Cambridge University Press.

Nye, David E. 1994. *American Technological Sublime*. Cambridge, MA: MIT Press.

O'Byrne, Tamsin Kilner. 2008. 'Empire of the Imagination: Victorian popular fiction and the occult, 1880–1910'. Unpublished PhD thesis, University of Exeter.

O'Donoghue, Diane. 2009. 'The Magic of the Manifest: Freud's Egyptian dream book'. *American Imago* 66 (2): 211–30.

Ogden, Daniel. 2013. *Drakōn: dragon myth and serpent cult in the Greek and Roman worlds*. Oxford: Oxford University Press.

Oppenheim, Janet. 1985. *The Other World: spiritualism and psychical research in England, 1850–1914*. Cambridge: Cambridge University Press.

Orczy, E. 1900. 'The Revenge of Ur-Tasen'. *Pearson's Magazine* 3 (6) (June): 558–66.

Osmond, Suzanne. 2011. '"Her Infinite Variety": representations of Shakespeare's Cleopatra in fashion, film and theatre'. *Film, Fashion & Consumption* 1 (1): 55–79.

Otis, Laura. 1994. *Organic Memory: history and the body in the late nineteenth and early twentieth centuries*. Lincoln, NE: University of Nebraska Press.

Owen, Alex. 2004. *The Place of Enchantment: British occultism and the culture of the modern*. Chicago, IL: University of Chicago Press.

Parker, Louis N. 1913. *Joseph and His Brethren: a pageant play*. New York: John Lane.

Parramore, Lynn. 2008. *Reading the Sphinx: ancient Egypt in nineteenth-century literary culture*. Basingstoke: Palgrave Macmillan.

Parrinder, Patrick. 1995. *Shadows of the Future: H. G. Wells, science fiction and prophecy*. Liverpool: Liverpool University Press.

Paul, Joanna. 2015. '"Time is only a mode of thought, you know": ancient history, imagination and empire in E. Nesbit's literature for children'. In *The Reception of Ancient Greece and Rome in Children's Literature: heroes and eagles*, edited by Lisa Maurice, 30–55. Leiden: Brill.

Pearsall, Ronald. 2004. *The Table-Rappers: the Victorians and the occult*. Stroud: Sutton Publishing.

Penfield, Frederic Courtland. 1899. 'In Fascinating Cairo'. *The Century Illustrated Monthly Magazine* 48 (6): 811–31.

'Photographed as Sphinxes and Mummies'. *Popular Mechanics* 10 (7) (July 1908): 429.

Pick, Daniel. 2000. *Svengali's Web: the alien enchanter in modern culture*. New Haven, CT: Yale University Press.

Pittard, Christopher. 2016. 'The Travelling Doll Wonder: Dickens, secular magic, and *Bleak House*'. *Studies in the Novel* 48 (3): 279–300.

Plunkett, John. 2007. 'Moving Books/Moving Images: optical recreation and children's publishing 1800–1900'. *19: Interdisciplinary Studies in the Long Nineteenth Century* 5, https://doi.org/10.16995/ntn.463 (last accessed 13 April 2022).

Podmore, Frank. 1897. *Studies in Psychical Research*. London: G. P. Putnam's Sons.

Poe, Edgar A. 1845. 'Some Words with a Mummy'. *American Review: A Whig Journal* 1 (4): 363–70.

Pollock, Griselda. 2007. 'Freud's Egypt: mummies and m/others'. *Parallax* 13 (2): 56–79.

Price, Harry. 1933. *Leaves from a Psychist's Case Book*. London: Victor Gollancz.

Principe, Lawrence, M. 2011. 'Alchemy Restored'. *Isis* 102 (2): 305–12.

Proctor, Richard A. 1883. 'The Pyramid of Cheops'. *The North American Review* 136 (316) (March): 257–69.

Proctor, Richard A. 1892. *Old and New Astronomy*. London: Longmans, Green and Co.

'Programme: Messrs Maskelyne and Cooke from England's Home of Mystery'. 1887. Evan 96, *British Library*, http://www.bl.uk/catalogues/evanion/Record.aspx?EvanID=024-000000 085 (last accessed 15 April 2022).

'Public Amusements'. *South Wales Daily News*, 18 July 1892, 4.

Punter, David, and Glennis Byron. 2006. *The Gothic*. Oxford: Blackwell.

Rauch, Alan. 1995. 'The Monstrous Body of Knowledge in Mary Shelley's "Frankenstein"'. *Studies in Romanticism* 34 (2): 227–53.

Rauch, Alan. 2001. *Useful Knowledge: the Victorians, morality, and the march of intellect*. Durham, NC: Duke University Press.

Rebry, Natasha. 2016. 'Playing the Man: manliness and mesmerism in Richard Marsh's *The Beetle*'. *Gothic Studies* 18 (1): 1–15.

Reid, Donald Malcolm. 2002. *Whose Pharaohs?: archaeology, museums, and Egyptian national identity from Napoleon to World War I*. Berkeley, CA: University of California Press.

Richards, Jeffrey. 2009. *The Ancient World on the Victorian and Edwardian Stage*. Basingstoke: Palgrave Macmillan.

Rieser, Klaus. 2019. 'Significant Absence in Narrative Fiction Film'. In *Meaningful Absence Across Arts and Media: the significance of missing signifiers*, edited by Werner Wolf, Nassim Balestrini and Walter Bernhart, 101–25. Leiden: Brill.

Robinson, Charles Mulford. 1902. 'Art Effort in British Cities'. *Harper's Monthly Magazine* 105 (629) (October): 787–96.

Robinson, Mike, and David Picard. 2009. 'Moments, Magic and Memories: photographing tourists, tourist photographs and making worlds'. In *The Framed World: Tourism, Tourists and Photography*, edited by Mike Robinson and David Picard, 1–37. Farnham: Ashgate.

Rodgers, Terrence. 1997. 'Queer Fascinations: Rider Haggard, imperial gothic and the orient'. In *Decadence and Danger*, edited by Tracey Hill, 46–63. Bath: Sulis Press.

Rohmer, Sax. 1924. *Brood of the Witch-Queen*. New York: McKinlay, Stone & Mackenzie.

Rolleston, Frances. 1867. *Letters of Miss Frances Rolleston of Keswick*, edited by Caroline Dent. London: Rivingtons.

Rossell, Deac. 1998. 'Double Think: the cinema and magic lantern culture'. In *Celebrating 1895: the centenary of the cinema*, edited by John Fullerton, 27–36. London: John Libbey.

Roy, Dinendrakumar. 1910. *Pishach purohit*. Calcutta.

Ruffles, Tom. 2004. *Ghost Images: cinema of the afterlife*. Jefferson, NC: McFarland.

Said, Edward W. 2014. *Orientalism*. New York: Knopf Doubleday.

Saler, Michael. 2012. *As If: modern enchantment and the literary prehistory of virtual reality*. Oxford: Oxford University Press.

Sarton, George. 1953. 'Why Isis'. *Isis* 44 (3): 232–42.

Satz, Aura. 2013. 'Typewriter, Pianola, Slate, Phonograph: recording technologies and automisation'. In *The Machine and the Ghost: technology and spiritualism in nineteenth- to twenty-first-century art and culture*, edited by Sas Mays and Neil Matheson, 37–56. Manchester: Manchester University Press.

Scafella, Frank. 1981. 'The White Sphinx and "The Time Machine" (Le Sphynx blanc et "la Machine à remonter le temps")'. *Science Fiction Studies* 8 (3): 255–65.

Scarab Seal Finger Ring, c.1186BC–715BC, *National Museums Liverpool*, 56.20.575, https://www.liverpoolmuseums.org.uk/artifact/scarab-seal-finger-ring (last accessed 13 April 2022).

Schaffer, Simon. 1997. 'Metrology, Metrication, and Victorian Values'. In *Victorian Science in Context*, edited by Bernard Lightman, 438–74. Chicago, IL: University of Chicago Press.

Schivelbusch, Wolfgang. 1995. *Disenchanted Night: the industrialization of light in the nineteenth century*, translated by Angela Davies. Berkeley, CA: University of California Press.

The Secrets of Ancient and Modern Magic: or the art of conjuring unveilled. c.1880. New York: M. Young.

Senf, Carol A. 2002. *Science and Social Science in Bram Stoker's Fiction*. Westport, CT: Greenwood.

Serpell, James A. 2013. 'Domestication and History of the Cat'. In *The Domestic Cat*, 3rd edn, edited by Dennis C. Turner and Patrick Bateson, 83–100. Cambridge: Cambridge University Press.

Serviss, Garrett P. 1912. *The Second Deluge*. New York: McBride, Nast & Co.

Serviss, Garrett Putnam. 1947. *Edison's Conquest of Mars*. Los Angeles, CA: Carcosa House.

Sety, Omm, and Hanny El Zeini. 1981. *Abydos: holy city of ancient Egypt*. Los Angeles, CA: L. L. Company.

Shackleton, David. 2017. 'H. G. Wells, Geology, and the Ruins of Time'. *Victorian Literature and Culture* 45 (4): 839–55.

Sharpe, William Chapman. 2008. *New York Nocturne: the city after dark in literature, painting, and photography*. Princeton, NJ: Princeton University Press.

Shelley, Mary Wollstonecraft. 1823. *Frankenstein: or, the modern Prometheus*, i. London: G. and W. B. Whittaker.

Sichel, N. 1888. 'An Egyptian Princess'. *The Illustrated London News*, 16 June 1888, 649.

Sitch, Bryan. 2013. 'The Inspiration for Bram Stoker's *The Jewel of Seven Stars*?'. *Ancient Worlds: ancient worlds at Manchester Museum*, 8 December 2013, https://ancientworldsmanchester.wordpress.com/2013/12/08/the-inspiration-for-bram-stokers-the-jewel-of-seven-stars/ (last accessed 13 April 2022).

Smith, G. Elliot. 1912. *Catalogue général des antiquités égyptiennes du Musée du Caire: The Royal Mummies*. Cairo: Le Caire Impr. De l'Institut français d'archéologie orientale.

Snell, Arthur Bartram. 1890–4. 'What is wanted in Darkest Africa is the Electric Light'. Victoria and Albert Museum, E.1519–1919.

S. S. D. D. [Florence Farr]. 1896. *Egyptian Magic*. London: Theosophical Publishing Society.

Stafford, Barbara Maria. 2001. 'Revealing Technologies/Magical Domains'. In *Devices of Wonder: from the world in a box to images on a screen*, edited by Barbara Maria Stafford and Frances Terpak, 1–142. Los Angeles, CA: Getty Research Institute.

Stayton, Kevin. 1990. 'Revivalism and The Egyptian Movement'. In *The Sphinx and the Lotus: the Egyptian movement in American decorative arts: 1865–1935*, 5–10. New York: Hudson River Museum.

Steinmeyer, Jim. 2004. *Hiding the Elephant: how magicians invented the impossible*. London: William Heinemann.

Stiles, Anne. 2012. *Popular Fiction and Brain Science in the Late Nineteenth Century*. Cambridge: Cambridge University Press.

Stoker, Bram. 1904. *The Jewel of Seven Stars*. New York: Harper & Brothers.

Stoker, Bram. 1996. *The Jewel of Seven Stars: complete and unabridged*, edited by Clive Leatherdale. Westcliff-on-Sea: Desert Island.

Stoker, Bram. 2012. *The Lost Journal of Bram Stoker: the Dublin years*, edited by Elizabeth Miller and Dacre Stoker. London: Robson.

Stover, Leon. 1996. 'Introduction'. In H. G. Wells, *The Time Machine: an invention*, edited by Leon Stover, 1–17. Jefferson, NC: McFarland.

Strobridge Lithographing Company. c.1900. *Kellar. Library of Congress*, https://www.loc.gov/item/2014637364/ (last accessed 13 April 2022).

Strobridge Lithographing Company. 1894. *Kellar/Levitation*. Harry Ransom Centre, The University of Texas at Austin, https://hrc.contentdm.oclc.org/digital/collection/p15878coll5/id/112/ (last accessed 13 April 2022).

Strobridge Lithographing Company. c.1914. *Thurston*. Library of Congress, https://www.loc.gov/item/2014636952/ (last accessed 13 April 2022).

Suffling, Ernest Richard. 1896. *The Story Hunter; or, Tales of the Weird and Wild*. London: Jarrold & Sons.

Tattersdill, Will. 2016. *Science, Fiction, and the* Fin-de-Siecle *Periodical Press*. Cambridge: Cambridge University Press.

Taylor, C. Bryson. 1904. *In the Dwellings of the Wilderness*. New York: Henry Holt.

'Tesla at the Royal Institution'. *Scientific American*, 12 March 1892, 168.

Tesla, Nikola. 1915. 'The Wonder World to be Created by Electricity'. *Manufacturer's Record*, 9 September 1915, 37–8.

Thompson, Terry W. 2001. '"I Determined to Descend": devolution in "The Time Machine". *CEA Critic* 63 (3): 13–22.

'Through the Opera Glass'. *Pick-Me-Up*, 5 September 1896, 358–9.

Thurschwell, Pamela. 2001. *Literature, Technology and Magical Thinking, 1880–1920*. Cambridge: Cambridge University Press.

Thurston, Howard. 1926. 'Revealing the Mysteries of Magic'. *The Day*, 1 January 1926, 12.

Tompkins, Matthew L. 2019. 'Mediums, Magicians and the All-Too-Fallible Mind'. *Financial Times Magazine*, 15 March 2019, https://www.ft.com/content/1f90bdfe-4522-11e9-b168-96a37d002cd3 (last accessed 13 April 2022).

Trafton, Scott. 2004. *Egypt Land: race and nineteenth-century American Egyptomania*. Durham, NC: Duke University Press.

Trent, Tiffany. 2017. 'The Lights of Dendera'. In *Clockwork Cairo: steampunk tales of Egypt*, edited by Matthew Bright, 81–99. Tarpon Springs, FL: Twopenny.

Trotter, David. 2001. *Paranoid Modernism: literary experiment, psychosis, and the professionalization of English Society*. Oxford: Oxford University Press.

Ulmer, Rivka B. Kern. 2003. 'The Divine Eye in Ancient Egypt and in the Midrashic Interpretation of Formative Judaism'. *Journal of Religion and Society* 5 (5): 1–17.

Van Ash, Cay, and Elizabeth Sax Rohmer. 1972. *Master of Villainy: a biography of Sax Rohmer*. Bowling Green, OH: Bowling Green University Popular Press.

Van Tiggelen, R. 2004. 'Ancient Egypt and Radiology, a Future for the Past!'. *Nuclear Instruments and Methods in Physics Research B* 226: 10–14.

Verne, Jules. 1897. *Le Sphinx des glaces*. Paris: J. Hetzel et Cie.

Verne, Jules. 1899. *An Antarctic Mystery*, translated by Cashel Hoey. Philadelphia, PA: J. B Lippincott.

Vinson, Steve. 2018. *The Craft of a Good Scribe: history, narrative and meaning in the first tale of Setne Khaemwas*. Leiden: Brill.

Von Reichenbach, Charles. 1851. *Physico-Physiological Researches on the Dynamics of Magnetism, Electricity, Heat, Light, Crystallization, and Chemism, in their Relations to Vital Force*. New York: J. S. Redfield, Clinton-Hall.

Von Siemens, Werner. 1893. *Personal Recollections of Werner von Siemens*, translated by W. C. Coupland. London: Asher & Co.

Vyver, Bertha. 1930. *Memoirs of Marie Corelli*. London: Alston Rivers.

Walker, Nathaniel Robert. 2015. 'Babylon Electrified: orientalist hybridity as futurism in Victorian utopian architecture'. In *Revival: memories, identities, utopias*, edited by Ayla Lepine, Matt Lodder and Rosalind McKever, 222–38. London: Courtauld Institute of Art.

Warner, Marina. 2006. *Phantasmagoria: spirit visions, metaphors, and media into the twenty-first century*. Oxford: Oxford University Press.

Warner, William Henry. 1919. *The Bridge of Time*. New York: Scott & Seltzer.

Watson, Henry Sumner. 1902. 'Illuminated Advertisements, Ludgate Circus – London Night'. In Charles Mulford Robinson, 'Art Effort in British Cities', *Harper's Monthly Magazine* 105 (629) (October): 789.

[Webb, Jane.] 1828. *The Mummy!: a tale of the twenty-second century*, 2nd edn. i. London: Henry Colburn.

Weintraub, David A. 2020. *Life on Mars: what to know before we go*. Princeton, NJ: Princeton University Press.

Wells, H. G. 1895. *The Time Machine: an invention*. London: William Heinemann.

'The Western Electric Company's Exhibit in the Electricity Building'. *Electrical Industries* 1 (1) (15 June 1893): 1–5.

White, Trumbull, and W[illia]m Igleheart. 1893. *The World's Columbian Exposition, Chicago, 1893*. Philadelphia, PA: P.W. Ziegler.

Willis, Martin. 2006. *Mesmerists, Monsters, and Machines: science fiction and the cultures of science in the nineteenth century*. Kent, OH: Kent State University Press.

Willis, Martin. 2011. *Vision, Science and Literature, 1870–1920: ocular horizons*. London: Pickering & Chatto.

Wilson, J. Arbuthnot [Grant Allen]. 1878. 'My New Year's Eve Among the Mummies'. *Belgravia* 37 (148) Christmas Annual: 93–105.

Winter, Alison. 1998. *Mesmerized: powers of mind in Victorian Britain*. Chicago, IL: University of Chicago Press.

Wolfe, S. J. 2016. 'Bringing Egypt to America: George Gliddon and the *Panorama of the Nile*'. *Journal of Ancient Egyptian Interconnections* 8: 1–20.

Woloshyn, Tania Anne. 2017. *Soaking Up the Rays: light therapy and visual culture in Britain, c. 1890–1940*. Manchester: Manchester University Press.

Woodbury, Walter E. 1896. *Photographic Amusements: including a description of novel effects obtainable with the camera*. New York: Scovill & Adams.

Wynne, Catherine. 2013. *Bram Stoker, Dracula and the Victorian Gothic Stage*. Basingstoke: Palgrave Macmillan.

Wynne, Catherine. 2020. 'Victorian Stage Magic, Adventure and the Mutilated Body'. In *The Palgrave Handbook of Steam Age Gothic*, edited by Clive Bloom, 691–710. Basingstoke: Palgrave Macmillan.

York & Son. *Sir (Henry) Rider Haggard*, 1890s, *National Portrait Gallery*, NPG x3647, https://www.npg.org.uk/collections/search/portrait/mw57025/Sir-Henry-Rider-Haggard (last accessed 13 April).

Yoxall, J. H. 1892. *The Lonely Pyramid: a tale of adventures*. London: Blackie & Son.

Zimmerman, Virginia. 2008. *Excavating Victorians*. Albany, NY: State University of New York Press.

Zimmerman, Virginia. 2019. 'Excavating Children: archaeological imagination and time-slip in the early 1900s'. In *Excavating Modernity: physical, temporal and psychological strata in literature, 1900–1930*, edited by Eleanor Dobson and Gemma Banks, 63–82. New York: Routledge.

Index

Adams, Henry Cadwallader 98
Akhenaten 56, 227n118
alchemy 4, 6, 10–12, 13, 33, 34, 47, 97, 112,
    113, 121, 124, 125, 127, 145, 153, 167–8,
    169, 170, 171, 212, 213, 236, 242
    see also philosopher's stone
aliens *see* extraterrestrials
Allen, Grant 12, 43, 123, 138
Amenhotep III 211
ancient Greece 6, 11, 23, 77, 89, 99, 101, 104,
    106, 109, 172n5, 185, 198
    as foil to ancient Egypt 132, 140
    as inheritor of Egyptian knowledge 4, 7, 11,
        83, 84–5, 86, 87
ancient Rome 23, 99, 101, 143, 176n197
    as foil to ancient Egypt 81, 132, 140
Anderson, John Henry 153
animal magnetism *see* mesmerism
Anubis 89, 240
Apis 89
archaeology 45, 46, 77, 78, 79, 82, 83, 87,
    98, 100, 102, 106, 107, 116, 161, 172n5,
    184, 187, 210
    in fiction 39, 92, 113, 114, 239
    pseudoarchaeology 231, 234–5, 236
astral projection 189, 241
astrology 4, 7, 22, 68, 211
astronomy 6, 16, 78, 79, 85, 86, 87, 89, 90, 92,
    94, 98, 107, 115, 231
    ancient Egyptian knowledge of 7, 84–5, 85,
        86, 88, 90, 116
Atlantis 79, 81–2, 93, 111–12, 170, 235
automata 17, 183, 194, 195–6, 217
Les Aventures extraordinaires d'Adèle Blanc-Sec
    18, 240–2

Bacon, Gertrude 27
Ball, Alec 156
Bangs sisters 59
Bara, Theda 215–16, 215
Bayard, Émile 5, 6
Becquerel, Henri 164, 165
Belzoni, Giovanni Battista 24, 82
Benson, E. F. 210
Bernheim, Hippolyte 206, 221
Besant, Annie 32, 111
Besson, Luc 240
Betiero, Thomas Jasper 15, 17, 183, 211–12

Blackwood, Algernon 14, 15, 40–1, 42, 43, 44,
    46, 69, 70
Blavatsky, Helena 4, 9, 60, 111, 124, 155, 166,
    189, 208, 213, 232, 235
    and fiction 125, 149, 189, 190
Bonaparte, Napoleon 80, 92
Bonomi, Joseph 43, 100
Booth, Walter R. 65, 66
Boothby, Guy 15, 149, 214, 217
British Museum 31, 32, 59–60, 101, 108,
    161, 206
    lighting of 127, 131–3, 132, 147
    and Wells's Palace of Green Porcelain 106–8
Budge, E. A. Wallis 31, 228n148, 239
Bulwer-Lytton, Edward 12, 78, 81, 124–5, 138,
    149, 150, 239

Cairo Museum 155, 161m 162
Carpenter, William Benjamin 193–4
Carrière, Eva 42
Carter, Charles Joseph 29
Carter, Howard 72n26, 161, 217
cats 183, 187, 201, 203, 203, 204–6, 220, 222
Caviglia, Giovanni Battista 77, 107
Chabas, François 217
Champollion, Jean-François 82, 187
Charcot, Jean-Martin 161, 205, 206, 221
Cheiro *see* Warner, William John
chemistry 11, 12, 17, 92, 95, 113, 147, 168,
    170, 192, 232
    see also alchemy
Cheops 115, 123, 141, 142, 212 *see also* Great
    Pyramid of Giza
Christian, Paul *see* Pitois, Jean-Baptiste
Christianity 5, 99, 113, 124, 141, 144, 171
    the Bible 80, 81, 92–3, 142, 143, 154, 171,
        177, 178, 179–80, 179, 186, 230n215
    see also Joseph; Moses
cinema 15, 17, 20, 21, 22, 43, 44, 46, 64–70,
    146, 171, 215–16, 217
clairvoyance 13, 82, 180, 184, 187, 189, 190,
    191, 198, 210, 224, 234
Clemens, Samuel *see* Twain, Mark
Cleopatra VII 50, 58, 59, 65, 73n61, 156, 157,
    187–8, 214–16, 215, 217, 226n59
Cleveland, Lucy 14, 183, 210–11
Colossi of Memnon 29
Cook, Florence 39

258

Cooke, George Alfred 28, 30, 35, 60, 95
Copland, Alexander 115, 144
Corelli, Marie 14, 60, 70, 124, 125, 149, 187–9
  The Sorrows of Satan 217
  Ziska 15, 22, 60, 61–3, 64, 136, 217
Crookes, William 151, 158, 159, 164, 165, 191
Crowley, Aleister 208
crystals 113, 165, 168, 175n173, 183, 206,
  207, 212, 213
crystal balls 178, *179*, 182, 216, 232
Crystal Palace 100–1, 106, 109
Curie, Marie 17, 120, 159, 164, 165, 168–9,
  171, 176n209
Curie, Pierre 159, 164, 165, 168, 176n209,
  176n221
Cutcliffe-Hyne, C. J. 118n107, 192–3

d'Espérance, Elizabeth 32
Däniken, Erich von 17, 235, 236
Darwin, Charles 5, 123
Davenport brothers 28, 39–40, 66
Davy, Humphry 150
de Philipsthal, Paul 45–6
De Quincey 187
degeneration 17, 125, 148, 184, 213, 214,
  222–3, 224
Dessoir, Max
Devant, David 30, 31, 65
Dickens, Charles 25, 177
Dieudonné, Florance Carpenter 14, 183, 196
dioramas 20, 42–3, 149, 233
Donnelly, Ignatius L. 81–2, 93, 94, 95, 111
Dreams 42, 43, 67, 186–8, 189, 190, 199, 212,
  220, 221, 222, 238
  interpretation of 177, 183, 186, 190, 221
  prophetic 40, 121, 180, 186, 199, 213, 215
  and reincarnation 187–9, 192
  see also prophecy
Doughty, Francis Worcester 78, 79–80
Douglas, Theo *see* Everett, Henrietta Dorothy
Doyle, Arthur Conan 12, 123, 146–7, 168,
  195–6, 214, 217
Du Bois, W. E. B. 211
du Maurier, George 180, 198
Durbin, William W. 29

Edison, Thomas 3, 16, 92, 127, 154–5, 159, 193
Edwards, Amelia B. 136
Egyptian Court *see* Crystal Palace
Egyptian Hall 15, 21, 22, 23–4, 25, 27, 28–30,
  34, 42, 52, 60, 70, 72n17, 73n54
  architecture of 23–4, *24*, 25
  and early cinema 65, 66, 68
Egyptology 5, 33, 37, 79, 80, 81, 82, 98, 107,
  108, 112, 143, 155, 160, 161, 162, 163,
  164, 184, 187, 191, 192, 195, 198, 203,
  206, 217, 228n148, 239, 240, 241
electricity 1, 4, 13, 120, 121, 122–3, 124–5,
  127, 130–1, 133–5, 139, 140, 141, 142,
  145, 146–9, 150, 151, 155, 156, 158, 169,
  181, 193, 197–8, 201, 210, 236
  see also lightning
electric light 16, 74n114, 120, 124, 126,
  127–8, 129, *129*, 130–8, *132*, *134*, *137*,
  139, 140, 147, 152, 154, 156–7, *166*, 170,
  236, 237, 240

Eliot, George 210
Elliotson, John 201
Ellis, Havelock 214
engineering 7, 12, 82, 90, 93, 97, 139,
  147, 151
Evans, Henry Ridgely 7, 11–12, 15, 21, 25,
  44, 45, 52
Everett, Henrietta Dorothy 14, 15, 31, 39, 43,
  63, 238s
evolution 17, 185, 213, 222–3, 224
extraterrestrials 16, 90, *91*, 92–3,
  94, *96*, 98, 232, 233, 234, 235, 238
eyes 17, 23, 30, *33*, 163, 180, 183, 187,
  196, 198–9, 201, 206, 207, *209*, 210,
  212, 213–14, 215, *215*, 216, 224–5,
  228n149, 238
  eye of Horus 198, 208, 225
  luminous 4, 48, 60, 93, 141, 189, 195,
  197–9, 203, *203*, 204, 205, 206, 207, 208,
  213, 222, 237–8, 239

Faraday, Michael 150
Farr, Florence 182
The Fifth Element 240, 241
Figuier, Louis 84, 85, 86
Fiorelli, Giuseppe 77
fire 31, 32, 41, 63, 64, 67, 69, 76n172, 93,
  136, 150, 165, 169, 175n173
  for occult visualisation 183, 206, 209,
  210, 213
  see also eyes, luminous
Flammarion, Camille 16, 78, 115–16
France, Anatole 203
Franklin, Benjamin 140
Franz Ferdinand 56
Freemasonry 5, 23, 29, 36, 47–8, 71,
  181, 211
Frederick, Pauline 178, *179*
Freud, Sigmund 17, 183, 190, 217, 219, 221

Galvani, Lucia 145, 146
Galvani, Luigi 145, 146
galvanism 123, 140, 141, 142, 144, 145–6,
  147, 150
gas light *2*, 12–13, 129, 138
Gautier, Théophile 145, 185
gemstones 45, 64, 114, 165, 168, 198, 207,
  208–9, 210, 211, 212, 213, 216
  see also crystals
geology 5, 78, 102, 106, 109, 116, 142, 184
Gérard, Jean-Ignace Isidore 99
Ghost Club 40
Goble, Warwick 154
Golden Dawn *see* Hermetic Order of the
  Golden Dawn
Great Pyramid of Giza 61, 87, *88*, 90, 94, 115,
  126, 141, 142, 147–8, 149, 212
  see also pyramids
Great Sphinx of Giza 5, 29, 43, 67, 77,
  79, 83, *91*, 93, 105, 107, 139,
  196, 216
  as Martian monument 90, 92, 98, 114
  see also sphinxes
Greiffenhagen, Maurice 37, *50*, 199, *200*
Griffith, George 12, 17, 34, 97, 168,
  194, 207–8

INDEX 259

H.D. 219, 221, 229n119, 229n203
Haggard, H. Rider 14, 36, 43, 44, 47, 48, 60,
    70, 75n121, 105, 122, 149, 162–3, 171,
    188, 189–90, 192, 208, 215, 217, 224
  Ayesha: The Return of She 17, 122, 125,
    169–70, 212–13
  Cleopatra 15, 21, 36, 37, 39, 47, 48, 51, 69,
    183, 214–15, 216, 217
  She 16, 60, 64, 76n172, 78, 79, 114, 116n3,
    169, 180, 183, 189–91, 197–8, 199, 201,
    207, 222
  'Smith and the Pharaohs' 17, 122, 125, 155,
    156, 161–4, 168, 171, 172
  The World's Desire 198–9, *200*, 207
Hale, Edward Everett 98–9
Hall, Granville Stanley 184
Hamon, Count Louis *see* Warner, William John
Hardy, Paul *2*, 3, 193
Hathor 23, 89, 156
Hatshepsut 217
Herbertson, Mallard *see* Hutcheson, Marie
Hermetic Order of the Golden Dawn 5, 22,
    23, 24, 39, 40, 131, 139, 158, 182, 184,
    208, 211
Herodotus 80
hieroglyphs 16, 37, *38*, 79, 81, *85*, 86, 93, 98,
    105, 112, 124, 165, 183, 187, 207, 208,
    217, 220–1
  decorative 25, 45, 74n110, 138
Hoffmann, Louis 25
Holmes, T. W. 193
Hopkins, Albert A. 56, 66
Horus 47, 98, 198, 208, 225
Hospitalier, Édouard 151–2
Hutcheson, Marie 14, 15, 53, 69, 185–6
hyperdiffusionism 80–1, 82
hypnotism 34, 111, 178–80, *179*, 181–3, 191,
    192, 193, 194, 195, 196–7, 198, 203, 204,
    205–6, 207–9, 211, 212, 213–14, 216,
    218, 221, 222–4, *223*, 226n67, 238
hysteria 193, 206, 214, 218, 219

illusion 21, 23, 27, 29, 34–9, 40, 42, 43, 44,
    47, 48, 52, 53, 60, 65, 66, 71, 72, 153
  see also Pepper's Ghost; stage magic;
    Stodare's Sphinx
Isis 5–7, *6*, 12, 32, 47, 52, 80, 89, 112, 156,
    168, 169, 195, 214
  and the Egyptian Hall 25, 27
  mysteries of 21, 36, 45, 48, 51
  as scientist 7

James, William 184
Jane, Fred T. 11, 16, 78, 87, 94–8, *96*, 237
Janet, Pierre 189
jewels *see* gemstones
Johnson, Robert Underwood 153
Jones, Owen 100
Joseph 57, *99*, 109, 143, 177, 180, 215, 221,
    224, 225
Jung, Karl 220

Kant, Immanuel 140
Kellar, Harry 28, 29
Khaemuas 163
Kipling, Rudyard 190
Kircher, Athanasius 45

Laborde, Albert 168
Lampen, Charles Dudley 80
Lang, Andrew 190, 198–9, 201
  see also Haggard, H. Rider, *The
    World's Desire*
Leadbeater, Charles Webster 15, 21, 44, 51,
    82, 208
Lepsius, Karl Richard 82
Liégeois, Jules 206
light 3, 16, 53, 97, 129, 131, 137, 138, 140,
    147, 150, 151, 153–4, 155–6, 163, 164,
    165, 166–7, 168, 169, 170, 195, 198–9,
    203, 204, 208, 212, 213
  as metaphor for enlightenment 3, 126, 131,
    137, 140
  see also electric light; eyes, luminous;
    gas light
lightning 124, 131, 140, 142, 143–5, *143*, *144*,
    154, 237
Lockyer, Norman 123, 236
Lodge, Oliver 151, 188, 191
Lombroso, Cesare 159
Londe, Albert 160, 161
Loti, Pierre 136
Lovecraft, H. P. 233, 235
Lowell, Percival 89–90, 107, 117n24
Lumière brothers 64

Mackay, Charles 4, 13
magic lanterns 20, 21, 22, 32, 44, 45, 46, 47,
    48–50, 51, 52, 53, 63, 65, 68, 70, 102,
    137, 149, 171
  see also phantasmagoria
magic wands *see* wands
Mariette, Auguste 217
Mars 3–4, 78, 83, 87, 89–90, 92, 93, 94, 115,
    155, 235, 239
Marsh, Richard 17, 148, 180, 183, 194, 195,
    198, 217, 221
Martin, John 142, 143, *143*, 144, 147
Maskelyne, John Nevil 22, 28, 29, 30, 35,
    60, 66, 95
Maspero, Gaston 161, 162, 217
Mayo, Herbert 201
medicine 4, 13, 95, 159, 179, 180, 181, 185,
    189, 193, 194, 201, 204, 211, 218, 221,
    224, 241, 242
Medusa 201, 207, 216, 217
Méliès, Georges 65–6, 67–9, 232
Meneptah 162
Mesmer, Franz Anton 181, 223, *223*
mesmerism 1, 7, 178–80, 181–3, 184, 189,
    191, 193, 194, 195, 197, 198, 201, 203,
    204, 206, 207, 211, 212, 215, 216
Millar, H. R. 33, *33*, 109, *110*
Minor, Thomas C. 13
mirrors 24, 52, 67, 70, 124, 183, 206, 209,
    210–11, 212, 213, 232
  as bringing about trance states 183, 206
  as revealing occult truths 209, 210–11, 212
  employed in illusions 24, *26*, 45, 67, 73n54
Mitchell, T. W. 185
Mohamed Tewfik Pasha 87
Montgomery, Richard R *see* Doughty, Francis
    Worcester
Moreau, Mathurin 137, 138
Moses 142, 143, 155

260   INDEX

Moses, William Stainton 190
moving pictures *see* cinema
mummies 3, 11, 12, 16, 21, 24, 32, 41, 42,
    45, 51, 53, 54, 61, 63–4, 66, 68, 69, 106,
    108, 115, 135, 149, 155, 165, 173n73,
    175n173, 185, 198, 201, 203, *203*, 205,
    210, 214, 218–19, 220, 232, 238
    application of X-rays to 125, 159–61, *160*,
        162–3, 164, 175n178
    communication with 1, *2*, 192–3
    reanimated 12, 14, 16, 43, 113, 122–3, 131,
        139, 140–2, 144–7, 148, 154, 164, 181,
        195, 196–7, 241, 242
    'Unlucky Mummy' 59–60, 70
Musée du Louvre 206, 237, 241
museums 13, 29, 79, 80, 84, 100, 101–2, 106,
    107, 128, 135, 140, 147, 163, 175n173,
    218, 233
    see also British Museum; Cairo Museum;
        Musée du Louvre
Myers, Frederic 190, 210

Nefertiti 240
Nephthys 89
Nesbit, E. 14, 15, 16, 21, 30, 31, 34, 69, 78,
    99, 100, 101, 107–12, 165, 167
nightmares *see* dreams
Nile, River 25, 48, 82, 86, 89, 109, *110*,
    126, 209
Nobel Prize 150, 164, 165, 169
Nordau, Max 214

obelisks 52, 81, 84, 97, 105, 128–31, *129*, 138,
    139, 143, 156, 171
Orczy, Baroness 16, 78, 80
Orientalism 10, 24, 97, 105, 135, 139,
    216, 239
Osiris 25, 27, 155, 156, 163, 168
Ouija boards 35
Owen, Richard 82

Palladino, Eusapia 39, 159
panorama 20, 21, 23, 42–3, 44, 149, 171, 233
Parker, Louis N. 178, 224
Pepper, John Henry 27, 30
Pepper's Ghost 22, 27, 48, 232
Peters, Christian Heinrich Friedrich 89
Petrie, Flinders 161, 217
phantasmagoria 21, 44, 45–6, 48, *49*, *50*, 51,
    52, 53–4, 64, 68, 102, 233
    see also magic lantern
philosopher's stone 12, 167–8, 226n59
    see also alchemy
phonograph 124, 192, 193, 197
photography 15, 20, 21, 41–2, 46, 47, 48, 53,
    55, 56, *57*, 59, 60, 61, 69, 70, 71, 92, 136,
    152–3, 154, 163, 178, 191, 197, 212, 218
    see also spirit photography
physics 16, 17, 92, 115, 125, 145, 148, 150,
    153, 158, 164, 182, 241
Piper, Leonora 194
Pitois, Jean-Baptiste 5–7
Plato 81, 112
Podmore, Frank 28
Poe, Edgar Allan 12, 83, 123, 145–6, 149, 181,
    193, 241

Pogson, Elizabeth Isis 89
Pogson, Norman Robert 89
Pompeii 77, 80, 101, 219
Poole, Reginald Stuart Poole 82
Poyet, Louis 7, *8*, 87, *88*, 89, 152
priests 5, 7, 15, 23, 30, 31, 33, 39–40, 45, 47,
    48, *49*, 60, 65, 84, *88*, 99–100, 112, 113,
    120, 121, 149, 169, 175n173, 185, 186,
    197, 220, 222, *223*
Proctor, Richard A. 79, 87, 89, 94, 117n24
prophecy 177, 181, 189, 199, 210, 215
psychical research 7, 9, 42, 60, 62, 159, 179,
    182, 184, 185, 191, 194
    see also Society for Psychical Research
psychology 9, 17, 178, 180, 181, 182, 184,
    185, 189, 190, 194, 198, 222, 231
pyramids 5, *6*, 7, 22, 29, 43, 49–50, 67,
    75n152, 78, 79, 82, 86, *86*, 92, 94, 95, 98,
    107, 124–5, 126, 127, 130, 138, 141–2,
    143, *143*, *144*, 147, 196, *202*, 208, *209*,
    232, 234, 235, 236, 237, 239
    see also Great Pyramid of Giza

Ra 121, 239
radioactivity 9, 16, 121, 122, 125, 158, 164,
    165, 166–7, 169, 234
Ramses II 29, 133, 162
Reichenbach, Karl von 207, 209
reincarnation 111, 113, 114, 115, 121, 163,
    189, 204, 208–10, 211, 212, 226n59, 238
Renenutet 198
Renouf, Peter le Page 81
Robert-Houdin, Jean Eugène 22, 37
Robertson, Étienne-Gaspard 45
Rohmer, Sax 14, 53, 183, 217–21, 224, 236
Röntgen, Wilhelm 147, 153, 158, 160, 163, 165
Roux, George 82–3
Roy, Dinendra Kumar 15, 149
Royal Polytechnic Institution 27, 46, 65
Rutherford, Ernest 164, 167

Sarcophagi *2*, *55*, 56, 59, 67, 69, 138, 164
Sarton, George 7
Schiaparelli, Giovanni 89, 90
science fiction 1, 13, 14, 231
Schliemann, Heinrich 77
Scott-Elliot, William 82
séances 21, 22, 28, 32, 33, *33*, 34, 35, 36, 39,
    41–2, 44, 51, 56, 60, 66, 67, 71, 151, 165,
    171, 184, 190, 195, 218, 231
Serviss, Garrett P. 16, 78, 87, 90, 92, 93, 95,
    98, 114, 234–5
Set 221, 230n220, 240
Seti I 24
Seti II 162
Shakespeare, William 187, 216
Shelley, Mary 123, 140–1, 142, 149
Sichel, Nathaniel 57–9
Siemens, Werner von 147–8, 149
Sloane, Hans 106
Smeaton, Oliphant 78, 81
Smedley, William T. 195
Smith, Grafton Elliot 17, 81, 161–2
snakes 5, *6*, 28, 36, 37, *38*, 178, *179*, 183,
    198–9, *200*, 201, *202*, 203, 206, 208, 212,
    214–15, *215*, 216, 220

INDEX   **261**

Society for Psychical Research 5, 9, 28, 34, 40, 42, 62, 119n124, 150, 158, 159, 185, 189–91, 192, 194, 195, 210
see also psychical research
Soddy, Frederick 164, 167, 170
Spencer, William Call 81
sphinxes 5, 16, 21, 24, 25, 29, 47, *49*, 52, 54, *55*, 56, 67, 69, 72n17, 78, 82–3, 84, *85*, 102–5, *103*, 106, 107, 108, 114, 116, 138, 189, 233, 238
see also Great Sphinx of Giza
spirit photography 46, 56–7, *57*, 59, 60, 62–3, 65, 66, 70, 159, 191
spiritualism 5, 7, 8, 15, 20, 22, 23, 24, 28, 32, 34, 35, 36, 39–40, 41, 42, 44, 56, *57*, 59, 70, 115, 124, 131, 139, 151, 158, 159, 170, 171, 182, 184, 189–90, 193, 194, 195, 199, 218
stage magic 7, 15, 20, 21, 22, 23, 24–5, 27–8, 29, 31, 32, 34–9, 43–4, 51, 65, 66, 70, 131, 135, 148, 153, 189, 218, 231
Stargate 17, 234, 235, 237, 238–9, 240
Stevenson, Robert Louis 199
Stodare's Sphinx 24–5, *26*, 27, 29, 66, 69, 73n54, 232
Stoddart, Joseph 24, 25
Stoker, Bram 14, 149, 168, 207, 208, 213, 217, 224, 238, 239
Dracula 180, 198, 217
The Jewel of Seven Stars 17, 122, 125, 164–6, 167–9, 171–2, 183, 185, 186, 207, 208, 217, 234, 238, 239
Suez Canal 90, 126, 139
Suffling, Ernest Richard 1, 3, 4, 192–3

Taia *see* Tiye
Tardi, Jacques 240
Taylor, Charlotte Bryson 14, 15, 63, 166, 167
telegraphy 9, 133, 134, 136, 147, 196, 197
ancient Egyptians as having knowledge of 12, 120
and spiritualism 158, 191, 193
telekinesis 234, 241
telepathy 3, 17, 111, 158, 159, 170, 180, 181, 182, 186, 190–1, 195, 197, 198, 212, 234, 238, 241
between the living and mummified individuals 3, 195
telephone 124, 133, 190, 191, 192–3, 197
teleportation 233
temples 5, *6*, 7, *8*, 12, 15, *24*, 28, 29, 51, 71, 74n72, 74n110, 77, 80, 82, 84, *85*, 97, 114, *202*, 218
modern constructions 23, 25, 27, 29, 52, 67, 68, 113–6, *134*, 137
Tesla, Nikola 17, 149, 150–5, *152*, 164, 168, 171, 172, 191, 233, 240
theatre 13, 29, 39, 42, 44, 51, 71, 100, 127, 132, 133, 136, 146, 147, 149, 150, 152, 153, 154, 177, 178, 207–8, 216, 218, 224, 231
theosophy 4, 5, 7, 9, 14, 15, 32, 34, 40, 44, 49, 51, 60, 111, 115, 131, 139, 158, 182, 183, 184, 185, 189, 190, 208, 211, 232
and Atlantis 81, 82, 11
and reincarnation 111, 115, 163

Theosophical Society 4, 5, 51, 124, 158
Thomas Cook & Son 54, 60
Thoth 6–7, 89, 95, 236
thought transference *see* telepathy
Thurston, Howard 29
Thutmose IV 161
time travel 16, 30, 32, 42, 78, 98, 99–101, 102, 107, *110*, 111, 112, 114, 116, 232, 233, 240
by ancient Egyptians 16, 78, 99–100, 112–14, 120, 121, 186, 209, 233, 240
Tiye 199
trance 13, 17, 178, 181, 182, 183, 185, 187, 191, 193, 194, 201, 215, 224
and mummification 40, 192
and occult visions 51, 52, 178, 189, 212
and telepathic communication 180, 181
Turner, J. M. W. 143, *144*
Tutankhamun 72n26, 229n189, 234
Twain, Mark 153
typewriters 196

Uhlemann, Max 98

Varian, George 93
Venus 78, 83, 94, 95, 98, 129
Verdi, Giuseppe 89
Verne, Jules 16, 78, 82–3, 93, 114, 241
Victoria, Queen of the United Kingdom 25
Volta, Alessandro 125, 145
Vyver, Bertha 187–8

wands 37, *38*, 39, 150, *152*, 156, 171, 181
Warner, William Henry 16, 78, 112–14, 120, 208
Warner, William John 165, 167, 201, *202*
Watson, James Craig 89
Webb, Jane 14, 123, 141–2, 144, 146, 147, 148
Wedgwood 104
Wedjat 198
Wells, H. G. 14, 19n48
The Time Machine 16, 73n36, 78, 101–6, *103*, 107–8, 113, 114, 115, 223
The War of the Worlds 92, 93, 117n34, 154
Whymper, Edward 37, *38*
Wilde, Oscar 62
Wilson, J. Arbuthnot *see* Allen, Grant
Wilson, John 201
Winter, Charles Allen 199
Wolf, Max 89
Woodbury, Walter E. 56
Woodville, R. Caton 37, *49*
World's Columbian Exposition 237

X-rays 13, 16, 120, 121, 122, 125, 147, 153, 157, 158, 159, 160, 162–4, 165, 167, 169, 175n178, 234
as applied to mummified remains 16, 125, 159–61, *160*, 163

Yoxall, James Henry 49